National Theatre Connections
2017

NEW PLAYS FOR YOUNG PEOPLE

Three

#YOLO

FOMO

Status Update

Musical Differences

Extremism

The School Film

Zero for the Young Dudes!

The Snow Dragons

The Monstrum

with an introduction by
ANTHONY BANKS

Bloomsbury Methuen Drama
An imprint of Bloomsbury Publishing Plc

B L O O M S B U R Y

Bloomsbury Methuen Drama

An imprint of Bloomsbury Publishing Plc

Imprint previously known as Methuen Drama

50 Bedford Square	1385 Broadway
London	New York
WC1B 3DP	NY 10018
UK	USA

www.bloomsbury.com

**BLOOMSBURY, METHUEN DRAMA and the Diana logo
are registered trade marks of Bloomsbury Publishing Plc**

First published 2017

For details of copyright of individual plays, see page 656.

Introduction copyright © National Theatre 2017
Resource material copyright © National Theatre 2017

British Library Cataloguing-in-Publication Data
A catalogue record for this book is available from the British Library

ISBN: PB: 978-1-3500-3359-7
ePDF: 978-1-3500-3360-3
ePub: 978-1-3500-3361-0

Library of Congress Cataloging-in-Publication Data
A catalog record for this book is available from the Library of Congress.

Cover design by National Theatre Graphic Design Studio
Photographs by Sorted

Typeset by Country Setting, Kingsdown, Kent CT14 8ES
Printed and bound in Great Britain

Contents

National Theatre Connections

Connections is the National Theatre's nationwide youth theatre festival and it has been at the heart of our work for young people for the last two decades. Each year it offers a unique opportunity for youth theatres and school theatre groups to stage new plays written specifically for young people by some of the most exciting playwrights working today, and then to perform them in leading theatres across the UK. Ten new plays are commissioned each year, building up a repertoire permanently available to schools, colleges and youth theatres.

Each year more than 250 companies from across the UK (and beyond) take up the challenge of staging a brand new Connections play. The young people are involved not just as actors, but as stage managers, designers, and lighting and sound technicians – all the roles required for a professional theatre production.

At the beginning of the rehearsal process, the NT hosts a weekend in London for the directors of all the companies in the Connections programme, giving them the chance to work with a leading director and the playwright of their chosen play, as well as to meet everyone involved with Connections. The weekend includes a range of practical professional development workshops to enhance their practice and to give them new ideas and skills to share with their young company.

When the plays are performed in the companies' home venues, a director from the National Theatre travels to see the performance, and provides detailed Development Notes. All productions then transfer to a Connections Festival held at one of twenty-eight Partner Theatres, giving all the young people the opportunity to work with theatre experts and perform on a professional stage.

One production of each play is invited to perform at the National Theatre Festival in London in a week-long celebration of Connections and of young people's theatre.

**For more information and to get involved please visit:
connections.nationaltheatre.org.uk**

Ros Terry
Connections Producer
National Theatre
March 2017

Introduction

Each year the National Theatre invites playwrights whose work excites us to write new plays for Connections. Playwrights take many different approaches to the commission, but all Connections writers have the opportunity to test their ideas with young people through research, rehearsed readings and workshops. The ten new plays in the 2017 collection were developed with young people across the UK.

HARRIET BRAUN created the award-winning BBC Three television series *Lip Service*, set in Glasgow, which is about three young women looking for love. For Connections, Harriet has written *Three*, a series of snapshots of three plucky young potential couples navigating the ups and downs of love and friendship. Her play was workshopped with students from Leyton Sixth Form College at the National Theatre Studio.

MATTHEW BULGO is a playwright and an actor. He began writing plays for the Sherman Theatre Advanced Writers Group in Cardiff and his *Last Christmas* was a smash hit at the Edinburgh Festival. His idea for writing *#YOLO* came shortly afterwards and the first draft of the play was performed in a rehearsed reading followed by a discussion with the West Glamorgan Youth Theatre Company.

SUHAYLA EL-BUSHRA wrote three successful plays about young people in quick succession: *Pigeons* for the Royal Court, *The Kilburn Passion* for the Tricycle and *Cuckoo* for the Unicorn. Before this, she wrote many episodes of the television drama series *Hollyoaks* focusing on the lives of young people. Suhayla lives in Hove, near Brighton, and workshopped the events of her new play *FOMO* in her local school, Blatchington Mill School, with some very imaginative Year Ten drama students who explored through improvisation the potential outcomes of the internet being switched off.

TIM ETCHELLS has led the world-renowned performance group Forced Entertainment for thirty years. Based in Sheffield, they've performed extensively across the world and collaborated with many leading international companies. Tim created a play for a group of Belgian children aged eight to fourteen called *That Night Follows Day* in which there was an extraordinary collaboration between writer and young performers. His new play for Connections, *Status Update*, continues to explore that territory for teenage performers. It was co-commissioned and developed with Cuturgest in Portugal as part of their version of the Connections programme, which is called Panos, while he was artist-in-residence in Lisbon. The script was further developed with the Young People's Theatre at the Sheffield Crucible.

ROBIN FRENCH wrote his first play, *Bear Hug*, for the Royal Court. It was an acerbic, absurdist comedy in which a mother and father persevere optimistically to bring up their depressed son even though he's been transformed into a bear. Robin went on to create and write the award-winning television series *Cuckoo*, which appealed to a large young audience on BBC3. He went back to his old school in the Midlands for inspiration for *Musical Differences*. He wanted to create a script which could be realised differently by each young company of actors who perform it. Robin discussed early ideas for his play with Year Nine students at the Petchey Academy in Hackney.

ANDERS LUSTGARTEN is a political activist and playwright. His award-winning early play *A Day at the Racists* explored the gap between the BNP's subtle tactics and their extremist views. His first play for Connections, *Socialism Is Great*, was an exacting satire about young people living in present-day China. His new play, *Extremism*, began through research into the organisations that have been set up in response to the 'Prevent Duty' section of the Counter-Terrorism and Security Act of 2015 and the impact it has on pupils, teachers, parents and families. The play was workshopped extensively with a Year Eleven class over the course of a year while Anders was writing it.

PATRICK MARBER is an experienced writer and director and has worked regularly at the National Theatre for the last twenty years. He has written for Connections before and was keen to create a large ensemble piece in which the actors were in view throughout the performance and would need to 'speak out' to the audience, rather than speaking to each other in naturalistic scenes. *The School Film* is written for an ensemble of school-children who are assembled to watch David Lean's film *Great Expectations*.

ALISTAIR MCDOWALL burst on to the stage with his plays *Brilliant Adventures* and *Captain Amazing* and followed these with *Pomana*, which began life in Cardiff. It later transferred to the Orange Tree Theatre in Richmond, the National Theatre and the Royal Exchange, where he workshopped his new play for Connections, *Zero for the Young Dudes!* While writing his Connections play he simultaneously wrote an extraordinary play set in an imagined future in outer space called *X* for the Royal Court.

LIZZIE NUNNERY is a playwright and songwriter who has worked with companies including Liverpool Everyman, Manchester Royal Exchange, Paines Plough, Cardboard Citizens and Theatre503. Through visits to Norway she became aware of the story of King Haakon who escaped the Nazis through the woods above the fjord town of Molde at the beginning of the Second World War. She has transformed this historic truth into a folktale with songs. *The Snow Dragons* was workshopped by talented drama students at Loreto College in Hulme, Manchester.

KELLIE SMITH is the Channel Four playwright-in-residence at the Royal Exchange where her play *Jonestown* was shortlisted for the Bruntwood Prize. Kellie began her Connections play by researching the various types of bullying which take place in schools and the pressures many young people face due to targeted marketing that implies perfect body image. An early idea for the play was explored with puppeteer Toby Olié at the Liverpool Everyman, which followed a similar story to the creation of Frankenstein's creature. Later developments of *The Monstrum* were explored with the talented ensemble of actors at Chickenshed Theatre Company in North London.

ANTHONY BANKS

Three
by Harriet Braun

It's a long, hot summer. Six teenagers are in various states of lust, longing and unrequited love. A boy has a crush on the girl next door; only she's going out with the school heart-throb. Two teenagers meet for a blind date but they're both thinking about someone else. A shy girl with a secret makes friends with the most popular girl in her class. Only these are love stories with a difference: thanks to the inner voice trailing around after each character, we get to hear what they're all saying and thinking. Fortunately there's a narrator to keep us all on track, but there's a small problem: our narrator would much rather be on reality TV.

Cast size
8F, 4M + Narrator M or F

Harriet Braun created the BBC3 TV series *Lip Service* with Kudos, and wrote on and executive produced the second series. She has written extensively for TV and was also one of the co-creators of the World Productions series *Attachments*. She has numerous TV and film projects in development and is currently part of the writers' room for *Trust*, a TV series for FX. Harriet wrote and directed the play *Love Me Tender*, which was staged at the Finborough Theatre.

Notes on the text

This play needs minimal scenery – just enough to indicate the environment the characters are in.

Depending on where and when in time this is performed, popular culture references, with the exception of *Lost in Translation*, such as *Britain's got Talent*, may be changed if it is evident something else will resonate better with the audience.

The inner voices should wear something that marks them out – the same colour, perhaps, or the same clothes as their character. Although ideally they should be the same gender and around the same age as their character, they do not need to resemble their character in any other way. They stand or sit close to their character throughout. When the characters are mentioned in the stage directions, it is a given that their inner voices are with them.

What the inner voices do when they aren't speaking is a choice for the company, although they may at times reflect the feelings of their characters, both conscious and unconscious, through actions and gestures.

When not speaking, the Narrator sits on the side of the stage. Similarly what she does when not speaking is a choice for the company, although at times she might be engrossed in the action or alternatively reading a magazine, texting, listening to music on headphones, etc.

The performers playing the characters should not rely on their inner voices to play the subtext for them. Although the inner voices are an integral part of the piece, the performances of the characters should be as layered as if the inner voices weren't there. Running some scenes during rehearsal without the inner voices may help facilitate this.

Characters

Narrator, *sixteen or seventeen, referred to as 'she' for ease, but can be male or female*

Lena, *sixteen, female*

Lena's Inner Voice, *female*

Jamie, *seventeen, male*

Jamie's Inner Voice, *male*

Jo, *seventeen, female*

Jo's Inner Voice, *female*

Gina, *seventeen, female*

Gina's Inner Voice, *female*

Caz, *eighteen, female*

Caz's Inner Voice, *female*

Topsy, *nineteen, male*

Topsy's Inner Voice, *male*

Scene One

The **Narrator** *takes centre stage.*

Narrator So I'm sitting in front of the telly watching Jeremy Kyle and Mum comes in and she's all 'I said if you leave school you can't just sit around the house. Have you filled out that application for WH Smith's?' My mum hasn't got a clue, I'm going to be a star, the only application I want to fill out is for *Britain's Got Talent*. I'm not sure what my talent is yet, but I'm bound to have one.

Anyway, to shut my mum up I said I was going down the job centre. Instead I went and got a drink in this local caff and what do I see on the notice board – 'Narrator Wanted for Theatre Production'. So I think – HELLO! Anyway, I call the number and I go in for this audition and the director says the narrator's job is to help tell the story – and I say I love telling stories, that my mum says I can talk the hind legs off a donkey. Although why anyone would want a donkey's hind legs I dunno.

He gets me to prance about reading some stuff, and I kill that, cos it's showing off and I am definitely good at showing off. And cos it's all going well I ask whether I get to wear a fancy costume and he says the narrator's role isn't so much about being in the limelight as 'facilitating others in telling their stories'. So I'm like I'm not one for the limelight, which is a big fat lie, but I'm thinking once I'm on stage who says I won't be in the limelight.

Like now for instance, I was just meant to come on and introduce the characters, but I figured first you'd want to hear about me. Although I suppose we better get on with the show.

She turns to stage left and shouts:

You can come out now!

Lena *and* **Jamie** *walk out accompanied by their* **Inner Voices**.
Lena *lays out a towel and lies down on it, sunglasses propped on her head, wearing headphones that are plugged in to her phone. She flicks through a magazine.* **Jamie**, *who is on the other side of the garden fence, is doing some gardening. They ignore the* **Narrator** *as she walks around them talking and pointing things out.*

Narrator   So this is what's gonna happen. These are some of our characters. In a minute you're gonna see three stories which are mostly about love and friendship and stuff, which I'm sure you're relieved about. People pretend to want to know about war and politics but they don't really.

Anyway – (*Points.*) This is Lena and this is Jamie and next to them are their inner voices. Inner voices, can I borrow you a minute.

The **Inner Voices** *come over and stand either side of her.*

Narrator   You know how when you're telling your mates a funny story and they're all laughing and a voice in your head says . . .

Lena's Inner Voice   Check you out, you are hilarious.

Narrator   Well, that's your inner voice. Or sometimes it says shit things. Like the time I was walking round the park and I thought everyone was eyeing me up but I'd been eating a doughnut and I had jam all over my face. Then it said . . .

Jamie's Inner Voice   Oh God, embarrassing or what, everyone must think you're a right idiot.

The **Narrator**   *turns to the inner voices.*

Narrator   You can go back now.

The **Inner Voices** *go and join their characters again.*

Narrator   Anyway, on account of being the voices in the characters' heads, no one else on stage can see or hear them apart from their character, which I think is weird, but whatever.

So this is where we're at. (*Pointing.*) Lena, over there, is the year below Jamie at school and there's no way she'd usually hang out with him cos she's like the prettiest girl in the school and she dates Daz in Jamie's year, who is like a total hunk. Only a few weeks ago Jamie's family moved in next door, so they got chatting over the garden fence which Jamie is well pleased about cos he luuuurves Lena.

OK, best get started, I'll be over there, I would say just ignore me but I'm hard to ignore.

The **Narrator** *walks to the side of the stage and sits down.*

Lena *is looking at her phone.*

Lena's Inner Voice   Why doesn't he text? Maybe he's with some other girl. He can't be, there's no way he'd fancy another girl more than you, is there?

Jamie *stands up, trowel in hand and notices that* **Lena** *is now in her garden.*

Jamie's Inner Voice   Shit, it's Lena. Quick. Look cool.

Jamie *attempts to take up a cool pose, but it's a disaster.*

Jamie's Inner Voice   What are you doing? You look like an idiot.

Jamie *relaxes again.*

Jamie   Hey Lena.

Lena *hears him but pretends not to as she has her headphones in.*

Lena's Inner Voice   Jamie's sweet but he's bound to fancy you, you probably shouldn't encourage him.

Jamie   Lena.

Lena *doesn't respond.*

Jamie's Inner Voice   Try again.

Jamie   What if she's ignoring me?

Jamie's Inner Voice   Are you a man or a mouse?

Jamie   A mouse, obviously.

Jamie's Inner Voice   Just do it!

Jamie   Lena.

Lena's Inner Voice   Then again, if Daz *is* off chatting up other girls two can play at that game.

Lena *looks up, takes her headphones off, approaching the fence*

Lena   Tell me you're not gardening. My grandad gardens.

Jamie's Inner Voice   Oh great, that well-known turn-on, looking like someone's grandad.

Jamie   I'm not gardening.

Lena   You're holding a trowel.

Jamie   It's the new must-have accessory. I'm surprised you haven't got one.

Lena *smiles, amused.*

Lena's Inner Voice   He's funny. Who knew a brainiac would be so funny.

Jamie's Inner Voice   She's smiling – keep her smiling.

Jamie   Actually, don't tell anyone, but my little brother's been making noises about wanting the big bedroom, so I killed him. I was just burying him. I'm going to tell my parents he ran away.

Lena *laughs.*

Lena's Inner Voice   I suppose there's no harm in being friendly. There's no one around to see.

Lena   Wanna jump over here and hang out.

Jamie's Inner Voice (*excited – possibly punching the air or doing a victory dance or both*)   Yes! Yes! Result!

Jamie (*feigning nonchalance*)   Sure, why not.

He hops over the fence and they sit down together.

Lena   So what you up to the rest of the day?

Jamie's Inner Voice   Obsessively thinking about you probably.

Jamie   Well, I'm either going to charter a private jet and head off on a round-the-world adventure where I do James Bond style stuff, or I might help my nan put up an IKEA cabinet, it's a tough call.

Lena   I'd love to travel round the world.

Jamie   Me too. Actually I've got this plan that one day I'm gonna do it and write a blog called 'Jamie's Here, You're Not'. I thought I'd take selfies in front of –

Lena   – every famous monument?

Jamie   Yeah, how did you know?

Lena   Cos that's what I wanna do too. Only my blog's gonna be called 'Lena's Luvvin It'.

Both surprised to share the same dream.

Jamie's Inner Voice   Weird.

Lena's Inner Voice (*simultaneously*)   Weird.

Jamie   So give me your best in-front-of-a-monument selfie face.

Lena *poses, smiling and looking carefree.*

Jamie   Nice, it's a sort of an 'I'm definitely having a better time than you' look.

Lena   So what's yours?

Jamie   Mine's . . .

He poses looking serious and clever.

Lena   Interesting choice.

Jamie   I'm going for 'I've grown a lot wiser through my travels and now I'm an intriguing and deep person'.

Lena *laughs*

Lena's Inner Voice   Who knew hanging with Jamie'd be so much fun. When you told Daz about travelling he said he'd never want to go somewhere they don't serve fish and chips.

Jamie's Inner Voice   Who knew you'd have so much in common. Maybe *you are* in with a chance.

Jamie   The place I most want to go is Japan. There's this cool hotel I saw in this film . . .

Lena   *Lost in Translation?*

Jamie   Yeah! You know that film? It's really old. No one ever knows that film.

Lena   I've seen it like a million times. The whole idea of two people meeting so randomly and getting on so brilliantly, it's really romantic.

Jamie   Yeah.

Both of them suddenly look a bit awkward

Jamie's Inner Voice   It sounds like she's talking about you!

Lena's Inner Voice   Why did you say that? He might think you're talking about him! This is Daz's fault, why hasn't he texted? (**Lena***'s phone beeps.)* Ooh, maybe that's him.

Lena *hurriedly grabs her phone. Then looks really annoyed when it's not Daz and chucks it aside.*

Lena   Why do mobile phone providers text you *all* the bloody time. No one wants to read their crap.

Jamie   Were you expecting someone else?

Lena   No, well, sort of.

Lena's Inner Voice   You can't tell him, it's embarrassing. Then again it is only Jamie.

Lena   Daz went caravanning in the Isle of Wight with his parents yesterday and he hasn't texted me back all day. D'you think that's weird?

Jamie's Inner Voice   Daz, Daz, stupid, horrible, better-looking-than-you, boyfriend Daz. Any luck he's been run over in a freak caravanning accident.

Jamie   He probably just hasn't got any reception.

Lena   I thought that but he posted some pics on Facebook earlier. He's probably just busy, right?

Jamie's Inner Voice   Busy chasing other girls.

Jamie   Yeah, probably.

Lena   Maybe he just needs some space, I mean when people are going out they need space sometimes, don't they?

Jamie   Yeah, I suppose.

Lena's Inner Voice   Why does he look weird? Maybe he knows something, maybe Daz *is* with some other girl.

Lena   Why d'you look like that?

Jamie   Like what?

Lena   I dunno, weird.

Jamie's Inner Voice   Because Daz is a bastard who's always flirting with other girls and she deserves better.

Jamie   I don't.

Lena   Yeah, you do.

Jamie's Inner Voice   Don't say it. Don't say it, she won't want to hear it.

Jamie   Well, it's just –

Jamie's Inner Voice   Oh shit, you're saying it.

Jamie   – a bit rude, isn't it, not to text. If I loved someone I'd want to respect them and that means I'd keep in touch not leave them worrying something was wrong.

Lena's Inner Voice   What! Daz does respect you. He loves you. He told you. Jamie's just jealous. And he's a geek, what does he know?

Jamie's Inner Voice   You *so* shouldn't have said that.

Lena   You just don't like him.

Jamie's Inner Voice   Don't like him! You hate him more than you've ever hated anyone.

Jamie   Look, forget I said that, I hardly know him.

Lena   Exactly, so you shouldn't be judging him, or talking about stuff you don't understand.

She hastily gets up, grabs her towel and phone and headphones.

I've gotta go, I've got stuff to do.

As she makes her way inside, **Jamie** *watches her go, distressed.*

Jamie's Inner Voice   Well, someone shouldn't have opened their big mouth. Looked like you were in with a chance and now you've blown it.

Jamie *sticks his fingers up at his inner voice.*

Scene Two

The **Narrator** *gets up and runs to the centre of the stage. As she talks, in the background we see* **Jamie** *get up and make his way back over the fence and then offstage.*

Narrator   Oooh – 'methinks the lady doth protest too much'. That's Shakespeare, bet you didn't expect me to know any Shakespeare. I saw it on a game show. That's my back-up plan, if *Britain's Got Talent* doesn't work out I'm gonna win big on a game show.

Anyway, what about those two. I dated this good-looking bloke like Daz once. Well, not exactly dated, he bought me a Nandos. But I thought it was a bit weird cos he looked really bored, before I'd even said anything. Anyway turns out he was never even interested. I was doing a Saturday job at the gym and my friend Lianne heard him telling his mate Leo that he was only after me getting him in half price. Well, the joke was on him cos they sacked me after two weeks, so he got nothing and I got a free peri peri chicken burger.

OK, so I suppose we should get on with the show, which is kind of a shame, cos there's a lot you still don't know about me. It's OK though, when I'm on *Britain's Got Talent* they'll do one of those little films where they show your mum's house and your dog and stuff and then you get to say loads.

She turns to the side of the stage.

Can you come out, please?

Jo *walks on to the stage accompanied by her* **Inner Voice**. *They sit down.* **Jo** *gets out a book and reads as the* **Narrator** *talks.*

Narrator   So this is Jo and she's just moved away from London with her parents. She likes to come and sit by this river cos she's the shy and reserved type and they do stuff like that. Anyway, Jo's had to start at a new sixth form and in the wings over there is Gina. She's at Jo's school in the same year, but she's a really confident party girl, not like Jo at all, and well, she likes to come to the river too.

So enjoy. I'll be over there if you need me.

As the **Narrator** *walks to the side of the stage,* **Jo** *flicks through her book, then puts it down and stares into the distance.*

Jo's Inner Voice   Could you be any more miserable?
Maybe you'll always feel like this. Maybe you'll never be
happy again.

Gina *walks on to the stage looking at her mobile. She hasn't noticed*
Jo *yet.*

Jo's Inner Voice   Oh God, it's Gina from school. Great,
now she's gonna see you here alone and think you're more of
a friendless freak than she probably already does.

Jo *quickly looks away.* **Gina** *looks up and sees her.*

Gina's Inner Voice   Wicked, it's that new girl from
school. Your chance to check things out, see if she's as stuck-
up as she seems. Just when you think life can't be any more
fun, suddenly it is!

Gina *approaches* **Jo** *and sits down next to her.*

Gina   So finally I get to talk to the mystery woman.

Jo   Me?

Gina   Yeah, you, arriving from London, not talking to
anyone at school, disappearing every lunch break.

Jo's Inner Voice   Oh shit, she thinks you're rude, don't
say you're shy – you'll look like a tit.

Jo   Well, it's just, you know, everyone knows everyone
already and I didn't really want to, well, muscle in.

Gina's Inner Voice   Oh, she's shy, that's why she's been
so weird.

Gina   We don't bite you know. I'm Gina by the way, and
you're Jo, right.

Jo *nods.*

Gina   D'you live near here?

Jo   Yeah. My parents took over the Yew Tree restaurant up
the road, so we live above that now.

Gina   Shit, that's so posh. I've always wanted to go there. Does that mean you get free meals?

Jo   Yeah, if I want I can go in the kitchen and ask for something. Although it also means I have to get eyed up by our chef. He's called Wolfgang, he wears a white leather jacket with studs on and white cowboy boots and he's got a moustache.

Gina   Mmmh – *hot*!

Jo   The sad thing is he thinks he is. He's from Germany – maybe a big tash and cowboy boots are a hit with the fräuleins.

Gina *and* **Jo** *laugh*

Jo's Inner Voice   She's actually being really nice to you. She's got the loveliest smile.

Gina's Inner Voice   She's not stuck-up at all, in fact she seems really nice. She's really pretty too.

Gina   So where *do* you go at lunchtime. We've all been really intrigued. No wait, let me guess, you've got a secret bloke, he's older and you're meeting in the Premier Inn for a lunchtime liaison

Jo's Inner Voice   You can't tell her, you'll look like a total saddo.

Jo   Um . . . I go to that greasy spoon down by the station.

Gina   That weird-looking one where all the lorry drivers go?

Jo's Inner Voice   What did I tell you.

Jo   All the lorry drivers and me. I take a book. They do a great fry-up, and you know lunchtimes are kind of awkward, for me, at school.

Jo's Inner Voice   Well. she obviously thinks you're a total loser now, she probably wants to leave.

Gina's Inner Voice   She's obviously having a really hard time, you should've spoken to her before.

Gina   I'm guessing you didn't really want to move?

Jo   I'm not a big fan of the countryside.

Gina's Inner Voice   Hilarious, she thinks you're a bumpkin.

Gina   We have a good time here as well you know. (*Smiles.*) We have electricity and running water and everything. If you go into town there's even shops

Jo   It didn't help that when I came for the interview at the school the headmistress told me I could meet people by joining the young farmers' association.

Gina   Mrs Barker! She's such a fossil. I've never even met a farmer. I doubt even farmers join it. It's probably just an empty room.

Jo   Well, empty apart from the new students Mrs Barker sends there.

Gina *and* **Jo** *smile enjoying themselves. Simultaneous:*

Jo's Inner Voice   This is great, it's like you've known her forever.

Gina's Inner Voice   This is great, it's like you've known her forever.

Gina   So d'you still go and visit your friends in London?

Jo's Inner Voice   Shit. Now what d'you say?

Jo   Well, I thought I would, but it didn't really turn out that way.

Gina   What d'you mean?

Jo's Inner Voice   What did you open your big mouth for? It's not like you can tell her the truth.

Jo   Well, my best friend was all excited about going to this new sixth form and, well, I don't really hear from her much now.

Gina's Inner Voice   Why does it seem like she's hiding something? She's so mysterious and intriguing. Maybe you could work on being mysterious. Yeah, right, you're about as mysterious as a pair of socks.

Gina   Sounds like you're well shot of her. D'you have a boyfriend in London?

Jo's Inner Voice   Red alert, the boyfriend question.

Jo   Yeah. No.

Gina   So which one is it?

Jo's Inner Voice   Don't ever take up espionage, you'd totally suck at it.

Jo   No, no one special.

Jo's Inner Voice   Quick, change the subject.

Jo   What about you?

Gina   Nah, I've got off with loads of lads, but I haven't got serious with anyone.

Gina's Inner Voice   What d'you say that for?! It sounds like you'll snog anyone.

Jo   How come?

Gina's Inner Voice   Well, this is tricky. It's like you're interested but then you're not any more and you don't know why.

Gina   I dunno, guess I'm too busy having fun. So many lads too little time, know what I mean.

Jo's Inner Voice   No, you don't. That's the problem.

Gina *looks at her watch;* **Jo** *notices.*

Gina's Inner Voice   You better get back for dinner. Mum's making spag bog, yum.

Jo's Inner Voice   She obviously wants to leave. She's got better things to do than talk to you.

Gina   I've gotta get back for dinner.

Jo's Inner Voice   That's probably just an excuse.

Jo   No worries.

Gina   But look, there's a party later at a mate's house. D'you wanna come?

Jo's Inner Voice   She's asking you to a party!

Gina   I live just down the road from the Yew Tree, you could come to mine and we could get ready together.

Jo's Inner Voice   Oh shit, a party, with loads of people you don't know.

Gina's Inner Voice   Maybe she doesn't want to come, maybe she doesn't like you after all! (*Beat.*) Bollocks, this is just what shy people do.

Gina (*off* **Jo***'s worried expression*)   Don't worry, I won't leave you on your own.

Jo   Sure, sounds great.

Gina's Inner Voice   See!

Gina   I'm 9 Elmer Close, see you at eight?

She walks off.

Scene Three

As the **Narrator** *makes her way centre stage,* **Jo** *sits in the background for a moment, smiling, unable to believe the turn things have taken for the better. As the* **Narrator** *talks,* **Jo** *slowly picks up* *her book and makes her way offstage, and* **Caz** *makes her way onstage and sits down.*

Narrator   Well, I'm glad Jo's got a new mate. It's terrible falling out with your friends. I fell out with my best mate Lianne once. We were at this party and this bloke had a huge spliff and I don't take drugs cos it's stupid but Lianna said we should try some and then I felt terrible, like I was paralysed. Lianne kept laughing and telling me I wasn't paralysed cos I was rubbing my nose. But when I told her I definitely was she threw a bucket of water over my head cos apparently she thought it would help. So then I was paralysed *and* I had bad hair.

Anyway, now we're gonna meet Caz and Topsy. That's Caz sitting over there in a café looking awkward. Caz and Topsy's sisters are mates and they've set them up on a blind date. You see, they were both dumped a few months ago and their sisters reckon this might cheer them up – shows how much sisters know. You'll see what I mean.

The **Narrator** *walks to the side of the stage and sits down.*

Caz's Inner Voice   He's late. Great. You knew this was a bad idea.

Topsy *comes hurrying into the café and looks around.*

Topsy's Inner Voice   Is that her? Pretty. But not as pretty as Soph.

Caz's Inner Voice   That must be him. Well, he's definitely got nothing on Kev.

Topsy *approaches the table.*

Topsy   Caz?

Caz   Topsy?

Topsy   Sorry I'm late, it was murder getting the curlers out of my hair.

Caz *doesn't laugh.*

Topsy   I'm joking, I don't use curlers.

Caz *forces a smile.*

Caz   Right.

As **Topsy** *sits down:*

Topsy's Inner Voice   Wow, looks like she's gonna be a tough crowd.

Caz's Inner Voice   You just have to get through this, then you can get out of here.

Topsy   So . . . you're Ellie's sister.

Caz   Yup.

Topsy's Inner Voice   Oh, nice opening gambit, Casanova, state the obvious why don't you.

Caz   And you're Mandy's brother.

Topsy   Yup, that's me. Mandy's brother. One and the same. One *and* the same.

Topsy's Inner Voice   Now you're just babbling utter shite.

Caz's Inner Voice   Who is this loser? What was Ellie thinking?

Topsy's Inner Voice   What's the matter with you? You used to have game, now you're totally lame. Pull it together.

Topsy   It's boiling out there. Not that I'm complaining. I love the heat.

Topsy's Inner Voice   I said pull it together not talk about the weather!

Caz's Inner Voice   It's official, your sister's set you up on a date with your grandad.

Caz   I'm a bit too hot actually. I shouldn't have worn this top.

Topsy   It's OK, we all make fashion errors.

Caz   I meant cos it's too warm.

Topsy   Right. Sorry.

Topsy's Inner Voice   Look on the bright side, the ground could open up and swallow you.

Caz's Inner Voice   It's official, this bloke has *no* game.

Topsy   Oh shit, sorry, d'you wanna drink?

Caz   A Coke would be good.

Topsy   One Coke coming up.

As he gets up and heads away from the table:

Topsy's Inner Voice   Man, this is a disaster, I mean she's a tough crowd but can you blame her. You have let this whole Soph thing get to you. You have got to stop thinking about her or you are *never getting laid again.*

As **Topsy** *disappears offstage,* **Caz** *is left on her own.*

Caz's Inner Voice   Could he be any sadder? Wonder what Kev's doing now. He's probably with that girl. They're probably in the park, holding hands, snogging. He's probably not thinking about you at all.

Topsy *reappears with two cans of Coke.*

Topsy's Inner Voice   Right, confidence my man, confidence. That's what women want. Time to get the Topsy magic back.

He hands a can of Coke to **Caz**.

Topsy   Here you go.

Caz   Thanks.

Topsy   So . . . what d'you when you're not sitting here, you know, hobbies and that.

Topsy's Inner Voice   Hobbies? That's your play?

Caz's Inner Voice   What is this, a job interview?

Caz   Well, I guess I like TV and films and stuff.

Topsy   Films, great, who doesn't love a good film.

Topsy's Inner Voice   You, you never watch them.

Caz   So what films you into?

Caz's Inner Voice   Now *you're* sounding like someone's gran. It's catching.

Topsy   Um . . . Um . . .

Topsy's Inner Voice   That's two ums so far.

Topsy   Um . . .

Topsy's Inner Voice   Woo hoo, the hat-trick, well done. It's *obvious*, just name some film girls like. Anything.

Topsy   I quite liked those *Pitch Perfect* ones.

Caz's Inner Voice   He can't be serious.

Caz   Right.

Topsy   Not your bag?

Caz   Not really, no.

Topsy's Inner Voice   Well, not all girls I guess.

Topsy   To be honest I'm not that good at sitting around, I'm sort of into sport, you know, running, the gym, and football.

Caz   Who do you support?

Topsy   You're into football?

Caz Well, not really, any more, my ex, Kev, was a footballer.

Topsy's Inner Voice Oh great, her ex is a footballer. As if you weren't feeling shit enough.

Topsy When did you break up?

Caz About four months ago.

Caz's Inner Voice Four months, three days and six hours to be exact.

Topsy's Inner Voice Same as you and Soph. So you do have *one* thing in common.

Caz's Inner Voice Don't show him you're upset.

Caz It's fine, we just drifted apart, we're friends.

Another awkward silence.

Topsy's Inner Voice No! Not another silence! Think man, think, there must be something you can talk about.

The silence continues

Why is there nothing in your brain? It's empty in here.

Topsy*'s mobile beeps, signalling a text. He gets it out and reads.*

Topsy Shit.

Caz Something the matter?

Topsy Our cat's been ill. My mum's gonna take her to the vet. Thinks she might have to be put down.

Caz's Inner Voice That's fantastic, he might need to leave.

Caz I guess you wanna get back, say goodbye.

Topsy Nah, it's OK.

Topsy's Inner Voice What are you saying? This is your chance. Cut your losses, call it a day, get out of here.

Topsy   Actually, yeah, it would be good.

Caz   No worries.

Topsy *hastily gets up,* **Caz** *doesn't.*

Caz   I'm just gonna finish my Coke.

Topsy   Cool, we can always do this again some other time.

Topsy's Inner Voice   As if.

Caz   Sure.

Caz's Inner Voice   Like hell.

Topsy   See ya.

Caz   Bye.

Topsy *heads out of the café.*

Scene Four

Caz *sits sipping her Coke and texting as the* **Narrator** *walks centre stage.*

Narrator   So I would tell you about the time I went on a blind date but the director's had a word. He said my job's to tell the stories and I've got to stop with the ad libbing and I said, well, it's improvisation, that's when you make shit up in the theatre. But he wasn't having any of it and told me to just get on with the show. So I will, but I'm telling you he's gonna be sorry when I'm famous.

Caz *gets up and leaves the stage as* **Lena** *walks into her garden in the background and sits under a tree. She has her headphones on and rests her head in her folded arms, unhappy.*

Narrator   OK, so now it's time to catch up with Lena and Jamie. It's been a week since Lena and Jamie had that spat in her garden and they haven't spoken since. Fact is they don't talk much at school anyway. Jamie hangs out with Big Sam who wears a *Call of Duty* T-shirt and plays loads of video games and no girl would ever talk to Big Sam unless they were like dead or mad. Jamie doesn't care cos Big Sam's really nice and very clever, but there's no way Lena wants to be seen anywhere near Big Sam cos her mates would laugh. Anyway, now a lot has happened, which I can't tell you cos you're about to find out.

The **Narrator** *makes her way to the side of the stage and we hear that* **Lena** *is crying.* **Jamie** *walks out into his garden.*

Jamie's Inner Voice   What's that?

Jamie *looks around and sees* **Lena***, who doesn't see him as she's too busy sobbing.*

Jamie's Inner Voice   Shit, it's Lena. You need to go over there.

Jamie   I can't, she's angry with me.

Jamie's Inner Voice   She's probably crying about Daz. This is your chance. She'll realise Daz is a shit and you're a much better idea.

Jamie   She might shout at me.

Jamie's Inner Voice   What would James Bond do?

Jamie *braces himself, climbs over the fence and approaches* **Lena** *who still has her head in her arms, crying. She senses someone approaching and looks up. She takes her headphones out, annoyed.*

Jamie   Lena?

Lena's Inner Voice   You can't talk to Jamie – you can't talk to anyone. You look like a total fool.

Lena   Go away.

Jamie's Inner Voice   *Do not* even think about going away! People always say that when they're upset but they don't mean it.

Jamie   I'm not gonna leave you here crying.

Lena's Inner Voice (*quietly*)   No, don't leave me.

Lena   You're trespassing, this is my garden.

Jamie *sits down.*

Jamie   You'll just have to call the police then. But I'm warning you it could get ugly. I'm armed and dangerous and I won't leave without a fight.

Lena *looks up and wipes her eyes. She can't help but smile.*

Lena   What are you armed with?

Jamie *picks up a twig on the grass beside him.*

Jamie   This. It may just look like a twig but in my hands it's so much more than that.

Jamie's Inner Voice   Great, she's smiling. God she's so beautiful when she smiles.

Lena's Inner Voice   He always makes you laugh, Daz didn't make you laugh, but then Daz is cool and, well, Jamie just isn't.

Jamie   Are you gonna tell me why you're crying?

Lena   So you can laugh at me.

Jamie   Yeah, cos that's always what I do with my friends, laugh at them.

Jamie's Inner Voice   Don't use the friend word, you idiot.

Lena's Inner Voice   You could ask him but you might find out things you don't wanna know. Just saying.

Lena   Have you heard anything about Daz? At school? Him and some girl?

Jamie *hesitates*

Jamie's Inner Voice   Don't say anything! Look what happened last time.

Lena   Look, I'm sorry I bit your head off, I promise not to do that again. Please, Jamie, I wanna know.

Jamie   Well, if you're sure.

Lena's Inner Voice   Told you. This doesn't sound good.

Jamie   He was sort of telling his mates he copped off with some girl on his weekend away. But he might've just been boasting, who knows if it was even true.

Lena's Inner Voice   This can't be happening. Things like this happen to losers not people like you.

Lena   It is true, he was being really weird and then I found this text on his mobile from some girl. He denied it but I know he was lying. I guess you're gonna tell me I told you so. That I'm an idiot and I should've known.

Jamie's Inner Voice   You'd never think she's an idiot. You luurrve her.

Jamie   It's him who's the idiot, Lena, not you.

Lena's Inner Voice   Everyone knew apart from you, they've all been laughing at you behind your back.

Lena *starts to cry again.*

Jamie's Inner Voice   Give her a hug.

Jamie *(mouthing at inner voice)*   No!

Jamie's Inner Voice   Man up and just do it. Do it now!

Jamie *edges towards* **Lena** *and tentatively puts his arm around her. She moves into his arms and he hugs her.*

Jamie's Inner Voice   Oh my God, you're hugging Lena. This is actually happening.

Lena's Inner Voice   Now that feels surprisingly good, safe and happy and . . . but it's Jamie. What would your mates say if they saw you hugging Jamie? Everyone's already laughing at you, wanna make them laugh some more?

Lena *quickly pulls away, drying her eyes, looking a little awkward.* **Jamie**, *seeing she's awkward, looks awkward too. Quickly deflecting he picks up her phone.*

Jamie   What you listening to?

Lena *quickly grabs it off him.*

Lena   No way, then you'll definitely laugh at me.

Jamie   OK, let's get one thing straight, I don't laugh at my friends.

Jamie's Inner Voice   Will you stop with the friend word!

Lena   It's Katie X – she's my guilty pleasure.

Jamie   Why guilty? She's the queen of pop, she's great.

Lena   Well, my mates aren't really into pop, they think it's shit.

Jamie   I don't care what my mates think. Then again, Sam isn't really in a position to judge anyone. He still wears Spiderman pyjamas.

Lena's Inner Voice   Why does he hang out with Big Sam, doesn't he realise it's embarrassing?

Lena   Is he like your best mate?

Jamie's Inner Voice   Oh God, she thinks Sam's uncool. You could say he just tags around after you. That you don't really like him.

Jamie *surreptitiously sticks his finger up at his* **Inner Voice**.

Jamie   Yeah – he's really nice – I know he looks weird but he'd do anything for anyone.

Lena's Inner Voice   You don't feel like that about your mates, do you? In fact now Daz has shat on you some of them are telling you I told you so.

Jamie's Inner Voice   This is your chance. Daz is out the picture and there's the tickets. Mention the tickets. Do it. Do it now!

Jamie   You know my uncle works for Katie X's record label.

Lena   No way! Bury the headline.

Jamie's Inner Voice   Go on, now, before you lose your bottle.

Jamie   Well, it's just he's got me two tickets to her concert on the 14th and I thought maybe, you know, to cheer you up, you might wanna go.

Lena's Inner Voice   Oh my God, is this Jamie asking you out? You can't go on a date with Jamie.

Jamie's Inner Voice   Shit, she doesn't look happy, quick, do something, anything

Jamie   Oh not as a date, just as a friend, I've got a girlfriend.

Jamie's Inner Voice   What?! Since when?!

Lena's Inner Voice   He's seeing someone?! Who? And why do you care?!

Lena   Who – who is she?

Jamie's Inner Voice   Yeah – who the hell is she?

Jamie   She's, um . . . the daughter of some friends of my parents. We met the, um . . . other week. She's called . . . Marigold.

Jamie's Inner Voice   Marigold!

Lena   Cool.

She gets up.

I just remembered I said I'd help my mum with something. But that sounds good, let's go. I'll text you.

As she walks off:

Jamie I can't believe it. I've got a date with Lena.

Jamie's Inner Voice Well, not really, you've got a girlfriend, remember. I don't think Marigold will be amused.

Jamie Shut up.

Scene Five

*As **Jamie** walks off the **Narrator** takes centre stage.*

Narrator Not being funny, but Lena's just been lied to by Daz and now Jamie's lied to her, I'm not sure that's gonna turn out well. I was gonna tell you about the time I told this massive lie but, well, I've told you about the little director problem, so you'll be missing out on that treat.

Anyway, since Jo and Gina had that chat by the river they've been thick as thieves, and now they're on a school history trip to London. They get to stay in a hotel for two nights and everything and go to these lectures for sixth formers which I *never* got to do at school. Anyway, Gina asked Jo if she'd share a room with her and she said yes and, well, they've just arrived at the hotel room.

Gina *and* **Jo** *let themselves into the room.* .

Gina I thought it'd be minging but it's all right.

Jo It is, isn't it. Although I don't think much of the orange bedspreads.

*As **Jo** sits on a bed and **Gina** wanders around checking things out:*

Jo's Inner Voice   Check you out. Two whole days in a hotel with Gina. Shame you can't stay here forever.

Gina   I don't believe it, there's a minibar!

As she rifles through the minibar and pulls out some drinks:

Gina's Inner Voice   Perfect, why didn't you think of this before, you both need to get drunk.

Jo   Put them back. They'll go on the bill.

Gina   We'll just say it was a mistake and we didn't touch them.

Jo's Inner Voice   Should you show her the wine? What if she thinks you're trying to get her drunk? Don't be stupid, she doesn't know what you're thinking.

Jo *gets up and takes them out of her hand.*

Jo   No! We don't need them anyway, I filched this from the restaurant.

She pulls a bottle of wine out of her bag.

Gina's Inner Voice   Hello! Maybe she wants you to get drunk too.

Gina   You're a genius.

She throws her a corkscrew.

Crack it open.

Jo   We can't drink it now, we've gotta go to that lecture at six.

Gina's Inner Voice   Lecture! Is she mad? This is your chance to hang out alone.

Gina   Forget that, it's some boring shit about Tudor food.

Jo   Mrs Heaver might be there.

Gina   No, she won't. She's way too lazy.

Jo   You don't know that.

Gina   I do. You know last year before you were here we had to do this history project, four thousand words about whatever we wanted, like any of us wanted to do any of it. Anyway we had this joke Mrs Heaver just weighed them and gave a mark that way. I thought I'd test it out so I wrote 'Two pints of lager and a packet of crisps please', right in the middle of a paragraph. She never noticed, I even got a tick on that page.

Jo   No way.

Gina   Yes way.

As the two of them laugh, having a great time:

Jo's Inner Voice   It's great, isn't it? How she just does what she likes. You've always wanted to be like that.

Gina's Inner Voice   It's so sweet, how scared she is of everything. You've never really been scared, well, not until now.

Jo *opens the bottle of wine. She takes out some plastic glasses, pours some wine in and hands one to* **Gina**.

Jo   Let's celebrate.

Gina   What are we celebrating?

Jo   Getting to know each other.

Gina   I will definitely drink to that. To us.

Jo's Inner Voice   She said us!

Jo   To us.

Gina   I've got a surprise for you. A present.

Jo's Inner Voice   A present. She must've been thinking about you when you're not there?

As **Gina** *rifles in her bag:*

Gina's Inner Voice   Look at you, all nervous, this is a first. .

Gina *pulls an envelope out of her bag, then sits down next to* **Jo** *on the bed and hands it to her.* **Jo** *opens it.*

Jo   Tickets to the Katie X concert. I can't believe it. No one can get these. How d'you pull that off?

Gina's Inner Voice   By spending forever on the internet trying to make it happen.

Gina   Just got lucky I guess.

Jo *spontaneously throws her arms around* **Gina**. *They hug for a moment.*

Jo's Inner Voice   Mmmh, she smells like roses. Pull yourself together, she'll think you're weird. She got off with Jason at that party on Saturday, she likes lads.

Jo *pulls away and looks awkward, quickly changing the subject.*

Jo   So what's happening with Jason?

Gina's Inner Voice   Who? Oh him.

Gina   Nothing.

Jo   How come?

Gina's Inner Voice   Tell her!

Gina   I was just pissed, I'm not really into him.

Gina's Inner Voice   Wow, you are really bottling it!

Gina   What about you, did you snog anyone?

Jo   Nah.

Gina   It's just you never mention any lads you like.

Jo's Inner Voice   Don't tell her, don't tell her, you can't ever tell her. You know what'll happen.

Jo   I guess I'm fussy.

Gina *glances at* **Jo**.

Gina's Inner Voice   God, she's *sooo* pretty.

Jo's Inner Voice   Why is she looking at you like that? Maybe you've got something on your face?

Gina's Inner Voice   Oh come on, enough of the nerves, do it, just do it.

Gina *lies back on the bed.*

Gina   Did you read that thing in *Heat*, said Katie X might be bisexual.

Jo's Inner Voice   Only five times!

Jo   Don't think I saw it.

Gina   It's just I think I might be bisexual.

Gina's Inner Voice   Woo hoo, get in.

Jo   Yeah?

Jo's Inner Voice   Is this happening? Is this really happening?

Gina   Well, sometimes I fancy girls.

Jo's Inner Voice   Breathe. Breathe.

Jo   Yeah?

Gina   Yeah, actually I kind of fancy you.

Jo, *dumbstruck, says nothing.*

Jo's Inner Voice   This is too amazing – good things like this don't happen.

Gina's Inner Voice   Why isn't she saying anything? Well, you can't stop now, you've got to be in it to win it.

Gina   And I was wondering if maybe, you know, you feel the same?

Jo's Inner Voice   It is happening. It's actually happening.

Gina   Well are you gonna say anything or do I have to die of embarrassment.

Jo *turns towards* **Gina**.

Jo   Yeah, yeah I do.

Jo *and* **Gina** *look at each other. They may or may not already have started kissing as the* **Narrator** *comes hurrying centre stage.*

Scene Six

Narrator   Well, I'm gonna stop that right there. Off you go, you two. We don't want things getting X-rated. Cos I can see the way that was going. Anyway, now we're going to another part of the country where Caz is standing alone at a bus stop waiting to get a bus home.

Caz *walks onstage and stands at the bus stop.*

Narrator   Unfortunately for her Topsy doesn't live that far from her and he needs to get home too. And as you can imagine they are the last people either of them wants to see.

As the **Narrator** *makes her way to the side of the stage,* **Topsy** *arrives at the bus stop and sees* **Caz**.

Caz's Inner Voice   You have got be kidding.

Topsy's Inner Voice   Is this some kind of cosmic joke?

Caz   Hi.

Topsy   Fancy meeting you here.

Caz   Getting the bus?

Topsy   Yeah.

Topsy's Inner Voice   What d'you say that for? Now you have to stand here, you idiot!

As **Caz** *and* **Topsy** *stand there, awkward:*

Caz's Inner Voice   Come on, bus. *Come on.*

Topsy's Inner Voice   Oh no, you can't go through this again. You have to do something. Anything.

Topsy   Look, I'm sorry about the other day. I mean that was a really bad date. Oh, not cos of you. I mean I can normally, you know, hold a conversation. I was dumped by my girlfriend and my sister thought a date would help but I guess she was wrong. And that makes me sound sad, I know, but I figured you already think I'm sad, so, well . . .

Topsy's Inner Voice   I said do something, not bleat your heart out like someone on Jeremy Kyle.

Caz   It's OK. Me too.

Topsy   You were dumped by my girlfriend too?

Caz *smiles; it's one of the first we've seen from her.*

Caz   No. My boyfriend dumped me.

Topsy   Well, that's a relief, if I'd found out she was seeing you behind my back too, that would've been too much.

Caz *laughs again.*

Topsy's Inner Voice   So she does have a sense of humour!

But then **Caz***'s laughter soon turns to tears as she start to cry.*

Topsy's Inner Voice   Shit. What the hell?

Topsy   You OK?

Caz *shakes her head, no.*

Caz's Inner Voice *looks totally horrified and disgusted.*

Caz's Inner Voice   No, you really aren't, crying in the street, talk about tragic.

Topsy   Hey.

Topsy *hugs* **Caz**.

Caz's Inner Voice   OK, just so you know, you are making a total embarrassment of yourself.

Over **Topsy**'*s shoulder* **Caz** *holds her finger up at her* **Inner Voice***, who looks affronted.*

Caz's Inner Voice   Just saying.

Topsy's Inner Voice   Mmmh, this feels good. Ooops. Red alert, potential trouser snake problem.

Topsy *pulls away from* **Caz** *who tries to clean up her tears.*

Topsy   Wow, you had me fooled with all that 'we drifted apart, we're friends' stuff.

Caz   What was I supposed to say? He dumped me for someone prettier.

Topsy   I'm sure that's not true. I mean the prettier bit.

Caz   She's a lingerie model.

Topsy's Inner Voice   A footballer with a lingerie model – some lads have it too good.

Topsy   Well I'm sure she's ugly on the inside.

Caz *smiles, really warming to him.*

Caz   I'm sorry I was such a bitch, you know, when we met. I'm just so furious all the time. He told me he needed some time alone and then two days later I hear he's with her. There's like this angry voice in my head and it won't shut up.

Caz's Inner Voice   Too right I won't. You were fucked over.

Caz   I hate him but then I can't stop thinking about him, so then I hate myself.

Caz's Inner Voice   So you should, you're a loser who was taken in by some dickhead.

Topsy   If it's any consolation, my girlfriend dumped me for one of my mates.

Topsy's Inner Voice   Hey, what's with all the soul-baring? This is so not cool.

Caz   That sucks. You must be really angry with her.

Topsy   I should be but for some reason I seem to be obsessed with getting her back.

Topsy's Inner Voice   What did I just say!

Caz   Do you think you will?

Topsy   No. Unless the new boyfriend falls off a cliff, or I push him off.

Caz *amused.*

Caz   I guess that could work.

Topsy   Nice idea, but I don't think I'm up for it. Apparently prison food sucks and you're not allowed a mobile.

Caz   Cos that's the biggest problem with prison, the food and the lack of a smartphone.

Topsy   I'm a hungry guy and I like to stay in touch.

Caz *laughs.*

Caz's Inner Voice   Hey, what's with all the laughing and having fun? I'm still here you know, still angry. Are you just gonna ignore me?

She crosses her arms and looks affronted.

Topsy's Inner Voice   Look man, I'm your inner voice, all this saying what you really feel is making me redundant.

He also crosses his arms, fed up.

Topsy   The worst thing is her birthday's next week and I got her present months ago.

Caz   Look on the bright side, now you can take it back and get yourself something instead. What d'you get her?

Topsy   Tickets to Katie X.

Caz   No way.

Topsy   I know, I was a bloody great boyfriend. Don't get me wrong, I wanted to go, but still.

Caz   So what you gonna do?

Topsy   Dunno, flog 'em on eBay. Go on my own.

Caz   I like Katie X, I mean we could, you know, go, I could do with a friend who's as miserable as me.

Topsy   Yeah, why not, sounds good.

Topsy's Inner Voice, *who has been sulking, springs back into life.*

Topsy's Inner Voice   A friend! You're meant to be moving on, finding a new girlfriend, not making friends!

Topsy *surreptitiously turns to his inner voice and mouths:*

Topsy   Go away.

Caz's Inner Voice, *who has also been sulking, also springs back to life.*

Caz's Inner Voice   What are you doing? What if you get hurt again? Better to be miserable forever than have that happen.

Caz *surreptitiously turns to her inner voice and mouths:*

Caz   Shut up.

Topsy *and* **Caz** *see a bus approaching.*

Topsy   That's my bus.

Caz   I get the sixty-two.

Topsy   Well, I'm really glad I ran into you. I'll text you about the gig.

Caz   Cool.

Scene Seven

*As the **Narrator** comes onstage, **Caz** and **Topsy** and their **Inner Voices** sit down together. They are followed by **Gina** and **Jo** and their **Inner Voices** who sit down together a little further along the stage, and then **Lena** and **Jamie** and their **Inner Voices**, who also sit down together, a little further along still.*

Narrator   OK, so now we're reaching our gripping climax, we're going to jump in time, like on *Dr Who*. It's the day of Katie X's gig. Picture the scene, behind me is a load of grass. It's in a park and it's hot. Got it? And Jamie and Lena, Gina and Jo, and Topsy and Caz are all there. They're waiting for Katie X, who is late on, so they're chatting and chilling. And cos things are speeding up, when I clap my hands I get to freeze time like a wizard and we jump from one couple to another. OK, so we're kicking off with Lena and Jamie on their date not date.

*The **Narrator** walks to the side of the stage and sits down.*

Lena   Why d'you reckon she's so late on?

Jamie   Pop star's prerogative. If I was a pop star I'd be a total diva.

Lena   You would not.

Jamie   I would. I'd say things like 'The holes in these hoola hoops aren't big enough'.

Lena   Rubbish. I can't ever imagine you being nasty, you're too lovely.

Jamie's Inner Voice   She called you lovely!

Lena's Inner Voice   Did you just say he's lovely?!

Jamie   You're right, I am totally lovely.

Lena   Shut up.

She pushes him on the arm; he laughs.

Jamie   It's true, everyone says so.

They look at each other. The atmosphere is heavy with sexual tension.

Jamie's Inner Voice   Shit, how much d'you want to kiss her?

Lena's Inner Voice   He looks like he might kiss you and, stop press, you want him to. But what if someone sees you?

Lena *suddenly glances around her.* **Jamie** *notices.*

Jamie's Inner Voice   Why's she looking around?

Lena's Inner Voice   Chill, he's got a girlfriend anyway, remember.

Lena   So does your girlfriend not mind, you being here with me?

Jamie's Inner Voice   What do you do now, Pinocchio?

Jamie   Nah, she's cool like that. Anyway, she's away on a school trip.

Jamie's Inner Voice   Quick. Change the subject.

Jamie   I'm gonna get another Coke, d'you fancy one?

Lena   Sure.

Jamie   Look after my jacket, will you?

He gets up and walks offstage, leaving his jacket behind. As he disappears offstage his phone beeps in his pocket, signalling a text.

Lena's Inner Voice   That could be his girlfriend – aren't you curious to know what she's like?

Lena   I can't look.

Lena's Inner Voice   Yeah you can, he'll never know.

Lena *looks around and then reaches into* **Jamie**'s *pocket and pulls out the phone. She reads the text.*

Lena's Inner Voice   Whoa. No bloody way!

Jamie *walks back over holding a can of Coke.* **Lena** *holds the phone up, furious.*

Lena   What the hell is this?

Jamie *stops in his tracks, uncertain what's happened but looking alarmed.*

Lena   A text from your mate Sam – 'How's it going – hope your ruse with the made-up girlfriend is working out.' Did you make her up?

Jamie's Inner Voice   Oh no, this is bad, this is really, really bad.

Lena   Well?

Jamie *says nothing, caught.*

Lena   Oh great, so all that shit about respect and you're just a liar too.

She gets up and makes to walk off.

Jamie's Inner Voice   Do something. Stop her.

Jamie   Would you have come with me if I hadn't lied?

Lena *hesitates.*

Lena's Inner Voice   No.

Lena   Yes.

Jamie   Now who's the liar? If you thought this was a date you wouldn't have come, even though, I think you . . . well, I think you like me too.

Jamie's Inner Voice   Woo hoo, brave.

Jamie   Only you're worried about what people'll think, aren't you? When have we ever spent any time outside our back gardens? D'you think I don't see you avoiding me in the corridor at school. D'you think I didn't notice you looking around earlier in case anyone saw us? Yeah, I shouldn't have lied and I'm sorry, but I'm also sorry I had so little self-respect I'd hang out with someone who's embarrassed of me. So fine, be angry with me, cos I don't wanna know you any more anyway.

He turns and starts to walk off.

Lena's Inner Voice   Jamie. Out of your life. For good. You have to stop him.

Lena   Wait.

Jamie   What?

Lena *walks up to* **Jamie** *and kisses him.*

The **Narrator** *gets up and claps her hands.*

Narrator   OK you two lovebirds, stop right there. Sit down. Plenty of time for that later. Moving swiftly on to Gina and Jo, who only got back from their school trip yesterday and this is the first time they've seen each other.

The **Narrator** *sits down again.*

Gina *and* **Jo** *lounge on the grass.* **Gina** *looks totally chilled,* **Jo** *less so.*

Gina's Inner Voice   This is the life, Jo, the sunshine, being in love.

Gina   You OK?

Jo's Inner Voice   No.

Jo   Yeah, fine.

As **Gina** *looks around:*

Gina   It's weird, isn't it. All these people in the world and we'll only ever get to meet a tiny fraction of them.

Jo's Inner Voice   Why hasn't she mentioned the weekend?

Gina   I mean, there's probably people in, say, Japan or Iceland we'd get on really well with and we'll never know.

Jo's Inner Voice   Why's she talking about meeting other people? Does she mean some lad?

Gina's Inner Voice   She looks great today. You should just kiss her, but will she mind? What are the rules? This is all new. Look at you being all insecure.

Jo's Inner Voice   She's regretting it. I mean, she gave you a hug when you met up but she didn't kiss you. You've been here before. She's hoping if she doesn't mention it, it will all go away.

Gina's Inner Voice   Enough sitting here wondering, just talk to her.

Gina   Look, about the weekend.

Jo's Inner Voice   Don't let this happen again, get in there first.

Jo   I know what you're gonna say. It was a mistake. And you can chill cos I think so too.

Gina's Inner Voice   What?! Ouch.

Jo   I mean we can just be mates again, it's fine.

Gina's Inner Voice   Save face. Just save face.

Gina   Sure. Great. Course.

Jo's Inner Voice   See, you knew this would happen.

Gina's Inner Voice   Shit, this is what lads must feel like when you give them the old let's-be-friends speech. It sucks.

Jo's Inner Voice   Don't look sad, you'll look like a loser. Just chat like everything's normal.

Jo   So what did you get up to last night?

Gina's Inner Voice   Wait a minute. This is bullshit. You gonna let her get away with this?

Gina   Actually, it wasn't a mistake. Not for me.

Jo   It wasn't?

Gina   No! And I can't believe it was for you either.

Jo   Well . . . it wasn't really.

Gina's Inner Voice   What?!

Gina   So why did you say it was?

Jo   I thought that's what you were gonna say.

Gina   But why?

Jo   You know that mate in London I mentioned, well something happened before I left, you know, between us, and then she just stopped calling. I heard she's seeing some lad now.

Gina   Well I'm here, aren't I, and I haven't stopped calling and I'm not gonna be seeing any lad, cos, well, I think I'm, you know, gay. And I kind of thought you were too. Aren't you?

Jo *looks around a bit nervous.*

Jo   Well, yeah.

Gina   Hey, chill. We can get married now and everything.

Jo   You proposing?

Gina   Well, I think maybe we should try holding hands in public first.

She reaches out and takes **Jo**'s *hand.* **Jo** *smiles.* **Gina** *smiles.*

The **Narrator** *gets up and claps her hands.*

Narrator   OK, you two stay there. You can keep holding hands if you like. God, I wish my love life went this well. Last bloke I went on a date with had bad breath and kept talking about *Star Wars*. Let's see if we can score a hat-trick of happy endings, shall we? Caz, Topsy, you're on.

The **Narrator** *sits down.*

Topsy *looks at his watch.*

Topsy She's taking the piss now.

Caz Anyone would think you weren't having a nice time.

Topsy I'm having a great time, but she is taking the piss.

Topsy *flashes* **Caz** *a big smile.*

Caz's Inner Voice Stop admiring his lovely smile, you're not interested.

Topsy's Inner Voice It's true, you are having a great time. In fact you haven't thought about Soph all day. This is progress, my man, progress.

Caz So you been on any more dates?

Topsy Nah, I'm in no rush.

Caz's Inner Voice Now that could be cos he's interested in you, but you don't care, remember.

Topsy What about you?

Caz Nah, I've sworn off men for a while.

Caz's Inner Voice Exactly my point! So stop looking at him like that.

Topsy's Inner Voice The way she's looking at you, I think she might be lying.

He looks across at **Caz**'s *necklace.*

Topsy That's nice.

He reaches across and picks up the pendant on her necklace.

Topsy's Inner Voice This is more like it, my man, someone has his mojo back.

As **Topsy** *removes his hand:*

Caz Well, I'm glad you don't think this is a fashion error.

Topsy   You're never gonna let me forget that, are you?

Caz   Probably not.

Caz's Inner Voice   What's with the butterflies in your stomach? You need to be on your guard.

Topsy   So what did your sister say about us meeting up again?

Caz   She was pretty smug, said she knew we'd get on, that you're really nice.

Topsy   And what do you think? Am I nice?

Caz   Maybe.

Caz's Inner Voice   What the hell. Fluttering your eyelashes, flirty voice – rein this in now!

Topsy's Inner Voice   How did you not notice how hot she is before? Great eyes.

Topsy   Your neck's getting a bit burnt.

Caz   What you doing noticing my neck?

Topsy   Just looking out for you, that's all.

Caz's Inner Voice (*outraged*)   OK. This is now out-and-out flirting. This has to stop.

Topsy *picks up some sun cream.*

Topsy   Want me to put some on for you?

Caz's Inner Voice   No! You are taking a break from men, remember.

Caz   Sure.

As **Topsy** *rubs the cream in.*

Topsy's Inner Voice   Smooth, very smooth, nice work.

Caz's Inner Voice   I give up. If you don't wanna be angry any more, that's your business.

Topsy's Inner Voice   You know, I think my work here is done, someone is back on track.

The lights change as Katie X prepares to come on stage. **Caz** *looks up and smiles*

Caz   Something's happening.

We go to **Lena** *and* **Jamie**

Lena   I think she's coming on.

She looks at **Jamie** *and smiles*

Lena   What you thinking?

Jamie   That whatever else happens I'm gonna remember this moment.

We go to **Gina** *and* **Jo** *who also notice the lights.*

Gina   Finally.

Jo   I'm glad she was on late, you know, that we got a chance to chat.

Gina   Me too, but if you ever give me a heart attack like that again I'll kill you.

We go to **Jo** *and* **Topsy**.

Caz   What you thinking?

Topsy   That this turned into the best bad date I ever had.

Topsy *and* **Jo** *smile at each other as* **Topsy** *takes* **Jo**'s *hand.*

A voice booms out over the stage.

Voice   Ladies and gents, please welcome to the stage Katie X.

Simultaneously: **Lena** *and* **Jamie**, *holding hands, stand up.* **Gina** *and* **Jo**, *holding hands, stand up.* **Topsy** *and* **Caz**, *holding hands, stand up.*

Lights down then spotlight on the **Narrator**.

Narrator   So that, ladeez and gents, is the end of the show. I think it's a shame we don't get to find out what happens next like you do on the telly. But the director says that's the beauty of theatre, you get to imagine the rest for yourselves. Talking of telly. If there's anyone out there from, you know, reality TV, and you're looking for contestants, or maybe a presenter or, you know, anything really, I am totally available. Just catch me afterwards.

The End.

Three

BY HARRIET BRAUN

Notes on rehearsal and staging, drawn from a workshop with the writer, held at the National Theatre, October 2016

How Harriet came to write the play

Harriet explained that as a teenager she wrote extensive diaries and when she was asked to write a play for Connections, she revisited them. What struck her was the extreme self-consciousness and angst, alongside a distinction between how we present ourselves on the surface and who we would truly like to be. This was the initial idea for the inner voices. The title comes from the idea of an individual with two conflicting voices on their shoulders.

The Narrator was the first character that Harriet wrote. She describes their voice as 'just arriving'. The Narrator has no separate inner voice because they are the closest match between inner and outer; they honestly say what they feel. They are an unsuited, or unlikely, Narrator, who doesn't want to solely facilitate the other characters' stories; they also want to be heard.

Harriet described the play as a tragicomedy. It treads the line between self-consciousness, pain, worry, loss and comedy.

Approaching the play

Iqbal Khan, lead director, praised the play for its extraordinary range; he began by highlighting that whilst it is a very funny play, it is also serious and dangerous, and needs tension in order to be funny. Firstly, it is a play that requires intimacy between the actors, so a level of trust needs to be established early on in the rehearsal room. As well as being physically comfortable with one another, they need to be able to work closely and delicately together.

Secondly, structurally it needs to be technically and musically taut. Iqbal described the play as having a 'fantastic game' of inner and outer time for each of the characters. There are lots of questions to be considered about how structurally and rhythmically the inner voices and characters work. What do characters do when their inner voices are speaking? Do they act naturalistically? Does time stop? How does the play work rhythmically?

Iqbal advised thinking really carefully and truthfully about your own reasons for doing the play – and encouraging the actors to do the same. It is really important to think about why you want to do the play, before you think about how. He used the 'seven sentences' exercise below to explore the group's interests and priorities in the play.

EXERCISE 1: SEVEN SENTENCES

- Write down seven sentences that summarise the play. Doing this can be very revealing as different people will structure along plot, or themes, or motifs; Iqbal called it 'different privileging of the story'. Once you have your seven sentences, examine what you have prioritised. Do you give more sentences to the first half of the play? Do you focus on particular characters? What ideas for discussion come out of it? Phrasing can often be revealing too.

- Next, write down three sentences to summarise the play. Again, this reveals the priorities even further. Unpick the loaded comments. For example, what do we mean by words like 'proper', 'want' or 'manageable'? What judgements are we making through 'honest', 'true' or 'correct'? Why have we chosen interesting or unusual words like 'headspace' and 'ridicule'?

- Finally, write a single sentence to summarise the play. These are usually more poetic and capture the essence of the play. Every word becomes important.

This exercise can be quite challenging. When facilitating it, it is very important to really engage with what individuals are saying and allow for contradictions. They will begin to care and engage with the play – not just from the perspective of the part they are playing – and become committed to a complex matrix of ideas. It is also useful for pushing the group beyond the initial fun and comic responses to the play to exploring something much more deeply connected.

Themes

The play deals with themes of sexuality and mental health. It is therefore important to protect and support the actors during the potentially sensitive scenes. Iqbal suggested that if a comment is made or people laugh, try to make a discussion point of it rather than blaming. Explore why it makes people feel uncomfortable. This can sometimes be turned into a strength too. The audience may have this reaction, so what does it mean?

Iqbal also encouraged the group to think of ways to make all three relationships exciting and dangerous in their own way. Intimacy is the taboo and the challenge. Iqbal advised establishing an ease and comfort with being open with one another early on in rehearsals, so that when it comes to an intimate onstage moment, such as a kiss, the actors can have a conversation about the moment together; this can take the pressure off improvising it 'free form' too, as it becomes part of the action.

Below are a number of exercises for use in the rehearsal room to explore intimacy and trust.

Establishing trust and intimacy in rehearsal

Iqbal stressed the importance of gaining trust as the director; if the actors feel cared about, they will leap further. Remember that different people in the company will take different journeys and take different amounts of time. Allow people to surprise, challenge and shift you. He suggested gently addressing the natural groups that inevitably form in the rehearsal room (i.e. boys vs girls); a game like Fruit Bowl mixes up everyone without making a comment about where they stood initially. He also suggested considering drawing up a contract between the company – not something imposed by the director, but rather constructed by the company. They set their own rules about listening, lateness, sensitivity, etc., so it imposes structure and responsibility in the room.

EXERCISE 2: VOCAL WARM-UPS

Iqbal advised directors not to overlook voice work in their rehearsals; they can be exposing, liberating, and build confidence within the group. Often in front of an audience, young performers' voices can disappear and it can be tempting to tell them to speak up, but he advised that actually they need to be more comfortable with sharing themselves with an audience, so that they can find placement with ease, rather than shouting.

Vocal exercises which were shared within the group:

1 Chewing an imaginary 'magic sweet' using the teeth and tongue.

2 Yawning and adding in voice to play with resonance.

3 Making an 'mmm' hum, then dropping the lower jaw to create an open 'mah' sound.

4 Sending vowel sounds across the space.

5 Sirening in an 'ng' sound, going into falsetto and aiming to even out the break between chest and head (Iqbal used this exercise as it is slightly more exposing, and pulled people out individually to listen to. This is initially intimidating, but very liberating. It's also a great warm-up and can't hurt the voice.)

6   Call and response. (Again, this can be done with
    individuals to develop intimacy and trust.)

EXERCISE 3: THREE-BALL GAME

- In a circle, set up a route of throwing a ball across the
  circle. This is Path A. Remember and repeat the route.

- With a second ball, create a different route for this ball.
  This is Path B. Remember and repeat the route. Next, try
  to get both Path A and Path B going at the same time.

- With a third ball, create Path C. Try to get all three
  routes going at the same time.

When three balls are introduced, often anxiety increases and
people begin to talk and lose focus. This establishes
concentration; it needs to be done calmly.

To add a further element to the game and encourage the
group to take risks and support each other, add in a rule that
the balls now have to be bounced to one another along the
same routes, but the group will have no chance to practise it.
They have to focus and help one another.

EXERCISE 4: TRUST EXERCISE

- In pairs, one person falls backwards and the other stands
  behind them to catch them. To begin with, the person
  falling can shut their eyes (as it's easier). The catcher
  should aim to reassure their partner with their hands and
  lower them down carefully.

Be careful that this doesn't turn into a competition. It needs
to be gentle. The catcher needs to be responsible for the
person falling.

This can also be done in a group with one person falling in
the middle of a circle of catchers. As they grow in confidence,
the catchers could advance to lifting the person into the air.

EXERCISE 5: TAXI GAME

- Set up an obstacle course in the room. In pairs, one person is the 'taxi driver', and the other is the 'passenger'. The passenger closes their eyes. The taxi driver stands behind them. To start and stop the passenger moving, the driver presses between their shoulder blades; to turn them left and right, they tap the respective shoulder. Without speaking and without the passenger looking, they must be guided around the obstacle course.

The aim is to strengthen the company through shared problem-solving, but also gently get them to begin to touch each other.

EXERCISE 6: UNRAVELLING

- In a circle, remember the person to your right and left. Play another game where everyone moves around. Then stop. Grab the hands of the person who was originally to left and right. There will be a tangle of bodies. Now, the group must unravel themselves without breaking hands to return to a circle.

EXERCISE 7: MIRRORING

- In pairs, face one another. One person begins making very slow movements and the other follows. Get to a point where the pairs are very close together, exploring different levels and moving different body parts – not just their arms. Initially, the instinct is often to look at the body part which is moving, but try to look at the face and use peripheral vision. Synchronise breath. The more silence there is during the exercise, the more dangerous it becomes.

EXERCISE 8: KEEPING A DIARY

As Harriet used her own diaries as a starting point for writing the play, it might be useful to ask the actors to keep a diary during rehearsals. If they are self-conscious about this, ask them to keep a diary about how they are feeling about the rehearsal process, as this can still be revealing. You could ask volunteers to read from their diaries. Others may see a difference in how the individual expresses themself in their inner, diary voice and in their outer, public voice.

Structure

The structure of the play is surprising; the audience receives one set of expectations and this is undermined. For example, we see two characters getting on, followed by a terrible date. When Gina and Jo initially meet it feels potentially like a bullying scene, but then turns into a burgeoning love story. Sometimes the inner voices set up an expectation which the characters then undermine.

Language

Harriet has tried not to use any slang that is too specific to a certain area or age group to allow it to be transferable to different regions.

Characters and characterisation

NARRATOR   The Narrator has an opportunity at the start of the play to establish a relationship with the audience.

Iqbal encouraged participants to think about the quality of that first entrance. Establishing this relationship with the audience can be very useful in letting the audience in, particularly as the Narrator identifies their own personal experiences with the other characters.

The Narrator sets up the rules of the play regarding what the inner voices are and how they operate. Structurally, they are necessary to define the conventions. Iqbal recommended thinking about the relationship between the Narrator and the characters. Are they always 'in character' or do we see them take on the role? If they do come in and out of role, he pointed out that it adds an extra dimension and potential difficulty; most importantly it needs to be clear.

A particular challenge of this play is to make the Narrator look like they're improvising, but Iqbal advised caution about actually letting them improvise '– the narrator needs to feature less and less as the play progresses. It will also be important to consider how to deal with the Narrator's presence during the play. Where do they go? How do they remain present without upstaging? Can it help the audience focus?

The following exercise was used to explore the relationship between Narrator and acting company.

EXERCISE 9: STORYTELLING

* One person acts as the Narrator (and playwright) who is going to tell us a story. Four others play the acting company, who are allowed to make sounds but cannot use dialogue. They can take on different roles throughout the story. The group works together to tell a completely improvised piece.

Through doing this exercise, the participants observed that the Narrator can shift the audience focus by moving in and around the acting company. They can also take brilliant ideas from the actors and use them in the storytelling, rather than having to drive the whole thing alone.

The exercise was repeated with two narrators and six actors. This time the actors could say text but only lines that were given to them by the narrators. Iqbal encouraged participants to drop characters and become someone else, and to be bold with the vocalisation.

The game can develop further by adding dialogue until eventually the group are all improvising together, and finding an instinctive rhythm to pass around the storytelling.

Inner Voices

When the characters talk to their inner voices, it is intended to be an aside, or a surreptitious talking to self. It is important to define the psychological and physical rules between the inner voice and character. Can they touch? Can they look at each other? Keep it consistent (although you may choose to break the rules in moments of tension). It may be that different inner voice and character partners have different rules.

Iqbal suggested exploring how invested the inner voices are in the lives of the characters. Do they care about them? Do they become increasingly redundant? If there is a really strong connection between character and inner voice, when this is broken the audience will really feel the loss. He advised to beware focusing solely on the humour, and explore the darkness, truth and anxiety of the inner voices.

The participants looked at versions of the first scene with and without the inner voices.

EXERCISE 10: REMOVING THE INNER VOICES

- Iqbal asked four volunteers to read through the first Lena and Jamie scene. Lena and Jamie were sitting opposite each other on chairs, whilst their inner voices stood behind. The inner voices were allowed to move wherever they liked within their respective half of the stage. The inner voices were also given permission to be as inappropriate as they liked and to use the audience. They could be as loud as they wanted too; no one other than their character can hear them.

Through this exercise, it was discovered that a big contrast between inner voice and character can be very revealing or funny. The inner voices can be really liberated in their behaviour too as they are invisible.

After this exercise, Iqbal gave the actors playing Lena and Jamie a version of the script with the inner voices removed. He asked them to play the scene but try to keep their inner monologue with the inner voices alive. The biggest difference was that the actors now played the subtext. In the first version, the actors handed over the subtext to the inner voices. In the second version, they played the tension, intimacy and inner emotion. The play needs both the inner voice and character to play each thought. Also, when the character was playing their inner monologue it gave silences to the scene, which created danger and tension for the other character. It may be useful to explore the scene without the inner voices to give them truth.

Casting

During the workshop, several participants asked about changing the gender or number of actors playing a part. While Harriet is flexible to some degree, as detailed below, she has written with a sensibility of gender in mind.

GENDER   The narrator can be played as either female or male. The important qualities are that they are gregarious, talkative, not macho, playful, open and naively excited. They should enjoy the comedy of it.

Each inner voice and character has been written for the same gender. Harriet is flexible about the inner voices being of a different gender, but asks the director to really consider the implications of this decision. She feels that the inner voices for Jo and Gina should ideally be female, because it adds a potentially difficult dimension if those female characters have male inner voices.

CHORUS   The Narrator needs to be played by an individual, but it is possible to consider using a chorus element for the inner voices. Again, Iqbal added that if a choice like this is made to cater for the group's needs, it is important to be aware that this does change the nature of the play.

Production, staging and design

Harriet wrote the play in a minimalist way to make it accessible for any budget and size of space. It moves quickly between place and scenes, so the set can be symbolic and use whatever the company feels is necessary to tell the story. Iqbal added that using minimal set allows the production to concentrate on the psychological and imaginative space. It asks the audience to use their imagination, so it needs to be playful, especially when creating the comedy. Do you use soundscape to indicate place? Does the set arrive with the characters? Iqbal suggested the following exercise to facilitate creating ways of using objects to tell a story.

EXERCISE 11: OBJECT GAME

* There is an object in the room. The other person has to define what it is, and use or respond to it appropriately. Perhaps a ball becomes a baby. This allows inventiveness and playfulness, but most importantly the ingenuity has to be clear.

Improvisation

Iqbal recommend using improvisation in the rehearsal room to build confidence, prepare for unexpected things, allow ideas to develop that can then be used in the production, and create a character freely before placing the text on top. It can often be difficult to play and move with an unfamiliar script in hand; improvisation allows an actor to trust their instincts and impulses and share with an audience.

EXERCISE 12: OBJECTIVES AND SHARING WITH AN AUDIENCE

When setting up an improvisation, it is important to give clear rules. For this exercise, two actors are given a series of objects (we had: a basketball, a chair, scissors, a bottle, masking tape, a pen). They are told that they are a world-famous visual artist. Individually and privately, they must decide how they would like their art work (made up of the objects) to look. It must be a great masterpiece that sums up the artist. Now, both artists have to try to make their masterpiece and try not to compromise on their vision. Importantly, they cannot fight or grab things from the other person, they have to negotiate and persuade.

For the first version, the actors improvise without any words, although sounds are allowed. A further version is to allow the actors one phrase – but whatever phrase first comes out of their mouth is the only thing they can repeat.

Iqbal described negotiation as the DNA of drama: two people with objectives and agendas trying to negotiate with each other. In this improvisation game, we see sneaky strategies coming into play and it becomes exciting to watch as it is more than pure confrontation. Everything is also played for the audience.

A further version of the game can be played with four people. They are on a late-night arts programme, and all four artists are coming together to make a work of art. There are microphones and cameras everywhere so everything that they do and say is public. Individually, each person is privately told what type of artist they are: the autobiographical Tracey Emin-type artist, the political artist, the anti-artist, the student of the artist who was meant to be there. They cannot be explicit about what type of artist they are, but can speak to negotiate with the others. They will begin to create characters outside themselves. At the end, the audience can guess what type of artist they think each person is.

The exercise can also be adapted to explore themes appropriate to the play. The game could be played with one person in love, or lust. This may also allow them to begin to develop a physical vocabulary of how they can be intimate together.

Suggested references

Harriet recommended Phoebe Waller-Bridge's *Fleabag* as a
potentially useful reference point for a sense of inner voice
and character.

From a workshop led by Iqbal Khan
with notes by Anna Marsland

#YOLO

by Matthew Bulgo

'How am I supposed to deal with . . . that . . . with the idea of . . . when I haven't dealt with life yet?!'

It's A-level results day and Jack has it all laid out in front of him. After a summer of love and laughter with his mates, he's off to university. He can't wait for Freshers' Week and all the adventures that will follow. Life is just beginning and it couldn't be better. But when Jack gets blind-sided by a revelation about his health, he gets propelled into an adult world before he's had a chance to enjoy his youth.

Will Jack be able to become an adult in time to save himself?

Cast size
11 (6f, 4m, 1m/f)

Matthew Bulgo trained at LAMDA and works as an actor and playwright. Credits as a playwright include: *Constellation Street* at The Other Room; *Last Christmas* for Dirty Protest/Theatr Clwyd, Edinburgh Fringe/Soho Theatre; *The Knowledge* for Dirty Protest/Royal Court Theatre, 'Surprise Theatre' Season; *My Father's Hands* for Paines Plough, Come To Where I'm From; *Lacuna* for Three Streets Productions, New Wimbledon Studio. In addition, he has written short plays for National Theatre Wales, Dirty Protest, Not Too Tame and Ugly Sisters, among many others. He was the recipient of the Best Playwright in the English Language award at the Wales Theatre Awards 2015 and his debut play *Last Christmas* was nominated in the Best Production in the English Language category at the inaugural Theatre Critics of Wales Awards in 2013. He is an Associate Director of Dirty Protest.

Notes on the text

Location

I wrote this play with my home city of Swansea in mind. It
could be quite easily transposed to any city or town that's by
the sea. Feel free to change any location-specific references
to fit your production – e.g. *Evening Post*, Bluebirds, The Full
Moon.

Music

I think music in theatre/film can be extremely powerful but
be careful you don't manipulate the audience with it.

I saw the play being soundtracked by Jack's iPod. Maybe he
has headphones around his neck for the entire play. Maybe
all the music should be of a similar style or genre. Maybe it
should be really eclectic. I envisaged the music being pre-
recorded, existing songs, but if you have a cast of particularly
talented singers, maybe they could sing all of the songs *a
capella*. Maybe they never leave the stage. Lots of maybes.
Have fun with the maybes.

If you do consider using copyright material, then the usual
copyright rules will apply.

Dialogue

An ellipsis (. . .) indicates a loss for words.

A forward slash (/) indicates a point of interruption meaning
text will overlap.

A dash (–) indicates an interruption, either a character
interrupting themselves if mid-line or another character
interrupting if it's at the end of a line.

Italics indicates a soft emphasis.

SMALL CAPS indicate a hard emphasis.

Dialogue in brackets is not to be spoken and is included for
the sake of clarity.

Characters

Jack, *male, seventeen, probably watches too many funny videos on YouTube*

Johnno, *male, eighteen, intelligent and fun-loving*

Daf, *male, nineteen, if he was any more laid-back he'd be lying down*

Luke, *male, eighteen, highly strung, a worrier*

Molly, *female, eighteen, sensitive, soft-hearted, warm*

Nat, *female, eighteen, she and Tash are inseparable, spiky but soft-centred*

Tash, *female, eighteen, she and Nat are inseparable, spiky but soft-centred*

Lydia, *female, eighteen, no one messes with her, formidable*

Lucy *female, eighteen, a force of nature, never stops to breathe*

Josie, *Jack's sister, mid-twenties*

Doctor, *could be male or female*

Jack and **Lucy** *have been an item for just under a year*

Luke and **Lydia** *have been going out for about four years*

Daf and **Nat** *are brother and sister*

Nat and **Tash** *often finish each other's sentences*

Daf *has just taken a year out*

The 'f' in **Daf** *is pronounced like a 'v'*

Scene One

Music.

A pool of light.

Jack *with headphones on holds an envelope.*

A strange moment . . . interrupted by **Johnno**.

Outside college/sixth form.

Johnno   What you doing out here, you knobber?
Everyone's inside.

Jack   Just – headache.

Hot in there, everyone screaming about what they got.

Johnno   Well?

Jack   What?

Johnno   How'd you get on, you numpty?

Jack   Dunno. Haven't opened it.

Johnno   Well, what you waiting for? Christmas?!

Jack   Hey! 'S alright for you, brainiac. Oxford – big news
that is.

Johnno   Whatever.

Jack   You'll be in the *Evening Post* and everything.

Johnno   Seriously. You going to open that or am I going to
have to get you in some sort of death-lock?

Jack   I will! (*Beat.*) In a minute.

Johnno   Just do it! What's the worst / that could happen?

Jack   Yeah, no, but.

Johnno   Not going to be the end of the world, / is it?

Jack   I know, but . . .

Johnno   So open it!

Enter **Nat**, **Tash**, **Lydia** *and* **Molly** *closely followed by* **Daf** *and* **Luke**.

Nat   Here you are!

Tash   Well, what / did you get?

Lydia   Yeah, what'd you / get, Jack?

Luke   Here / he is!

Daf   How'd you get on, mate?

Beat.

Johnno   He won't open it.

They all encourage him to open it: 'Come on!', 'Just open it!' 'What you waiting for?', etc.

Jack   Alright! Alright! I'll . . .

He opens it. Slides the sheet out slowly. He almost can't look. He looks blankly.

He looks crestfallen.

Johnno   Ah, crap. Sorry, mate.

Jack   Yeah . . . it's fine . . . don't worry about it . . . because I ONLY BLOODY GOT IT! Three 'C's.

Improvised lines from all: 'Nice one!', 'Get in!' 'Good one, Jack', etc.

Get in! You beauty!

He celebrates like he's scored a goal in the FA Cup Final.

Johnno   Nice one, mate.

Molly   Good one, Jacko.

Jack   Three 'C's. Nailed it!

Nat (*teasing him*)   Hardly!

Jack   Hey, 's all I needed. No point in over-achieving, is there? No point in breaking into a sweat.

Tash   Nah, you sweat enough as it is.

Luke   Owned!

Jack   Funny.

Nat   I'm teasing! Nice one.

Tash   You deserve it.

Johnno   Never in doubt, mate. I mean, I did half the coursework for you so –

Nat   You what?!

Jack   Helped! He helped, that's all.

He notices for the first time that **Daf** *is wearing a onesie.*

Jack   Woah! Who've you come as? Mate – you could've got dressed for the occasion.

Luke   One–nil.

Johnno   Get in the sea!

Jack   You staying the night or what?

Daf   That's what your mother said.

Luke   Ooo!

Johnno   Good comeback.

Luke   Late equaliser.

Nat   Ah, don't go there. He's been wearing that all summer.

Molly   Ewwww.

Lydia   Gross!

Daf   It's comfy!

Nat   He's been dressed like that playing World of Wow all day / every day.

Daf   Warcraft! It's called *World of Warcraft*! They call it *WOW* for short.

Nat   Whatever.

Daf   You're *so* embarrassing.

Nat   Says the guy wearing a onesie.

Luke   And there it is! She shoots, she scores. A late winner in injury time.

Lydia   Are you still talking?

Luke   Yes, Lyds. Sorry, Lyds.

Nat   Right! Come on, my mother's waiting in the car.

Molly (*to* **Jack** *and* **Johnno**)   Hey! Don't forget. House party at mine tonight.

Nat   It's fancy / dress.

Tash   Yeah! It's fancy dress.

Jack   Is there an echo in here?

Nat   Funny.

Tash   Yeah, funny.

Molly   You two better be coming.

Jack   Try and stop us!

Improvised goodbyes from all.

Exit everyone except **Johnno** *and* **Jack**.

Jack *looks at his grades.*

Johnno   What happened to Luce?

Jack   She was here first thing. Got what she was predicted so . . .

Johnno   You should text her. She'll be chuffed for you.

Jack   Yeah.

What you smiling at, you weirdo?

Johnno   Nothing. Just . . . good to have the old Jack back, that's all.

We all thought you were going to blow a fuse. All that revising. Just chuffed you got what you needed.

Hey, Josie'll be on cloud nine too. Finally having you out from under her feet.

Jack   Yeah! Right enough.

Johnno   What you doing now? Might go cinema or –

Jack   Hospital appointment. These headaches. Know exactly what they're gonna – gonna tell me I need glasses.

Johnno   Brilliant! You're going to look like a Minion.

Jack   Funny.

Johnno   There's your fancy dress sorted right there.

Jack gives **Johnno** *a playful punch on the arm.*

Johnno   Well done, mate. (*Of the envelope.*) You deserve those.

I'll see you at Mol's then.

Jack   Bringing my A-game.

Johnno   'Go hard or go home'.

Jack   That's what your mother said.

Johnno   Dick!

Music.

Scene Two

*The new scene forms around **Jack**.*

*A **Doctor**'s consulting room.*

Same day.

Jack *sits staring into space* . . .

Doctor   I'd hoped you might have brought someone along with you.

Jack   . . .

Doctor   A parent? Or guardian? Bit of moral support.

Jack   . . .

Doctor   We do recommend it. Even with adults. I think I did say that on the phone . . .

Jack   Thought you were just saying that 'cause . . . thought that was just something doctors say to . . . y'know . . .

The **Doctor** *fills the silence by flicking through some notes.*

Doctor   The headaches. How long have you been having them?

Jack   Uh. Dunno. Months?

Doctor   Two? . . . Three? . . . Six? . . .

Jack   Six. Maybe six. I . . . I don't know.

Beat, **Doctor** *writes.*

Doctor   What about 'night sweats'?

Jack   What's that?

Doctor   Sweating . . . in the night . . .

Jack   Right! Maybe. Uh. Sometimes, yeah.

Doctor *starts to write.*

Jack   I do sweat quite a lot though so . . .

Beat, **Doctor** *makes some notes.*

Jack   Thought I might need glasses, thought that might've been it – the headaches. I'd look stupid in glasses so I just, yeah, thought it might've been that.

Doctor   If the headaches were persisting, you really should have come to us sooner.

Jack   This isn't (happening) . . . This is – there must be . . . Has there been some sort of a, some sort of mistake? I mean, I don't smoke, I don't *really* drink, not *really*. Don't do . . . anything, I'm just, you know . . . I'm quite active, bit of footie and that, five-a-side.

I . . . I don't really . . .

Doctor   These things can happen to the healthy, these things can happen to the young. There aren't really any 'rules', I'm afraid. But this has happened, *is* happening, and now, well now we need to think about what happens next.

Jack   But – I mean – I feel fine! It's just these headaches / so . . .

Doctor   Is / there – ?

Jack   So maybe if you just gave me something for the headaches and / then –

Doctor   Is there anything you'd like me to repeat?

Jack   I don't –

To be honest, I sort of stopped listening after – when you said – what you said about the –

Beat.

Doctor   Tumour.

A relatively small one – at present.

Beat. **Jack** *nods.*

Jack   . . .

Doctor   It is operable – I think I did mention that.

Jack   I don't . . . ?

Doctor   That means that we can operate on it –

Jack   Right.

Doctor   – but we're going to need to move quite quickly on this. Looking at it's placement, normally we'd try to reduce it down to a more manageable size. That would mean a course or two of chemotherapy . . .

Jack   Chemo.

Doctor   -therapy. Yes. Chemotherapy.

Jack   That's, like, that makes your hair fall out, right?

Doctor   There are a number of side-effects.

Jack   It does though, doesn't it?

Doctor   Hair loss being one of the most visible, yes.

Jack (*breathless*)   Fuck.

I . . .

Sorry.

Beat.

Doctor   As I was saying, that would be the normal course of action . . . but time isn't really our friend, I'm afraid.

Jack   I'm not sure what you're . . .

Doctor   I'm saying we need to go ahead and operate. I'd like to get you in here over the next seven days if I can. I'm confident we can move some things around.

Jack   Right.

Beat.

I'm – I'm supposed to be starting uni in a few weeks . . . Is that? Does that mean . . . ?

Doctor   We should probably take things one step at a time. Maybe – I don't know – deferring your place would be an option? I'm sure they'd be sympathetic to your . . . situation.

Beat.

Jack *laughs suddenly.*

Jack   Is this a wind-up?

Did Johnno put you up to this? Or Daf? Is this a joke?

Doctor   No, I'm afraid it isn't.

Beat.

There are a lot of things in your favour. You're young.
You're healthy.

Until we get 'in there', so to speak, we won't know exactly
what we're dealing with, so . . .

Is there someone I can call? A parent?

Jack   No. No parent.

Doctor   Or a guardian?

Beat.

Jack   My sister. She's . . . It's just the two of us, so . . .

Doctor   I'd hoped you might've brought her / along.

Jack   I'm eighteen. Almost.

Doctor   Is there a number I can speak / to her on . . . ?

Jack   She can't – I don't want you to – I don't want you to
speak to her – I want to – I'll do it – I can do it – I'll speak to
her. I will.

Beat.

Doctor   OK.

Well, if there's anything else you'd like to – ?

Jack   The operation.

What are the odds that . . . That's what they always ask, isn't
it . . . ?

Doctor   I'm never very comfortable speaking in those terms. A procedure like this . . . can go a number of ways. There are a lot of factors. It's . . . a lot more complicated than a couple of numbers.

Beat.

These things do come as a massive shock.

There are some leaflets you could read, if you like. In the meantime. They might be useful.

Jack   I don't really – not really a big reader so . . .

Beat.

He stands.

Doctor   Would you like to call your sister? She could come and pick you up.

Jack   You know what?

I'm fine.

I'll walk.

Music.

*The **Doctor**'s consulting room dissolves around him.*

The music segues into . . .

Scene Three

*A party at **Molly**'s house.*

Nat *and* **Tash** *are talking to* **Molly**, **Daf** *and* **Luke** *are chatting conspiratorially. There could be others if you have a bigger ensemble.*

Nat   New Zealand.

Tash   Then Australia.

Nat   Then we're thinking about Thailand on the way back.

Tash   If we can afford it . . .

Nat   Yeah, if we can afford it.

Molly   I'm well jel. Gap year.

Tash   You must start pretty soon?

Molly   In, like, three weeks or something. Decided on UCL in the end. (*Slurring.*) Sociology and Psychology. (*She laughs at herself and tries again. Still slurring.*) Psychology and Sociology.

They all laugh. **Johnno** *enters and sneaks up behind* **Molly** *holding a glass with a bit of water in it.*

Tash   Molly! Are you wasted?!

Nat   Good girl!

Molly   You try! It's really hard!

Daf (*overhearing*)   That's what your mother said!

Nat   Shut it!

Molly (*to* **Johnno**)   They're making fun.

Tash   We're only teasing!

Molly   You try –

She notices **Johnno** *is holding the glass above her head; she shrieks and runs off.*

Nat   Aww, leave her alone.

Johnno *starts to leave.*

Daf   Hey, Johnno. What's fifty-seven multiplied by ninety-six?

Beat.

Johnno   5,472.

Nat   Freak!

Daf   That's good! (*To* **Luke**.) He's good!

Johnno *pursues* **Molly**.

Daf (*shouting after him*)   Johnno! You're not drunk enough!

Luke *is drunk. So's* **Daf** *but not as drunk as* **Luke**.

Luke   Listen, though. What if she says no? That'd just, that'd be, that'd just be, like, a a a a a disaster. Am I stuttering? Was I just stuttering just then? Shiiiit, I'm stuttering. My brain is stuttering. I can't talk to her like this.

Daf   You're not stuttering.

Luke   But I heard myself.

Daf   Yeah, but you're – *listen* to me. YOU – are – not – stuttering.

Beat.

Luke   What do you mean? You meant something then – the way you said that.

Daf   I mean, you ain't stuttering, bro! Your mouth ain't stuttering and your brain that ain't stuttering neither. You can't think like that. Shut it out. If anything your ears are stuttering – yeah? You get me? Because they, THEY are hearing things that ain't happening. Yeah?

Luke   Yeah. Yeah! That, that's starting to make some sense now . . . I think.

Daf   Woahwoahwoah! Don't think! Don't start thinking, bro. You think too much as it is.

Luke   Yeah, I suppose I do, don't I! (*Beat.*) Do I?

Daf   Sure you do. Now, you just gotta do it, gotta speak to her tonight, yeah? Special night, all of us here together, you want to celebrate it with your friends, don't you? Only live once, mate. Now, relax.

Luke   Yeah, yeah, I will. Relax, yeah . . .

He jiggles nervously. There's a loud knock at the door. He nearly jumps out of his skin.

That's her!

He nervously swigs. **Molly** *enters yelping, pursued by* **Johnno**, *still with the glass of water. He moves wherever she goes so the glass is almost always over her head. Even though she's complaining,* **Molly** *is enjoying the attention. One minute she's yelping, the next she's giggling. They end up near the front door.*

Molly Stop! Stop it!

Johnno Stop what? I don't know what you're / on about.

Molly Stop it. Stop being a dick. You're going to give me a wet T-shirt.

People cheer and applaud at the phrase 'wet T-shirt'. **Johnno** *acknowledges the applause and* **Molly** *pulls his trousers down. They cheer and applaud and laugh even louder.* **Molly** *panics, grabs the glass of water and throws it in his face. She is as shocked as he is. Then she runs off, cackling.*

Another knock at the door. Louder this time.

Luke (*standing bolt upright*) Oh, God. It's Lyds. I know it is.

Tash What's the matter with him?

Nat Get the door, will you, Johnno.

Johnno What did your last servant die of?

Nat Not doing as they were told.

Johnno Funny.

He answers the door; it's **Lydia**

Johnno Good cossie, Lyds!

Lydia You're wet.

Johnno Well spotted.

Lydia What happened to your trousers?

Johnno Nothing gets past you.

Luke Lyds! Alright? How's it going?

Lydia   Who put ten pence in you?

Luke   Nice one, Lyds!

Lydia   What have you done?

Luke   Nothing! I just . . . I, I, I, I, I . . .

Daf   He thinks he's got a stutter.

Luke   Am I stuttering, Lyds?

Lydia   Are you wasted?!

Luke   Only a little bit. It tasted so good . . .

Lydia   Well, you can sleep on the sofa if you're going to be farting and snoring all night.

Nat (*aside*)   Check them out!

Tash (*aside*)   Like a married couple.

Daf   Shhh.

Nat   What?!

Luke   Lyds. Gotta talk to you.

Lydia   Well can I, like, get a drink first or − ?

Luke (*pulling her by an arm towards the kitchen*)   No. Gotta talk to you now.

Lydia   Alright! Don't dislocate my shoulder.

*As **Luke** and **Lydia** are exiting to the kitchen, **Molly** enters. Unseen, **Jack** enters at the front door.*

Molly (*over-excited*)   Lyyyyyyds! Let's get this party started!

She does a little dance by herself with her eyes closed and giggles.

Lydia   Have you all been spiked or what?

Luke and **Lydia** exit. **Molly** opens her eyes; they've gone.

Johnno   Hey! Here he is! What time do you call this? You know the party doesn't start until you get here.

Jack Right.

Johnno Where's your costume?

Jack Dunno. Forgot.

Johnno Ah, you're such a lame-arse!

Come on – come in the kitchen. There's some black bags and Sellotape. Reckon I can make you look like Lady Gaga.

Jack You're alright.

Johnno It's no bother. Made Chris a mean Julius Caesar earlier. Shoulda seen it. Couple of bed sheets tied together, stuck some of those flowers from the front garden in his hair.

Molly (*suddenly sober*) What flowers? Not the – my mother *loves* those flowers, you numpty? She's gonna freak.

She chases **Johnno** *out of the room*

Jack You guys seen Luce? Need to talk to her.

Nat She's been trying to call you all night.

Tash Her dad just got here.

Nat They're taking her to Paris.

Tash For the weekend.

Nat As a surprise.

Tash Yeah.

Nat 'Cause she got her grades.

Jack She never said.

Nat She didn't know, you doughnut!

Tash Wouldn't be a surprise then, would it, Sherlock?

Jack Right. Yeah.

Enter **Lucy**.

Lucy There you are!

Jack   Luce. I need to talk, / can we –

Lucy   Did you get my voicemails?

Jack   No, I've been – I wanted / to –

Lucy   YAY! Paris! Did they tell you?

Jack   Yeah, they said. Luce, / listen –

Lucy   Anyway. Gotta go. My dad's waiting for me in the car. Listen, I'll call you on Monday when I'm back, yeah? We can do something. and don't forget to text me, it's just my normal number but it shouldn't cost you anything extra and you've still got free texts haven't you and, ooo, let me know what you want me to bring you back, and, oh, yeah, if Daf tries to make you play drinking games again –

Daf   Hey!

Lucy   Because you know what happened last time.

Re-enter **Johnno**.

Daf   Did someone just say 'drinking games'?

Lucy   Shut it, Daf.

Daf   'Shut it, Daf.'

Lucy   Just tell him 'no'. My dad's still trying to get the smell of spew out of the back of his car. Ooo, Dad, he's waiting. (*Kisses him.*) Text me, yeah?

Bye!

Improvised responses from everyone as she exits.

Johnno   No wonder you've been getting headaches! Seriously, does she come up for air or what?

Daf (*standing up on his chair*)   Hey! Jack!

Nat   Luce could talk for Wales.

Tash   Olympic standard.

Daf Jack! You are now looking at a Level Capped, Raid Geared Warlock.

Jack What?

Daf *does a little victory dance.*

Nat (*embarrased*) Oh God.

Daf Well, aren't you happy for me?

Johnno Is that the actual time? I've got my paper round in five hours!

He starts gathering his stuff.

Daf Paper round? Where do you live?! The 1980s?

Nat Woah! Stop everything! Daf did a funny!

Daf Me? I'm Mr Funny! Funny's my middle name!

Nat It's also your surname if you're name's Mr Funny, you pleb.

Molly (*to* **Johnno**, *in private*) You can stay . . . if you want? Go straight from here in the morning?

Johnno Ah, I'd like that . . . but . . .

Daf (*of* **Jack**) Is someone going to get this guy a drink or what?

Molly Text me then, yeah?

Johnno Yeah. Course.

Improvised farewell to **Johnno** *as he exits.*

Nat *notices* **Daf** *isn't wearing any shoes.*

Tash You OK, Mols?

Nat (*to* **Daf**) Where are your shoes?

Molly I – I don't feel so good.

Daf Under your mother's bed!

Tash (*giving her some*)   Have some water.

Nat   That doesn't make any sense. She's your mother too, you knob-jockey.

Daf   Oh yeah.

Tash (*finding this very funny*)   Haha! You sicko!

Molly *is sick into something . . . maybe the hat of her costume.*

Daf   Woah!

Nat (*exiting*)   I'll get a cloth.

Molly   I'm drrrrrrunk.

Nat   Oh-my-God! Think I almost walked in on something.

A blood-curdling scream from the kitchen. They all freeze. After a beat, **Lydia** *comes hurtling into the room holding up her ring-finger.*

Lydia   He propoooooosed.

They cheer, ad lib.

Tash   About time. Been going out since Year 9.

Nat (*to* **Daf**)   So that's what you two were —fair play, where is the little charmer?

Lydia (*showing off her ring to someone*)   In the kitchen, having a panic attack.

Daf   I'll get him.

He exits and returns with **Luke** *over the next few lines.* **Tash** *gets her camera out.*

Molly   Amazeballs!

Nat   She's feeling better.

Molly   Is this what a second wind feels like?

Nat   What you doing?

Tash   Getting a close-up! I'm Instagramming the shit out of this.

Nat   Hey, come on! Oscar selfie! Everyone squeeze in. Come on, Jack.

Jack *has hardly moved since he last spoke. The chaos has happened around him.*

Nat   Jack?

Jack   Why?

Tash   You what?

Jack   Why would I want to do that?

Daf   'S up with you?

Jack   This is – this is it to you, isn't it?

Nat   Jack – you feeling alright?

Jack   Getting so drunk you can't remember what you did the night before and, and selfies and dressing up like a bunch of freaks. Is that all that matters to you?

Molly   Jacko – it's just a party – it's just –

Jack   You don't know what living is? None of you. You're just . . . floating around, spouting bullshit at each other, that's all you're doing. And what's the fucking point in that?

Daf   Woah, where's all this coming from, mate?

Lydia   Think it might be best if you went.

Molly   Daf – please make him go.

Daf   I'm calling you a cab, mate.

Jack *snatches* **Tash**'s *camera out of her hand.*

Jack   You want a photo? There! (*Showing them.*) Look at yourselves. Take a good look. You're pointless. You're fucking pathetic. All of you.

Daf *advances.*

Daf   Mate . . .

Jack   Don't bother.

He throws the camera. **Daf** *catches it.*

Jack   I'm out of here . . .

Music. The party dissolves around him . . .

Scene Four

A beach.

Next day.

Jack *is sitting looking out towards the sea.* **Johnno** *stands behind.*

Jack   How'd you know I'd be here?

Johnno   'Cause this is where you always come when you've got the 'Gary Guilts'.

Beat.

What was it? Nat and Tash pushing your buttons again? Sounds like you had a proper shit-fit! The way my phone was beeping this morning I thought someone had died.

He sits next to **Jack**.

Johnno   I come in peace!

Listen. Bunch of us are going down the bowling alley. Walk off the hangovers. Bit of air-hockey, foosball, shoot some pool, whatever.

You keen?

Beat.

Sure they'd all like to see you. Chance to say I'm sorry, whatever.

Jack   Got nothing to be sorry about.

Johnno   You weren't *that* drunk were you?

Sounds like you made a bit of a dick of yourself to be honest, mate.

Come on, we've all done it: drunk too much, got a bit fighty.

Beat. **Johnno** *lightly punches* **Jack** *on the arm.* **Jack** *doesn't respond, doesn't even move.*

Johnno   What's up? Come on – I know you like the back of my hand and something's –

Ahhh, you're not getting all down 'cause we're all off to uni? We'll see each other at Christmas, you bell-end. Lyds is already talking about booking somewhere. You know what she's like. Be just like old times. Anyway – scratch that – it's your birthday next week in case you've forgotten. We're not going to miss the big one-eight, are we? It's gonna be carnage.

Beat.

Jack   How many days is that?

Johnno   You what?

Jack   How many days – eighteen years – how many days is that?

Johnno   Jesus! I thought school was out for the summer.

Jack   How many?

Johnno   Uh, well . . . eighteen times 365 is 6,570 . . . but then you've got to remember to add one on for each leap year / so –

Jack   That's nothing, is it. That's fuck-all – six thousand – that's like, that's *nothing*, that's –

Johnno   You feeling alright?

Beat.

(*Going to get up.*) Look, I've gotta –

Jack   Do you remember us coming down here when we kids?

Johnno   Yeah . . .

Jack   That one time when we'd built this like . . . mega-castle, out of sand, it was massive, and we'd put pebbles all round the edge . . . decorated it with shells and seaweed, all sorts of shit . . . and then we'd got all our toys, Lego men and Power Rangers and – *everything* – and we'd put them all inside, all stood up like a, like a little army and then we'd run back up here to tell our parents. We wanted to show them what we'd made, 'cause we were just chuffed to bits with it. Really chuffed. But by the time we'd got back down there . . . it was gone, the tide must have come in quick, it'd come out of nowhere and just flattened it, washed it all away and there was nothing . . . there was nothing left. We could see a few of them floating on the surface, the coloured plastic, but they were going. They were going and then they were gone.

Do you remember?

Johnno   Yeah. I think so.

Jack   It just came to me. Haven't thought about that in years.

Johnno   That's a funny thing to think.

Jack   Is it?

Beat.

Johnno   Look, if you don't fancy it, I'll give you a text later, maybe we can –

Jack   You seen the sky. 'S like a painting. 'S like someone's painted it.

Johnno (*with a laugh*)   Seriously. Are you feeling / alright?

Jack   Yeah. I'm fine.

Just . . . never really looked at it before, that's all.

Johnno   Right.

Beat.

Look. I'd better go, said I'd meet Daf at one so –

Come along later if you want.

Jack   Don't think so.

Johnno   Well, if you change your mind.

Jack   Probably stay here for a bit, I reckon.

Beat, **Johnno** *gets up*

Johnno   Well, don't stay too long.

Don't want the tide washing you away!

Beat. **Johnno** *leaves.* **Jack** *puts his headphones on.*

Music. The beach dissolves around him . . .

Scene Five

Jack *and* **Josie***'s house.*

Josie *is getting ready for work*

Josie   Have you been listening to a word I've said?! I'm
running late as it is. That'll be the third time this week. Three
strikes and / I'm –

Jack   Yeah, well, I need to talk to you.

Josie   And it can't wait?

Jack   Not really.

Josie   Matter of life or death, is it?

Jack   I / don't know . . .

Josie   Then I'm sure it can wait a few hours.

Jack   Jose!

Josie   God! You're such a child sometimes, you know that?

Jack   Jose – just – please –

Josie   Make it quick.

Jack   Sit down.

Josie   Sit down?

Beat.

Aww, God. Lucy's not pregnant, is she. You haven't / gone and –

Jack   Jose! Will you just – please – sit down?

FINE – STAND UP – WHATEVER – JUST –

Josie *is halted by the size of his emotion.*

Josie   What, what is it?

Beat.

Jack   I'm . . . I'm not well, Jose.

Josie (*with a laugh*)   So stay in bed. You're wasting my time with – ? You're not / in school any more, Jack. You don't have to ask my – do what you want!

Jack   No. Jose. Listen – you're not listening!. Will you just shut up and listen to me for one minute. It's not – it's – it's – it's bigger than that – it's . . .

Josie   What then?

Jack   And see, I thought they might have got things mixed up, got it all wrong because, well, I mean I'm not, like, pissing blood or anything and I / thought –

Josie   Wait, what?

Jack   And I thought maybe you could call them, talk to them, 'cause I –

Josie   Who's 'them', Jack?

Beat.

Jack   Hospital. That appointment I –

They said –

Jose –

They said it's a tumour.

Beat.

That's – that's cancer, Jose. That's *cancer* cancer. That's – and I don't know what I'm –

A short, sharp, breathy laugh.

I thought saying it out loud would – but it's not – it hasn't – it's just –

Beat.

Jose – I didn't know who to – so I thought –

Are you going to say *anything*?

Josie   What did they – what did they say / exactly?

Jack   They said – they said it might be benign / but –

Josie   Well, that's good. Benign is good.

Jack   Yeah, but, yeah, they said they can't, they can't be sure, until they, until they 'get in there', and . . .

Josie   Where?

Silence

Get in where, Jack?

Beat. He indicates his head. **Josie** *is poleaxed.*

Jack   The thing they said – big-long-word – I googled it and –

Josie   You shouldn't / have –

Jack   It said – listen – it said in some cases it was fifty-fifty.

Josie   You don't want to go doing that.

Jack   Fifty–fifty.

That's what it said.

That's like . . . like flipping a coin, like, like heads you live and tails you – that's – that's what that means, isn't it – fifty–fifty.

Josie   You shouldn't have done that!

Jack   What should I have done, Jose?

You tell me and I'll –

'Cause I don't know, I don't know what to, I don't know, I don't know.

Beat.

I mean . . .

How am I supposed to deal with . . . *that* . . . with the idea of . . . when I haven't dealt with LIFE yet?!

I haven't started . . . have I? I'm just starting . . . so . . .

I mean, I might want kids for all I know! Does that sound – ? But, who knows, yeah, I might want kids, get married, all that . . . who knows?

Beat.

Say something.

You're the one who, you're supposed to . . .

You're supposed to say something now to make everything – you're supposed to say something!

Josie (*barely audible*)   I . . . I don't know.

Jack   Is that – ? You don't know. Is that all – ?

Josie   It's going to be fine . . .

Jack   No! You can't – you can't say that, you don't know, so don't say that –

Josie *goes to hug* **Jack**.

Jack   No! No, I don't want a hug. I want you to help me, Jose. To fucking *help* me.

Josie   This is all – it's a lot to – I don't know how to –

Jack   You *have* to.

Josie   I'm a kid myself, Jack . . . I'm . . . I don't know where to start . . . I –

Jack   You have to . . . 'cause if you don't . . . 'cause this is big, Jose. This is bigger than me and I . . .

He slumps in a chair, head in hands.

Silence.

Josie   I . . .

Jack *looks to* **Josie**.

I'm going to be late for work.

Music. The living room dissolves around him . . .

Scene Six

A Starbucks.

Lucy *sits opposite* **Jack**. *Untouched cups in front of them. She stares at him. He stares at his hands in his lap.*

Lucy   I don't know what to say.

Beat.

I don't know what you want me to say, Jack.

Beat.

I can't believe – am I going red, I'm going red aren't I, I can feel it.

Beat.

Well, are you going to say *anything*?

Beat.

Jack – are you just going to sit there staring at your fucking hands or what?

Beat.

Couldn't you have even thought of a better place to meet?

Starbucks. I hate Starbucks. Their coffee's shit.

Beat.

Nothing?

Nothing you want to say?

Well, I think I can figure it out for myself – I go away for the weekend and when I get back you break up with me – doesn't exactly take a rocket scientist, does it? I mean, how dumb do you think I am?

Beat.

It was Thursday night, wasn't it? Results night – it was, wasn't it? Something happened at that party. I know it did, because Johnno told me, so what was it?

Beat.

Ha!

As soon as my back was turned. You are lower than a snake's arse, you really are, you know that?

Well, it wouldn't be Nat or Tash. They wouldn't touch you with a bargepole. Can't be Lydia. Oh, my God. Who was it? Was it Molly?!

You *know* she's head over heels for Johnno! That's just, that is so –

Jack It wasn't Molly.

Lucy He speaks!

Not Molly. So someone else then.

Jack I meant / that –

Lucy You said 'it wasn't Molly' – that implies it was someone else, Jack. So who was it?

Beat.

I am not going to cry I am not going to cry I am not going to cry I am not going to cry I am not going to fucking cry –

Beat.

Rrrrrrrrrrrr.

Beat.

Does she look like Taylor Swift? I bet she looks like Taylor Swift, she looks like Taylor Swift, doesn't she? She does, doesn't she?

Oh my God! I can't believe you've taken me for a mug, you fucking *arsehole*!

Beat.

I'm not upset.

It's funny . . . when you didn't text me this weekend – you said you would and you didn't, and I thought –

You wanna know what I think?

I'm thinking that this, whatever this is, has probably been going on for a while, hasn't it?

You wanna know why I think that? Because I'm smarter than you. Yeah, sorta knew all that shit you were spouting about keeping 'us' going long distance, seeing each other every other weekend, yeah, I think I sort of knew all that was just bullshit.

Silence.

Jack   It's not as simple as that.

Lucy   Isn't it?

Jack   You've got me wrong, Luce.

Lucy   Have I?

Beat.

Jack   It's not – breaking up. I'm not breaking up with you.

Lucy   I'm sorry?!

Jack   I don't want to be with you / right now.

Lucy   That sounds like breaking up, Jack. That is absolutely what that sounds like.

Jack   I *can't* be / with you.

Lucy   That is *totally* what that / is.

Jack   You're not listening. I don't want you to – to be with me – right now – / because

Lucy   Right now? So what? In a couple of days, you might change your mind?

I'm not going to hang on, Jack, until you've shagged around and got this, whatever this is, out of your system. I'm not going be dicked around. Do you understand?

I'm a one-way street, Jack, and you know what, right now, you are going in completely the wrong direction.

Beat.

You've got ten seconds to try and save this, and then that's it. Ten.

She waits ten seconds.

She does well to hold herself together.

(*She types a text on her phone while she says this.*) You know what? I nearly loved you. Might not have said it but I thought about it.

And I'm glad I didn't waste my breath.

She sends her text and puts her phone down.

He wobbles. He almost says something. He doesn't .

Silence.

Jack   You can – you can go if you like.

Lucy   I'm not going anywhere. I'm going to stay right here. Going to finish my shit coffee.

Jack   I'll go, then.

He stands, starts to go.

Lucy   You are such a coward. You know that?

Beat.

Jack   Yeah. Yeah, I am.

Music. The café dissolves around him . . .

Scene Seven

Daf *and* **Nat**'s *house.*

Jack *is motionless.* **Luke** *is holding his nose, which is bleeding. He is in a lot of pain.* **Johnno** *has the beginnings of a black eye.* **Daf** *is dressed for bed.*

Jack, **Luke** *and* **Johnno** *are out of breath.*

Johnno   We didn't know where else to –

Daf   Do you know what time it is?

Luke   Rrrrr.

Daf   Is he alright?

Johnno   He's –

Daf   Is he – ? Is he bleeding?!

Johnno   He'll be fine.

Daf   Mate –

Johnno   Luke – you're gonna be fine.

Daf   Mate. You're dripping on the carpet – can you –

Luke   Ah!

Daf   Will someone tell me what's going on?

Luke   Mmm.

Daf   Please!

Johnno (*to* **Jack**)   Are you going to tell him or am I?

Luke   Shiiiit.

Johnno (*to* **Jack**)   I said, are you going to tell him or am I?

Daf   Mate. Do you want to keep your voice down?

Beat, nothing but the sound of **Luke** *snivelling and sniffing.*

Daf   Well? Is *someone* going to tell me what you're doing banging down my front door at ten to midnight?!

(*To* **Luke**.) Mate! You're dripping on the – my mum's gonna go ape.

Luke *uses the bottom of the T-shirt to absorb the blood.*

Johnno (*looking at* **Jack**)   Well, me and Luke, we'd been to watch the match, and we were having a quiet pint in The Full Moon. Weren't we, Luke?

Daf   And?

Johnno   And Jack here thought it'd be a bright idea to walk through the door and start shouting 'Bluebirds'!

Daf   Yeah?

Johnno   The 'Bluebirds' are Cardiff, you muppet. You don't go in a Swansea pub, *any* Swansea pub, and shout 'Bluebirds' unless you want to be picking your teeth up off the floor.

Jack   I didn't ask you to step in.

Johnno   Sorry?!

Jack   Said, I didn't ask you to / step in, did I?

Johnno   Yeah, well I did because otherwise you were going to get your head ripped off – and look what I got for my troubles! Couple of lads squared up to him and he just – you just stood there! Tried to cool things down and one of them clocks me. Luke tries to pick me up off the floor and he gets a boot in the face for his troubles. Got his nose spread halfway across / his face.

Luke   Lydia's going to kill me.

Johnno   So, we ran. (*Of* **Jack**.) Dragging him behind us. (*To* **Jack**.) Did I miss anything?

Daf   They didn't see you come in here, did they?

Johnno   We lost them.

Daf   You're sure, 'cause –

Johnno   Anything you want to throw in the mix? Like what you thought you were doing picking a fight with a bunch of meat-heads? You can't reason with people like that, Jack. Football hooligans aren't renowned for their sense of humour. They're not big fans of irony! They're big fans of punching people. In the face. What did you think you were doing pulling something like that? BLUEBIRDS?!

Luke *uncovers his nose; the bleeding has stopped, his T-shirt is covered in blood.*

Luke   Johnno – does it look alright? Does it? Like if I clean it up, do you think she'll – she probably won't even notice will she, / if I –

Jack   Who said I was picking a fight?

Johnno   If you weren't picking a fight, you were asking for a good kick-in!

Jack   Maybe I was.

Johnno   The hell's that supposed to mean?

Luke   It's – it's clicking. Should it be / clicking . . . ?

Johnno   What is wrong with you?! The party, then Luce, then this –

Jack   Luce. You spoke to –

Johnno   She called me – obviously – she was in bits.

Luke   Johnno – it's not . . . you don't think it's broken, do you?

Johnno   It's not broken, Luke. It's – it's just a bit messed up, that's all.

So, there's nothing you want to say.

Like . . . maybe . . . 'Thanks for saving my arse.'

Like, 'Sorry you're going to wake up with a black eye tomorrow.'

Like, 'Sorry, it's my fault that Luke's got a broken fucking nose'!

Luke   You said it – you said it wasn't broken / you said –

Johnno   Of course it's fucking broken, Luke!

Luke   But you said –

Johnno   I think you owe us both an apology for starters – or a bit of gratitude, at the very least – don't you think?

Jack   I didn't ask you to. You butted in. That was your choice. Why should I apologise?

Luke   (*with sudden vigour*)   Because you're being a dick is why! You were being a dick at the party and I thought, I just thought it was the drink, I just put it down to that – but this?!

I've got blood pouring out of my face, Jack. I've got a broken fucking nose. I – I was trying to be your mate. I didn't ask for this.

Jack (*surging up*)   Yeah, and I didn't ask for this either, mate. Any of this. But this is what I've got and that's what you've got so – sometimes bad shit happens – / Live with it. *Live* with it.

Johnno   And what's *that* supposed to – ?

Voice of **Nat** *upstairs.*

Nat   Daf . . . is that Jack and Johnno? . . .

Daf   Yeah, they're just . . . we're just chatting . . .

Nat   Yeah, well can you 'chat' a bit more quietly.

Beat.

Daf   Mate. I don't know what's up with you. I really don't. But I think you need to leave.

Now.

Beat.

Johnno   Did you hear what he said?

Now you can walk out of that door . . . or I can help you on your way.

Your call.

Music. **Daf**'s *house dissolves around* **Jack** . . .

Scene Eight

A beach. Same night.

We can hear the wind and the waves slamming on to the shore.

Jack *zips up against the cold.*

His phone rings. He pulls it out. Doesn't answer it. It rings off.

It rings again. This time he 'declines' it.

It rings a third time. The noise of it seems to pierce louder. Pain. He holds it in his hand and squeezes it tight. Suddenly, he throws it as far as he can into the sea. He watches it land in the water.

He watches the sea.

He closes his eyes and buries his hands deep into his pockets. He opens his eyes.

He pulls out a bottle of vodka, unscrews it, psychs himself up and then takes a big glug of it.

He pulls his headphones on.

He presses play and we hear the music – you choose. After a moment he turns the volume up to drown out the sound of the sea.

(I was listening to 'Death' by White Lies and 'Rebellion (Lies)' by Arcade Fire when I wrote this section. Use those . . . or use those as a starting point and find what works for your production. Think something that builds in size and scale. The sort of song that swallows you up and drags you along with it.)

The sound of the sea seems to swell and compete with the music.

Pain.

He turns up the volume.

He drinks some more. A lot more.

He closes his eyes and starts to gently move to the music.

Pain.

He turns the music up to try and drown the pain out. He starts to move with more determination.

He drinks some more without stopping dancing, maybe it spills a little.

The dancing grows.

Maybe he kicks his shoes off.

He dances.

Pain.

He dances through it.

Pain.

He dances with all his might. He dances like he'll never get the chance to do it again.

(It shouldn't be good dancing but it should be utterly heartfelt and every fibre of his being should be engaged. I was thinking about Ian Curtis from Joy Division – find what works for you.)

He starts to spin. Like a whirling dervish. It's verging on the maniacal. He spins, he drinks, he dances he spins, he drinks, he dances. Maybe he mouths some of the words.

Pain. He throws it off. And dances, dances, dances . . .

The music grows louder and more distorted. It merges with the sound of the sea swelling.

The sound and the darkness swallow him up as the beach dissolves . . .

Silence .

Scene Nine

Jack *and* **Josie***'s house. Later.* **Jack** *sits with his head in his hands.*

Josie *in her work clothes.*

Josie   What were you thinking?

Jack   I / wasn't –

Josie   You're lucky I was on nights, lucky I came home and found you.

Jack   I / didn't –

Josie   Could've swallowed your tongue.

Jack   Will you / just –

Josie   You do know that, don't you?

Jack Shut up / a minute –

Josie Could've choked on your own spew. You didn't think of that, did you?

Jack Jose!

Josie Is that what you want?

Jack You're not listening, / you're not –

Josie You're a fucking idiot, Jack.

Jack They want me in tomorrow.

Beat.

The hospital. They want me in.

He takes an envelope out of his pocket and holds it out to **Josie** *without looking at her. She doesn't take it.*

Josie Tomorrow?

Jack (*realising the time*) Today.

Josie Right.

Jack Yeah and – I can't . . . they want to cut this open, Jose. This! . . . And that . . . I don't know . . .

He's all out of words.

He places his hands on the back of his head and holds it in towards his chest.

Silence.

Josie I don't know either.

Don't know what I'm supposed to do, or say . . . but I'm here.

And I'm going to hold on tight – I'm going to hold on tight – because you're all I've . . .

A chance! That's something. It's a chance. That's better than nothing, that's –

She sits next to **Jack**.

Josie   You know what? I don't care if I have to drag you there kicking and screaming tomorrow . . . if that's how this has to happen then that's what I'm going to do so . . .

Jack *collapses into her lap. He holds on to her so tight. It sucks the air out of her. She holds herself together for him. He sobs like a child.*

They cling on to each other for dear life.

Josie   You're right. I can't promise everything will be fine. I can't.

But I can promise I'll be here.

Every step.

Jack *settles. It takes as long as it takes. She rests her hand on his head. It's the tenderest thing.*

Josie (*putting on a brave face*)   Right. I'll tell you what's going to happen now. You're going to get in the shower and I'm gonna make us some food. Get some stodge in that belly of yours. Soak up the booze.

Then me and you, we're going to sit down here and we're gonna talk, talk it all through. We'll talk all night if we have to. And tomorrow I'm going to pack you a bag and I'm going to drive you there and I'm going to wait for you . . . I'm going to wait . . .

Beat. **Josie** *untangles herself from* **Jack**.

Josie   How about a pizza?

Beat.

I think we've got Hawaiian, Four Cheese . . .

Beat.

I will take your silence to mean you have no objections to a pizza.

He nods. He smiles. She starts to leave.

Jack　Jose.

Josie　Yeah?

Beat.

Jack　I'm scared.

Josie　I know you are.

Let's be scared together.

Beat. He nods.

Silence.

Right! What do you want?

Beat.

Jack　I want to live.

They hold each other's gaze. She smiles; it covers something else.

Music.

Josie *exits.*

The living room dissolves around **Jack**, *leaving him in a pool of light.*

He stands alone holding the envelope.

Scene Ten

Morning.

Josie *joins* **Jack** *in the pool of light. A hospital waiting room forms around them.*

They sit on a long row of plastic chairs. **Jack** *has his headphones around his neck.*

Silence.

Josie (*standing*)　Do you want something from the machine? Crisps or – ?

Jack I'm good.

Josie You didn't have breakfast. Or lunch. You should eat something.

Jack They said not to. In the letter.

Beat.

Josie Can of Coke then?

He gives her a look. She leaves him be. It's a warm moment.

Beat.

Josie *yawns but tries to quash it.*

Jack You were up early this morning. Could hear you rumbling about downstairs.

Josie Couldn't sleep.

I went for a walk. Down along the front. It was gorgeous out there. I was sat out there on the sea wall at seven. Just closed my eyes and felt the breeze . . . then the heat on my face as the sun came up. The two things together – it was funny, you know. The hot and the cold.

I'd never thought to do that before. Just sit there and . . . breathe. It was nice.

Beat. He nods.

You OK?

Jack Yeah. Fine. It's just weird. The waiting.

Beat. She nods.

Enter **Johnno**. *They both look to him – maybe* **Jack** *stands expecting the* **Doctor**.

Josie I'll give you two a minute. I could do with stretching my legs.

She exits.

Johnno *and* **Jack** *stand opposite each other awkwardly.*

Silence.

Jack   She told you?

Johnno   Yeah, she, yeah.

Jack   Right.

Johnno   Shit.

Jack   Yeah, it's –

Johnno   Mate.

Jack   Yeah.

Johnno   Maaaaaaate.

Jack   Yeah, I know.

Silence.

Johnno   So, it's like –

Jack   Yeah.

Johnno   Like a proper –

Jack   Yeah, it's a tumour, it's –

Johnno   That's like –

Jack   Yeah.

Johnno   Like.

Jack   I know, yeah, I know.

Silence.

Johnno   Can you . . . can you see it? Is there, like, a lump or – ?

Jack   No, it's –

Johnno   So, it's –

Jack   Inside, yeah, it's –

Johnno Right. Course. Idiot.

Beat.

Don't know what to –

Beat.

Fuck.

Jack Yeah.

Johnno Sorry.

Jack Yeah.

Beat.

I'm sorry too. Your eye.

Johnno Nah, it's –

Jack Don't know what I was –

Johnno You don't have to –

Jack Head's been in pieces.

Johnno Course, don't worry about it, you don't need to –

Beat.

Molly thinks it's quite sexy so . . .

They share a smile.

Johnno's *smiles turns into a short laugh.*

Jack What?

Johnno Nothing, it's . . .

Was walking here and I was thinking . . .

Do you remember our first day? In nursery? Didn't even know each other's names and you, you came over and said I should eat some of the Lego, so I did, and then I said you should pee in the pot plants –

Jack   Yeah –

Johnno   And you did!

Jack   Ha.

Johnno   The ones in Storybook Corner. Do you remember?

Jack   Mrs Williams was raging.

Johnno   Spent the rest of the day sat on the 'Naughty Mat' together.

Jack   Yeah!

Beat.

That's a funny thing to think.

Johnno   Don't know. Just popped into my head.

Beat.

Jack   I feel older. Isn't that – ? Just a few days and I feel –

Beat.

Did she tell you – (that it could be fifty–fifty?)

Johnno   Yeah. Everything.

Silence – neither of them knows what to do or say.

Eventually, **Johnno** *clears his throat and . . .*

Johnno   I told them it'd probably be better if – but they wanted to come so . . .

He moves towards the entrance.

Guys.

The gang shuffles in awkwardly, **Nat**, **Tash**, **Molly**, **Lydia**, **Luke** *and* **Daf**. *A couple of them are carrying pillows or bags. No one knows what to say.*

Nat   We wanted to see you.

Tash   Before the – before your –

Silence.

Molly   Don't know what to say, Jacko.

Beat.

Jack   You – you don't have to say anything.

Enter **Lucy***, unseen at first.*

Johnno   There's someone else too.

Lucy *moves towards* **Jack***. This conversation should feel private. Maybe the others give them a bit of space.*

Jack   Did Johnno – ?

Lucy   Yeah, he –

Jack   You don't have to – I didn't want you to feel you had to –

Lucy   You're not getting rid of me that easy. You're stuck with me.

Jack   But I'm –

Lucy   I'm not going anywhere so –

Jack   But I'm just saying –

She stops him speaking with a kiss.

They're all just standing around.

Beat.

Noticing **Daf** *in his onesie.*

Jack (*with a small laugh*)   You staying the night or what?

Daf   Yeah.

If I have to.

We all are.

Molly   We didn't know what to – so we –

Lydia   We just want to be here . . . just want to sit here and . . .

Luke   If that's OK with you? I mean, we don't want to –

Lydia   Luke.

Luke   Yeah, sorry.

Jack   . . .

He nods faintly.

A moment of stillness and silence.

Gradually, they all start to move, quietly, towards the plastic chairs and get settled. Last to leave **Jack** *are* **Johnno** *and* **Lucy**. **Jack** *remains standing. Maybe there aren't enough chairs for all of them. They leave one centre for* **Jack**.

Once they're settled the **Doctor** *enters.*

Doctor   Jack? We can take you through now.

Jack   I'm . . .

Beat.

I don't think I'm ready.

My sister, she's just –

Doctor   Whenever you're ready. In your own time.

Beat.

Jack   I might just sit here for five minutes if that's – ? Is that – ?

Doctor *smiles and leaves.*

Jack *sits and listens to the silence of his friends sitting around him.*

He slides his headphones on and presses play.

Music.

(I was listening to 'South' by Hippo Campus when I was thinking about this final moment. A song that feels like it's about not knowing what lies ahead but facing it head-on anyway, a song about possibilities. You could use whatever you like but try and get the right tone. It shouldn't necessarily be a downbeat song.)

All of the following should have its own little pocket of time but should happen in quick succession. It could happen in any order.

Luke *puts his arm around* **Lydia***.*

Johnno *takes* **Molly***'s hand and gives it a squeeze, then holds on to it. She tears up and puts her head on his shoulder.*

Someone hugs a pillow.

Nat *gives* **Tash** *a tissue.*

Daf *puts the hood of his onesie up.*

Someone stretches their legs and takes a few steps before sitting down again.

Daf *sits on the floor against the end of the row of chairs.* **Luke** *gives him his pillow to lean on. He accepts it with a faint smile.*

Lucy *rests her head on* **Jack***'s shoulder and closes her eyes.*

You might find other moments that you would like to incorporate.

Jack *has surveyed them all. He sits up straight . . . something lifts. He closes his eyes.*

The music swells.

The he opens them.

He lives or he dies . . . we never know . . . but he faces it head-on.

Slow fade to blackout as the music continues.

#YOLO

BY MATTHEW BULGO

Notes on rehearsal and staging, drawn from a workshop with the writer, held at the National Theatre, October 2016

How Matthew came to write the play

Matthew began by saying that he knows an emotionally complex piece is difficult for a young company to access and perform truthfully. However, he felt he wanted to make a virtue of this fact by creating a piece which follows a young adult coming to terms with huge emotional decisions that they may well be unable to articulate.

When writing the play he was thinking about his own teenage years and his transition from carefree teenager to responsible adult. He was interested in exploring the period of time 'when you are forced to be an adult but all you want to be is a kid'.

Approaching the play

Adele Thomas, lead director, suggested that it was important to find the light as well as the shade in the play. Although the subject matter appears intense, there is camaraderie between the characters and a sense of exuberance in their interactions. It is – at its heart – a play about a group of friends. Part of the director's job is to explore the lightness in the play by paying heed to the final stage direction *'He lives or he dies . . . we never know . . . but he faces it head on.'*

It is also important to create real relationships on stage and to try and avoid playing 'best friends' or 'boyfriend/girlfriend' dynamics. You should focus on what the text says about each character and avoid being led by assumptions like 'this is how siblings behave'. You should be careful to avoid paraphrasing the text and encourage your company to be really specific about what is written on the page. This is challenging because although the dialogue is naturalistic and comes tumbling out of the characters' mouths, there is a rhythmic and poetic aspect to how it is written.

Themes

The playwright Arthur Miller would place one sentence
about his work above his typewriter. When he felt he might
have lost his focus, he would refer back to this as his guiding
principle and use it to stimulate his thought process. The
workshop participants attempted to locate the key themes and
motifs of *#YOLO* so that they could be used as both catalysts
and lights in the dark during moments of doubt. Here are
some of the ideas the participants came up with:

THEMES (what the play is about)

* Mortality.
* Friendship.
* Isolation.
* Youth to adulthood.
* Time.
* Arrested development.

TIPPING POINTS (key moments of change in the play)

* End of an era.
* Jack's emotional control.
* The beach scene.
* A-level results.
* Lucy's holiday.
* Friends' attendance at hospital.
* The engagement of Lydia and Luke.
* The bloody nose (aftermath of pub brawl).

FAILURE OF LANGUAGE

* The missing adult support in Jack's situation.
* No one listens (characters tend to talk but not converse.
  with each other).
* Luke's drunken stutter
* Trying to articulate grief.

- Jack lashing out.
- Comedy, the pressure to be funny.
- Competitive friendship (the violence of banter).
- The unspoken (the proliferation of pauses in the play).
- The burden of the news (Jack doesn't articulate what is going on).

The group discussed the need to present Jack as a multifaceted character and to resist the urge to paint him as a saint. He still has/needs flaws.

Understanding the text

The group discussed some of the aspects of language that might not be instantly understandable. The main points were:

- You may wish to alter Daf to a more suitable variation for your company/region.
- Matthew confirmed that he was happy for roles to be gender swapped if this was a requirement of the company.
- The 'Gary Guilts' could be a way of describing hangover guilt.
- The reference to the *Evening Post* can be altered to the local paper of your area.
- The Full Moon pub was described as a 'rough football' pub in your home town that you have never been into (and may not want to!)
- The beach: it was briefly discussed whether companies from areas not near the coast needed to replace the beach with another location. It was decided that it was better to ask the audience to suspend their disbelief.

Punctuation and rhythm

See the author's notes on the text (p. 69). One way to engage your company in the play's specific rhythm of speech is to ensure that they drive through to the very ends of lines and pay careful attention to punctuation as well as content.

Music

The music is an important part of the play. You are free to find music that represents your company rather than sticking to the songs in the script; however, the songs you choose should match the tone/intention of the original songs. If you do consider using copyright material, then the usual copyright rules will apply.

Matthew described how the songs tap into the 'flavour' of the scenes and mirror the drive or intensity of the characters' own experiences.

Swearing

Matthew stated that he would rather the swearing was kept in, but acknowledged there may be situations that require it to be taken out. He emphasised that the swearing is not gratuitous and is an important part of the rhythm and emotionally serves the characters.

Exercises

The following exercises are designed to get your company analysing the text on their feet and generating a sense of pace and dynamism in the rehearsal room.

EXERCISE 1: THROWING LINES (CUE ENERGY)

Ask individuals to select a favourite line from the play, then to form a circle and say their line to the next person. Ensure this happens swiftly and avoiding pauses. Experiment with running it 'twice as fast' or in the opposite direction. Add pointing so the line is thrown randomly across the circle and everyone in the room is engaged. It is OK to get the line wrong in this exercise; the focus should be on the energy in the room instead.

EXERCISE 2: CHARACTER ANALYSIS

Use this exercise to lock actors' character choices into the text. This should prevent the company from making assumptions about characters.

Ask each actor to note down:

1   Everything they say about themselves.
2   Everything that character says about everyone else.
3   Facts about their character. These must be completely
    indisputable. Be very disciplined with this aspect as it can
    be tricky: e.g. it is a *fact* that Jack got three 'C's in his A-
    levels. It is a *supposition* that Jack got good A-levels.

After listing these, ask actors to consider how this information
changes what they think about the characters. For example. it
is a fact that Jack went to nursery with Johnno. How does this
alter their understanding of their relationship/timeline?

EXERCISE 3: SPEAKING/LISTENING

Encourages eye contact/allows actors to discover the nuances
between them.

• Ask the group to get into pairs and sit opposite each
  other. First, ask the actors to sit for one minute looking at
  each other. Then give them two minutes to speak the
  lines that they say about each other in the play. Do not
  allow them to embellish the lines. Do not allow them to
  improvise. At the end resist the temptation to analyse or
  discuss the character/exercise. Instead sit in silence with
  eye contact. When it has concluded ask what has become
  clearer as a result of the process. Repeat the process until
  all the characters have met.

EXERCISE 4: EXPLORING THE DETAIL

• Part A: In pairs (or the number of people necessary for the
  scene) start whispering lines to each other. Whispering
  encourages the actors to connect to each other.
• Part B: Then repeat, this time at normal volume. Ask
  them to pay attention to the geographical references in
  the dialogue. For example, if they say *you*, they should
  point to the person they are referring to. For *me*, point at
  themselves. For *there* – they point where it is. Interpret

these rules liberally. For example 'not going to be the end of the *world*, is it' may include a reference to outside/or the whole world. This process encourages the actors to engage with the world that the characters inhabit.

- Part C: Then repeat the scene focusing on the status/ power dynamic. At the start of every sentence, ask actors to take a step forwards/backwards. Try and make the decision before they speak so the move is attached to the line. Encourage the group to be instinctive and not to overthink the movements. Encourage the actors to play with their choices. What is revealed by their movements?

- Part D: Ask the actors to use the same scene overlapping each other and interrupting the lines. This encourages an explosive energy and a questioning of how each character's thoughts interact.

- Part E: Ask the actors in the scene to say the phrase 'I want to be here', then move, then speak their character's line of dialogue. This explores the relationships between the characters and how close/distant they may be from each other. Ask them to make sure they 'play the situation not the geography'. E.g. if someone says 'out there' do not necessarily move outside.

- Part F: Further development of this work could be to instruct the company to always maintain physical contact while speaking their lines. This deepens the exploration of their relationships.

MOVEMENT EXERCISE

This exercise could be useful as a way of approaching Jack's dance. It offers a way of freeing inhibitions and developing a theatrical language for your company. It could be done by the whole group, perhaps even as a group warm-up before each rehearsal. This would not only help the performer playing Jack to feel less inhibited, but may also be a great way of generating possible material through what other people come up with. Maybe every rehearsal should start with five minutes of dancing!

The workshop used the song 'Rebellion (Lies)' by Arcade Fire during this exercise. The participants established five stages of movement:

- Abandonment: open, relaxed, embracing the enormity of the moment.
- Pulse: engaging with the music's rhythm in the body.
- Arms: adding arm movements into the pulse.
- Amplification: heightening the intensity of the dance.
- Round: using space to turn around after we have. amplified the movements.

They then identified two further instructions to layer on top:

- 'Drink' – incorporating the character's need to drink into the movements.
- 'Pain' – embracing the character's moments of pain into the movement.

While the song played, different numbers were called and participants moved up and down the scale. While in each state they experimented with the commands to 'drink' or feel 'pain'.

SCENE CHANGE EXERCISE

Scene changes are an important part of the play and staging them represents a significant challenge. The workshop participants split into groups and took half an hour to explore the staging of every scene change, including the 'strange moment' as one continual movement. They paid particular attention to Matthew's descriptions of the stage directions in the text as 'dissolving, 'form[ing] around' and 'segueing' into one another.

Some of the group feedback was as follows:

Group 1   This group maintained a constant connection between all the scenes, with the final image of one scene shaping the initial image of the other. They incorporated the movements of chairs into each scene change rather than attempting to conceal them.

Group 2   This group used sound to mark the change of each scene. This helped reinforce the idea that each of the scenes begins in the middle of the action.

Group 3   This group experimented with using their bodies to create the physical space of each scene.

Group 4   This group used a single stationary figure in every change whilst the scene morphed around them. The phrase 'limiting your palette' felt useful in response to this choice: i.e. the value of making use of a single motif for the scene changes.

Group 5   This group used their bodies to create the effect of the wave on the beach. They crossed over scenes, with elements of the ending scene taking place as the next scene began.

Uniting

Uniting can be defined as a process of breaking down the script into beats to facilitate a deeper understanding of the piece's subtext. It also allows easy chunks to rehearse with. The workshop group focused on 'uniting' Scene Four of the play.

The group's working definition for the titling of the units was '*Who* is doing what to *whom*?' – e.g. Johnno probes Jack on his behaviour.

As a development of this work it was suggested you might want to stick to using transitive verbs to help ensure the unit titles remain active, i.e. a verb that sits between 'I' and 'You'.

To ensure the unit titles help further the company's understanding of the characters, try to avoid cerebral descriptions (keep it about what they are doing) and 'wishy washy' words like 'try' or 'bid'. Uniting works best when the character is active and you always assume success.

This process can then help your actors

- Learn their lines afresh.
- Reveal subtext.
- Add texture.

Objectives and obstacles

As a further extension, you could add 'objectives and obstacles'. These cover the entire scene and define what the character wants and what is preventing them from getting what they want. E.g. Objective: Johnno wants to find out what is wrong with Jack.

Once objectives are established you can begin to think of what obstacles exist to prevent the character from achieving this aim. The obstacles 'force' conflict and enhance the drama.

For Johnno in Scene Four, obstacles may include:

TIME: he has to meet Daf.

JACK: is not ready to open up.

INTERNAL: his own inexperience in handling this sort of situation.

As you explore these options you could read the scene again to see what has been revealed.

MEMORY EXERCISE

To help further your understanding of character, you could explore what has happened before the play for each of them. One way of doing this may be to improvise memories that the characters mention, or draw a timeline of key events preceding the play.

Make the realisation of these memories as real as possible. Ensure that actors know the place, who is involved, where and possible dialogue that may have taken place.

The aim of this exercise is to add detail, content and believability.

From a workshop led by Adele Thomas
with notes by Tom King

FOMO
by Suhayla El-Bushra

Dani and Josh are the perfect high-school couple. Their friends look on in envy as their love story unfolds on social media. But when the government switches off the internet for reasons of national security, the truth of their relationship is revealed. Told almost entirely through tweets, texts and status updates, *FOMO* takes a light, humorous look at the futility of comparing your own life to someone else's Instagram feed.

Cast size
9 (5m, 4f + ensemble)

Suhayla El-Bushra was writer in residence at the National Theatre Studio from April 2015 to August 2016, during which time her adaptation of Nikolai Erdman's *The Suicide* was staged in the Lyttelton Theatre. Other stage work includes *Pigeons* at the Royal Court Theatre and on tour; *Cuckoo* at the Unicorn Theatre; *The Kilburn Passion* at the Tricycle Theatre; and *Fingertips* for Clean Break at Latitude Festival. She has developed an original drama series with Headstrong/E4 and worked on *The ABC* for The Forge and Channel 4. Other TV and film work includes *Hollyoaks*, feature screenplays and children's drama.

Notes on the text

Until the final part of the play, when the internet is turned off, every scene is an online interaction of some kind. It is up to the companies how they choose to dramatise this, although the use of actual screens is forbidden.

It's up to each company to apportion speaking lines to whomever they see fit in the online chorus sections. The named characters do sometimes contribute to these sections, but it is up to the companies if they want to have them speaking their 'lines' or not.

The play isn't set anywhere specific. Words like 'bruv' and 'fam' can be used ironically and should not be considered an indication of any particular region.

A dash (–) indicates an interruption.

A slash (/) indicates overlapping dialogue.

Characters

Dani
Hayley
Fran
Steph
Sonali (*pronounced Shon-aa-li*)

Josh
Fraser
Hal
Lurch

The Online Chorus (can be made up of as many performers as needed – I would suggest between four and eight, but more or less would still work)

Scene One

Dani   DaniHotstuffMacmuffin

Danielle Macmillan

'Pretty hurts, we shine the light on whatever's worst'

1,201 posts

523 followers

212 following

Hayley   HayHay2001

Hayley Saunders

I'm a basic bitch

967 posts

348 followers

195 following

Fran   Frimps_123

Fran Simpson

I love shopping. And Nando's.

1,143 posts

516 followers

3,24l following

Steph   Steffiweffnumber1

Steph Dallimore

Right now I really fancy a ham sandwich

456 posts

82 followers

118 following

Josh   J-Bra

Josh Braun

Football legend

104 posts

642 followers

203 following

Fraser   snapfrazzlep0p

Fraser Newley

Nothing to see here

112 posts

581 followers

317 following

Hal   hal-tha-don

Hal Baker

lovemachine

317 posts

234 followers

193 following

Lurch   Lurch-D-Dogg

Lawrence Davis

thuglife

12 posts

27 followers

7 following

Sonali   Sonali_b

Sonali Bates

'It's the cracks that let the light in'

46 posts

3 followers

12 following

Scene Two

ONLINE CHORUS

DaniHotstuffMacmuffin

Hashtagnewshorts hashtag1stdayofsummer hashtagstarbuckscaramelfrap hashtagscrewthediet

27 likes

U LOOK HAWTTTTT! Winky face ice-cream heart heart sun heart

Schmoking!

Flame sun sun lips lips lips sunglasses sunglasses sunglasses sunglasses sunglasses cat with love hearts for eyes smiley face with love hearts for eyes smiley face with love hearts for eyes two love hearts two love hearts two love hearts two love hearts two love hearts red love heart yellow love heart green love heart green love heart purple love heartpink love heart with diamonds tiger

Where did you get ur shorts dani?

NU LOOK

WANT!

35 likes

47 likes

243 followers

259 followers

Dani Hotstuff Macmuffin was at Villa Rosa, Portugal, with Kyra Macmillan and two others

Dani Hotstuff Macmuffin changed her profile picture

Hayley Saunders, Fran Simpson, Sasha Myers, Steph Dallimore and twelve others reacted to Dani Hotstuff Macmuffin's picture

HAWTTTT.

Bootifalll!

OMG THIGH GAP!

HOW R U SO PRITI??!! Pusheen with love heart above head.

Where did u get your bikini?

TopShop

WANT

Two love hearts two love hearts two love hearts bikini bikini bikini sunglasses sunglasses sun sun sun sun sun pink love heart with diamonds

87 people liked Dani Hotstuff Macmuffin's photo

HayHay2000

DaniHotstuffMacmuffin hashtagfriendsforever

17 likes

Heart heart heart heart heart

Hashtaghotubparty!!!!!!!

12 likes

Noooo! I look SO FAT. Pusheen in a donut.

You look scha-mazing Frimps_123!

You can see my cellulite!

u look fit gyal

weightlifter weightlifter weightlifter

Oh my LIFE wot is going on with Steph in this photo?

Forgot my waterproof mascara

Hashtagracooneyes

Hashtagulooklikethatgrimgothgirlinmaths

Who?

The grim one

name?

How shd i no?

Shanita Shapali or sum shit

Shitali

Turd with a face turd with a face turd with a face

LOLZZZZZZ winky face

Hashtaghotubparty!!!!!!! J-Bra hashtagsixpack

27 likes

SO. FINE.

Smiley face with love hearts for eyes

Hashtaghotubparty!!!!!!! J-Bra snapfrazzlep0p Hal-Tha-Don lurch-d-dogg hashtagboyzintrunks hashtagsixpack hashtagbbq

Hashtaghotubparty!!!!!!! Hal-Tha-Don lurch-d-dogg hashtaghotdogeatingcompetition hashtaghowmanybangerscanufitinyourmouth?

GIF of **Hal** *and* **Lurch***, shoving two hot dogs into their mouths. GIF of* **Hal** *and* **Lurch***, shoving two hot dogs into their mouths. GIF of* **Hal** *and* **Lurch***, shoving two hot dogs into their mouths. GIF of* **Hal** *and* **Lurch***, shoving two hot dogs into their mouths.*

47 likes

Hotdog hotdog

Hashtaghotubparty!!!!!!! J-Bra DaniHotstuffMacmuffin hashtagcaughtsmooching hashtaglovesyoungdream

22 likes

Wow.

Smooooooooch

Well in

LAD!

Smiley face with love hearts for eyes smiley face with love hearts for eyes smiley face with love hearts for eyes

Such a cute couple!!!!!

LAD!

Hearts hearts hearts

32 likes

57 likes

64 likes

Scene Three

JOSH AND HAL PLAY 'CALL OF DUTY' ONLINE

Hal What were they like? Go on, you must have felt 'em.

Josh Argh!

Hal Are you dead again? Mate. You are shit at this.

Josh Prepare to die suckaaa

Hal Change your load out

Josh I'm good

Hal Looked like your hand was pretty close to you know. Hitting the jackpot.

Josh Boom!

Hal He was one of ours, you dick. So? Did you?

Josh Gentleman never tells

Hal Don't give me that. We all saw the photo. You definitely went over the bikini, that's a given, right?

Josh Not up for discussion, bruv

Hal Booom! I'm cleaning up here. Fraser said you weren't man enough to go for it

Josh Fraser's a little queer

Hal I knew you'd style it out. How far d'you get?

Josh Hang on

Hal Top half? Bottom half?

Josh Trying to concentrate here

Hal You gonna see her again?

Josh I did not see that one coming

Hal   Mate. Sort it out. You're costing us dear. You and her gonna –

Josh   Dunno

Hal   The way she looks in a bikini? Only a gay could turn that down – HOW COULD YOU NOT SEE THAT COMING?

Scene Four
ONLINE CHORUS

Dani Hotstuff Macmuffin changed her status to 'in a relationship'.

Josh Braun changed his status to 'in a relationship'.

Hayley Saunders reacted to Dani Hotstuff Macmuffin's post. Love heart.

Hayley Saunders reacted to Josh Braun's post. Love heart.

Hal Baker likes Josh Braun's post.

LAD.

Hand with forefinger pointing. Hand making circle with thumb and forefinger

Get in son

You dirty dawggg

Fran Simpson reacted to Dani Hotstuff Macmuffin's post. Love heart.

Fran Simpson reacted to Josh Braun's post. Love heart.

Steph Dallimore reacted to Dani Hotstuff Macmuffin's post. Love heart.

So CA-YOOOOT Dani!

I LOVE YOU GUYS!!!!!!!!!!!

Dani Hotstuff Macmuffin likes a comment on her own post

Steph Dallimore and 72 other people reacted to Dani
Hotstuff Macmuffin's post

Scene Five

DANI AND JOSH (SNAPCHAT STORY)

Josh *and* **Dani** *on the pier, with ice-cream cones, posing for the
camera.* **Dani** *dabs* **Josh**'s *nose with ice cream. He wipes some on her
chin. She splats him right in the face with her cone, they're both laughing.
He rubs his ice cream into her hair, she screams, laughing.*

Scene Six

LURCH, HAL, FRASER AND JOSH
(FACEBOOK GROUP MESSAGE)

Lurch   LAD!

Hal   Did you do it tho?

Lurch   FILM IT NEXT TIME

Hal   But did u actually do it?

Lurch   SWEAR DOWN JOEL BARKHAM FILMED
HIM AND TASH DOIN IT ON A WEBCAM

Hal   SLag

Fraser   Harsh

Lurch   SHE DIDN'T NO HE WAS FILMIN

Fraser   That was a fake!

Hal   Still a slag

How was it fake?

Fraser   Did you even see her face, bruv?

Hal   R U doin it or not j?

Lurch   FACE WAS OUT OF SHOT!

Fraser   U R SO DUMB.

Hal   R U & DANI DOIN IT?

Fraser   That was blatantly a porn

Lurch   R U DOIN IT BRUV?

Hal   We need to no!

Josh   YYY??? So u can fap urself off?

Fraser   Yeah Hal put ur little weener away

Hal   Shut Up Frasaaaaah!

Fraser   Fagit

Hal   Homo

Lurch   Queer

Josh   Batti rida

Scene Seven
SONALI AND FRASER (FACETIME VIDEO CALL)

Fraser   Hi. What is that behind you?

Sonali   Oh. That's Herman.

Fraser   Herman.

Sonali   He's a cheese plant. My mum like had him for about twenty years and then he got too big so my dad was gonna throw him out but I was like nooo, he's one of the family and he was all, OK but he goes in your room.

Fraser's *phone pings.*

Sonali   So now I've got like zero space for anything else?

Fraser   Dick.

Sonali   Excuse me?

Fraser   Not you. Sorry. Looks like he could turn nasty

Sonali   I know

Fraser   You're gonna wake up in the night and find he's wrapped his fronds around you, like some crazy sci-fi movie

Sonali *laughs.*

Fraser   Is that even a word? Fronds?

Sonali   Er I think it is yeah

She freezes with an unattractive facial expression.

Fraser   Hello? Hi.

Sonali   Hello?

Fraser   Yeah sorry you just froze

Sonali   Was I pulling like a really bad expression?

Fraser   Uhm. It wasn't the most flattering. (*His phone pings.*) Swear down that plant's moved like, a foot closer. You should probably get out of there.

Sonali *laughs.*

Fraser   Your mum's got a lot to answer for. (*Phone pings again.*)

Sonali   Yep

Fraser   Does she know she's put you in mortal danger?

Sonali   Er. She's not around. Any more.

Fraser *is sending a message on his phone.*

Sonali   She's not. She's still alive. I haven't seen her in a couple of years. It's kind of complicated. It's OK. My dad's pretty cool so. Do you want to do this another time?

Fraser   Huh? Sorry. My mates. Hal is *so* dumb sometimes.

Sonali   What is that? On the wall? Behind you?

Fraser   That? Er. That's my brother's?

Sonali   You don't have a brother

Fraser   He's dead.

Sonali   Shit. I'm really sorry.

Fraser   I'm only messing. All boys have rude posters in their bedroom.

Sonali   Right.

Fraser (*gets another message*)   Mate! (*Messaging back.*) Soz.

Sonali   So . . . have you thought who to do this project on?

Fraser   I thought seeing as you were the straight-A student you'd make all the decisions.

Sonali   Great thank you.

Fraser   And then do all the work

Sonali   Nice try. How about we meet tomorrow? After school?

Fraser   Got football training.

Sonali   I can do evening.

Fraser   Aren't you going to Sasha's party?

Sonali   Er. I'm not really on her radar.

Fraser   Awkward.

Sonali   It's OK I can live with it.

Scene Eight
ONLINE CHORUS

HayHay2000

hashtagsasha's16th hashtaggettingready

A GIF of **Dani** *applying mascara while* **Hayley** *smacks her lip-glossed lips.*

A GIF of **Dani** *applying mascara while* **Hayley** *smacks her lip-glossed lips.*

A GIF of **Dani** *applying mascara while* **Hayley** *smacks her lip-glossed lips.*

A GIF of **Dani** *applying mascara while* **Hayley** *smacks her lip-glossed lips.*

32 likes

hashtagsasha's16th hashtagpartyon hashtagbestnightever

17 likes

u all look so beeaaaaoooootifullllllll!

Lips lipstick red stiletto red stiletto white sandal green dress green dress lipstick flamenco dancer flamenco dancer twin playboy bunnies lips lips lipstick

OMG do i look that fat in real life?

Green dress lipstick lipstick

U honestly don't fran!

hashtagfatlense

hashtagtakeitdown!

Hashtagnever!

Hashtagwotabitch

Lol

hashtagsasha's16th hashtagpartyon hashtagbestnightever

hashtagdoesn'tnormallydrink Snapfrazzlep0p

48 likes

Fraser wtf??

mate

u look hammered!

LAD!

Fraser u lightweight

Scene Nine
SONALI AND FRASER (WHATSAPP)

Sonali   U OK? good party?

Fraser   . . . .

Sonali   Saw that photo of u. Hope ur not dead or anything. Winky face.

Fraser   . . . .

Sonali   Do u want to meet at library tmrw?

Fraser   . . . .

Scene Ten
ONLINE CHORUS

Fraser Newley posted a video to Dani's timeline.

Video footage of **Dani** *and* **Josh***, at* **Sasha***'s party.* **Dani** *in his arms.* **Josh** *looks directly into the 'camera'. He looks down at* **Dani***. She looks back at him. Intense. They move in for a kiss.*

Steph Dallimore reacted to Fraser Newley's post. Love heart.

Fran Simpson reacted to Fraser Newley's post. Love heart.

So ROMANTIC smiley face with love hearts for eyes

Hal Baker reacted to Fraser Newley's post. LAD! Shocked face looking around

Dani-Hotstuff Macmuffin liked Fraser Newley's post on her wall

Josh Braun liked Fraser Newley's post

Hayley Saunders reacted to Fraser Newley's post. Love heart

You guys!

Hayley Saunders and 47 other people reacted to Fraser Newley's post.

Scene Eleven

HAYLEY, DANI, STEPH, FRAN (SKYPE GROUP CHAT)

Fran   Is that ice cream?

Steph   Müller peach

Fran   Vom

Steph   Guess what I found when I was helping Sasha clear up this morning?

She holds up an empty Durex wrapper.

Fran   OK. Wow.

Steph   It was in the living room. Under. The sofa. Where a certain loving couple were filmed making out last night.

Fran   Instagram it!

Mum (*just heard in background*)   Stephi, are you playing tennis today, Daddy's / waiting

Steph   Get out of my room, this is a private call!

Fran   Ohmygod are you serious? You call your dad 'Daddy'?

Steph   She was joking.

Incoming call from **Hayley***:*

Fran   Mate

Hayley   Dude

Steph   Guess what I found? (*Waves condom packet aloft.*)

Fran   I need ice cream

Steph   It was by the sofa.

Hayley   Someone had sex. Big deal

Steph   Not just / 'someone'

Fran   Yeah, Steph. Can you believe she was going to Instagram it?

Steph   No I / wasn't

Hayley   Ohmygod you're so immature you're like some little twelve-year-old / or something

Steph   It was Dani and Josh!

Hayley (*screams*)   Call her quick!

Steph   Yes!

Hayley *tries to connect with* **Dani***. No answer.*

Hayley (*texting her*)   She never misses Sunday chat

Steph   Fran, are you OK?

Hayley (*calling her*)   Where are you, Dani?

Steph   I think Fran's like passed out

Hayley   Maybe her screen's frozen

Steph   No she's breathing

Fran *groans.*

Hayley   Mate, what's wrong?

Fran   I was up all night puking

Steph   Gross!

Fran   Mum found me on the bathroom floor and now she's totally flipped, like, balls out batshit

Hayley   No way, bra

Fran   I am SO grounded

Steph   How long?

Fran   Indefinite –

Hayley *(throwing something)*   JACOB GET OUT OF MY ROOM!

Sound of a child crying.

It didn't even hit you!

Her phone pings.

Ohmygod Dani

Steph   What she say?

Hayley   '2 secs just drying my hair'

Hayley *and* **Steph** *squeal.*

Fran   I really need some crisps.

Steph   Müller peach?

Hayley   I honestly don't know how you can even eat that shit

Fran   Like they call it low fat but it's actually way / full of sugar

Incoming call from **Dani**. *They all squeal.*

Hayley   Oh my God!

Dani   Hi.

Fran   How do you look so good?

Hayley   You are glowing, baby girl.

Dani   Uh . . . I went for a run this morning?

Steph   Yeah right. It was the run

Hayley   Not the kind of work-out we had in mind

Fran   Something you want to tell us, Dani?

Hayley   Yes. Macmuffin. Spill now.

Dani   Uhm . . .

All (*impression of her*)   Uhm . . . !

Hayley   We all know what happened

Steph   We saw the big smooch Fraser posted on your wall today

Dani   Yeah, what the hell was up with him?

Steph   Don't change the subject

Dani   Seriously. He was acting really weird

Fran   Tell us what happened after the smooch

Steph   And don't lie. Because I would like to present – (*Holds up the empty Durex wrapper.*) Exhibit A!

Fran   Busted!

Hayley   I can't believe you didn't tell me like, straight away??!!

Dani   That's not –

Fran   What was it like?

Hayley   Did you enjoy it?

Steph   Did it hurt?

Hayley   How big was it?

Dani   Oh my God!

Fran   Come on, Dani

Hayley   I tell you everything!

Fran   Yeah and me

Steph   Spill bitch.

Hayley   Tell us!

Dani   It was nice.

Hayley   Nice?

Dani   Yeah.

Fran   That's so / cute!

Dani*'s phone rings.*

Dani   That's him now, better go.

Steph   Probably calling him to say how much he loves her!

Dani   Bye

Hayley   Message me later, yeah?

Dani*'s gone. The others all look at each other and squeal.*

Scene Twelve
SONALI AND FRASER (WHATSAPP)

Fraser   I'm fine

Sonali   Cool I thought u might have choked on ur own vomit or something? Sad face with bead of sweat. Sad face with bead of sweat.

Fraser   . . . .

Sonali   was it a good party?

Fraser   . . . .

Sonali   library tmrw?

Fraser   sure

Sonali   cool.

Scene Thirteen

ONLINE CHORUS

Fraser Newley checked in to the Odeon Cinema with one other person.

Dani Hotstuff MacMuffin liked Fraser Newley's post

Scene Fourteen

DANI, FRASER, HAYLEY

(FACEBOOK GROUP MESSAGE: GOSSIP!)

Dani   Er . . . CUZZIN. Were u on a DATE?

Hayley   No shit? Fray on a date who with?

Dani   U will die when u find out! Surprised face

Hayley   Tell us fray! That's SO cute I can't believe it love heart love heart love heart

Dani   Reply Fraser!

I KNOW UV SEEN THIS MESSAGE!!!

Hayley   Who is it?

Dani   Shitali Bates!

Hayley   OMG!!!!!!!!!! GOTH GIRL? WTF?? Purple and yellow scream face.

Dani   Wot u doin with her????

Hayley   Coulda done better fray.

Dani   Disappointed in u CUZZZ.

Scene Fifteen
FRASER, JOSH, HAL AND LURCH PLAY
'CALL OF DUTY' ONLINE

Hal   Boss

Fraser   Eat shit!

Josh   Cover me, lads, I'm going in

Hal   Did you do it, Fray?

Fraser   What?

Hal   Dani said you and the Goth Girl did it / didn't she, Josh?

Fraser   Don't call her that

Lurch   In the cemetery on the way home

Josh   Take cover take cover

Fraser   Dani's a bitch

Josh   Mate! You ballsed that right up

Hal   It true then?

Fraser   No!

Lurch   She has got a nice pair

Hal   Yeah they're a good size

Fraser   I'm sure she'll be very happy to hear that

Lurch   Tell her to wear tight tops more often

Josh   Mate

Hal   Fraser!

Fraser   If you'd stop asking me stupid questions. All I can hear is you going on in my ear

Josh   Change your load out

HL: So you and the Grim –

Fraser   We went to the cinema that's all

Lurch   Lad!

Hal   And did you . . . ?

Fraser   We watched a film, remarkable really

Josh   Guys, come on. We've got this. Concentrate

Lurch   How far d'you get?

Hal   Over or under?

Lurch   Top or bottom?

Josh   Shut up! Doing my head in.

Hal   What's your problem?

Josh   Can we just concentrate on the game?!

Scene Sixteen
SONALI AND FRASER (WHATSAPP)

Sonali   I had a really fun time. Smiley face.

Fraser   Me too

Sonali   Do u want to do somethng next wknd? My friend nuzzles picnic. Smiley face. Chicken drumstick. Donut. Cake.

Fraser   Your friend nuzzles picnic???!!

Sonali   Izzie's picnic!

Fraser   Say wha??!!!

Sonali   Guess it's not that rocknroll.

Fraser   Sounds fun. Smiley face. I'm away next wknd. Cuzin's wedding

Sonali   Another time?

Fraser   . . . .

Sonali   When's good?

Fraser   . . . .

Scene Seventeen
ONLINE CHORUS

Dani Hotstuff Macmuffin added 21 photos to the album 'my big sis just got married!!!!!'

Wow, Dani, she looks amazing

U look amazing!

Josh looks SO GOOD in a suit

Like Like Like! Check U2 out

OMG they're gonna be next lolz

Girl and boy with love heart top hat engagement ring two love hearts pink love heart love heart with two diamonds

Holy shit. Is that Fraser?

He scrubs up WELL

Fraser! U LOOK FINE

Loving the hair

Form an orderly queue, ladies

Behind Shitali??? No thanks turd with a face turd with a face

Like

Like

Like

Like

Like

Like

Like

Like

Like

Like

Like

Like

Dani Hotstuff Macmuffin was tagged in Sarah Hassan (friends with Kyra Macmillan)'s video

Footage of **Dani**, *extremely drunk, dancing with* **Josh**. *She's twerking away, winding and grinding; he's looking slightly uncomfortable.* **Fraser** *is at the bar, staring at them both.*

Girl U got tha MOOOOVES

Love this!

Dani ur so funny!

Dani Hotstuff Macmuffin was tagged in Sarah Hassan's album 'Kyra and Sam's wedding'

Drunk bridesmaid

Is that Kyra's little sis? Wow she looks so grown up

Who is that?

Kyra's sister's boyf!

Loving the topless look

We caught him leaving her bedroom at 2 a.m. dressed like this

LAD!

Naughty boy!!!!

Er Dani??! Caught in the act!

Hayley Saunders liked Sarah Hassan's photo

Hal Baker liked Sarah Hassan's photo

Lawrence Davis liked Sarah Hassan's photo

Kyra Hamilton (was Macmillan) liked Sarah Hassan's photo

Sam Hamilton liked Sarah Hassan's photo

Fran Simpson liked Sarah Hassan's photo

Steph Dallimore likes Sarah Hassan's photo

Fraser Newley liked Sarah Hassan's photo

84 people reacted to Sarah Hassan's photo

Scene Eighteen
SONALI AND FRASER (WHATSAPP)

Sonali   Why did u blank me at school today?

Fraser   . . . .

Sonali   You've been ignoring me all week

Fraser . . . .

Sonali   I saw u at lunch u walked right past me.

Fraser . . . .

Sonali   Is it because your 'friends' don't like me? I know
what they've been saying about me. You should tell them to
check their privacy settings.

Fraser . . . .

Sonali   You're pathetic.

Fraser   Come Fran's party with me?

Sonali   RU serious?

Fraser   This wknd.

Sonali . . . .

Fraser   Didn't mean 2 ignore u. Soz. Been busy with
football. Football football football

Sonali . . . .

Fraser   League final next week. Come 2 party. I'll make it
up 2 u.

Sonali . . . .

Fraser   Don't be moody.

Sonali . . . .

Fraser   Please? My friends are OK ull like em. Winky face.

Sonali   They hate me. Plus Fran's a bitch

Fraser   She speaks highly of u

Sonali . . . .

Fraser   Will u come?

Sonali   No thnx

Fraser   Her parents won't be there it's gonna be off tha chain. Beer beer beer champagne bottle cocktail

Sonali   . . . .

Fraser   Twist ur arm?

Sonali   What time?

Scene Nineteen
ONLINE CHORUS

Frimps_123

Hashtag16th hashtagcalmbeforethestorm

13 likes

balloon party popper party popper party popper cake

How many beers?

Cannot wait to get stuck into that! Smiling devil face smiling devil face smiling devil face

Hashtag16th hashtagcalmbeforethestorm hashtaggettingreadywithmabitches

16 likes

Cannot wait to get stuck into that! smiling devil face smiling devil face

Lad!

Ew.

Just being friendly

U all look so nice. Dunno what to wear now. Crying Pusheen

OMG Fran where did u get that dress?

Coast

WANT!

Dani you look so beautiful

Scene Twenty

JOSH, DANI, FRAN, HAYLEY, STEPH (SKYPE)

Dani   Hi

Josh   Where are you?

His phone pings.

Dani   Fran's

Fran   Hi Josh!

Hayley   Hi Joshi!

Josh   Didn't realise you were all –

His phone pings.

Dani   I told you we were coming here early to get ready

Fran   Tell him to come over

Josh's *phone pings.*

Dani   Who's that?

Josh   What's Hayley done to herself?

Fran   She wants to look hot for Hal!

Hayley   Shut up!

Josh's *phone pings.*

Dani   Who keeps messaging you?

Steph   Is that Josh?

Dani   When are you getting here?

Josh   Uhm (*Coughs.*)

Steph   Josh, can you bring me some cigarettes?

Josh   Yeah. I might. Might not come actually.

Hayley   You just bought twenty!

Dani   What's wrong?

Steph   Everyone ends up poncing off me

Josh   I don't feel that well

His phone pings.

Dani   Are you alright?

Fran   Steph what did you with my mascara?

Josh   Yeah. No. I feel a bit hot and cold

Steph   I dunno

Hayley   Steph, you're such a dumbass

Dani   Have you taken something for it?

Fran   You literally had it like two seconds ago

Josh   Just, just a Lemsip

Hayley   Can someone please take these crisps away from me?

Dani   D'you want me to come over?

Steph   I know they're so good

Josh   Nah I'll be alright.

His phone pings.

Probably just sleep to be honest

Dani   Who is that?

Steph   Josh can you bring me ten Silk Cut? I'll pay you back –

Dani   He's not coming

Steph   What?!

Hayley   Who's not coming?

Josh's *phone pings.*

Fran   Joshi?

Josh's *phone pings.*

Dani   He's ill

Josh   I'm ill

Hayley   Mate

Steph   You don't look great to be honest

Hayley   You can't leave Dani all on her lonesome?

Fran   She was looking forward to seeing you!

Hayley   How can you say no to this beautiful face?!

Dani   Shut up

Josh   Sorry girls.

Fran   Go back to bed. Josh

Steph   Maybe we'll send Dani round later

Laughter.

Josh   Happy birthday, Fran

Josh's *phone pings.*

His phone pings.

Dani   Bye. Get some re –

Steph   He's gone.

Scene Twenty-One
SONALI (INSTAGRAM)

Sonali   Sonali_b

Hashtagnewdress hashtagitsnotme

You ask me / to a party / full of people I hate. Who offer me /
a chance at cool / even though I silently berate / them, and I
/ like the phony I am / drop my mates / drop my clan.
Tempted. Seduced. A hypocrite.

Zero likes

Zero comments.

Scene Twenty-Two
HAL, FRASER, JOSH, LURCH
(GROUP MESSAGE: PARTAYYYYY!!!)

Hal   Guys help. This?

He posts a selfie, wearing his dad's jacket.

Fraser   Mate.

Lurch   Wot is that?

Hal   My dad's

Lurch   R U SERIOUS?

Hal   It's sharp

Fraser   Mate

Lurch   THAT'S A NO.

Fraser   I wouldn't

Hal   I'm on a promise with Hayley

Wot u wearin?

Fraser   Not in that u won't be

Ben Sherman mate.

Hal   Josh?

Fraser   Have it.

Lurch   NIKE HOODIE ALL THA WAY

Hal   Josh?

Josh   Not going bruv soz

Lurch   WOT?

Hal   WTF?

Josh   Feel shit lads soz

Hal   U gotta come

Josh   Nah man in bed got fever

Lurch   HAVE A JAGAR BOMB

Hal   Sort it out son

Lurch   IT'S FRAN'S PARTY!!!

Hal   No parents fam

Lurch   WE BE GETTING IT ON ALL NITE ALL NITE

Hal   U R COMING!!!

Fraser   lurch u need to manage ur expectatons

Josh   Can't fam got fever

Lurch   HAVE 2 JAGAR BOMBS

Hal   Tell him Fray

Fraser   If he's sick he's sick. Smiley with a green tongue.

Hal   I need a wing man

Josh   U got Fray!

Hal   He'll be busy with corpse girl

Fraser Newley left the conversation

Hal   can't take a joke since he started seein her

Josh   U got lurch

Hal   Lurch is a liability

Lurch   STILL HERE BRUV!

Hal   This why I need u fam

Josh   Soz bro. have fun.

Hal   This ain't right. Calling u.

Josh   Mate seriously

Hal   Ansa ur phone

Josh   Lost my voice!

Hal   I'm comin round

Josh   Bad idea

Hal   U better be ready

Josh   I got the shits bad!!!!!!

Hal   U got ten minutes fam

Josh   Aint pretty bruv no joke

Hal   I WILL SEE U IN 10.

Scene Twenty-Three
ONLINE CHORUS

HayHay2000

Hashtagnewdress, hashtagitsnotme
Hashtagwhydidyouevencomebitch?
Hashtagyourdresslooksshitanyway

12 likes

wot a loser

that's her in her new dress? New from where?

Oxfam

Lol

Can't believe she turned up after slating u all

Ye if u hate us bitch

Angry red face downward thumb angry cat

Wot is snapfrazzlep0p even doing with her?

Ye snapfrazzlep0p ditch dis btch now!

Scene Twenty-Four
INSTAGRAM FEED

Steffiwef posted a video

Fraser and **Sonali**'s *backs as they argue in the corridor.*

Fraser   Why d'you put it online?

Sonali   I always post my poems

Fraser   Didn't you think people might see?

Sonali   No one ever looks at them

Fraser   People are always looking. All the time.

Sonali   I wanna go home

Fraser   Go then.

Sonali   I don't know how to get back from here.

Fraser   Get a cab

Josh and **Hal** *come in.*

Steph (*from behind the camera*)   Joshi! Thought you weren't coming. Dani's in the kitchen.

Hal   Alright, Fray. See you brought your girl

Fraser   She was just leaving.

Sonali *leaves.* **Josh** *and* **Fraser** *exchange a look. Blackout.*

32 likes

Awkward!

Bitch got told!

Scream face

WTF is Hal wearing?????

LOL.

Scene Twenty-Five
YOUTUBE FOOTAGE

YouTube video – 'bitchslap'. Sound of the party going on in the background. Some sense of a camera moving through a crowd of people – they're dancing or snogging or smoking.

The camera moves through the crowd until it comes to **Dani**, *standing on her own; she's looking at something, shell-shocked.*

Lurch (*from behind the camera*)   What's up Dan? (*As she pushes past upset.*) Dani?

We follow **Dani** *out, as she pushes through everyone, making her way to* **Sonali**, *who's outside, texting.*

Dani   Did you know?

Sonali   Huh?

Dani   You're sick. Were you trying to cover for him?

Sonali   I genuinely have no idea / what you're –

Dani *slaps* **Sonali** *in the face. Sound of collective 'oohs' and 'that's gotta hurt' coming from behind the camera.* **Dani** *turns to face the camera.*

Dani   Fuck. Off!

Blackout.

All comments 172

Top comments

Ouch!

She got told!

I wanna no wot she did?!!!!

That girl got bare beats

'Fuck. OFFFF!' Brilliant.

Her face is gonna sting for days

High school drama

Love it

Scene Twenty-Six
ONLINE CHORUS

Danielle Macmillan changed her relationship status to single

Hayley Saunders reacted to Danielle Macmillan's status. Sad face.

Hayley Saunders wrote on Danielle's wall.

Oh hun R U OK???

Fran Simpson wrote on Danielle's wall.

I heard u were upset what happened? Sad face. Broken heart.

42 people reacted to Danielle's post

Dani? Message me hun?

Dan u OK?

Love u

Hugs

Hugs

Broken heart broken heart sad face angry red face crying face crying face crying face crying cat

126 people reacted to Danielle Macmillan's post

Scene Twenty-Seven
SKYPE CALL (FRAN, STEPH, HAYLEY, LURCH)

Fran   Oh my God

Steph   Like. Oh. My God

Fran   MY. GOD.

Steph   I know, right?

Fran   Right?

Steph   I actually know

Fran   What the hell happened?

Steph   I. Literally. Have no idea

Fran   OK OK OK. You're gonna have to talk me through the last few stages of the evening because I honestly can't remember anything beyond, like, dancing in my kitchen?

Steph   You must remember Fraser turning up with the Grimm

Fran   Ohmygod, did I say something to her? What did I say to her?

Steph   You told her if she hated us so much she should crawl back under her gravestone? And then you were like 'FYI? Your poems are shit.' Then her and Fraser had like this really big row in the hall?

Fran   I don't remember that at all

Steph   I put it on Instagram don't worry

Fran   So what happened with Dani?

Steph   I genuinely don't know? Like, one minute Dani was dancing in the kitchen with the rest of us, then she just like stopped. She went over to the window and that's when she flipped –

Incoming call from Hayley.

Fran   Oh my God she'll know something

Steph   Hayley

Hayley   OH MY GOD

Fran   I know

Hayley   THERE ARE NO WORDS.

Steph   We know!

Hayley   I'm like SO shocked

Fran   Us too

Hayley   I'm totally devastated

Steph   Totally

Hayley   I literally feel like I did when my mum and dad got divorced. Worse, because they argued like the whole time and it wasn't even a surprise

Fran   What happened?

Hayley   I genuinely have no idea.

Her phone bings. They all scream.

Fran   Is it her is it her?

Hayley *checks her phone.*

Hayley   Hal. 'You seen J-Dog he's gone AWOL.' What is going on? She won't answer my calls, texts, messages anything. I'm like so worried

Steph   Poor Dani

Fran   Poor thing

Hayley   Who filmed it? Someone filmed it and put it in YouTube they must know

Steph   Lurch

Fran   Yeah it was Lurch

Hayley   Call him

Fran   What's his Skype name?

Steph   I've got it I've got it

Hayley   Add him!

Connecting to Lurch . . .

Fran   Ohmygod is that his picture?

Hayley   That's gross

Steph   What even is / that?

Lurch   Well. Hello / ladies

Hayley   Lurch what / happened?

Fran   What did you / see?

Steph   What the hell was going on with Dani?

Lurch   I dunno

Fran   Did Josh dump her?

Hayley   No way would / that happen

Fran   Why did she punch goth girl?

Steph   You filmed it, you must know something

Lurch   All I saw was –

Camera freezes on his face.

Fran   No. Don't do this to me

Steph   Not now

Fran   Retry retry

Hayley   Work, you dumb machine

Lurch   I went in the kitchen to tell her Josh had turned up, only she was looking out the window and I don't know what she saw but she was properly freaked out, you know when people get –

Can you guys hear me? Shit. Hello. Guys?

Fran   Muuuuum!!

Steph   Daddy!

Hayley   Jacob you little arsewipe have you been messing about with the computer?

Steph   Mummy. Can you get online?

Lurch   Hello?

Fran   The wifi's down!

Hayley   Mum, Jacob's been downloading *Minecraft* mods and the laptop's crashed AGAIN

Steph   I can't get online!

Hayley   I need to REVISE.

Scene Twenty-Eight
ONLINE CHORUS

At first no one minded

There'd been a lot of storms

We thought it was, like, a local thing?

Then we saw the news

The prime minister

The heads of state had all got together and made a decision

In the interest of national and international security

To turn the internet off

With immediate effect

It was the only way to stop the terrorists

Apparently.

And no mobile phones

Landlines only

Only everyone had got rid of their landlines

We had to wait till we saw each other on Monday at school

Like, what's the point if there's no internet?

How are we supposed to learn?

It must have been how it was in the war

Or like, Tudor times

We were really pissed off

We wanted to know what happened with Dani?

Only no one would tell us.

She wouldn't talk to any of us

She looked awful

Really thin

Not in a good way

Is that even possible?

Yes.

I used to think she was so pretty but now

Now she looks kind of scrawny when you see her up close

And spotty

Puffy eyes from crying

Josh missed the football match, against St Bartholomew's

We lost the cup

Coach was furious

The team were furious

Everyone thought it was

You know

Drugs

Apparently some sixth formers were handing out pills at
Fran's party

We were all really shocked

We didn't think Josh did things like that

But once we heard

It all fell into place.

We asked Fraser

He said it was true!

He didn't exactly say it was true

He didn't deny it either

He didn't deny it in such a way

In such a way that suggests

It was actually true.

We tried to ask Sonali

Now she is a stuck-up cow

She totally thinks she's better than everyone else

Even though she's a blatant freak

We were like perfectly nice to her

But she wouldn't tell us anything

Lurch kind of ruined it by asking her bra size

And then we kind of ruined it by laughing.

We asked Hayley

She told us to get lost

Can you believe that?

She told us to mind our own business

Which is actually like really rude?

Because it is our business actually

Dani is our friend

We're friends on Facebook

We follow her on Instagram

On Snapchat

We're friends

No one would tell us anything

And

This is the worst bit

There was no way of finding out

No posts

No photos

No videos

No chats to eavesdrop on

We couldn't lurk

We had nowhere to lurk.

Scene Twenty-Nine
ART ROOM

Fraser   It's really good.

Sonali   How long have you been standing there?

Fraser   Couple of minutes. Five. Ever since you started on the flowers. Been nice. Watching you paint.

Sonali   I'm gonna pack up now.

Fraser   I'm really sorry.

Sonali   Why didn't you just tell me?

Fraser   It's not that easy –

Sonali   It kind of is actually. You just open your mouth and try not to lie –

Fraser   I'm not like you, alright?

Sonali   Clearly.

Fraser   You go out of your way to stand out.

Sonali   I can't help being me.

Fraser   I thought I could.

Sonali   Maybe it's time to stop pretending –

Fraser   I'm not pretending. Apart from that one thing, this is who I am. I support Chelsea. I like sport and *Grand Theft Auto* and bants with the lads. I don't wanna lose my mates.

Sonali   So tell them. They might surprise you.

Fraser   Yeah, right.

Scene Thirty
DANI'S ROOM

Dani   We only kissed, like, four times.

Hayley   But you told me you'd –

Dani   You assumed.

Hayley   Why didn't you say?

Dani   Felt stupid.

Hayley   Didn't you think it was weird?

Dani   Thought he was shy. Then I thought. Maybe he just didn't like me

Hayley   But all your. All your photos, all that . . . That snog at Sasha's party –

Dani   That was the only time he kissed me like that. And you know why he did, don't you? I watched it back. The video. I wanted to see. If he'd been lying all along or if he'd meant it.

Hayley   And?

Dani   That look he gave. Just before. That look he gave into the camera. Like he was trying to prove something. You know who was filming it don't you? You remember who posted it on my wall? Fraser. He was staring at Fraser.

Scene Thirty-One
BOYS' CHANGING ROOMS

Fraser   You're brave. Showing up here.

Josh   Waited till everyone had gone.

Fraser   Better not let Coach see you.

Josh   He still not forgiven me?

Fraser   We lost five–nil cos of your no-show.

Josh   Couldn't face seeing you after. After the party.

Fraser   Dani said anything?

Josh   To me?

Fraser   No, I mean, to anyone else.

Josh   Right. No I don't think so. What about Grimmy?

Fraser   Sonali. No.

Scene Thirty-Two
DANI'S ROOM

Hayley   What about your sister's wedding?

Dani   I passed out drunk.

Hayley   That photo of him outside your room, with no top on.

Dani   Yeah, I puked all over his shirt.

That's when it first happened apparently. When I was unconscious.

Hayley   Nice.

Dani   Yeah.

Scene Thirty-Three
BOYS' CHANGING ROOMS

Fraser   She thinks I should tell people.

Josh   Is she mental?

Fraser   She says worrying what other people think is no way to live your life. Says you just gotta be yourself and not try and second guess how everyone's gonna react.

Josh   She said all that?

Fraser   She's been seeing a counsellor. Since her mum left.

Josh   Freak.

Scene Thirty-Four
ONLINE CHORUS

After a while we get used to it

We forget we ever had it

We talk to each other face to face

And when we go home

We know we're all at home

We know there isn't some secret conversation happening somewhere else

So we don't feel like we're missing out

We're actually a lot more relaxed?

We can sleep at night.

No waking up at three in the morning

Reaching for our phones

Just to check

Just a quick check.

And when we say like really dumb things

And do really dumb things

They're over

They don't hang around to haunt us

It's actually loads better

We still gossip

And speculate

And just cos something's not being recorded

Doesn't mean it didn't happen

Like the ball

The leavers' ball!

We were really looking forward to the ball

Who was wearing what

Who was going with who

Who was gonna end up doing it

We thought Fraser and Sonali were back together again

They had been hanging out loads

And we thought

We hoped

We thought Josh and Dani might

We hoped

They made such a cute couple

And they'd been spotted chatting recently.

On the night of the ball

The hall all decorated

Music playing loud

Drunk on smuggled vodka

We saw them arrive

Fraser and Sonali

What was she wearing?

It was like a bin bag or something

They walked in together

Followed by

Josh

Alone

Only guess what

He wasn't alone

Sonali went off to talk to her friends

That gang of freaks in the corner

And Fraser and Josh

Held hands

Like actually held hands!

And then Fraser put his arm around Josh's shoulder?

It was disgusting

It was actually really sweet

And they leant in.

And they kissed

On the lips.

And they looked at each other

And that was that.

We can't show you it

No one filmed it

No one took a photo.

You'll just have to trust us.

It happened.

The End.

FOMO

BY SUHAYLA EL-BUSHRA

Notes on rehearsal and staging, drawn from a workshop with the writer, held at the National Theatre, October 2016

How Suhayla came to write the play

At the beginning of this project, Suhayla wanted to write a romantic comedy. She was thinking about films she loved when she was growing up, like *The Breakfast Club* and *Pretty in Pink*. She wanted to prove that plays for young people don't have to be dark and moody, they can be light and romantic. She was also interested in exploring the different cliques in a school.

Suhayla wanted to tell a story for a generation that has grown up with the internet. She wanted to imagine what would happen if the internet was switched off. What is left when you switch off access to the hive mind and you are left with individuals who have to interact in the real world? She decided to tell a love story online and then follow it in real life after the internet is switched off.

She was excited by the challenge of showing the internet onstage. She was inspired by seeing *Teh Internet Is Serious Business* by Tim Price at the Royal Court. She enjoyed the way the internet was shown without any screens, instead using ball ponds and zany costumes to show how we are constantly bombarded in the online world. For Suhayla, this play opened up the possibility of showing the internet onstage. She feels that we are just at the start of this conversation between theatricality and the online world and that there is lots of exciting exploration ahead of us.

Suhayla was interested in the difference between what people choose to show online and their real lives. She observed that our obsession with social media can leave us feeling vulnerable and bad about ourselves. Even though what we see from our friends is polished PR, it can still leave us feeling like we are lacking.

As part of her research process, Suhayla did a workshop in a school. The young people said they felt more relaxed in places where they didn't have online access (e.g. in their granny's house) and one girl said she felt constantly under attack by the internet.

Suhayla didn't want to write a play in which adults tell teenagers what is wrong with their lives – because actually this affects all of us. We are all not seeing the full picture. We are all made to feel like we're not good enough.

The play is a love story about a gay romance, however it is not an 'issue'-led play. It is a story about feeling that you're not good enough, which just happens to have a gay protagonist.

Games and exercises

The following games and exercises could be useful starting points to find a way into the play.

THE 'YO' GAME

- Participants stand in a circle. One person starts in the middle and spins around. They eyeball someone in the circle and run towards them. Both have to jump and do a double high-five and shout 'Yo'. The person in the middle and the person in the circle swap places. Gradually add to the number of people in the middle of the circle.

- You can then introduce the idea of 'keeping the ball in the air' – how can they make sure they don't drop energy or bump into each other?

WALKING AROUND THE SPACE

- Participants walk around the room and fill the space. Ask them to blow out something bad that's happened this week. Then ask them to blow out something good that they are bringing into the room.

- Then ask them to walk with the energy of Suhayla's writing, thinking about the pace of the dialogue and the speed of the internet. When you clap your hands, the internet has been switched off. What is the energy in the room now? (Encourage individuals to do whatever feels right for them and to resist following anyone else's energy.)

- The next time you clap your hands, only one person can move at a time. 'Keep the ball in the air' – as soon as one person stops moving, another starts. If two people move at the same time, they have to stop and a brand new person starts to walk. Be strict (a twitch counts as moving). Rufus Norris often talks about 'finding the promise' – can you be open to what is being offered and see how it might inform the next stage of your thinking? Play with different energies, eye contact, relationships, invite participants to feed off moments and see where they can be taken.

This exercise encourages participants to explore the potential in small moments, to build an awareness of each other and to develop the ensemble dynamic.

NB. You could also try this when your company is starting to get off book. The actors move on their line and stop when their line finishes, handing over their energy to the actor who has the next line.

You could also think about what might happen if you add character into this exercise? What might happen if you bring a world into this exercise? (For example you could run this exercise in the online world.)

TALKING AND DRAWING

- In pairs, participants have 90 seconds to talk about the online world. Person A starts. They should try to talk in a stream of consciousness; if they get stuck, they should go back to the phrase 'The online world is . . .' or 'The world of social media is . . .' Person B has a pen and paper and draws what person A is talking about. After 90 seconds, stop and repeat the exercise with B talking and A drawing. Take time to show back and reflect. What does the online world look like?

FREEWRITING

- Participants have 90 seconds to write about the offline world. They are not allowed to take their pen off the paper. If they get stuck, go back to the phrase 'the offline world is . . .' There is no need to write in full sentences or to be articulate.

WRITING LISTS

You could do this as preparation, or with your company. Repeat the freewriting exercise, but this time you are creating lists. Start with list number one. As you start to add two, three, etc. you can move between different lists if more ideas come to you. Try to write without stopping and to focus on just getting ideas down without worrying about committing yourself to anything.

- Write a list of smells.

- Write a list of 'things I know.

- Write a list of things in *FOMO*.

- Write a list of things people will hear in my/our production of *FOMO*.

- Write a list of things people will feel when they come to watch my/our show.

- Write a list of things people will see in my/our show.

- Write a list of questions people will ask when they come out of my/our show.

If doing this with your company, invite them to take a moment to reflect back on what they have written. Then share this with a partner and report back to the group.

This is a useful exercise to remind yourself that as a director, half your time is spent listening to the script and half your time is spent thinking about the audience – how will they receive your play?

Visual language

The visual language and design is at the heart of the play and therefore requires careful thought. In the workshop, Emily Lim, lead director, split participants into groups of four or five. Each group was given a simple provocation and had 15 minutes to create a design for the show with pens and paper.

Group 1 had to design the show on a fiver.

Group 2 had to design the show thinking about the weather.

Group 3 had to design the show on the vertical.

Group 4 had to design the show with the Olympic Opening Ceremony budget.

Group 5 had to design the RSC version of the show.

Emily encouraged the groups to think about colours, atmospheres, textures, pictures and to get all their ideas out, without censoring themselves. At this stage, not a bad idea!

Vocal warm-ups

1) Participants stand in a circle. Together, make a big face (opening mouths and eyes wide), a small face (closing their mouths and eyes tight), a long face (pulling their chins down), a wide face (making their mouths wide), an out face (puffing their cheeks out) and an in face (sucking their cheeks in).

2) Participants stand in two lines, with everyone opposite a partner. Ask them to have a conversation with each other

that is mouthed, not spoken. Ask those who can't understand their partner to put their hand up. Try it with a couple of lines from the play.

Still standing opposite their partner, ask them to speak a line each from the play. Then take a step back and speak them again. If they can hear their partner, they take another step back and so on. If they can't hear them, they take a step in again. N.B. this exercise is not about shouting, it's about projecting.

3) It is helpful to mix voice work with physical action. For example, try chanting 'ba ba ba ba ba ba bounce the ball' (*bouncing ball*) 'da da da da da da don't do that' (*wagging finger*) 'ga ga ga ga ga ga ga get the goal' (*throwing a ball into a goal*).

Scene work: part one

The workshop participants divided into groups to look at scenes and explore different forms of online communication. They then showed their work and reflected on each version.

Each group was given a different starting point.

Facebook group message

This group was given the starting point of creating two versions, firstly using a phone as a prop, secondly banning the use of a phone as a prop.

This group made the discovery that sometimes the audience joins the characters halfway through a conversation.

Facebook online chorus

This group was given sound as their starting point.

They then did a version of the scene where Dani stood as a silent presence in the middle of the chorus.

Through this group's work, participants noticed that sound was a particularly effective way of creating the world of the internet. For example, a breaking heart was achieved with a crunching sound and words were delivered with varying levels of enthusiasm and sarcasm.

Instagram

This group was given the starting point of chairs.

Whatsapp

This group was given the starting point of thinking about different types of space and different spatial relationships with the audience.

They played with how much eye contact and physical contact the characters had while they were chatting on Whatsapp.

Skype

This group was given the starting point of thinking about eye contact vs no eye contact.

The question 'Is Skype the closest online interaction to a real-world interaction?' was raised. You have to look someone in the eye, but it is hard to avoid looking at yourself on the screen. What is it like if you are constantly looking at your own face and seeing your own reactions instead of the other person's?

Call of Duty

This group was given the starting point of creating one version of the scene in the bedroom and one version in the game.

The group noted that the version in the game felt more successful and interesting because real life could intrude on the game at any moment – for example, someone's mum could walk through with a basket of washing in the middle of the game.

Scene work: part two

Suhayla took a story from her Facebook feed and told the story how it looked online (happy families, a birthday party). She then told the reality of the story as she knew it (an argument, a vomiting child).

Participants took out their phones and found a story on their Facebook. They imagined the reality behind that story. The group reflected back, talking about how online communication is sometimes blocked rather than enabled.

In groups of three, participants took a scene from the play and wrote out a timeline of events that are reported in the scene.

For example, here are the events that are reported as taking place in Scene Two:

- Dani posts a picture of herself on holiday with her sister.
- The girls tag posts about the party.
- The boys tag posts about the party.
- There is a Twitter post saying that Dani and Josh have been caught smooching.

There was then a discussion about what might have really happened:

- Is the family holiday actually really boring?
- Are the girls feeling insecure?
- Are the boys feeling insecure?
- Did people throw up in the hot tub?
- Were the boys too scared to talk to the girls?
- At this point we don't know if they really snogged or if it's just a rumour

- Was the snog really awkward and did they have hot dog breath?
- Has Frazer been watching Josh and has he been in love with Josh for quite some time?

The reported events in Scene Seventeen are:

- Dani's sister gets married.
- Frazer and Josh go to the wedding (Frazer is her cousin)
- They look smart.
- Dani gets really drunk.
- Josh is caught leaving Dani's room at 2 a.m., with no shirt on.

What might have really happened:

- Dani's sister gets married.
- Dani gets drunk because Josh is not giving her much attention.
- Dani is sick over Josh's shirt.
- Josh takes his shirt off.
- Dani passes out in bed.
- Josh and Fraser have their first kiss – referenced on page 180: 'That's when it first happened apparently.'

The reported events in Scene Twenty-One:

- Sonali buys a new dress.
- She posts a poem about how much of a phoney she feels.
- Nobody likes or comments on it.

What might have really happened:

- Sonali is perhaps more truthful than the other characters, her online self is more unfiltered, and closer to her offline self.

- Is it easier to be bold and emo online? Might she have been more hurt at the party than she is letting on? Might she be more confident in her online self?

The reported events in Scene Twenty-Three:

- The girls slag off Sonali.
- They tag Frazer in on it.

What might have really happened:

- The girls felt hurt by Sonali's poem.
- Perhaps they were quite nice to her face at the party but they are slagging her off behind her back.
- Frazer felt awkward having her there; perhaps he was angry with her for posting the poem.

Observations that came out of the scene work:

The storytelling has to be very clear at the start of the play, when the audience is attuning to the language of the online world.

Big exaggerated gestures could work well for the emoticons.

It was enjoyable when there was a clear distinction between the chorus's conversation and snippets of action. There is room to be playful about how and when you switch from chorus to a moment of action – how quickly and sharply can these switches happen and can you choose the most dramatic moment to cut from one to the other, e.g. just before a kiss?

The online world has a fast pace. If you keep the pace up you will earn moments of suspension.

Scenes were more satisfying when characters were allowed to interact. A version of the play in which characters only spoke out to the audience may not be the most successful.

TRUFFLE DOWN

This exercise was used in the workshop to brainstorm ideas
for showing what it feels like when the internet is switched off.
The participants walked around the space. When someone
had an idea, they shouted 'truffle down' and everyone ran
into the middle of the space to hear their idea.

These are some ideas that the participants came up with:

- There could be a change of pace.

- The house lights could go on.

- There could be more eye contact and physical contact.

- Or there could be less eye contact.

- There could be a change of costume.

- There could be white noise.

- There could be rain.

- It could become very naturalistic.

- The chorus could disappear through a trap door.

- There could be music and movement.

Question and answer with Suhayla

*How important is it to you that the different digital forms are always
made clear?*

SUHAYLA EL-BUSHRA   'The most important thing is to
delineate between the video clips vs. the messages.'

How far can we change the text?

'The dialogue should stay the same, everything that is written
should be heard, but you can play with the texture.'

Is it OK to stage the play with twelve- and thirteen-year-olds?

Suhayla wondered whether twelve-year-olds are as enmeshed in the online world as slightly older age groups? But she encouraged directors to judge it according to their own groups.

Could you explain the note about 'bruv' and 'fam' at the start of the play?

'The girls call each other bruv ironically. It's fine to play with that according to how the groups would use those words.'

With a smaller cast, can the actors playing named roles become the chorus?

'Yes. Think about whether they are going to present as the character when they are delivering chorus lines or if they will multi-role and play a chorus character alongside their designated character.'

Could this play be performed with different genders to those specified?

'Sonali seems to be the most "real" character. The other girls perform their gender so it might be interesting to see them be played by boys. There are some interesting reference points in contemporary performance practice – e.g. Glenda Jackson, Phyllida Lloyd. We want the characters to feel truthful.'

Were you thinking about any music when you wrote the piece?

'I love music in my plays, but it's totally up to you and the company to choose particular tracks.'

Can we use recorded lines as part of the soundscape?

'Yes, completely up to you! There are lots of interesting things you could do with sound – perhaps there is a hum under the online world that disappears in the offline world for example.'

How could you feed in the young people's experiences of using different forms of online interaction and enlist them in helping differentiate between Facebook, Whatsapp, etc.?

It would be interesting to know how far they distinguish between different ways of communication. Are we getting too hung up on pinning down the different qualities of interacting online? For them is it much more fluid?

From a workshop led by Emily Lim
with notes by Jane Fallowfield

Status Update
by Tim Etchells

We know facts. We know secrets. We have opinions, we have intuition and we have the stage. *Status Update* is an unflinching and funny catalogue of the things teenagers learn, believe and have sussed out about the world. From the ridiculous to the highly charged, all these truths and half-truths are laid bare before us, without the safety net of character or fiction.

Cast size
Variable size ensemble

Tim Etchells is an artist whose work shifts between performance, visual art and fiction. He has worked in a wide variety of contexts, notably as the leader of the world-renowned, Sheffield-based performance group Forced Entertainment. Publications include *Vacuum Days* (Story things, 2012) and *While You Are with Us Here Tonight* (LADA, 2013). Etchells' work has been shown recently at Cubitt, Hayward Gallery and Bloomberg SPACE in London, at Turner Contemporary and Compton Verney in the UK, at Witte de With (Rotterdam), Netherlands Media Art Institute (Amsterdam) and MUHKA (Antwerp).

He became Professor of Performance and Writing at Lancaster University, he was a Tate/ Live Art Development Agency Legacy: Thinker in Residence Award winner in 2008, Artist of the City of Lisbon in 2014, and received the prestigious Spalding Gray Award in February 2016. Forced Entertainment were recently announced as the winners of the Ibsen Award for their groundbreaking contribution to the field of contemporary theatre and performance.

timetchells.com

Characters

A
B
C
D
E
F
G
H
J

A   We know that there are **237** people in the audience tonight.

B   We don't know yet if you'll all still be here at the end.

A   We know that there are roughly **150** people who booked in advance –

B   And around **87** of you just bought tickets at the door.

C   We know that the room we're standing in is about **6** metres wide, **18** metres long, and between **3** metres and **5** metres high.

D   We know that the carpets are **red**.

E   We know that the seats are uncomfortable.

D   We know that some parts of the dressing rooms haven't been cleaned for a long time.

F   We know that there are **9** of us on stage.

G   We know that if you add our ages together it makes a number greater than **150**.

E   But smaller than **200**.

G   We don't know your ages.

H   We do know that later, when the lights on stage fade, there will be a clicking sound from up there above us as the metal of the lanterns starts to cool.

J   We know that on the back of seat **D19 or 20** someone has scratched something – with a penknife maybe, or with a pen that's not working –

A   – or with a piece of glass.

J   Not writing, just a few horizontal lines.

F   We know that **near the back of the room**, to the left there are some inexplicable **marks** on the floor.

B   We don't know what caused those **marks** . . .

F   We don't know how they got there.

G   We don't know the right word for the colour of **the curtains**.

A   We know that the temperature on stage is now **20** degrees.

C   We know that the windows are closed.

D   We know that the air conditioning is off.

C   We know that if all of us were all trapped in here, with the doors and windows completely sealed, there'd only be enough oxygen to last a group of people this size for two and a half days.

D   We know that none of us suffers from claustrophobia.

C   We know that none of us is particularly frightened of the dark.

F   We know that two of us are frightened of spiders.

E   That one of us is frightened of moths.

A   That another of us is frightened of moths *and* snakes.

H   That four are frightened of heights.

B   That several faint or go queasy at the sight of blood.

J   That six are uneasy with silence.

G   That four like screaming on rollercoasters.

B   That two are frightened of shadows.

J   That three are uneasy about flying.

G   We know the difference between 'frightened' and 'uneasy'.

C   We know our own names.

D   We know each other's names.

C   We know each other's nicknames, past and present.

J   In some cases we know your names.

A   **John and Jackie** are here – **Karen's** parents.

F   So are a small group of **Jose's** relatives including **Aunt Flora**.

A   Navraj – **Sonia's** boyfriend.

F   Jim – **Yvette's** younger brother.

H   Others people's names we know from the box office.

J   **Mrs Smith or Mr Jeardon**.

H   **T. E. Hastings.**

B   We know which of us has brothers and sisters.

G   And we know which of us has living parents.

B   We know about our own grandparents.

G   In the sense of living or dead.

B   But we're hazy about the grandparents of others in the group.

G   And hazy about other relations – cousins, aunts, uncles.

C   **We know that none of us has a twin.**

F   We know which of us has boyfriends or girlfriends. Except in a few cases where there is ambiguity or some kind of secrecy.

C   We know which of us identifies as gay. Except in a few cases where there is ambiguity or some kind of secrecy.

D   We know which of us eats meat, which of us is vegetarian, which is a smoker, which of us drinks or takes drugs, which of us is promiscuous, which of us is into this or that kind of music, which of us is into politics, which of us reads or plays sports or is into games or . . .

A   We don't know what the future will bring.

G   We don't know which of us will get married.

A   Which of us will stay single. Which of us will divorce.

C   We don't know which of us might find out only later, or only later come to terms with the fact that we're actually gay.

B   We don't know which of us will stay here in **England** and which of us will move away.

G   We don't know which of us will have kids.

F   We don't know which of us will be happy.

G   We don't know which of us will live life as a tragedy.

F   We don't know which of us will sell his soul or her soul to the devil.

G   We don't know which of us will work at an investment bank.

F   Or which of us will earn money taking off clothes, or waiting tables.

D   Or which of us will end up sleeping in a doorway.

B   Or sleeping on the beach.

C   We don't know which of us is going to be rich.

B   Or which of us might end up being poor.

C   Though we can take an educated guess.

J   We don't know which of us is going to have a lot of difficulty to deal with, through illnesses or accidents.

A   We don't know which of us will have good luck

J   Or which will have bad luck.

A   Or which will have good luck disguised as bad luck.

J   We don't know which of us will fall on ice.

A   Or get hands caught in machinery.

J   We don't know which of us will have big car crashes.

A   Or which of us will have small car crashes.

E   We don't know which of us will have red skin rashes.

H   Or which of us will become addicts to something.

E   Which of us might win money in the lottery.

D   Which of us might discover something – a new planet, a new dimension, a new way of making computer chips, a new branch of mathematics.

F   We don't know which of us will die first.

H   We don't know which of us will still be alive in ten years' time.

F   Or in ten minutes time.

H   Or in twenty years time.

F   Or in fifty years time.

J   We know that **Michel** has a motorbike.

B   We know which of us has a good sense of humour.

C   We know that **Jorge** has an old Nokia phone.

A   We know which of us laughs the easiest and which argues the hardest.

E   We know that people who stop you in town asking for change to pay their train fare home are probably lying.

D   We know that anything an automated phone system says – that you are seventy-third in the queue and that 'your call is important' – is also a kind of lie.

E   We know that politicians lie.

F   We know how things work.

J   We know what people tell us.

F   We know what time it is.

B   We know that **Karen** and **Jose** are friends.

D   We know that **Michel** and **Yvette** used to be neighbours.

A   We know that it's not a good idea to hang around the railway station at night.

H   We know that in many cities the rich people live on the hills or facing the sea. And the poor people live in the valleys.

G   We know that in many cities the traffic chokes the centre, polluting the air, making things hard for cyclists and pedestrians, making it hard to breathe, especially in the summer.

F   We know that alcohol leads to some funny stuff happening.

D   We know that some kids like to fight.

J   We know that the sun sets in the west, rises in the east.

E   We know that none of us has been to **America**.

J   We know that none of us has been to **Hong Kong**.

D   We know that none of us has been refused entrance to a country because of criminal records or visa irregularities.

A   We know that one of us has had regular dealings with the police.

C   We know that some of us have had friction from particular neighbours, or from people living in the same building or street and that some of us have had trouble with various local shopkeepers.

B   We know that two of us have been excluded from school at one time or another.

D   We don't know so much about you.

H   We don't know who you are, where you came from –

D   – or why.

H   We don't know if you can be trusted, if you're trouble makers.

F   For the most part we don't know if you came here by chance or if you planned it for a long time.

G   We don't know if you came from far away or from nearby.

A   We don't know if you are drifters, or loners, or travellers.

J   We don't know if you're hard workers or lazy fools.

A   We don't know if you're bus drivers, comedians, office workers, teachers.

J   We don't know if you pay your taxes.

C   Or if you cheat on your taxes.

D   We don't know if you are racists.

C   Or if you're kind people.

D   If you're murderers.

C   If you play football on the weekends.

F   If you like to cook, or work in the garden.

A   We have no clue.

G   We don't know a thing.

B   We don't know if you're superstitious, if you go to church, if you keep your fingers crossed behind your backs when you are making promises, or if you're into witchcraft.

H   We're not sure if any of you has a criminal record.

J   We're not sure if any of you are under investigation by the police.

B   We're not sure if any of you are actually members of the police.

C   We are not sure if you're perhaps here as undercover police while following other people in the audience.

H   Or if perhaps you're police undercover following *us* as part of your investigations.

J   But we do think that's pretty unlikely.

D   We know that you are here and we know that you are watching.

E   We know what's happening in this room.

D   We don't know what's happening in this room.

E   We're pretty sure what's happening in this room.

D   We don't know what's happening in this room.

E   We are not completely sure what is happening.

A   We have no idea at all what is happening.

E   We are confident we know what is happening.

B   We don't know what's happening in this room.

E   We are pretty sure what is happening.

D   We can feel your attention.

E   And your inattention.

C   We know that you're looking with your eyes.

F   We know that the light from the scene enters your eye through the pupil.

J   The iris changes the size of the pupil, depending on how bright the light is.

F   Opening and closing like a shutter.

J   The lens focuses light from the scene on to the back of the eye –

F   – the retina.

J   The retina is a mass of light-sensitive neurons called photoreceptors, which change light signals into electrical ones.

F   We know these signals are then processed by the brain.

C   We know that if you look right into someone's eyes you can't tell what they are thinking.

H   We know that sometimes, if you look deeply into someone's eyes, you can tell what they are thinking.

E   We know that if you look into someone's eyes you can't tell what they are thinking.

H   We know that sometimes, on specific occasions, if you look really deeply into someone's eyes, you can tell what they are thinking

C   We know that if you look into someone's eyes you can't tell what they are thinking.

H   We know that sometimes, on specific occasions, if you look really deeply into someone's eyes, you can get the impression that you know what they're thinking.

A   We know that sometimes, on specific occasions, if you look really deeply into someone's eyes, you can persuade yourself that you know what they are thinking.

H   We know that if you look into someone's eyes you can't tell what they are thinking.

B   We know that if you look into someone's eyes you can take a guess as to what they are thinking.

H   We know that if you look into someone's eyes you can't tell a thing about what they are thinking.

F   If you cough we hear it. And if you laugh we hear that too.

C   Any movements, we also hear.

D   Except very small movements of course.

J   Or very slow ones.

D   The tiny movement of your eyelashes –

J   – or the steady movement of your breathing.

A   We know that silence and stillness are a sign of concentration.

C   We know that you are listening.

A   We know that sound travels more slowly than light.

G   We know that sound waves are produced when the air is moving . . .

A   When the air is 'mechanically disturbed'.

G   We know that sound draws the human eye.

A   Taking it from one place –

F   to another.

A   We know that sound waves enter the human ear through the ear canal, making the eardrum vibrate.

F   The vibrations pass through a set of bones in the middle ear, moving the fluid in the inner ear and bending the hair-like cells there to turn vibration into nerve impulses.

A   These nerve impulses are sent to the brain by the auditory nerve where this information is converted into what people 'hear' and understand as 'sound'.

H   You can most likely hear us speaking that way or perhaps you can just see our lips moving, and make out what we are saying from the movement of our mouths.

A   We know that most vocal sounds are made by a stream of air that flows from the lungs through the mouth or nose. We use this stream of air to form specific sounds by changing the shape of our mouths.

D   We know that typically people think a little before they start to speak . . .

C   People don't start talking for no reason, without thinking.

B   They spend time . . . considering thoughts or ideas they might want to convey.

G   And we know that after this initial time of interior reflection comes the task of word-finding –

B   – through which the person chooses the right words with which to articulate all the things they are thinking.

H   We don't know what you're thinking, though. We don't know if you're daydreaming or concentrating, thinking hard about what's happening –

G   – or if you are drifting off. We know that the warm and dark of the theatre can make it tempting to sleep, to fall back, to let the darkness fold around you.

B   We know you're out there.

J   Watching.

C   The neurons in your retinas turning what you see into electrical signals to be processed by your brains.

D   We know for sure that you're there in front of us.

E   But what's happening behind us we can't be so sure of.

C   Technically someone could cross the stage behind us, slowly, quietly and we wouldn't be aware of it.

J   Unless we set up a camera.

D   Or unless we look round.

F   What's happening backstage is also completely out of our grasp. We can't know about it unless someone yells, maybe, or coughs, or drops something heavy.

J Or unless someone breaks something noisily. Glass. Or crockery. A mirror. Something metal.

A We don't know what's happening in the foyer right now either.

H Or under the stage.

D And we don't know what is happening in South Africa.

B Or in the car park.

E Or in Paris.

G Or on the other side of the street. Or on the other side of the city.

A Or on Mount Everest.

J We don't know what's happening in Glasgow. Or in Porto. Or in the toilets downstairs. Or in **Leicester**.

C Or under the seats at the back now, or under the stage. Or Shanghai. Or in Bosnia. Or on the mountains of the Moon. Or in Faro. Or in Kinshasa. Or at the bottom of the ocean.

A We don't know what's happening on the International Space Station.

B We don't know anything about the International Space Station.

F We know that the International Space Station is the largest artificial body in Earth orbit, and from here, from the Earth, it can often be seen with the naked eye.

A The ISS is the size of a football field –

F – an American football field.

A It weighs the same as 330 cars –

B – but we're not sure what kind of cars.

F We know it's up there.

C   But we don't know what's happening.

B   We don't know much about the International Space Station.

F   We know that the ISS consists of pressurised modules, trusses and large solar panels, maintaining an orbital altitude of 380 kilometres and completing fifteen and a half Earth orbits a day. We know that it's been up there **X** months since October 2000, continuously occupied for **X** years, **X** months and **X** days, representing the longest continuous human presence in space.

A   You can see it with the naked eye.

B   We don't know what it would be like to be up there.

D   We don't know how it would be to spend a six-month expedition up there with just four to six other people.

J   We don't know what prison would be like.

E   Or solitary confinement.

B   We know a bit about the passage of time.

J   We don't know so much about the passage of time.

B   We know a bit about spending time with other people.

E   We don't know much about spending time with other people.

H   We know time with family and suchlike. Or time at school.

E   We know a lot about our own time.

H   We do know a lot about time with each other.

J   About time talking and time fooling around and time sleeping.

C   We know that time seems to go slowly sometimes. And sometimes seems to go faster.

F   It goes slowly when waiting for news, or waiting for people to arrive.

C   Faster during periods of excitement.

F   Slower during boring events.

J   We know that the human sense of time is linked to the movement of the earth – its rotation on its axis, which produces day and night, its orbit around the sun which takes a year to complete.

D   We know that the human heart beats faster when a person is excited.

J   That physical exercise, sleep, anxiety, stress, illness, food and drugs all change the human heartbeat.

D   We know the average human hearbeat is 60 to 100 beats per minute.

J   We know that this performance lasts around 3,375 heartbeats, around 45 minutes in clock time.

D   Unless something goes wrong, in which case the performance can be longer or shorter.

J   For example the duration changes if people say things they aren't supposed to say.

D   Or if someone jumps ahead a few pages.

J   Or if someone skips everything and jumps to the end.

D   Or if someone loops backwards in the text, so that something that should be said only once gets repeated, perhaps a number of times.

B   We know that sometimes, in the rehearsals, we have got stuck in a loop.

F   We know that in those loops it sometimes takes a little while for anyone to realise what is happening.

B We know that loops happen when a sentence doesn't go to a new place –

H – but instead takes us back where we've already been.

F And we know that in a loop time seems to go slowly.

B And that sometimes it seems to go faster.

E We know that the performance lasts about 45 minutes.

A Unless something goes wrong.

E For example if someone says something they aren't really supposed to say.

A Or if something that should be said gets repeated.

E We know that sometimes, in the rehearsals we have got stuck in loops.

D We know that in loops it can a little while before anyone notices.

E But eventually, usually, someone does.

J We know that round about now is probably the hardest part of the performance. You know what the parameters are. The rules. The possibilities. The stall of it is all laid out. It's clear what we can do, where we can stretch to, the kinds of topics we can reach to, without breaking our own rules. But at the same time we know you've seen enough to feel that our capacity to generate surprise is slowly getting reduced, that we're not pulling rabbits out of hats any more but rather walking the borders of a space that has its limits.

F We know that C's favourite TV show is ———.

C We know that A's favourite game is ———.

B We know that D is the best ——— player here.

D We know that B can only play three songs on the guitar.

C We know that E's favourite book is ———.

A   We know that J can dance.

D   We know that H likes to dance but can't really, at least not very well.

H   We know that from F's bedroom you can hear the sound of the broken air conditioning from the hotel next door.

C   We know that of all of us the most likely person to cry, in any situation, is D.

F   We know that in A's bedroom it's never really dark – because the curtains are thin and because there is a street lamp right outside.

E   We know that C sometimes sneaks boys up to her room so that they can fool around.

G   We know that J claims never to have had sex.

E   We know that A shares a bedroom with her sister.

G   That E shared a bedroom with his brother.

H   That B made marks on the bathroom wall.

E   We know that ———— would be a good person to ask about the things that go missing from the kitchen in the house where she lives.

A   We know that there are some private things – a diary and so on – hidden in the cupboard in F's sister's room.

E   We know that the most often used number in D's phone is **0654 721 8346**.

A   But most of us don't know whose number that is.

B   We know that if the seats are full you're closer to each other than we are.

F   We know that the distance between us here on the stage is about 20 centimetres.

B   And down there where you are, with the seats all occupied, you're sitting more or less shoulder to shoulder.

D   From where the first row sits to where we are standing it's **3 and a half** metres.

C   From our feet to the back of the room it's **10** metres.

D   The fastest sprinter in the world could cover that distance in .2 seconds.

C   A spider could spin a web from here to that wall in **X** minutes.

H   We know there are **9** of us.

A   And more or less **137** of you.

F   We know that the world's population is around **7.125** billion and that the world's land mass is just under 150,000 million square kilometres.

D   From these facts we can figure out that if all land-space were divided equally there'd be roughly **21,000 square metres** for each person.

F   But we know that space on earth is not divided in this way.

B   It's more unequal.

D   Some people have a lot of space. And others have none.

F   We know that some people have all money, and others have none.

B   We know that although people criticise inequality this doesn't really lead to change.

E   We know that what people say isn't always reflected in what they do.

B   We know that people's actions don't always match their principles

E   We know that the smooth running of the world depends on this fact not being made too explicit. We know that true things should not be said too often or too forcefully.

J   We know that some people get off on hurting others –

B   – on exerting power over them, directly, or indirectly.

H   We know that some people are arseholes and idiots.

J   We know that some people are selfish.

H   That some people are bigmouths.

C   We know that sometimes it's hard to get taxis in the early morning.

A   We know that you can't trust boys.

B   We know that you can't trust girls.

C   We know that you can't trust girls or boys.

E   We think that we can trust you.

D   We know that we can't trust you.

G   We're not sure if we can trust you.

F   We know that sitting there in the dark as we're talking you let your eyes and your attention wander.

J   We don't know if you are really paying attention or just pretending to focus on the stage while doing other things.

F   We don't know if you're daydreaming.

J   Or drifting off.

F   We don't know if you're paying attention.

A   We know that things that seem like a bad idea when you're sober can start to seem like a great idea when you have been drinking.

B   We know that sometimes people cling to the facts, because uncertainty or questions are too much to bear.

C   We know that snow and rain both fall downwards, at least so long as there is no wind.

H   We know that the Second World War is over.

C   We know that the Trojan War is over.

A   We know that the Cold War has more or less started again.

D   That a war of words has been going on for a long time.

H   We know that the steam engine is obsolete.

E   We know that skin burns if exposed to too much sunlight.

D   Or too much radiation.

F   We know that if you eat too much you get sick.

E   Or fat.

C   We know that in darkness you can't see anything.

C   We know that items deleted from a computer are rarely actually deleted.

J   We know that some people cope better with stress than others.

G   We know that this morning the pound slipped against the dollar.

D   And that the FTSE 100 Index slipped a little too.

G   That the euro stayed stable.

F   That shares in Xerox took a tumble.

E   That stocks in Apple took a small fall of .3 cents on the share.

D   That there was a rise in the price of oil.

E   And a rise in the price of grain.

D   We don't know how the stock exchange is moving right now.

H   We know that most damage from a nuclear weapon comes from the explosive blast – a shock wave of air radiates outward from the explosion, producing sudden changes in air pressure that can crush objects, and high winds that can knock things down. Large buildings are destroyed by the change in air pressure, while people and objects like trees and telegraph poles are destroyed by the wind. The size of the bomb blast is related to the height at which the burst takes place above ground level.

B   We know that bombs make a sound.

A   We know that bombs make a terrible sound.

H   We don't know much.

B   We know plenty.

D   We don't know anything.

H   We don't know much.

B   We know plenty.

A   We don't know anything.

H   We don't know much.

B   We don't know anything.

A   We know what happens but we don't always know why.

E   We know that people get closer.

F   Or further away.

C   That bodies change.

D   That memories fade.

E   That economies rise and fall.

F   That colours fade.

G   That muscles waste.

F   That cities change.

G   That eyesight blurs.

D   That stone turns to dust.

C   That skin loosens.

E   That light fades.

F . That uncertainty, once present, rapidly multiplies.

A   We do know that in eighty-five years all of us here – the people on stage – will be dead. And we know that all of you – very likely – all of you will be dead before we are. In any case we know in eighty years or so, at the outside, you'll all be dead.

J   We know that people get very nervous if the talk is too much of death.

H   They get a bit nervous.

J   We know that people get nervous if there's too much talk about illness too, for similar reasons, for obvious reasons.

H   People get a bit nervous if someone is waving a gun around too.

C   They get a bit nervous if there's too much talk about love too, but for different reasons.

D   Or if there's too much talk about sex.

A   About penetration.

B   And pleasure.

D   Or orgasm.

E   Things that breach the border of the person cause this nervousness. Things that might be called improprietous. Especially in public. And without the cover of character.

F   People also get a bit nervous when there is too much talk about race. Or about politics. Or about money.

J   We know that people don't want to hear long descriptions of global warming and the effects that it's having.

H   Or long descriptions of a YouTube clip in which someone gets killed.

J   Or long arguments about money and who has some and who has none.

H   We know that easy topics for conversation are the traffic yesterday.

J   And the sunlight the day before.

H   The food.

J   And plans for the summer.

B   We know that in some circumstances a difficult conversation is followed by a kind of awkward silence.

C   Like in a movie, when they make the tap drip or clock tick sound very very loud.

B   Or when silence seems very nervous. Like time itself is scratching the skin, awkward and uneasy. Or else time simply seems slow and echoing. Each second a big sharp sound.

J   We know that humans and animals are different.

H   Dolphins are intelligent. Bees are collective. Rats are resourceful.

A   We know that dogs are loyal.

G   We know that cats have personality.

B   We know that foxes kill sometimes for reasons other than hunger.

C   We know that spiders cannot swim.

A We know that some birds migrate tens of thousands of kilometres, working from some kind of radar in relation to the Earth's magnetic fields, using the stars and knowledge of the earth, navigating through some unknown system.

E We know that some people are better at reading maps than others.

D That some people can't find themselves on a mobile GPS.

B We know that the behaviour of animals can be changed or conditioned using the consistent application of particular systems of reward and punishment. Rats placed in a closed box – sometimes called a Skinner box or operant conditioning chamber – easily learn that pressing a particular lever is linked to the arrival of food, or with the cessation of an unpleasant electrical current. We know that there is no real difference between the learning that takes place in humans and that which takes place in other animals. B.F. Skinner proposed that humans learn behaviour in much the same way as rats learn to press a lever. Skinner believed that human free will was actually an illusion, maintaining instead that our actions are best understood as the result of their consequences. If the consequences of an action are bad, there's a good chance that action won't be repeated. If the consequences of an action are good, however, the actions that lead to it are more likely to be returned to in future. Skinner called this the principle of reinforcement.

H We know that time passes.

C That time is passing.

D We know that things are changing.

H We know that things are slowly closing down.

G We know that above and below us there's a certain amount of room. From the tops of our heads to the ceiling, is about **X** metres. From our feet here to the ground down below, is about **XX**. If we were to start digging – straight down –using spades and picks, by hand – we'd have to go 6,371 kilometres down before reaching the centre of the earth.

C   Assuming that all of us worked together, digging 2 metres per day on average, depending on the kind of ground we encountered, it would take us 872 years to reach the centre or core.

H   But of course, while that's all true, we know that we'd *all* be long dead from old age and exhaustion before then.

B   We know that time passes.

C   That time is passing.

D   That the time has probably passed.

A   We know that language is a trap.

F   And a way out of a trap.

B   We know that language is both a trap and a way out of a trap.

C   We know that language makes and shapes the world we're in.

D   It's also a tool to change it.

C   We know that B believes in ghosts,

E   We know that the world would be different if circumstances were to change. If the dinosaurs were still living. If the water levels rise.

A   Or if Hitler had not been born. If the Chinese Emperor Lizong of Song had died young. If the Palestinians had landed on the moon first. If Columbus never discovered America. If the First World War never happened. If Nelson Mandela was never freed.

B   We know that J saw a ghost, a figure in the corner of the room, sitting quietly and watching. Waiting.

D   We know that A has a recurring dream of falling.

E   We know that H has a dream that is only a sound.

B   We know that you're watching, waiting.

F   We know that strong electromagnetic fields, or electric shocks, can produce hallucinations.

G   We know that internet data is under heavy surveillance.

C   We know that chromosomes are made from DNA and that genes are short sections of DNA.

D   We know that DNA molecules are large and complex and that those molecules carry code which determines the characteristics of any living thing.

C   We know that other than identical twins, each person's DNA is unique.

F   We know that sometimes people get a feeling that something's wrong, a feeling not linked to a concrete event.

B   We know that at other times people get the opposite feeling – that things are going to be OK.

A   We know that neither of these feelings can be trusted.

J   We know that some people are optimists, others pessimists.

E   We know that things change.

A   We know that things stay the same.

C   We know that time passes.

A   That time is passing.

G   That time has certainly passed.

F   We know that people get a feeling sometimes, not linked to a concrete event.

A   We know that some people feel sure of themselves.

B   That some people know how to listen.

C   That some people watch carefully.

E   That some people close their eyes to concentrate.

F   That some people make wishes in the dark.

D   That some people get a feeling time is shifting.

H   That some people think that time is slowing.

J   That some people change.

E   That everyone changes.

A   That people change all the time.

B   That time has passed.

C   That time has moved on.

F   That some people change.

H   That people are change.

Status Update

BY TIM ETCHELLS

Notes on rehearsal and staging, drawn from a workshop with the writer, held at the National Theatre, October 2016

How Tim came to write the play

TIM ETCHELLS   'A lot of my work as a writer is in the context of the devising company Forced Entertainment, with whom I have been working in collaboration for thirty-two years. When we first started out, we came to theatre with the idea of creating extremely visual, different, closed-off worlds that you looked into, layering the stage as if it were an image. However after a while, little cracks started to appear in this work, drawing our attention to the relationship with the audience. We became interested in the audience's awareness that they were being watched or addressed directly, prompting the questions 'Who's here and what sort of contact is possible?' We started to focus on the space between the performers and the audience and the moment occurring between them. There seemed to be a huge potential for drama in this relationship.

'We developed the idea of what we came to call a "line game" in which a group of performers are talking to each other by talking to the audience. The performers propose things and stress opinions via a succession of statements. They appear to talk to the audience but at the same time it is also a dialogue between themselves – the audience becomes like a wall against which a ball is kicked, bounced off; they are in the firing zone. These successive, sometimes contradictory, statements create shifts of temperature in the room. The drama shifts from the relationship between performers and becomes about the changing temperature – who are the 'we' delivering the statements and who are the 'we' to which these statements are aimed? How does each new statement affect the relationship between performers and audience?

'One way of thinking about theatre is to focus on the limited number of things in the space – the actors with their props, costumes and scenery, and the audience with their bags, coats and whatever they have in their pockets. This is always a limited amount of stuff so theatre is always about finding ways to bring other things into the room – ideas, stories, images. One way to approach this is that we can make certain things visible in the room just by mentioning them. It's close to the speech Shakespeare has in *Henry V* in which the narrator asks the audience to use their imaginations to help make the scenes appear. In *Status Update* the text starts from describing the actual framework of the space or factual information about who and what is in this space. Once the performance is rooted in the room – in the real space and time of the performance – it then begins to go on excursions to other places: to ideas and images outside the room, out in the city, other countries, the International Space Station, before we come crashing back down into the room and are invited to question that we are still here but that possibly the temperature and the relationship between performers and audience has changed.

'Several of our shows have followed similar principles. *Speak Bitterness* was a performance in which a line of people had the task of making confessions to the audience, from the huge to the minute. *That Night Follows Day*, performed by young people aged eight to fourteen, directly addressed an adult audience to explore the relationship between young people and adults and how the adult world frames childhood.

'Think about *Status Update* in terms of a description of the world. It is an attempt to gather a catalogue or collection of what is known. It's a group of people saying 'What do we know?' Some of them seem sure of things and other less so. By attempting to consolidate or assert their knowledge they are trying to catch and question the world around them. By measuring the change in temperature this creates, they catch and explore the real moment that they are in, with each other and with the audience. Who are we? What do we know? What

do we know about each other? What can happen in the
encounter between performers and audience?'

Approaching the play: exercises

Below are a series of exercises that can be used at the beginning
of the rehearsal process. These exercises are designed to create
a language or framework within which to begin exploring the
text and the process of performing. They encourage the actors
to strip back their performance and to focus heavily on the
idea of being present and reflective of the space, the delivery
of text and their relationship with the audience. Importantly
much of the learning comes from watching others.

ESTABLISHING THE GAME: WHERE THE 'GROUND' IS AND MEASURING THE TEMPERATURE

Hester Chillingworth and Tim Etchells, co-lead directors, set
up a line of chairs facing the audience and asked half the
performers to sit. The instructions were that the performers
could either sit or stand, while dealing with the feelings of
being watched. In doing so they began to measure the space
between performer and audience. It is in essence an incredibly
simple 'game' but the challenge for the performers is to strip
back what they do and simply be present. By establishing
clear and simple ground rules or reference points, it provides
interesting opportunities to potentially depart from them.

A similar exercise directors might want to try in rehearsals is
for each performer to enter the space and stand alone for
two minutes in front of the audience. Again they should be
encouraged to own this situation and simply be there and
measure the gazes coming at them. This shouldn't be easy. In
reality our human instincts are to cover up this vulnerability
and so it is important to push the performer not to 'perform'.
Similarly the audience must be supportive and note what it is
like when the performer is genuinely vulnerable or when they
conceal it.

These exercises are useful both to the performer – to test stripping it back to just yourself on stage – but also for the group to witness this from an audience perspective. This raises the questions: who is watching whom and are the audience and performers together or apart? It should begin to create an awareness of the relationship between the audience and performer and the live process of both measuring this space and the temperature within it.

In the workshop, one of the key things that was drawn from the sitting/standing exercise was that everyone is compelling in their own way when they do not force trying to tell or show the audience something. When they are able to simply sit with themselves, little stories and offers begin to emerge. A sense of listening and connectivity down the line began to happen and we as the audience observed the groups' genuine little dramas, trying to understand their own behaviour, whilst in the context of being watched. This in essence is the group creating its own language, one that even in its simplicity can become utterly compelling to watch.

Hester reiterated the importance of insisting that even the simple parameters of sitting and standing can be enough – providing a whole series of games, problems, resolutions and relationships. We find the drama in a very refined set of minimalist rules – by crushing or limiting these parameters, small changes or events that wouldn't have been visible become visible and in turn have the potential to become a huge event.

Tim discussed how this idea is also reflected by the text, so that by limiting the statements to visible observations (about the room and the audience for example) at the beginning, suddenly talking in detail about the functioning of the human ear or the Space Station becomes a major event, a huge shift of ground. Experienced against the simple structure of the text the manner with which the performers choose to stand up – with a desire to, a reluctance to, or the massive range between – has a similar relationship to how the performers may choose to deliver the text. Again, small changes and inflections make a big difference.

INTRODUCING TEXT, STATEMENTS AND LEVELS OF KNOWING

This is a development of the first exercise, which begins to introduce text into the playing space. Again the group sat on a straight line of chairs facing the audience and had the same set of instructions – they could either sit or stand. One of the observations during the first exercise was that there were never more than two performers standing at one time, so Tim talked about pushing the extremes of the exercise – what would it feel like if the majority of people were standing without forcing it to happen?

In addition to the original game, each performer was also instructed to find one observation about the environment which they were in – similar to the text of the play, this might be a visible thing, e.g.'The clock says it is 3.23 p.m.' It might be more subjective, e.g. 'The colour of the walls is a horrible shade of green', or it might be more speculative, e.g. 'One person in this room is having an affair'. The actors were told to establish the original game before playing with the addition of their statements. Again it was stressed that the performers shouldn't try to hit anything in particular.

The group talked about how the second time round there was a temptation for performers to become more preoccupied with their own agenda – trying to be interesting or funny. The awareness of the audience became a predetermined response that they sought rather than simply gauging the audience responses and the temperature of the room. The group noted that often they were more interested or drawn to the people who did very little but were honest in their assessment of what was happening to themselves and around them. This lack of control over the situation allowed little moments or accidents to emerge which were often the most interesting.

This also happened with the introduction of the statements. When the group played their own individual agendas and forced their actions accordingly, the audience were left feeling that they didn't know 'where the ground was'. It therefore felt important to clearly define the 'ground' or establish the base rules of the game in order to build upon something. Without this we are unclear what is at stake with each choice made. Similarly Hester advised that, 'One or two rule breaks in a place that is effective, is more effective than ten, whereby we start to lose the stakes.' When the presentation of this excecise was most effective was when there was an economy in the build of moments that seemed to follow a logic of establishing a moment and then going up one step at a time. The actors only discovered these spontaneous moments by playing and trying things. They focused on simply dealing with themselves rather than the big agenda of trying to control the room. Their relationship to little tasks or projects becomes interesting if they are consistent and committed, rather than having lots of different impulses at once.

Tim referred to the idea of 'line testing' as being really important in approaching the text. This means that not only does the actor have an awareness of how the information they are delivering affects themselves but that they also allow themselves the space to see how the words land and change the temperature of the room and are alert to these shifts.

STAGING AND EXPERIMENTING

The group was split into three, each with a different cast size in order to experiment approaching the text with smaller or larger groups. Tim and Hester gave the following instructions:

- Make a simple choice about staging.
- Think about how you are breaking up the text and assigning it.

- Build a simple framework within which to test things and experiment.

The feedback both from audience and performers highlighted the following points, which may be useful when approaching rehearsals:

- Focus on the start position. It worked well to establish the starting position as one that was relatively chilled. This gave the performers somewhere to go in terms of building the stakes and ideas but also allowed them to clear the air and return to this place when needed.

- Hester reiterated that we learn more about people when they show us less. We were able to map human things on to them but if they kept trying to show or demonstrate to us, our suspicion radar goes up. Trusting what you do as a human is enough!

- When the performers were OK with just being there and recognised that that was enough, it meant that the audience didn't have to worry about them.

- It is easy for an audience to get lost when movement isn't logical to communicate intention. Certain movements made sense at certain points, for instance moving towards the audience when trying to persuade them or withdrawing when disagreeing or intimidated. These are natural human instincts that the audience can relate to. It becomes a barrier when movements don't seem to follow this logic.

- It worked well when it was clear who the performers were talking to.

- Silence and stillness were appreciated by the audience.

- Dynamic flurries of conversation worked well, where the performers were genuinely listening, discovering and responding to each other.

- It raised the question of what performers should be doing when they are not speaking and might have a significant amount of time before they do. While it is encouraged that they should be listening and engaging even in their responses, Tim also talked about letting performers be in a position of 'social comfortableness' or 'off-duty' state. This can be explored to see what colour or atmosphere this lends to the moment or text that is being spoken by others.

- The text that explains the science behind things can be genuinely interesting and it worked well when the performers actually tried to explain it to the audience rather than just throwing it away.

- A discovery was made by one of the groups when they played a section of the 'we know' statements with the objective of trying to persuade themselves. This had a really nice vulnerable quality as the group attempted to reconfirm and solidify their position.

- What are the subgroups in a larger group – age, gender, height, etc.? This might be something that can be played with, so that at certain points one subgroup might appear to take control or step back. This could also be a solution if you have extremely large casts and feel that there are too many people as a focus at all times.

PLAYING WITH DELIVERY OF TEXT

Hester asked two performers to read the text on page 221 as if it were written ABABAB. The first instruction was to read it at pace without any gaps between each statement. She then encouraged them to take their time and find the space between the lines. She really pushed them to make these gaps significant so that each statement became isolated.

The group considered how both versions had merit but that when we have space and time around the statements, we get a real sense of the performers considering what they are saying. This allows the audience to do the same. Tim spoke about how important it was to allow this space and the role the director has in finding which moments they want to give weight to.

This exercise also raised the idea of where you place things tonally – for instance the idea that you don't have to play the weight of a serious topic but can sometimes choose to fight the gravity of the scenario. However, dramatic events might shift the pace and tone of delivery and it is important that if this is the case, this shift is noted – if it becomes too easy to speak then the currency of words becomes cheap, so it is important to allow the weight of them at certain points. Similarly the actors should be clear about whether their lines are reported speech or if they are discovering them for the first time or anything in between.

Language

Tim is completely open to the redistribution of text depending on the numbers in your cast. The allocation of lines is simply a serving suggestion and directors are at liberty to shift this around, creating interesting possibilities about who is having a conversation with whom. There is no reference in the script to the first person 'I'. It is pooled knowledge that the group collectively knows. Within this there are individual voices pushing for autonomy.

It is suggested that actors use their real names and replace all the letters and gaps accordingly. It is up to your company as to whether you do this with audience names depending on whether you know this information, but it is not essential.

While the structure of the text and lines shouldn't be changed, Tim encourages companies to make small changes to factual information that is visible to the audience, for instance changing the measurements of the space you are in to something approximating your actual performance space or changing 'there are 237 people in the audience' to a figure closer to the reality of your audience. Tim stressed that this doesn't have to be exact but should be close enough so as to be believable for the audience.

Structure

There is a recurring structure within the writing which establishes the present moment by saying 'we are here'. It then drifts away from this, bringing other possibilities, places and ideas into the room, before abandoning these and being drawn back to the 'here'. Each time it asks 'what has changed?' and aims to measure the shift or change in temperature that has occurred. It asks the audience to sit with how OK, benign, stressful or provocative this situation is. There is a little war on stage between the people who want to push the boundaries and confront, and those who are keen to return to a more level place. This is constantly underpinned by the questions 'Who are we? What are we? What are we talking about? Is it OK?'

Tim divided the text into four sections, which he explained were not definitive but might be useful when breaking down the text and charting through the overall structure of the performance.

Part One

Page 201–8: start to 'But we think that's pretty unlikely.'

This section is about creating the 'ground' from which the work will proceed and setting initial parameters – where are we and what is going on. It sets up the game about knowledge and begins to explore the power relationship between the audience and performers – what we know, what we don't know and what the performers know about the audience.

- Starts with facts about the venue and the context what we all know and can visibly see.

- Attention turns to performers commenting on each other and the audience.

- The future – what we don't know or are less sure about.

- Returns to the facts – what we do know.

- Acknowledgement that we don't know everything about the audience.

Part Two

Pages 208–11: 'We know that you are here' to 'The neurons in your retinas . . .'

Having brought to the audience's attention an awareness of where we are and what is going on, this second section begins to explore the science behind how our sensory receptors are feeding us key parts of this information.

- Argument between performers about what we know and don't know.

- The eye.

- The ear.

- The mouth.

- Eyes.

Part Three

Pages 211–15:, 'We know for sure that you're there in front of us' to '. . . walking the borders of a space that has its limits'.

This section begins panning out from the performance space to the world outside. It explores the idea that we don't know what's happening elsewhere – pushing the audience into a new space, which they are unfamiliar with but also may have similarities to the experience of watching this performance. In this way the audience are brought crashing back down into the space. The final part of this section provides perhaps the biggest shift in the play – naming the game that is being played and vulnerably questioning whether it can be sustained for the remainder of the performance.

- What is happening elsewhere? We don't really know.

- Panning further away – what is happening under the stage? In the car park? In Glasgow? In South Africa? At the bottom of the ocean?

- The International Space Station – facts we do know about it. We don't know, for example what it's like to be trapped in space with a group of other people.

- However, we do know what it is like to be trapped with other people in a bounded situation – the performance space that the performers themselves and the audience currently occupy.

- 'The loop' – teasing the audience with the idea that something has gone wrong, making the game of the performance transparent and raising the question of how long the performers can keep this going.

- We know that round about now is probably the hardest part of the performance – everyone is aware of the rules and the potentials of the performance, a kind of deliberate stuck-point, it confronts the audience with the question of their expectations of what will come next.

Part Four

Pages 215–26: 'We know that C's favourite TV show is . . .' to end.

After the suggestion that there might be nowhere new to go, the text returns to the safety of stating basic facts – maybe this is because we're stuck or maybe it can still be interesting if we reinvest it with a different energy or approach? This section introduces the idea of animals and behaviour – is our behaviour conditioned or genetically determined? Do we have choice and the potential for change?

- Basics facts what we know about each other.

- What we know about the rest of the world.

- Introduces the notion of uncertainty: do we know anything?

- Taboo subjects – an attempt to make the audience feel awkward.

- In what sense are animals and humans different?

- Is our behaviour conditioned by systems or are we free?

- What makes humans do what they do?
- Change.

Within each of these four sections it is of course possible to subdivide them further into ideas and moments, often with clear shifts between them or with logical progressions and conversations. Often these can be grouped around levels of knowing or to whom the knowledge or lack of it belongs.

Character

Tim refers to the script as 'not having the safety net of character'. However, the allocation of text means an actor might develop certain emotions or motivations based on repetitive themes in what they are saying – the idea that 'if I say these words I will be coloured by them because I speak them'. In essence there is no 'character'. Instead we see a group of super-individuals rather than what the performers have imagined or are trying to sell us. The challenge for the performers is to learn that what they can bring as themselves and the relationship between 'them' and the words they are speaking is much more interesting than the fake.

Tim spoke about the idea that for him 'it is really lovely when I think you're really speaking to me. As a watcher I feel you are deeply implicated in what you're saying.' Performers would rather have something to hide behind but it creates a vulnerability and ambiguity to just put yourself forward. Tim stressed that this doesn't mean you can't still be inventive but that you have given yourself an authentic and grounded platform from which to explore the edges of theatricality.

This is a useful starting point to hold on to, where the focus is on the relationship the actor has with the text they are speaking and their awareness of the temperature shift their text produces, rather than looking for a character that is in some way predetermined or given by the text. Tim spoke about the idea that as a director what interests him is 'what the performer has already got rather than what I can make them do': what energy do they naturally bring and can this then be amplified in some way?

Who chooses to say which line might tell us about that person but what is implicit is that we are all individuals and that as a starting point the actors should try to use themselves as the characters. This is the real challenge, to put themselves on stage without hiding behind a story or character. By insisting on the collective 'we' within the text, we actually start to see the individuality through the game, as differences start to pop out or certain stories start to recur with certain individuals. As part of your rehearsal process, you should discover how lines fit with certain people and focus on this relationship as a means to discovering 'characters'.

How the actors deliver a line or receive a statement begins to shape their persona. As someone suggests a statement, someone else cuts in with their view which may be a contradiction or build on the same idea. Every line therefore becomes an opportunity in the game of 'yes or no' – are they trying to cause an argument, put a hole in the energy or back the previous speaker up? This again becomes instructive as to how this person behaves and who they are. Their 'character' is defined by their relationship to what they say, what is said and the context within which they find themselves. You could play with the lines as part of the process and discover who is drawn towards certain ideas and topics. The text is really a core set of thought experiments and an encounter with the public that asks:

- Who are you?

- Who are we?

- What do we know?

- What kinds of stories can we put on (or project on) you?

With each statement the temperature changes and should be taken. There is a sense that the performers know each other or are a collective body, a group. This is part of the game. It is potentially scary for the audience – the performers are comfortable with each other and the setting, they are able to play with the audience and tease them. They have a knowledge of each other and shared secrets through which they can raise the temperature. This turns the theatrical convention on its head – usually it is the audience who have the power to watch and judge but here the performers can turn it round on the audience to say: 'We can look at you, we have been watching you, we know about you.' Once the collective group is established, the text invites cracks to appear, which are further opportunities to reveal temperature shifts. The notion of character becomes something behavioural and reactionary based on the actual young person delivering the lines.

Similar attention should be paid to the performers when they are not delivering lines. As the sitting and standing exercises demonstrated, the audience are equally interested in what the performers are doing when they are not speaking and so abstaining or choosing not to speak becomes an active thing. Hester described this as: 'If they don't have a verbal line they should have a silent one.' Are the performers saying I am with that statement or not? 'You are a voter even when you are not speaking.' Therefore listening and thinking should be given equal weight to talking. If we take the idea of a 'thought experiment' then it is important that the performers leave the space for statements to be digested and to gauge how they are received. You can also experiment with the frequency with which someone delivers lines – what is the effect if a performer doesn't speak at all but then suddenly talks with real authority about the International Space Station?

Production, staging and design

Tim spoke about the simplicity with which he saw the staging of the piece – that it is possible to strip it right back and do it simply with a row of chairs at the front of the stage. While you might choose to impose a theatricality to the style of the piece, it is important that you attempt to create a sense of real time, in which the performers are genuinely addressing the audience. In this way it is again possible to do the play without the need for costumes or props. However, this shouldn't mean that creative discoveries can't happen within the process which then inform your piece. Tim Etchells added that sometimes a single simple device or staging idea – a gesture to more theatrical possibilities – can help to add a slight distance or spin to what's happening and in doing so help to articulate a piece like this one. There is potentially something interesting in creating a sense of theatre and then peeling it back again, so that theatre becomes a vehicle to expose what's underneath – the performers and the audience, in real space and time: 'It is always nice when theatre stops.'

The question was raised as to whether the audience should therefore be lit? This is completely up to you, however Tim suggested that it is not necessary and the feeling and idea of connecting is more important. By lighting the audience you also empower them hugely, which can be interesting but harder for the performers. It was advised that if you wanted to do this, to test it as part of your rehearsal process.

Hester Chillingworth spoke about how the text is just an occasion and it is up to each company approaching it to find out how and where to meet it. The workshop encouraged stripping back the performance and not trying to force creative decisions on to the text. Your rehearsals should be a process of discovery and testing and you should aim to carry this into the performance. What is important is that as a company you define where the 'ground' is, so that you can then jump up or land. Once you set the parameters of scale you can work within, you give yourself the opportunity to affect the temperature without potentially the need for big gestures. Tim Etchells spoke about how, during rehearsals, Forced Entertainment often have to remind themselves that they don't need to find ten OK ideas when one very good one would do.

From a workshop led by Hester Chillingworth and Tim Etchells
with notes by Richard Weinman

Musical Differences
by Robin French

In the summer of Year Ten, Alex Stokes takes the fateful step of buying an electric guitar and forming his own rock group. He teams up with a mysterious young singer by the name of Joel Lawrence. What follows could well be the most incredible saga in the school's musical history. The band survives different line-ups, impossible love affairs and brutal school politics. By Year Thirteen, they are a tightly knit four-piece, and their final gig is nothing short of remarkable – but have individual members paid too high a price?

Cast size
Variable size ensemble

Robin French spent several years in the music industry as the bassist of the UK band Mr Hudson and The Library, who appeared on Jools Holland, opened The Other Stage at the Glastonbury Festival and supported Amy Winehouse on a UK tour. His first play, *Bear Hug*, won the Royal Court Young Writers' Festival and was produced at the Royal Court Theatre in 2004. Subsequent productions include *Breakfast Hearts* at Theatre503; *Gilbert is Dead* at Hoxton Hall; *The Red Helicopter* at the Almeida; *The Get Out* at the Royal Court; and *Heather Gardner* at Birmingham Rep. He is also an award-winning screenwriter, who has twice been chosen as a *Broadcast* 'Hot Shot'. He co-created and co-writes the sitcom *Cuckoo*, starring Greg Davies, which has received nominations at BAFTA and the British Comedy Awards. The show has been recommissioned for a further two series. His film *Crocodile* won awards at Cannes, Encounters and Guanajuato festivals, and was BIFA nominated for Best British Short. Robin is currently writing a feature film about David Bowie and Iggy Pop.

Notes on the text

This is a play for a chorus. Productions can divide lines between actors however they see fit, but are encouraged to explore using the chorus or sections of the chorus speaking in unison. The variance of number of people speaking should provide a musical texture to the piece. Of course, some parts of the text may become monologues.

It may be that the entire chorus remains onstage for the whole production. It may not be.

The actors making up the chorus play members of the fictional school year. However, the following characters should not be represented on stage: Alex Stokes, Joel Lawrence, Mark Beevers, Christian Mbulu, Cathy Genovese, Nick Carter.

There are three exceptions to this rule:

First exception: when there is dialogue between these characters, then members of the chorus can 'act out' the scene. However, they are doing an impression, they are not the characters themselves.

Second exception: if these characters appear as musicians and play the songs of the fictional school band live. Do you have brilliant teenage musicians who could rehearse as a band and play some music live? Is live music going to be the charge of your production? But remember, the audience isn't going to be sympathetic to the band if they are no good.

Third exception: if these characters are represented by dancers. Could your production create a fitting choreography for the action?

But remember productions do not need to contain live music or dance. There should be a musicality in the piece without either, and some of the best productions will have neither. It's all up to you!

Summer's over.

Something's different about us.

Something's different every summer.

We got taller.

Or we never grew at all.

We got curves.

Or not.

Our bodies don't feel like our bodies any more.

So whose bodies are they?

Our voices changed.

They're alien.

Strangers speak out our mouths now.

Our skin cleared up

Or got worse.

No one's safe.

At any time, any of us could transition into full pizza face.

Blackheads punctuate our weeks.

Pus pours out of us.

The corridors stink the same.

Of sweat.

Of old trainers.

And perfume.

The air's heavy with pheromones.

Good friends are abandoned with no explanation.

We make new friends.

Everything is changing.

Second day of term, right, Matthew Byatt steals this bottle of hydrochloric acid from the science labs.

Top's not on properly. The acid burns a hole through his Adidas bag.

Dickhead gets expelled.

He could have burned a hole in his back!

Burned his skin off!

Would have probably died!

They all laugh.

You don't mess around at our school.

Our school's an academy.

Not like the one down the road.

Where the teachers carry knives.

We're lucky to be here.

We're lucky we're in the catchment area.

We weren't lucky. Our parents moved into the catchment area so we could enrol.

Most of us are lucky, OK?

We're scared of the future.

According to the teachers, the future is terrifying.

If you don't work hard now, your life's going to be tragic and unhappy

They talk about their high expectations for us.

They blather on about our 'potential'.

We're given coursework.

And assignments.

Every night there's more homework.

We have to get good grades.

If not, then.

We're told when to stand up.

When to sit down.

When to eat.

When to drink.

What to eat.

What to drink.

When to talk.

But we don't want to *talk*. We want to look at our phones.

Before lessons, we queue outside the classroom

Form an orderly queue

In complete silence

And if we talk or move or even feel for our phones in our pockets –

You there!

Saturday detention.

Just like that.

They don't even care

Because it's not about *this* Saturday

Apparently

It's about the horrendous soul-destroying Saturdays in your life if you don't do your homework

Your inevitable years trapped in sinkhole estates mired in drug addiction locked in brief unsatisfying relationships despised by your own children.

If you don't get a good grade for Geography GCSE.

If you don't form an orderly queue before lesson.

So we obey the rules.

*

First week of Year Ten.

Rains all week.

Remember that week?

We're stuck inside like cattle.

Watching everything changing.

We talk about football and fighting.

We talk about clothes and hair.

We boast and we bitch.

We think about sex.

All the time.

Some more than others.

No, all of us, all the time.

We fancy Stacy Calder.

And Nick Carter

And Darren Northcote.

Their names on our lips are like spells.

We think about them every night before we go to sleep.

When we pass them in the corridor, it's the best thing that happens all week.

Sometimes they nod back. Acknowledge us.

And we feel

For a moment

Like we exist.

But do we really exist?

We watch them whup their opponents at football.

At hockey.

At basketball.

At Sports Day, they win *everything*.

Nick Carter.

Darren Northcote.

Stacy Calder.

They don't even celebrate.

Because winning isn't surprising for them. Winning is what happens to you when you're perfect.

We're not perfect like they're perfect. Nobody is.

When we get the ball, we pass it to Stacy Calder.

And Darren Northcote.

And Nick Carter.

After the game, we talk about how the passes we passed them led to them scoring their goals.

They're tall – they can buy alcohol.

They take it to mysterious parties we only hear about on Monday morning.

Their hair is exactly right.

Skin glows.

They get into bars nobody gets into.

When they move, you move too.

When they sit, you sit.

They're physically attractive – so it's obvious they know important secrets about the world.

We talk about things we like that we only like because we know they like them.

We're madly in love with them.

We barely know them.

They are all joy and all truth and all reality and all happiness.

They are the end of the sexual rainbow.

Everybody agrees

No experience in life could possibly be greater than sex with Stacy Calder.

Or Nick Carter.

Or Darren Northcote.

We wish we had their lives. We wish we were born with cheekbones and great home lives and sporting ability so life could be easy.

Just like it's easy for Stacy Calder

And Darren Northcote

And Nick Carter.

*

Alex Stokes was on a flight back from family holiday in Andalusia when he committed himself to a life in rock music.

That's weird.

Don't really listen to rock music. Sort of prefer

Rihanna.

And Ed Sheeran.

We like Grime.

Grimes.

We like Kendrick Lamar.

And Kanye West.

Ellie Goulding.

Nah. She is wretched.

Alex Stokes starts dropping band names into conversations.

The Arctic Monkeys

The Strokes

Arcade Fire.

Never heard of them.

They're on the radio

Except at our school, we didn't listen to that kind of music.

Foals. Beach House. Bon Iver. Kurt Vile. Phoenix. The Mystery Jets.

You're not even starting with what's important. Alex Stokes is a complete nobody.

He's not cool.

No way.

Nope.

He is not hot.

Not yet.

He *never* gets hot.

He does. What about when the band gets really good?

He was hot then. It was just his braces.

He didn't have braces then, so . . .

No, I mean *then*.

He was in the football team in Year Eight.

He played like three matches.

No, he played two matches – and one when he was brought on because Nick Carter had an inflamed tendon.

Anyway, he was a nobody. Let's move on.

He scored a goal.

No, he didn't. As if.

He did actually.

Nope.

Anyway, he got dropped.

Start of school, he got in a few fights in break times, nothing big.

Nobody talks about him basically.

Nobody ever goes to his house.

I went to his house.

Nobody cool goes to his house.

OK, that's fair.

He's sort of a sidekick person really to –

Ateeq Javid

The most sarcastic human being who has ever existed

He goes to his place Monday nights. Their mums are friends.

Yeah, but Alex Stokes is closer to . . .

Sits next to Christian Mbulu in maths.

Piss themselves the whole lesson. They're tight.

Same sense of humour.

Plus Alex Stokes gets the same bus as Charlotte Randle, and Celine Cheng.

So at the bus stop

He doesn't talk to no one hardly

Just stares at his phone.

Or sometimes he talks about *Family Guy* with Vikram Kapadia.

We all talk about *Family Guy*

But he's the *Family Guy* guy. Always quoting it.

Making it unfunny. Spoiling it basically.

I like the news.

Shanika Samarasinghe sits next to Alex Stokes in history one time and he's listening to his headphones and he won't even turn them down.

Rude.

He should do.

Because Shanika Samarasinghe is mates with Stacy Calder and Lauren McIntyre and Charlotte Randle.

At this point.

And Alex Stokes is a nobody.

I like him. I play pool with him.

That was weird though – why did he start playing the guitar?

Random.

Lucy Graham lives on his road. Apparently, that summer, Alex Stokes washed car windows.

Like every Saturday the whole summer.

Exactly.

Random.

Christian Mbulu said he stayed over one weekend.

Yeah?

Because in Year Eight he used to stay over there loads.

He turns up with this electric guitar and this other thing –

An amplifier

He's getting it out the back of his mum's car.

And Christian Mbulu is like – what is that?

Says he got it off Gumtree for seventy quid. Says he's been saving up.

He can't even play one chord

Says he wants to start a band. With Christian Mbulu.

Apparently

But Christian Mbulu doesn't play no instruments.

And it's not like he likes guitar music anyway

So he says no

He prefers techno

So no

It's a no because he wants to concentrate on his sports.

It's just a no

The reasons for which include techno.

We're meant to be telling a story.

As if Christian Mbulu would want to be in a band with Alex Stokes. As if.

Nah, they're mates.

Saying you never saw them crease themselves in class? It was constant.

Christian Mbulu makes *everybody* crack up in class.

So funny.

What about that time . . .

Yeah.

He always stands outside class, right. Because of shit he's done.

He makes faces through the glass in the door.

It's actually rather immature.

Stupid shit.

Everybody seems to find him hilarious – bewilderingly

No, I'm telling you – it's funny shit

And you can tell – even the teachers –

Even though he ruins loads of lessons

But the way he does it –

Even the teachers have this look like

Fair enough – that's just factually funny.

Christian Mbulu would probably be mates with Darren Northcote.

Except Christian Mbulu is in love with Stacy Calder.

Like everybody.

And Stacy Calder goes out with Darren Northcote.

Or sometimes Nick Carter.

Depending on how she's feeling.

Anyway, we're getting stupidly off track.

Shut up.

Because . . .

Not really, because the band starts when Alex Stokes gets his guitar, you dick.

Yeah, that's sort of important.

Nah man, it starts with Joel Lawrence.

What?

According to Celine Cheng.

Pfft.

Joel Lawrence is a new kid.

Celine Cheng always makes stuff up.

He arrives in Year Nine.

Moon face. Should see it!

The kid has –

Massive face like a dinner plate.

Like an old male orang-utan. See them?

Like ninety per cent of what she says happened, never happened.

Celine Cheng.

You probably wouldn't believe it – if you saw him, you'd be like –

This guy is president of the moon faces. Seriously.

The circumference – wow – it's sort of magnificent.

He's got nice blue eyes

And his hair is messy

And he's always sort of grinning like he thinks something is funny.

Even when nothing is funny.

He's a new kid.

So nobody knows him.

I know nobody knows Alex Stokes but see we *know* Alex Stokes but nobody even *knows* Joel Lawrence.

Did anyone *ever* really know Joel Lawrence?

What about that science lesson?

Ha!

Yeah, OK, yeah. Mr Vittala is being annoying. Like he's repeating the same question.

Over and over.

'Why does hydrogen bind with water?'

And nobody knows the answer.

Because it's Chemistry – so obviously we don't.

Mr Vittala won't back down – he is *so* worked up

Face goes purple.

Veins on his forehead

He keeps asking the same question.

Bel-end.

Like somehow his whole life has been leading to this point

And if we get it right, all his life choices are vindicated

And if we don't know

Then teaching has been a mistake, and his marriage has been a mistake

If we don't know, then it's *all* been a mistake.

So he's up at the front, standing his ground.

'Why does hydrogen bind with water?'

'Will somebody please tell me, why does hydrogen bind with water?'

Over and over.

Until, Joel Lawrence stands up and says:

'Because you're a twat, sir,'

Picks up his bag, walks out the classroom.

You can tell Joel Lawrence likes music.

He always has one earphone in.

Always

Through every class. That's his thing. The earphone.

Nobody asks him what music he's listening to.

Nobody speaks to him.

He's a new kid.

Apparently, Joel Lawrence goes up to Alex Stokes during Geography.

Well, according to Celine Cheng.

Joel asks Alex one single question.

You play guitar?

Alex Stokes looks back at Joel Lawrence.

He stands up – raises himself to his full height.

Which at that time was five foot four.

Alex Stokes says

'Yeah, I play guitar.'

Joel puts a hand through his hair, sets his blue eyes on Alex Stokes.

Something is changing.

And Joel Lawrence says:

'We're starting a band. I'm the singer.'

*

We know parties are happening.

But it's impossible to get to them basically.

Depending on who you are

My advice – get booze. That is key

To get booze, you need to get fake ID off Vikram Kapadia

Twenty quid.

On Mondays, we check out photographs of the parties from that weekend

That we weren't at.

Everybody pools information.

Who got off with who?

Who felt who up?

And we all think about *our* Saturday night, when *we* were stuck at home

Watching TV with our mums and dads

Not feeling anybody up

In fact, looking at Facebook photos

While somewhere in town, people were being *in* Facebook photos.

When we have parties, our parents play evil tricks on us

Cancelling their romantic city break

Coming back early.

What the fuuuuuuck?!

Sitting in the next room with their sad lame friends

Laughing. You can hear them.

Because the sound of your parents' lame laughter is probably the most embarrassing sound anybody could ever hear ever.

And nobody takes any photographs to put on Facebook – because to be honest the whole sorry event is best forgotten.

Anyway, two years before this.

You're going to confuse them. Two years before what?

Before they started the band obviously.

For some random reason.

This is important actually.

Alex Stokes strikes gold.

His parents run into Lucy Graham's parents on the road, and apparently she's having a party.

This was two years before – so don't get jumbled, yeah. This guy looks jumbled. Are you jumbled? No? Good.

And so Alex Stokes goes along to Lucy Graham's party obviously

And . . .

He's the only boy there

You wait for this.

It's Charlotte Randle. It's Lucy Graham. It's Shanika Samarasinghe.

It's Lauren McIntyre.

It's Stacy fucking Calder.

If it had been me, I would have had a massive orgy with all of the assembled babes

But it's Alex Stokes.

He actually says nothing, we sort of forget he's even there.

He has lost the power of speech – he is so totally unprepared for witnessing that beauty all at once.

It's like dropping a five-year-old with armbands into the middle of the channel.

No chance

So we ask him about boys in our year

What's Darren Northcote really like?

What's Nick Carter into?

Who fancies them.

But then something weird happens.

Lauren McIntyre takes Alex Stokes to the bottom of the garden

French kisses him.

And since then

According to Celine Cheng

Nah, according to everybody because he never stops talking about it

Alex Stokes is in love with Lauren McIntyre.

Infatuated

Obsessed

Like you would not believe.

Nobody has ever loved anybody like Alex Stokes loves Lauren McIntyre.

When he stays over at Christian Mbulu's, the sole conversational topic is how amazing Lauren McIntyre and Stacy Calder are.

They give each other advice on seduction, even though neither has any experience whatsoever.

Lauren McIntyre is the star of the school basketball team.

She played in junior school – she had a headstart – it wasn't . . .

Scores more baskets than anyone.

True.

Even Stacy Calder.

Lauren McIntyre can spin a ball on the finger of one hand forever.

Make time stop.

She dribbles round us. Makes the ball invisible.

She can score from a thousand miles away.

She can score across time zones.

Celine Cheng and Charlotte Randle and Lucy Graham overhear Lauren's mum say she's going to have professional trials.

For England.

She would totally have got in.

Yeah, maybe in Year Eight.

But Lauren McIntyre didn't grow.

We grew.

We all grew

But Lauren McIntyre never grew.

So she's accurate – but all her shots get blocked.

By a forest of tall girls

Obscuring the light

Blocking out her future

Time out.

Lauren McIntyre's mum writes a lifestyle column for the local paper.

She once came in to talk to the school about body language in a business environment.

According to Christian Mbulu, when he went to Alex Stokes' house – Alex Stokes confessed

He always reads those lifestyle columns Mrs McIntyre writes

At least three times

Combing them for details about the home life of Lauren McIntyre.

Apparently

There was an article that summer

About how Lauren McIntyre took down all the basketball posters from her room.

And replaced them with posters of rock bands.

So we basically reckon

That is why Alex Stokes bought a guitar.

*

Gymnastics. Year Ten.

Charlotte Randle quizzes Alex Stokes about his Saturday afternoon.

Why does *she* want to know?

Maybe she fancies Alex Stokes.

More likely Christian Mbulu.

Or Joel Lawrence.

Seriously?

Joel Lawrence lives in a medium-sized house in the same area as Alex Stokes.

He opens the front door

They collect chocolate biscuits and proceed to his bedroom

Joel shows him the most –

A vintage Fender Jaguar.

Which must have cost . . .

Ones similar are on eBay for way over a thousand pounds

Apparently

Joel Lawrence doesn't let Alex Stokes touch his Fender Jaguar.

Not once the whole afternoon.

The room is piled high with sound-recording magazines.

He asks complicated questions about Alex's guitar, pedal and amp set-up that Alex Stokes has no idea how to answer.

They talk about bands they like.

They both like the song 'Aviation' by The Last Shadow Puppets, which is Alex Turner's side-project band.

Alex Stokes says he doesn't remember much.

Joel Lawrence likes the Foo Fighters and The Killers and Nirvana and The Smashing Pumpkins and The Red Hot Chili Peppers.

Alex Stokes plays the two chords he knows on loop. Joel Lawrence turns his amp up to full.

Closes his eyes

Plays a solo

Which lasts only eleven minutes, but feels like at least three hours.

After, Joel takes Alex to the loft

It's got this old-style record player.

Middle of the room. Big white rug.

And the walls are covered in shelves of vinyl.

Such a weird room.

Joel stops Alex at the door of the loft.

One pointed finger on his chest.

His dad owns the record player, and all the records – so Alex can't touch anything.

Says his dad works in London in the record industry and he will undoubtedly sign their band as soon as they work up some songs, and get themselves a healthy following.

Around five, Joel sets his Jaguar to one side, and tells Alex they're ready to find a drummer.

*

It's probably – what?

December

Probably

Year Ten.

Joel Lawrence and Alex Stokes are in class one lunch, discussing who's gonna be in the band.

Listening to their conversation:

Pawel Nowak

Ateeq Javid

Simon Heaton

The three dweebs wait in vain to hear their own names considered.

They even go without lunch.

He was already turned down flat, but Alex Stokes thinks he's going to get Christian Mbulu in the band.

This time on bass.

Christian Mbulu has only got nine fingers.

No, he's only got seven fingers you dick

Ring finger on his left hand. It's just a stub.

So he can never wear a wedding ring, so he says he can never get married.

Playa fo' life, I ain't thinking of wife

I ain't thinking of twice; bitch I'm thinkin tonight

Green light she ready, we on that Rozay Heavy

We goin' straight to the house it ain't no need for the telly.

I'm steak eggs and jelly, bitch I'ma fill that belly

She like 'Beeda, you nasty,' I'm like 'Bitch, you ready?'

Anyway, one missing finger

Says it was bitten off by a snake in Nigeria.

It got sliced off when Simon Heaton took everyone ice-skating for his eighth birthday party.

His stump is sort of amazing.

Christian Mbulu says it even itches sometimes.

Like a phantom limb.

Because sometimes you lose something, but your brain won't really accept that it's gone.

Joel Lawrence is well impressed when Christian Mbulu

Jeffrey Ferris dares him

Plunges a sharpened pencil

Because Christian Mbulu is usually all right with the teachers

Even though he takes the piss

Mr Desmond is leaning over Charlotte Randle's desk

And Mr Desmond always wears tracksuit bottoms.

And Christian Mbulu rams the pencil

Sharpened pencil.

Right up Mr Desmond's bum hole.

And Christian Mbulu says no way did he think he'd be so accurate

It actually goes through the material, it goes right up Mr Desmond's bum crack.

It goes deep, you know what I'm saying?

And the whole class cracks up.

And nobody ever saw Mr Desmond that angry

He was usually pretty chill

But he didn't like having a pencil in his arse

So Christian Mbulu almost gets suspended, right.

Joel Lawrence agreed with Alex Stokes – the pencil incident proved Christian Mbulu had the anti-establishment credentials that fitted the band's fuck-the-world ideology.

Christian Mbulu agrees to play the bass guitar, as long as he can fit it around his sporting commitments.

*

Problem.

No one in school plays drums

Says who?

Mark Beevers looks about eight.

He drinks full-fat milk.

He chews blocks of mature cheddar at break

He always smells of dairy.

Known for

Sticky-out ears.

Swimming. Fastest in the year at back stroke.

Breast stroke actually

As Pawel Novak tells it, Mark Beevers is planning to go up to Alex Stokes for weeks, ever since he hears Alex Stokes and Joel Lawrence have got the band started.

He's already Grade Six at the drums.

You get grades at the drums?

Obviously. So

He waits three weeks, planning his strategy. Finally.

Mark Beevers swaggers up to Alex Stokes and Joel Lawrence at the bus stop into town.

He never spoke to either of them before.

They weren't cool – but he *really* wasn't cool

And Mark Beevers freezes –

According to Charlotte Randle

He stands there. No words.

Face goes red

Finally he blurts out

In this high-pitched shriek

Because his voice was sort of unreliable back then

'I play the drums!'

And there are flecks of gob on Alex Stokes' blazer

And Beevers maybe looks eight, but he sounds six

And Mark Beevers tells Pawel Novak that was it – thought he'd totally fucked it.

But Alex Stokes gives Beevers a trial period.

A trial?

Beevers turns out to the best musician in the band

Mark Beevers is madly in love with Shanika Samarasinghe.

So there are negotiations of terms.

He will only join the band if nobody else in the band is in love with her.

That way, they avoid complications.

Should he ever summon up the courage to say one word to her.

But Alex Stokes is in love with Lauren McIntyre.

And Christian Mbulu is in love with Stacy Calder.

And Joel Lawrence has never expressed any opinion about any girl in the school.

Never?

Well, that was before . . .

Oh yeah.

So that was it – they're now a band.

*

We are connected

Always

We are inventing completely new systems of human
communication

We know everything about each other

But we know nothing

We WhatsApp

And Snapchat

And Facebook

And Instagram

And Skype

These are verbs

Because it's easier than talking

Because talking

You can say the wrong thing

And if you say the wrong thing

Even once

Then people can talk about it

And people can laugh about it

Which you do not want

Some of us are scared

Some of us hate ourselves

Some of us are gay

Some of us are cutting ourselves

Some of us are starving ourselves

I'm not scared. I have high self-esteem. I am straight. I eat properly. I don't cut myself.

Some of us are romantics.

Most of us are romantics.

Who think that our problems would be solved

If

The

Right

Person

Came

Along

But

The

Right

Person

Never

Comes

Along

Ever

*

Apparently

Mark Beevers is being annoying, going on about having the first rehearsal at his house.

His reasoning – there is a drum kit.

But for Alex Stokes and Joel Lawrence, starting proceedings chez Beevers gives the wrong message.

Anyway, he's on trial period.

He's not even really in the band.

They meet at Joel Lawrence's

Mark Beevers plays a wastepaper basket

Christian Mbulu is still saving for a bass.

He sits on Joel Lawrence's bed, nodding, providing good vibes.

Joel Lawrence can sort of sing

Sort of

He has confidence

He throws his hair around.

His blue eyes close on the expanse of his big moon face

Between choruses, he plays interminable solos on his Jaguar guitar.

The tunes they're covering don't actually have solos.

But Joel Lawrence says

We have to make the songs our own.

When Mrs Lawrence comes upstairs, the music stops.

Their hearts stop

Everything goes into slow motion

Mrs Lawrence is really really fit.

Like really really fit.

Properly fit.

Even though she is probably at least thirty.

Long, dark hair.

Her figure.

She smells

Amazing

She looks like

Penelope Cruz

Rachel Weisz

Her ass

Alex Stokes and Mark Beevers and Christian Mbulu watch her

And Joel Lawrence watches them watching her

When she goes downstairs, Christian Mbulu gets her to stay

Says they could do with some backing vocals.

She sings good. She dances too.

After rehearsal, she makes lasagne. Says

'That was fun!'

Says

'You're welcome to come and practise here every Saturday.'

Joel's retort is definitive.

'Fuck off, Mum. You're not in the band.'

Next Saturday, it's at Mark Beevers' house.

Mark Beevers' dad is fat and has coffee breath and only ever makes beans on toast.

Alex Stokes and Christian Mbulu secretly blame each other for staring at Joel Lawrence's mum too much.

*

No news about the band

They're not on the radar

They get together at Mark Beevers' place

Apparently

Christian Mbulu tells Ateeq Javid and Lucy Graham

Sound isn't coming together

Maybe because the band are on different drugs.

Joel Lawrence –

Skunk.

Alex Stokes –

Strongbow.

Mark Beevers –

Haribo.

Christian Mbulu doesn't smoke or drink because he's concentrating on his sports.

Lucy Graham and Celine Cheng see

Mark Beevers pin something on the school noticeboard.

Posters appear all over school.

The band's first gig.

The venue – the school gym.

The time – Thursday lunchtime.

So many Facebook Event reminders.

Why would we like their page on Facebook, when we haven't even heard them once?

But you have to . . .

Yeah, this is important

OK, so – two weeks before the gig, Joel Lawrence goes on one single solitary date with Stacy Calder.

How did Joel Lawrence get Stacy Calder to go on a date with him?

Makes no sense.

According to Charlotte Randle, his technique was simple.

Joel walked up to Stacy Calder by the lockers at lunchtime and asked her to go on a date with him.

We are outraged. This is not done.

If this could happen, then

Joel Lawrence is a new kid. Stacy Calder is Stacy Calder.

She goes out with Nick Carter or Darren Northcote depending on how she's feeling at the time.

We all look at Joel Lawrence again.

Who is this guy?

His blue eyes have captivated Stacy Calder.

His moon face seems less . . .

We no longer see the moon face.

Wasn't a problem for Stacy Calder – why have we been so anti extremely wide faces?

On Monday, classroom is silent, just amazed

Joel Lawrence got off with Stacy Calder

What?

At a bus stop

For at least ten minutes

And he felt her breasts over her top.

He felt her breasts over not under her top.

No, he was under her jumper, but he never actually removed her bra

Well, he was fumbling at the clasp for ages, so he would have

Then the bus came

Apparently, Stacy Calder told Charlotte Randle that Joel Lawrence is properly weird.

He *is* weird.

Apparently, he kept going on about his dad who is some big shot in the record industry in London.

He asked her to go back to his place to look at his thousand-pound guitar, but Stacey Calder was already disappearing into the bus.

Same week, Stacy Calder starts going out with Nick Carter again.

Still – it is now a fact. Joel Lawrence kissed Stacy Calder.

So either her reputation has to go down, or Joel Lawrence's up.

It was a complicated piece of mathematics.

Alex Stokes and Mark Beevers discuss band unity in the canteen.

They eat chicken pie and chips followed by apple crumble and custard followed by a Snickers bar followed by two packets of Monster Munch.

Christian Mbulu is in love with Stacy Calder, and now . . .

It's not like he actually got her bra undone

He got off with her

It's never going to happen again.

I mean – the singer and bassist in the same band . . .

Because remember Christian Mbulu loved Stacy Calder

He'd always loved her

Christian Mbulu and Joel Lawrence don't talk the whole sound check.

Somebody throws a basketball and it accidentally hits Mark Beevers in the face

I threw it deliberately

Stacy Calder appears in the gym that lunch.

So does Lauren McIntyre

So does Shanika Samarasinghe.

They play five songs.

Four covers. One Alex Stokes composition called . . .

Can't remember what . . .

Mr Desmond introduces the band. He is astonishingly lame.

The sound reverberates round the room.

Mark Beevers drums overpower everything else.

When he drums he grins almost constantly, pouring with sweat.

Joel Lawrence wears his guitar super low.

Turns it up super-loud.

His solos are super-long.

Alex Stokes plays competently and stays in time with Beevers, which just about –

Keeps the music listenable.

It's probably those two, you think . . .

Yeah. Have something maybe.

Christian Mbulu *looks* good

Yeah, he's the fittest

By far

But his playing is

Way out of time

Well, he missed a lot of practices because of his sporting commitments.

Nah, dude just has no rhythm.

What about his missing finger? Probably a handicap for bass playing.

Stacy Calder, Charlotte Randle and Celine Cheng walk out in the third song.

Lauren McIntyre stays until song four

A wave of feedback from Joel Lawrence's vocal mic stops the gig in its tracks.

Mr Desmond declares the band has potential – says they should get in the rehearsal studio, tighten up their sound.

The next day

At the bus stop into town

Alex Stokes goes up to Christian Mbulu. Says

'Mate, sorry, thing is

Don't take this the wrong way

Your bass playing is really bad so we're going to have to let you go.'

Alex Stokes and Christian Mbulu shake hands.

Says it's cool, it's not like he ever claimed to be musical.

They say they'll stay friends.

Christian Mbulu's mum phones Alex Stokes' mum. She asks whether Christian Mbulu can be let back in the band.

Alex Stokes' mum says

'Well, I think that's Alex's decision.'

Alex is never informed.

Christian Mbulu seems cool about it

But come on

Alex Stokes is well naive

Stay friends?

Because even though Christian Mbulu seems so funny and happy all the time

Thing is

Inside he isn't very happy, and things aren't very funny.

Alex Stokes' social life takes a dive.

Nobody nods when they pass him in the corridor

Nobody invites him to parties.

Measure for measure

Christian Mbulu poisons the cool kids against Alex Stokes.

So now the band is all Alex Stokes has got.

The week after the gig, Lauren McIntyre is picked up from school by a twenty-three year old guy with blue hair and a tongue piercing who works the till in WH Smith's.

Alex Stokes tells Ateeq Javid
'It's the worst day of my life.'
But it isn't – there's going to be a worse day than this.
A way worse day.

*

We start driving
In car parks with our mums
Or our dads
Mirror
Indicate
We put the car in the wrong gear
Nearly crash it into walls and bollards
We parallel park
We reverse park
We cram for our theory test
Darren Northcote and Nick Carter
And Stacy Calder
Pass their tests first time
Obviously
And are given small red cars
By their loving parents
As a reward for their good exam results.
Obviously
For finishing their coursework.
Obviously.

For just being themselves.

Now they drive to school themselves

Parking alongside teachers

Vikram Kapadia passes

Very next Saturday, he gets off with Charlotte Randle

Celine Cheng passes first time

We fail our first test

We get minor faults

We get major faults

We fail our second test

Everybody at school knows

Our instructor says that we'll definitely pass this time

Definitely

But we don't pass

We stop telling people at school we even have a test

Should have done that to start with to be honest

Until just when failure feels inevitable

We fail again

But the next time

We fail even worse

Then

We pass!

Yes!

Now we are adults

Now the world will give us everything we want

Except our parents don't get us cars

And we still wait at the bus stop into town with all the little kids

And nothing seems to change

But really, everything is changing.

*

Take the band

Cathy Genovese turns it around.

Such a swot.

She *was*.

Her mum's Italian, her dad's from Trinidad. They're on and off – that's why she keeps the surname Genovese.

She comes top in all her GCSEs.

She plays the oboe to Grade Eight.

She never goes to parties.

Or kisses guys.

Sometimes she even listens to classical music – for fun.

Until suddenly

Wonder why

She changes

Gets thrown out of wind band for smoking weed before a solo performance.

The concert captivates the audience of parents and teachers

Though it goes in some directions Johannes Brahms had not intended.

Now she's always got sunglasses on

Cosof the red eyes from the smoking.

Her sister works at Max Factor

She gets *heaps* of free stuff

And even though she wears hoodies now and is well scruffy

Her make-up is at all times *immaculate*.

Cathy Genovese loses her virginity to Darren Northcote during one of his periodical breaks from Stacy Calder.

She describes Northcote's perfect body to some Year Elevens during break-time.

Now, she gets detentions every week.

Because of dares

Puts fish behind radiators now.

Hides alarm clocks in the ceiling panels of the classrooms now.

Picks locks.

Shoplifts clothes.

Starts food fights in the canteen.

Sometimes Cathy Genovese doesn't even go to school now – hangs out with the kids from the graveyard.

Charlie Marriage – a skateboard freak who drinks all day.

He even drank aftershave once.

He has epileptic fits.

Emma Sell – she slept with three boys at the same party.

Apparently when you kiss her, her mouth tastes of burgers.

I confirm this.

Dom Wiley – he orders newly synthesised legal highs off the internet

Tests them on himself and anybody mental enough to join him.

He has mad eyes – but is that drugs, or were they already like that?

Cathy Genovese sells her oboe on Gumtree

For a fraction of its real value

Tells her parents she's storing it at school.

Buys a Precision Bass.

During rehearsals, she stops songs

And Alex Stokes gives her evils

So she tells him why some decision he's made is shit

You never saw him look so affronted

But he finds a way to make the songs better

Soon they trust each other.

The band recruit a friend of Mark Beevers' on keyboards.

He has wide teeth like a hippo.

His father recently died of cancer.

He doesn't get the gig.

Alex Stokes breaks the news

At the bus stop

According to Celine Cheng.

*

Anyway, even though Christian Mbulu avenged himself on Alex Stokes

Still outside rehearsals, there's Joel Lawrence

But he says it's always Joel Lawrence pestering him

Texting him

Daily

Snapchatting him

Daily

Facebooking him

Even calling his home on his parents' landline

Using a *landline*?!

Inviting him round *all the time*

And when he goes round – it's always the same deal.

The same one-way conversation

Alex Stokes tells Ateeq Javid that maybe he finds Joel Lawrence

A bit intense

Yeah?

Yeah

Apparently

Is this Year Eleven maybe?

Could be

So he goes round there. It's probably a Saturday night, and . . .

Yeah, he told *me* this – I sat next to him in History that year. I mean, it didn't happen to you. I'm sort of a primary source.

Go on then.

Yeah well

If you're going to interrupt

See he actually did tell me so, I'm just saying . . . no disrespect.

Continue.

Sorry.

Does it look like I care?

OK, yeah, so . . . Alex Stokes has dark hair, right, but he wants to dye it blue. And like a dick, he doesn't even google it, so he never bleached his hair before he did it.

So yeah, he goes to Joel's place Saturday, and his mum's going out – like on a date apparently. With some ancient dentist, which Alex Stokes is clearly jealous about because he goes on about that for like . . .

We know about that already, so hurry up.

Yeah, OK. So they raid the spirit cabinet, find this weird green spirit, which tastes like liquorice or aniseed.

What is it?

That's not important.

I think people would like to know.

Not really.

Anyway, usually Joel never answers direct questions, usually he just boasts about stuff which sounds like total bullshit – and he never really has a conversation. So they're getting totally pissed.

And Joel starts talking about his dad, who is this big shot in the record industry.

Yeah, like he already told Stacy Calder.

And it was his dad who apparently got him that guitar for his fourteenth birthday.

Yeah, we guessed that already.

And his dad has a new girlfriend and a new family in London. He has a new stepson same age as Joel. He's good at football and lost his virginity at thirteen. Sometimes, when he meets up with his dad, they play guitar together.

His dad is *really* good, he used to be a session musician.

So?

What else? He likes his dad more than his mum.

Joel's new stepbrother has a job at Pizza Express plus he had sex with a twenty-five-year-old motorcycle courier called Lotte.

Also his new stepbrother goes raving at Fabric nightclub in London, and takes loads of ketamine. Also he's going to Edinburgh University to study medicine.

Anyway, by now they're completely shit-faced on this green potion.

Alex Stokes says

'The room is swimming,'

And when he stands up he almost collapses.

And Joel Lawrence says

'Let's go up on the roof,'

And they go through the loft room with the white rug and the shelves of vinyl

And on the roof it's well windy and well cold.

And Alex Stokes looks out over the town, and the sky is swirling, and churning like

Van Gogh

Yeah. And Alex Stokes hears his own voice.

He's telling Joel Lawrence his solos are too long.

And Joel Lawrence says his solos are part of the signature sound.

And Alex Stokes' voice says Joel Lawrence needs to work on his singing, which would improve with more practice.

And his voice orders Joel Lawrence to stop changing the lyrics he writes.

Joel nods his huge moon face. His eyes two lakes.

And Alex Stokes says maybe he should sing alongside Joel Lawrence – sharing vocal duties. Like The Libertines. Because Alex is writing the songs, surely he should get to sing them too.

The atmosphere is strange

There are two stars for every star.

The wind tries to stop them lighting that spliff

The wind knows

Alex Stokes doesn't feel safe. He knows for sure he's going to fall off that roof.

Joel Lawrence becomes dead silent.

They go back down.

In the lounge, they are silent.

Alex Stokes examines the ceiling swirling

Joel says –

'I would say join me on centre stage, but Alex, man – you can't sing.

You write great songs. But you can't sing.'

And Joel says –

'Whereas me, I am a natural frontman.'

Alex Stokes stands up

'Except, Joel, you're a fake. You're so pretentious. Making it look like you know about music, because you have a posh guitar and all these guitar magazines, but the truth is you're not even that good at the guitar.'

And Joel Lawrence says

'I'm not a fake.'

And Alex Stokes says

'No? Except, look at the evidence. Look at that fucking earphone, you keep in your ear all the time. How pretentious could you possibly be? As if you're listening to music all the time.'

Joel Lawrence takes his earphone out of his ear

Which makes him look weirdly unlike Joel Lawrence

Like a stranger

Because Joel Lawrence always has an earphone in his ear.

Joel Lawrence's eyes flame with hatred.

Has Alex Stokes gone too far?

Joel Lawrence looks away

He lights a cigarette, which he's not allowed to do inside the house by the way.

And Alex Stokes starts puking. He hurls all over the house.

They go to bed.

And Joel Lawrence leaves a bucket by the bed for Alex Stokes, case he's sick again.

And Joel Lawrence leaves some water by the bed for Alex Stokes, case he's thirsty.

And Joel Lawrence gives Alex Stokes an eye mask, case the sun in the morning wakes him up.

Joel stops at the door.

The room swims above Alex Stokes, the ceiling is swirling with parallel universes like kaleidoscopes, he is travelling very fast.

And Joel Lawrence says to Alex Stokes,

Very clearly and very slowly in a voice that is almost certainly not his own,

'I wear my earphone all the time, so that I can block out the voices.'

And then Alex Stokes falls asleep.

They don't clean up. The house has taken a proper pasting.

Alex Stokes dreams and in his dreams

Apparently

He dreams about a guitar trapped at the back of a wardrobe – and somehow he has to get it out

And he dreams about a moonlit lake.

And he walks into it, and he wades up to his waist

And he searches desperately in the icy water

But he doesn't know what he's looking for

That's how he knows he can never find it

In the morning, Mrs Lawrence comes in with a glass of orange juice and a chocolate digestive.

Alex jolts awake.

There is blue hair dye all over the sheets.

The hair dye.

And he has wet the bed.

Oh my God, so embarrassing.

The sheets are ruined.

And last night – with the puking –

They never even cleared it up.

Is this the worst day?

No.

Mrs Lawrence puts the orange juice down.

And says

'Are you OK?'

Mrs. Lawrence isn't angry. She says he can stay as long as he likes. She hovers in the doorway.

'Are things OK at home?'

Alex Stokes tries to convince himself that even though he dyed her pillows blue and plastered her lounge with puke and is lying in his own cold piss, the sexual attraction between them is mutual.

Mrs Lawrence makes scrambled eggs, butcher's sausages, Portobello mushrooms, thick rashers of bacon.

Joel Lawrence wants to play guitar some more, maybe watch some Netflix.

Alex Stokes leaves after eating.

He's got a lunch date with Ateeq Javid. They're working on an idea for a graphic novel.

Before leaving, Alex Stokes masturbates in the toilet imagining Joel Lawrence's mum in the next room.

*

Is this Year Nine?

Probably.

Yeah, OK, so Mark Beevers shows up after summer.

Basically right – his dad gets this girlfriend who cooks all this Caribbean food.

Now he smells of goat curry.

Instead of dairy.

Mark Beevers is gaining weight.

Somebody has to talk to him.

He's turning into a fat kid.

Not an option.

Considering his recent transition to full pizza face.

His ongoing sticky-out ears.

Even behind the drums

Not an option.

Fat would be three strikes.

Nobody says this to his face, but somehow Mark Beevers finds out what we

Specifically Alex Stokes

Are saying about him.

Didn't Celine Cheng take that exact bus.

Yeah.

Anyway, Mark Beevers goes on a strict diet.

He forsakes the jerk chicken and the goat curry and the oxtail stew.

He forsakes the ackee and saltfish. The rice 'n' peas, the hard foods.

He forsakes the fish stew, and the coconut bread.

His dad is well needy. The girlfriend packs her bags.

Some nights, Mark Beevers hears his dad crying in the next room.

And Mark Beevers cries too. He cries for his lost meals.

But he gets back to band weight.

*

It's summer. The weather is beautiful

But we are revising.

Exams terrify us.

We talk about how we don't care.

We talk about how little we revised.

How we never listened in lessons.

But even Darren Northcote's beautiful eyes show fear.

We talk about the last horrifying hours before we hand in our coursework.

How shit it is.

Very very shit.

Oh my God!

We text each other.

Text back straight away.

No way!

We dream of escape.

But the trap was set years ago.

From the first day we ever went to school.

There is no way out.

Some of us have worked hard for years.

Some of us have basically done nothing.

Some of us say that we've done nothing when really we have worked hard for years.

Our parents are *obsessed* with our revision.

Why don't they get a life of their own?

They watch us from the minute we get in.

It is like a police state.

Stasi.

They take away our phones and our laptops and our TVs.

Stop us going out.

Even on Saturdays.

We make detailed revision timetables.

This is prison.

We encounter whole subjects for the first time.

Chemistry. History. Geography.

We read our textbooks for the first time, thinking . . .

Oh, so *this* is what this is about! That makes so much more sense.

And sometimes we actually *like* reading our textbooks.

And we think wow, I'd really like to do a course in this subject someday.

Like study it.

We stare into space.

We stare at clocks.

And walls.

We stare at pets.

We stare at carpets.

And duvet covers.

We stare into mirrors.

For the first time ever, we're jealous of younger siblings.

And older siblings.

Jealous of anybody not our age.

Which is the worst age anybody could possibly be.

Because of our exams.

Summer is poison.

If we are good at school

If we are rubbish at school

It doesn't matter who you are.

Exams come for everyone.

Society *will* put its stamp on you. There's nothing you can do to avoid it.

The headmistress takes a sudden interest in us.

Calls us by first names in the corridor.

Everybody talks about how much these exams matter.

For our futures.

For the school.

So why aren't we working?

We can't work.

Because we think about why we don't work.

Instead of working.

Time is running out.

Our parents get us sandwiches and biscuits and cups of tea.

They promise Augusts beyond our wildest imaginations.

If we get 'A's.

Everybody else is working. But we're not working.

We're staring

At clocks.

And walls.

And pets.

At carpets.

And duvet covers.

We're staring into mirrors.

*

Mark Beevers' physical transformations: part two.

Term before exams. Mark Beevers grows almost two feet.

Suddenly, he's six three.

His skin clears up.

His voice goes super low.

He develops a strong jawline

And stubble.

His hazel eyes are revealed as ridiculously beautiful.

His ears still sticky-outy – but . . .

Nobody ever got fitter at that accelerated rate before.

Seriously.

In one term, he starts getting off with all of the fit girls in the year below.

Emma Bevan. Lily Caldwell. Rianhan Matthews.

All certified foxes.

Charlotte Randle and Celine Cheng put Mark Beevers in the top three of the school.

Mark Beevers even becomes mates with Christian Mbulu.

He plays football on Tuesday lunchtimes with Christian Mbulu and Darren Northcote and Nick Carter.

He scores goals with headers

Something he thought he would never ever do.

And we watch them

All the girls watch them

They're magnificent

Alex Stokes worries that now Mark Beevers is getting so fit, him and Lauren McIntyre is inevitable.

Because Lauren McIntyre gets off with everybody that term.

Things are bad that term.

And Alex thinks things will get better.

Because things always get better in time.

But things are about to get way way worse.

He's about to get braces

Since that night with Joel Lawrence, he backed off – stuck to backing vocals.

The band play opening spots at rubbish pubs across town.

Usually disastrously, twice with almost no shame involved.

Nobody from school goes.

Whenever he sings, the crowd are dazzled by his braces.

And Joel Lawrence tells him not to worry, because that sort of thing isn't the end of the world.

But it actually is the end of the world.

Because at lunchtimes now, Christian Mbulu and Lauren McIntyre meet at the outside basketball court.

Alex Stokes watches them from the classroom window.

Point shots. Lauren McIntyre makes every basket. It's like the old days.

Christian Mbulu laughs in that beautiful way he has. And Lauren McIntyre giggles, you can see all her dimples.

And Christian Mbulu touches her on the small of her back when she gets a shot.

And their fingers brush against each other.

And they make each other laugh.

Just like Christian Mbulu and Alex Stokes used to laugh in class.

But how could it really be *that* funny?

And nobody else is ever invited to basketball.

And when Christian Mbulu walks beside Lauren McIntyre down the drive to school, he seems so happy that his walk is a beautiful poetry.

Lauren McIntyre starts making more effort with her appearance.

More make-up.

Starts smoking Camel Lights and listening to techno music.

Techno?

Christian Mbulu introduces her to more tunes – techno is after all his favourite type of music.

They go to a big club in town where no one from school has ever got in, and they get in even though Lauren McIntyre is basically a dwarf.

Alex Stokes tells Lauren McIntyre that Christian Mbulu is gay because once he had an erection in the showers after football and she just looks at Alex Stokes like he is weird, which he is.

Alex Stokes is in the multi-media lab. Vikram Kapadia solemnly informs him,

'Christian Mbulu walked Lauren McIntyre on to the playing fields at lunchtime after basketball and fingered her.'

It's like getting stabbed in the heart.

And stabbed again.

And it stabs Alex Stokes every time he wakes up in the morning.

Black day follows black day.

They're a couple now.

They're going out for one week

They're going out for two weeks

Apparently she –

Then three weeks

Then four weeks

Apparently, they –

And it's carrying on

When will it stop?

Because every second is agony.

Because it should be *him* with Lauren McIntyre.

Songs pour out of Alex Stokes. He doesn't write them, they just happen.

All he has to do is pick up the guitar. They are given to him.

He plays guitar all weekend. He limits time with his family to brisk dinnertimes.

Anyway, they don't like his music.

At all.

One night, an argument escalates.

Alex Stokes' mother breaks a dining chair on his back.

Mr Desmond invites Alex Stokes into his office at breaktime. And asks him

'Are you having problems at home?'

But even though Alex Stokes can write so many lyrics, and songs, and is so creative

It is very hard to answer that question.

*

Jeffrey Ferris' party.

Christian Mbulu is well pissed off with Alex Stokes for blabbing about his football boner with his girlfriend behind his back.

Christian Mbulu orders Alex Stokes not to come to Jeffrey Ferris' party.

And Christian Mbulu spreads it round that when Alex Stokes went to stay with him in Year Eight, he wet the bed twice.

In fact, it was only once.

Jeffrey Ferris invited Alex Stokes so if he doesn't go to the party, he'll look weak.

If he goes, he'll get beaten up by Christian Mbulu.

And Lauren Mcintyre is going to be there, and everybody is talking about how well Christian and Lauren have been getting along – and maybe people are thinking this could be one of those legendary school romances that become known in other years of the school. And people are talking about how Lauren McIntyre is going to shag Christian Mbulu at the party and even though that's the thing that will most hurt Alex Stokes in the world somehow it means Alex Stokes is compelled to witness it first hand and so he has to go to the party no matter what.

Jeffrey Ferris' massive house. Massive garden. Massive swimming pool. Massive television screen in every massive room.

Jeffrey Ferris' parents are on some romantic weekend in the Maldives.

Party is heaving.

We drink whisky and listen to Kanye West's 'Monster' and pour whisky in the fish tank so all the tropical fish float to the bottom.

We do a massive kung-fu kick and shatter the glass doors leading on to the garden.

We find Jeffrey Ferris' mum's bedside drawer and there are sex toys and crotchless panties and so we wear his mum's sexy knickers on our heads.

We steal Jeffrey Ferris' mum's camera which costs almost a thousand pounds.

We break the screen of Jeffrey Ferris' dad's tablet.

And when Alex Stokes gets there, Jeffrey Ferris opens the door to him, and kicks his head in.

And people say the only reason Alex Stokes still has teeth in his mouth, is the braces.

Alex Stokes is on the ground. One eye half closed.

He watches Lauren McIntyre kiss Christian Mbulu hello, link arms with him, and walk away together to join the party.

Joel Lawrence goes home with Alex in a taxi because he isn't enjoying the party much either.

That's the night Lauren McIntyre loses her virginity to Christian Mbulu.

*

So the band are playing gigs in pubs.

But like we said

Nobody from school goes.

So we don't know nothing about those really

Except Alex Stokes tells Ateeq Javid

'Yeah, sometimes, in rehearsals, it's better when Joel Lawrence doesn't turn up.'

Because he's started not turning up

He isn't turning up to school much then

He's hanging round with the kids from the graveyard

See when he turns up, truth is the music never gels.

Apparently

Just being honest, yeah

It goes on like this for a long time.

And without being nasty

Or disloyal

In any way

And giving careful consideration to Joel Lawrence's feelings

Alex Stokes consults with the other band members.

And even though they're fundamentally loyal to Joel Lawrence

And it's not like they won't stay friends.

They agree that he should be asked to leave the band immediately

So Alex Stokes goes up to Joel Lawrence

At the bus stop

Alex Stokes says Joel will always be important to the band

The problem is there are

Let's face it

Musical differences.

Joel looks into his eyes for like too long

A minute? Says finally

'Musical differences?'

And in those lakes of eyes are other worlds that Alex Stokes knows nothing about, parallel universes that terrify Alex Stokes.

And Joel Lawrence says:

'You can't sack me, Alex. It's my band.'

Alex Stokes arranges a rehearsal without Joel. The sound immediately gains new muscularity and vigour.

Joel Lawrence doesn't come back to school again that week. Or that month.

Or ever again in fact.

Now he goes to some sixth-form college down the road.

Oh yeah, Charlotte Randle told Mark Beevers. She'd heard from her mum.

So the story is Joel was heartbroken about Stacy Calder getting back together with Darren Northcote. So that's why he dropped out of school.

Which can no way be right.

Nah.

Because Joel never even mentions Stacy Calder, and anyway Stacy Calder is always either with Darren Northcote or Nick Carter.

So what does he expect?

Alex Stokes doesn't see Joel Lawrence for ages.

One day, out of the blue, Alex Stokes' mum says he should visit Joel Lawrence because Joel Lawrence has not been feeling well.

Alex is well excited about seeing Mrs Lawrence again.

There are bags under her eyes. She has some grey hairs.

Joel Lawrence looks at him morosely from a black leather armchair.

Conversation runs along predictable lines.

Joel Lawrence stares at the wall and listens to music on his iPod while they talk.

They don't have anything to say to each other. They never ever had.

Joel is forming another band. A completely new direction – ska.

His dad took him to see the re-formed Specials.

He's investigating personnel.

This band's going to be tight. No solos. None of that grunge shit.

Mrs Lawrence invites Alex Stokes to stay for dinner

Lasagne

Because she remembered he liked it before

Alex Stokes goes home after dinner, and he eats his mother's dinner too.

*

It's about then Lauren McIntyre and Stacy Calder become mortal enemies. Lauren McIntyre just bought two expensive bras and Stacy Calder stays at Lauren McIntyre's, and somehow one of her bras is missing, but Stacy Calder knows nothing about it − she *claims* − so the next weekend, Lauren McIntyre stays at Stacy Calder's and while Stacy Calder is in the shower, Lauren McIntyre goes through her drawer and finds the bra that got stolen and after that at school, she just stops speaking to Stacy Calder or even acknowledging her existence and Stacy Calder says to everybody:

'I've got bigger boobs, how would her bra fit me anyway?'

And Lauren McIntyre isn't popular like Stacy Calder so now people who would never have said anything bad to her say bad things to her, because Lauren McIntyre is tiny so there's nothing to be scared of anyway and in the changing rooms after PE, Lauren McIntyre is putting on her bra, and Celine Cheng watches her and Celine Cheng says:

'If you didn't have feet, would you wear socks?'

And everybody cracks up, and Lauren McIntyre doesn't even understand for about ten seconds and she even starts to laugh a bit too until she sees that the joke is on her.

*

Year Thirteen. Advert on the noticeboard.

'New singer required for best rock band in school history.'

Darren Northcote says he's up for it.

Darren Northcote?!

No, think about it. After his football injury, Darren likes to wear band T-shirts at weekends, and went to a T in the Park festival with his older brother, Kevin Northcote, a certified giant.

Nick Carter also signs up for auditions.

The two best-looking boys in the year.

Both amazing athletes.

Head to head.

To be the singer.

In theory they're best friends – but the wounds inflicted by six years competing for Stacy Calder run deep.

Now Alex Stokes and Mark Beevers and Cathy Genovese are invited to the best parties.

Auditions are in the multimedia lab.

Darren Northcote has a beautiful face – but from those bee-stung lips comes a voice of murderous ugliness.

He shows Cathy and Alex some of the poetry he writes. It is terrible.

He talks about bands they all like, but he makes them sound boring.

Everybody has the same strange realisation

Darren Northcote *is* boring, he possesses absolutely no mystique or charisma whatsoever.

Nick Carter turns up looking preppy.

Before the audition, he barely speaks. He has the same determined look he has just before a race.

His performance is electrifying.

He is a natural frontman.

Alex Stokes offers him the job on the spot.

They play the set, while Darren Northcote waits outside the multimedia lab, waiting for the penny to drop in his boring mind.

And the band members feel something for the first time

This feeling, which is almost religious it is so intense.

Which is the feeling that comes when you work really hard at something

And it works

When together you make something really special

Nick Carter.

Alex Stokes.

Cathy Genovese.

Mark Beevers.

This was the line-up they'd been waiting for all along.

Mark Beevers' dad asks to manage the band. The band decline.

Thing is – Mark Beevers' dad is a good roadie.

When they play pub gigs, Mark Beevers' dad takes the drums, picks up the rest of the members and their equipment, loads their amps into his car, drives them to the venue, loads the stuff into the venue, sets it all up, tunes the guitars, runs the sound check, loads the equipment back into his car, buys the band members a celebratory pint, drops them home generally pissed out of their skulls.

He was a great roadie. Why have him as the manager?

*

They play a new bar called Moonrise Kingdom.

Afterwards, the venue transitions into a club night.

Best night out in town –

Notorious for its strict door policy.

You can see the gig and get into the club on the same ticket.

Anyway, Nick Carter is in the band, so all the girls are coming.

The boys in love with the girls in love with Nick Carter therefore have to be there.

The band rehearse every day for two weeks.

Nick Carter is not your typical rock singer.

He is obedient.

He served in the school's cadet force, his psychology was forged in team sports.

When Alex Stokes or Cathy Genovese make observations about him −

Well, criticisms −

He listens conscientiously. The next rehearsal, the mistake is eliminated.

Alex Stokes and Cathy Genovese get Nick Carter to stop shaving, and they take him shopping.

Nick Carter says what Alex Stokes wants him to say between the songs

Cathy Genovese worries to Alex Stokes that the crowd will sniff Nick Carter out as a fake

But every time they worry about Nick Carter, somehow Nick Carter manages to raise his game and prove them wrong a thousand times over.

Alex Stokes wakes up with a terrible foreboding about the gig that night.

Everybody is coming.

That afternoon, he passes Joel Lawrence busking in town.

Joel has dyed his hair

Playing the song they used to cover in Year Ten

First time Alex Stokes ever went to Joel Lawrence's house

And they grin hello at each other

Very warm actually

And Alex gives him a thumbs-up

But Alex is in a hurry

In fact, he wasn't really in a hurry

So he doesn't stop to chat

But he could have, because he was actually just going to look at clothes.

It just isn't the moment OK?

Even though he's not seen him for over six months

And because he was in such a hurry, Alex Stokes gives him his thumbs-up

A very warm thumbs-up

And walks past.

And Joel Lawrence carries on singing.

That night at the gig, Alex Stokes knows in his gut that the gig will go badly.

He has a really bad feeling

The band is snapping at each other. They can't agree on anything.

Mark Beevers is pissed and he always speeds up when he's pissed.

Stage time nine-thirty

Second up.

They look good, better than we remembered

And Nick Carter is at peak fitness.

And Mark Beevers is also at peak fitness

And Cathy Genovese is of course possessed of her unique unassailable cool

And Alex Stokes looks

As good as he is ever going to look

And the music is authoritative

Undeniable.

And the lyrics are about our lives

About school

About love

And heartbreak

About everything we fear

About everything we want to be

And about everything we will never be

The band feel like they're ours

The songs – it seems like we have always known them.

And we don't want to be Stacy Calder any more, we want to be Cathy Genovese

And Stacy Calder doesn't want to be Stacy Calder any more, she wants to be Cathy Genovese.

They shouldn't go to university. They should go to London – and get famous.

Backstage after three encores, they can hear the crowd chanting the name of the band. Nick Carter wraps Mark

Beevers and Cathy Genovese and Alex Stokes into a group hug, like they're in the dressing room after a sports game. He says what a great team they make together.

And when Nick Carter says that, for the first time, it feels like they belong.

And for the first time ever, they feel no shame in just being themselves.

Because life is good and true and it will give them everything they want if they work hard and are patient and are kind to people.

Christian Mbulu congratulates Alex Stokes on the gig. They talk about a film they watched in Year Eight.

The management people at the pub book them in a superior slot for next week.

Vikram Kapadia offers to record them for free on Logic Pro Ten.

Lauren McIntyre smokes outside.

She sees Alex Stokes

They have a stupid conversation

Some episode of *Family Guy* Alex Stokes likes

Which Lauren McIntyre says is her favourite

And

They

Are

So

Near

To

Each

Other

And

Alex Stokes

Thinks

He

Will

Probably

Faint

Because

The

Moment

That

He's been waiting

For

And dreaming about

And let's be honest

Wanking about

Since that party in Year Nine

Finally

Comes

Lauren McIntyre tells Alex Stokes to meet her by the canal.

Alex Stokes

Borrows a condom from

Nick Carter

And

Nothing was ever as beautiful to Alex Stokes

As that fifteen minutes

When the world shifted on its axis

When he was transformed

And he spent his whole life chasing after

Anything that could compare

To that fifteen minutes

On the canal path

With Lauren McIntyre

But the chase would be in vain.

Mark Beevers gets off with Shanika Samarasinghe. They are boyfriend and girlfriend.

Alex Stokes gets in the taxi home. Two boys from the year below are singing the chorus to one of his songs.

Alex Stokes' parents are still up. Sitting at the kitchen table.

They want to know if Joel Lawrence has called him.

*

Alex gets his braces off on the morning of Joel Lawrence's funeral.

Apparently

Joel Lawrence was having some problems

That's why he'd changed school.

And recently Joel Lawrence had been acting weird.

Sleeping in the day

Walking round at nights

Singing

He never ate.

Sometimes he was very angry, and he smashed things for no reason

Sometimes he didn't come back home at nights

Mrs Lawrence didn't know what to do

And on the night of the gig, Mrs Lawrence came home and Joel Lawrence wasn't in the house and he hadn't taken his phone.

Which was weird because he always took his phone.

It is cold and frosty.

It is a full moon.

Apparently

He walks barefoot through town.

He walks fifteen miles along the hard shoulder of a motorway.

He walks the next day and the next night.

People see him throwing branches at passing cars.

And shouting angrily although nobody can see what he's shouting at

He walks until on the third night, he sees a farm, with a light in the hearth.

Next to it, a beautiful frozen lake, glittering in the moonlight.

And he walks into the middle of that frozen lake. And he drowns.

*

After the funeral, Alex Stokes goes to the reception at Mrs Lawrence's house.

Alex Stokes meets Joel Lawrence's dad. His face is like a perfect moon.

Mr Lawrence ushers Alex into Joel's old room.

Mrs Lawrence hovers near the door.

Mr Lawrence has blue eyes, just like Joel Lawrence.

He says

'I just want to know what Joel was really like.'

And Alex Stokes doesn't know what to say.

And Mrs Lawrence does a little laugh, and says

'Come on, Alex, you know better than anyone – you were his best friend.

Alex and Joel were best friends.'

And Alex Stokes doesn't know what to say.

And Joel's dad says he never spent as much time with Joel as he would have liked. That he'd love to know more about what Joel was like at school, anywhere.

And Alex Stokes tries to think of something to say, but he can't think of anything. He doesn't know.

And then, he bursts into tears. And people can hear him sobbing from the next room.

And Joel Lawrence's parents comfort Alex Stokes.

Alex Stokes can feel Mrs Laurence's boobs touching the top of his head.

The rest of the guests go, Alex Stokes and Mr Lawrence listen to records all evening and drink expensive whisky.

Alex talks about Joel's favourite records – though he moves quickly on to his own favourites.

Mr Lawrence knows all about music, because he owns a small independent record shop.

For the first time, Alex Stokes hears:

'Kashmir' by Led Zeppelin

'Let Him Run Wild' by The Beach Boys

The second side of *Low* by David Bowie.

'On the Beach' by Neil Young.

'London Calling' by The Clash.

The Stranglers version of 'Walk On By'.

Kraftwerk. The Smiths. The Stone Roses. Bob Dylan.
Marvin Gaye.

Stuff he'd never heard before.

Or never thought was cool before.

Alex Stokes wishes Mr Lawrence was his dad.

It's time to go. Mr Lawrence wants to give Alex Stokes
something.

It's Joel Lawrence's Fender Jaguar guitar.

So Alex Stokes finally gets to touch Joel Lawrence's amazing
guitar.

Alex Stokes takes the guitar home, and he buries it as deep as
he can in the back of his wardrobe, and he never tells his
parents he's been given it, and he never plays even one note
on it ever.

The End.

Musical Differences

BY ROBIN FRENCH

*Notes on rehearsal and staging, drawn from a workshop with the writer,
held at the National Theatre, October 2016*

Introduction exercise

Tessa Walker, lead director, gave the group three minutes to
find out as much as they could about someone in the room
who they didn't know before. After the conversation,
everyone took a turn to introduce their partner and tell the
group something that they were good at outside of their job.

Reading the play

Doing a read-through around the circle creates a shared
understanding of the play and forms a basis for the rest of the
work. Tessa invited participants to read the play line by line
around the circle, make a note of any questions they had
about the play and list the challenges that the text presents.

The workshop group identified the following challenges (you
might identify different ones with your company):

- How to make the chorus work.

- Creation and changes of location.

- Identifying the focal point of each bit of the story.

- Making sure that the story is clear.

- Pacing.

- How to bring music or musicality to the piece.

- Knowing how much is direct address and how much is
  among the characters onstage/dialogue.

- How to make the characters of the band exist when we
  don't see them on stage.

- Making clear the reality in which the characters tell the story – is it grounded in reality or is it an exploration of a shared dream, or something else?

- Maintaining the focus of the audience through the telling of the story.

- How to split up and assign the text.

- How to approach issues like self-harm, suicide and sex with young people.

- Shifts between poetic language and everyday language.

- Telling the story simply, but with theatricality.

Question and answer with the playwright

I love the play because of how it moves – how it's mapped according to the changes that teenagers experience. I think we can all identify with and remember those changes. How was it for you to hear it?

ROBIN FRENCH   'While you're writing something you're completely immersed, but once you've handed it in you tend to half forget about it. So it's exciting to meet it again and feel its impact like someone who doesn't know it. I don't think I realised how much of my life is in it before now.'

When you wrote it, did you imagine it in a theatre or in real life?

'I imagined it in a theatre. The characters address the audience directly so I always imagined a group of people being there listening and watching. In fact, there's a moment when they refer directly to someone in the audience. That's an important moment because it makes that relationship clear.'

Are the audience literally an audience? Or an imaginary group, like for example other kids at their school?

'It can be either.'

What we know for sure is that it's one group of people telling another group of people something. Beyond that fact, you can make your own choices.

'I think a big question here is who is getting to tell the story. It's like when something has happened to both you and a friend at the same time, then when you listen to your friend telling the anecdote and it's not your version of the story and you're like, "No, hang on." '

What's the space in time between chapters? Are the characters talking about something that's just happened?

'Time is an illusion in the play. It's designed in a way that feels good, not in a very logical way. A bit like an optical illusion.'

Did you picture certain characters telling the story when you imagined it?

'No. I feel excited to find out who the characters are that are telling the story. I felt like I heard certain characters starting to appear when I heard it read. I like the idea that different productions will make different choices and create different worlds.'

What ages did you imagine the characters?

'I was told the actors could be thirteen to nineteen for Connections, but I don't mind how old the characters are. It's tied to the time thing because in the play they grow and change but we don't have to see that for real.'

Did you always imagine it would be direct address?

'Yes, I always wanted it to be direct address.'

Do you have any advice on assigning lines?

'I would say experiment, and see what feels right. Some lines are funny – so give them to the funny people! But in general those choices will become clearer when you investigate who the characters are telling the story.'

Why did you write this particular story?

'I started thinking about what life really felt like when I was a teenager. I was in a school band so maybe that's where that came from. I was also fascinated by the first-person plural ('we') as a way to tell a story. I loved how it was used in novel *The Virgin Suicides*.'

What was your band name?

'The first one, when I was twelve, was called "Paralytic Rhino", but there were lots of incarnations with different names all the way through until I left school.'

How honest do you think the speakers are? Do they exaggerate or lie? Is Joel Lawrence's death a mythological version or what actually happened?

'That is constantly at play. There's a moment when someone says, "I'm the primary source." What's the story? What do they agree happened? One of the ways the play will have movement is seeing the fight over what the shared story is.'

How would you recommend tackling swear words or sexual language with younger actors or if you anticipate parents having a problem with it?

'If you feel you absolutely can't include certain words, I would always prefer finding an alternative way of expressing the same idea, instead of cutting the line. But this should be a last resort.'

Based on this discussion, Tessa categorised the questions and challenges into the following:

• Those relating to text and storytelling.
• Those relating to staging.

The following group exercises responded to these challenges.

Actioning exercise

Tessa suggested it is useful to discover the action of the line when working on the script with actors of any age and level of experience. This means designating specific verbs to each line or character thought, to give the actor a tactic that their character is employing when they say a line.

Why are they speaking, what do they want to *do* with the words? What is their intention towards each other and/or the audience – e.g. to provoke, to encourage, to illuminate? This can make what you're doing with each line very precise and it's also liberating because there are an infinite number of choices you can make. You may find it useful to include your actors in the process of choosing actions – to give them ownership of the text. It's also a good tool for you to use in your preparation for a scene, especially if you feel stuck on a particular section, or a section is feeling generalised.

In this play, the action can be described as telling us a story, but *why* are they telling us? What does each character want to achieve by telling us? How does this give clues to what they want to do with each line?

The participants formed groups of three and took a page of text each. They read the scene and gave each line an action. Groups shared what they worked on by first reading the action they had chosen and then reading the line.

Some reflections on the exercise:

- There is a difference between self-reflexive words like 'fantasising', which describe the state of the person who is talking, and words which direct the actor to do something to someone else on stage, like 'to provoke'. Both could be useful to you but note how much more active the latter is.

- There are so many ways that you want to individually interpret a line and it's exciting to be reminded of how many choices there are.

- The word 'fantasise' came up a few times. This might be an interesting route into the play.

Reflections on the play and its form

Tessa reflected on the story of the play and its form as a piece of direct address storytelling, i.e. a piece that works by one

group of people (performers) directly talking to another group
of people (audience).

TESSA WALKER   'The audience is like another character
because you can't tell the story without them. There's
something about really being told a story that you can't beat.
Why are they telling this story to *us*, *now*? How do they tell us
to make it feel urgent and relevant to us now?

'When you're a teenager and someone you know dies it is
profound and suicide is more complex. Along the way there's
a possibility that you contributed to the circumstances in
which that person died, and that stays with you. Something
about the exploration of that in the play is important. It's not
as much about a band as the suicide of a young man. This is
a momentous thing to happen in a group of young people.

'It could be told with everyone standing in a line very simply
and without music, or it could be told with huge transitions
and changes of location, but the relationship with the
audience is key.

'Directing is a very autobiographical process and you have to
bring yourself to it. I used to think writing was autobiographical
and directing wasn't. But now I realise that the difference
between a moment working for you and not working for you
is all about what you are bringing of yourself to the play.'

Splitting up the text exercise

The group was split into three and explored the following
exercises as a way of splitting up the text. Each group looked
at staging pages 254 to 257 and then shared what they found.
The notes below each exercise are a selection of responses
from the rest of the group to what was shared.

Group One DIVIDED UP THE THREE PAGES OF TEXT BY
ASSIGNING TEXT ACCORDING TO A SENSE OF CHARACTER

It was great. It came alive.

You can see character in the amount that someone has to say

When the group shared specific words it felt like they were a team. It felt like a useful way to 'play the positive', and avoid falling into 'sarcastic teenager' mode.

It felt like the characters know each other well.

Having one main storyteller helped make the story clear.

Point of view felt very important. One of them really didn't like Alex Stokes so took any negative lines about Alex.

Maybe there is a journey where at the beginning there is one main storyteller, and as it develops more people become co-opted into the storytelling or take more responsibility for it.

What is the character motivation for that person telling the story in that moment? Why are they communally and individually telling the story? There can be individual reasons for why each character is telling the story (e.g. I want everyone to know that Alex Stokes is an idiot) as well as a bigger group objective.

The desire to tell someone something is what makes people listen – it feels necessary. The events that happen are important to the people telling us. It's up to you to work on why.

Group Two EXPLORED VARIETY IN THE NUMBER OF PEOPLE SPEAKING, SOMETIMES ONE PERSON, TWO, THREE, ETC.

Speaking together in cannon was effective. The overlapping of everyone saying the band names was effective and everyone discussing the reasons Alex was hot.

It presented opportunities for chaos, which felt truthful to a teenage experience.

It was a sign of familiarity.

'He's not hot' – when everyone said it together – felt like a totally shared opinion.

ROBIN FRENCH   'There are certain sections that seem more obviously written to be choric but I really liked hearing other bits done in a choric way too. It's about exploring the relationship between the communal and individual, which is really important in the play.

'Who is speaking, how much they speak, what lines they get – all choices that contribute to the story and relationships that exist between the characters.'

Group Three DIVIDED THE TEXT INTO THREE MONOLOGUES

It was the most comical.

There's a joy in hearing somebody interrupt themselves.

Self-contradictions are really funny.

It suggests something has happened either in the character's head or in a response from the audience that means they have to change their mind.

It's a way of being playful with the text.

Is there a version where there's a moment where one person finds themselves alone onstage and suddenly gets the audience to themselves?

TESSA WALKER   'On the whole actors don't find direct address easy, but it's very important for this play. Sometimes actors create a false audience, making it look like direct address but they're not actually talking to anyone. Use the people in the room! And make sure they are telling them the story with eye contact. What will stop it working is if they are not really telling the story to the audience.'

Any of the above versions could work well in combination.

Tessa asked each group to stand in front of the rest (audience) and be playful with how they used eye contact with the audience, and genuinely tell them the story. If an audience member avoided eye contact, they were invited to see it as a good challenge; if another audience member made eye contact, they could choose to play with that.

The groups then repeated their earlier scene, but this time with the challenge of making genuine eye contact with the audience.

GROUP ONE REFLECTIONS

It was harder with scripts in hands.

There was a desire to come forward, and then a need to drop back. Where do you go with that?

Everyone on stage was a character.

It looks like the characters have rehearsed the story but it began to unravel when it doesn't go how everyone wants it to go.

It was like at school when you had to pretend you already knew all the gossip. The currency of telling a story in a school is big, being the one in the know. So the audience becomes a privileged group who are getting the narrative. There are some characters who only know bits of background knowledge, they don't know the main plot, but those people still want to be seen to be in the know, so their bits of the story are important to them.

Structurally, it's a long build-up to the core event of the story and then suddenly it's gone. There's a sense of circling the main story event. Emotionally there's a reason that they don't tell you right away. They need to work out how to be able to talk about it and maybe this audience can help them work out how to tell it.

ROBIN FRENCH   'I think this is really key. When something awful has happened to you, sometimes the first time you cry is when you tell someone else. That's the exact energy in the play. Telling this story is a hard thing for the characters to do.'

TESSA WALKER   'Staging – the line between the actors and the audience is very thin and this means you can be really adventurous with staging. How do you make sure the actors can be connected to the audience?'

GROUP TWO REFLECTIONS

Having to physically move past or through someone else on stage in order to connect with the audience was fun. Focusing on a certain audience member can be very effective. The group became playfully competitive with one another. It was really good fun to watch those games amongst the performers.

The act of telling is so important. In the simple act of telling, character and self is being revealed without setting psychological or logical decisions about who people are playing. It means very instinctive choices are happening just through the simple task of having to tell the story and be honest about how it feels.

GROUP THREE REFLECTIONS

It was spikey – there was more competition. Where are the power positions on the stage? The negotiation of the power positions became a part of the story. The stage felt like a dangerous place to be – like school.

When do you want to create an atmosphere of judgement amongst the storytellers and when are they complicit with one another?

Can the actors be co-operating while the characters are competing?

Using monologue made the stakes higher. It feels older. Can you track the characters' ages through using how much people say at a time? When are the characters comfortable enough to be the focus of attention? Does the line between complicity and competition shift over the course of the telling?

There's an age when genders mix well, and an age when they don't. Maybe we see that develop over the course of the play.

TESSA WALKER 'The number of speakers on stage really shifts the tone. It's in your gift as directors to decide who does what. If you need seventeen people to leave the stage because it's time for someone's monologue then they can just do it, they don't need an excuse to do it. It doesn't need to be explained.'

'What happens when three people are monologuing and the whole rest of the chorus is onstage? What's the relationship between a non-speaking chorus and a speaking chorus?'

Exploring speaking and non-speaking ensembles

The groups experimented with putting a character from the band onstage with the storytellers or played with separating the speaking chorus from a non-speaking chorus. The notes that follow each instruction are thoughts from the group.

ONE ACTOR PLAYED ALEX, EVERYONE ELSE WAS A
STORYTELLER

ROBIN FRENCH   'I specified in the production notes that we shouldn't see Alex or the main characters onstage. I think that was right. This exercise felt to me like having two TVs on at once. I struggled to see the story of the group politics because everything was focused on Alex Stokes. I think it's way more powerful for us to imagine our own version of Alex Stokes.'

The importance of surnames in storytelling became clear – is it about familiarity, gossip, specificity?

When Alex was there in the scene, we felt as an audience that we weren't being spoken to as clearly; there was less of a connection.

THE STORYTELLER PLAYING ALEX CHANGED
Each time Alex was mentioned, the storyteller became Alex.

This version also detracts from the relationship with the storytellers and the audience. Tessa's instinct was to resist the temptation to act things out at the expense of telling the story.

TWO ACTORS TOLD THE STORY
while everyone else was a non-speaking chorus

There was an interesting effect of creating allegiances, or gangs. Two influential forces driving the story and depending on who is onstage, the non-speaking characters raise the stakes, how do they respond? How do you show whose side they're on?

TESSA WALKER   'It feels important that you make a clear decision about who the actors are in relation to the audience. Be playful with how you choose to start the play, that's when you signal to an audience what the relationship with them will be like. Do you see the kids peeping out from behind the curtains, for example? How do you establish that they have a direct relationship?'

Tonal differences

The group worked on exercises to explore tonal differences in the language. Robin and Tessa identified some sections where the storytelling is in the 'we' voice, rather than the 'I' voice. It was useful to explore how the two were different.

The sections they chose were:

Pages 297–300: the exam revision section

Pages 284–286: the driving test section

Pages 274–275: the 'some of us are gay, some of us are cutting ourselves' section.

ROBIN FRENCH   'When I wrote them, I felt like these sections were sort of like the chorus. I imagined lots of people saying the lines at the same time. I think that gives a really interesting energy. That isn't a rule, but I would love people to explore how the text itself can feel musical, by playing with how many people are speaking.'

The groups made decisions about which bits were spoken in unison and which were independent, or anything in between (e.g. two or three people speaking).

Some reflections

There was a shared experience in these moments that felt different from other sections we've looked at when there's more push-and-pull or competition.

It was satisfying to hear the number of voices build as sentiments are repeated or re-enforced.

Hearing several people speak the same line cultivated various attitudes towards the same event.

It became clear that the storytellers are not the cool kids – they are the group talking about the cool kids. The difference between the cool kids and not-cool kids being that the cool kids are the main characters involved in this extraordinary story, whereas the storytellers are not the cool kids, but they are together.

The anonymity of the social media section was presented as one monotonous voice and everyone on stage facing different ways. This was interesting because they felt unified, defiant in their refusal to single out any individual for the audience's attention.

TESSA WALKER   'There is a lot of mileage in simple storytelling, playing with spatial rules like proximity. Simple choices that make the most of the relationship between actors and audience will serve you well.'

From a workshop led by Tessa Walker
with notes by James Blakey

Extremism
by Anders Lustgarten

The police just took Jamal away. Because Miss Tomlinson called them. Because she had to. Because of Prevent. But now Miss Tomlinson and the police are gone, and all that's left is a shell-shocked class. Who knew Jamal? What did he do? And what is gonna happen next? A play about fear, friendship and the creeping polarisation of our society.

Cast size
10 (5f, 5m, some gender changes possible)

Anders Lustgarten won the inaugural Harold Pinter Playwright's Award for *If You Don't Let Us Dream We Won't Let You Sleep* at the Royal Court Theatre Downstairs. His play *The Seven Acts of Mercy*, about Caravaggio and violent compassion, was at the Royal Shakespeare Company from November 2016 to February 2017. He adapted David Peace's *The Damned United* for the West Yorkshire Playhouse. His play about the current refugee crisis, *Lampedusa*, had two runs at the Soho Theatre and at HighTide. His play *The Secret Theatre*, about mass surveillance, will be staged at Shakespeare's Globe. He has also developed original projects for TV and radio.

Characters

Kirsty
Melina
Jordan
Darren
Suhayla
Evan
Rachel
Chris
Samuel
Olive

A classroom. Now. A door bangs loudly behind someone.

The rest of the class stares after the boy who was just escorted out of the door. A long moment. Everybody looks at everybody else. Pause.

Kirsty It might not be.

Melina It might not be?!

Kirsty What you think.

Jordan You don't know what I think.

Darren I know what *I* think.

Suhayla I bet you do.

Darren Peas in a pod, you two. Surprised they didn't take you with them.

Suhayla *does 'hand over yawning mouth which turns into the finger' at* **Darren**.

Suhayla *Now* you throw shade, when there's no teachers around. Big man.

Darren They'll be back for ya. Pack yer stuff.

Evan Is anybody else hungry?

Kirsty It could be nothing.

Melina Grow up, Kirsty.

Evan Cos I'm really hungry.

Rachel It's 10 a.m.

Evan I didn't have breakfast.

Rachel You sure about that? You know what they say, Evan: chips don't lie.

Chris Shut up, Rachel.

Kirsty It could be anything.

Melina   'It could be anything'?! So they just took him away for no reason? Jesus, Kirsty, the state of you.

Samuel   *yeSuS vIjatlh qengtaHbogh Duj'e' net maH. jatlh Miss Tomlinson. joH pong tlhap ropwI'qoq.* [We're not allowed to say Jesus. Miss Tomlinson said. Taking the Lord's name in vain.]

Olive   We're not allowed to say Jesus. Miss Tomlinson said. Taking the Lord's name in vain.

Evan   I'm on a diet.

Rachel   What are we allowed to say, then?

Samuel   *Shit.*

Olive   Shit.

Melina   Thanks for the translation.

Olive   Any time.

Darren   You can't say Jesus in class, but you can speak Klingon and say 'shit'. Modern life in a nutshell.

Evan   Been on it for a week now.

Rachel   You can't tell. Can we really swear in class?

Melina   I did on Wednesday and she didn't say anything.

Suhayla   Is the Klingon word for shit really 'shit'?

Samuel   *tlhIngan 'oHbe' Hol chenmoH motlh qech.* [Klingon is not a language suited to prosaic everyday concepts.]

Olive   Klingon is not a language suited to prosaic everyday concepts.

Samuel   *Qapbej net poQbej qech rur jolvoy'.* [It works better with ideas like 'transporter ioniser unit'.]

Olive   It works better with ideas like 'transporter ioniser unit'.

Kirsty   His mum might be ill.

Evan   I'm trying to get a beach body for the summer.

Rachel   You've already got one – a stranded whale's.

Olive   That is a really cruel thing to say, Rachel.

Suhayla   Specially cos you're more pint glass than hourglass yourself.

Rachel   Raghead.

Suhayla   'Scuse me?

Rachel   Can't take it, don't dish it out.

Kirsty   His dad might've been in an accident.

Melina   The Klingons have a word for 'transporter ioniser unit'?

Samuel/Olive   *'Jolvoy'*.

Melina   But not a word for shit. That is mental.

Kirsty   His dog might have died.

Suhayla   So what did they call it before they met the *Enterprise* then?

Chris   Was it an expensive dog, Kirsty?

Suhayla   Cos that must've been awkward.

Chris   A really special dog? The, like, Beyoncé of dogs?

Kirsty   I don't know about his dog, Chris.

Suhayla   'I really need a . . . '
   'What?'
   'I can't tell you yet! Where are the white space imperialists when you actually need one?'

Samuel   *Hov trek fun chenmoH DaH net poQbej mev SoH.*
[You'd better stop making fun of *Star Trek* now.]

Olive   You'd better stop making fun of *Star Trek* now.

Chris   When two police officers and your form teacher take you away, it ain't about a dog.

Suhayla   What? That's what *Star Trek* is about! It's literally a giant metaphor for American imperialism. I can't believe you don't know that.

Samuel *and* **Olive** *rise threateningly from their seats.*

Chris   This is about Prevent. Prevent just took Jamal away.

Sudden silence. **Samuel** *and* **Olive** *sit down. Everybody looks at each other. Pause.*

Kirsty   Poor Miss Tomlinson.

Rachel   I know.

Suhayla   Poor *Miss Tomlinson*?! That gimlet-eyed bitch has been sniffing all over us for weeks.

Darren   All over *you*.

Suhayla   Now they take Jamal away and you feel sorry for *her*? Nice.

Kirsty   Her face though. Pure fear.

Darren   She always looks like that.

Chris   Only when she looks at *you*.

Rachel   It's not her fault, is it? She's just doing her job.

Chris   No, Rachel, her job is to teach. Not to grass up her own pupils.

Jordan   Truth.

Melina   Who says she grassed?

Chris   Why else would they be here?

Rachel   Not her choice, is it?

Chris   How can we trust her now?

Jordan   Preach, brother.

Rachel   She has to report anything dodgy. It's the law.

Chris   She brought the *police* into our classroom!

Rachel   She's just doing what's she told.

Chris   How'm I gonna say anything in class now?

Rachel   You don't say anything anyway, Chris.

Chris   Well, I'm definitely not gonna say shit now! Who knows what some wanker teacher with an irrational grudge might do to me?

Melina   How is it an irrational grudge? You hate her.

Chris   A classroom is for teaching, man, not for spying.

Jordan   Preach!

Chris *and* **Jordan** *touch fists.* **Rachel** *shakes her head.* **Evan** *sighs deeply.*

Evan   You know what I really miss? Battenberg.

Chris   I'm keeping it zipped. No speaking in class, no coursework. Better fail than go to jail!

Rachel   Your loss.

Chris   I didn't *lose* anything, Rachel. Someone *took* it from me.

Rachel   She's only doing her *job*.

Jordan   Then she should have enough brains to do it properly and not get us into shit! Spreading rumours about us.

Darren   The police don't come for someone because of rumours.

Jordan   Don't they?

Darren   No. They don't. I know.

Suhayla   'I know.' Daddy's little boy.

Jordan   What about that kid in the terrorist house?

Suhayla   Oooh, don't say the T word, Jord. Go straight to jail, do not collect two hundred pounds.

Kirsty   What terrorist house?

Suhayla   A ten-year-old Muslim kid in Accrington tries to write, 'I live in a terraced house.' By mistake he writes, 'I live in a terrorist house.' His whole family are detained by the police.

Kirsty   Seriously?

Rachel   Spelling like that, he probably is a danger to society.

Suhayla   Funny. Till it happens to you.

Rachel   Not gonna happen to me though, is it? Because I'm not a . . .

Chris   Not a what, Rach?

Rachel   Not a terrorist, Chris. Why are you being like this?

Chris   Being like what?

Rachel   She won't give you any just for kissing her arse.

Chris   I can only agree with her if I want to shag her? Nice sisterhood there.

Rachel   Why else are you doing it then?

Chris   They just took our classmate away! That doesn't freak you out?

Rachel   He wasn't your mate, was he?

Chris   Are you really this shallow?

Rachel   Are you really this naive?

Jordan You wanna see about spreading rumours, Rachel? Let's see what happens when we spread some rumours about you.

He pulls his phone out and starts typing.

'I saw Rachel Cooke blowing Andy Thompson in the boys' lavs yesterday. No word of a lie!'

Rachel No! Don't you dare!

Melina No, Jordan.

Kirsty I don't think that's such a good –

Jordan Social experiment, innit.

He presses a button on his phone authoritatively. Several moments pass. Several phones start bleeping. The students look at them.

Chris Oh shit.

Evan I thought 'Slapper' only had one P in it? There you go. Who says you don't learn anything in school?

More phones bleep.

Kirsty Wow. Like wildfire.

Rachel *in horror as she looks at her bleeping phone.*

Rachel You wanker, Jordan. You absolute wanker.

She runs out of the room.

Melina That was so out of order.

Samuel *case HaD qaStaHvIS social media yapbe'mo' ghaH.* [That was a case study in the power of social media.]

Olive That was a case study in the power of social media.

Jordan Proved my point though.

Melina Proved *her* point.

She makes the wanker gesture at **Jordan***.*

Suhayla   This is why Prevent is so dangerous. The cuker-bum.

Kirsty   The what?

Suhayla   Look it up.

Kirsty and **Chris** *get their phones out and search. They start reading an article.*

Kirsty (*reading*)   'Staff at a nursery school threatened to refer a four-year-old boy to a de-radicalisation programme after he drew pictures which they thought showed his father making a "cooker bomb", according to the child's mother.'

Suhayla   Four. The kid was *four*.

Kirsty   'The drawing actually depicted his father cutting a cucumber, which the child referred to as a "cuker-bum", with a knife, but staff misheard his explanation and thought it referred to a type of improvised explosive device.'

Chris   Jesus.

Samuel *starts speaking Klingon.* **Chris** *holds up a hand.*

Chris   Whatever.

Suhayla   Because if you're gonna assemble an improvised explosive device, you always do it in front of your kids. Cos that's just what we're like. No regard for human life, even our own.

Chris (*reading*)   'I said to the assistant: "When you look at me, do I look like a terrorist?" And she said: "Well, did Jimmy Savile look like a paedophile?"' Yes! He did! Blatantly like a paedophile! That is literally the worst logic I've ever heard!

Evan (*dreamily*)   Dunkin' Donuts.

Darren   So why did they take him away then?

Chris   His *name* is Jamal.

Darren   Come on. If you're so clued in.

Chris   Why can't you say his name, Darren?

Darren   They're not making it up.

Suhayla   Aren't they? Seems like that's exactly what they're doing.

Darren   All those bombings are just bad dreams, yeah? All those terror threats just made up by the big bad government to scare us? Deluded. (*Turns to* **Jordan**.) He's your mate.

Jordan   No, he isn't.

Darren   Yes, he is.

Jordan   We hang out sometimes, that's all. He's not a 'mate'.

Darren   Why are you denying it? You have lunch together most days.

Melina   You do, Jordan. You sit with him almost every day.

Jordan   What are you trying to say?

Darren   What I'm trying to say is, now you've finished distracting us by making Rachel cry, maybe you can tell us a bit about your relationship with the suspect.

Suhayla   Oh my God, you are *such* a cringy little copper.

Kirsty   We're just trying to understand what's going on, Jordan.

Jordan   I don't know what's going on any more than you, Kirsty.

Melina (*holds up phone*)   Here's you and him tagged on Facebook. Yesterday. And again Tuesday.

Jordan   Are you accusing me of something, Melina?

Melina   And again . . . Woah.

Kirsty   What?

Melina   They just deleted his Facebook account.

Evan   'They'?

Melina   Someone. (*Jabbing at her phone.*) Not just his account. All the photos of him. On all our accounts. They've disappeared.

Others get out their phones too.

Suhayla   Oh shit. As the Klingons couldn't say till recently.

Chris   Any of them. With Jamal in. They're all gone.

Beat.

Samuel   *qatlh 'e' ta' chaH?* [How can they do that?]

Olive   How can they do that?

Kirsty   Maybe they didn't do it. Maybe he did it.

Melina   From the back of a police car?

Chris   They're not gonna expel you if you say his name, you know.

Melina   In handcuffs?

Kirsty   You don't know he's in handcuffs.

Chris   *His name is Jamal.*

Melina   Why do you care?

Chris   Why don't you?

Melina   I do care. I care about *us*. The group. You should be more worried about the group and less about some . . .

Chris   Some what?

Melina   Outsider. Stop putting words in our mouths, Chris.

Darren   If he didn't do it, they did it. Either way, it's not good for him.

Evan   Who is 'they'?

Suhayla   Ever heard of GCHQ?

Evan   No.

Suhayla   NSA?

Evan   Errrr . . .

Suhayla   Snowden?

Evan   Yes! I know all about it, *actually*. We climbed it last year for Duke of Edinburgh's.

Suhayla   Not Mount Snowdon. *Edward* Snowden.

Evan   Oh. Right. Never heard of him.

Suhayla   The guy who leaked all that shit about how the governments taps all our emails, all our tweets, all our Snapchats and WhatsApps and Instagrams. How they can read your browsing history for all our innermost secret desires. How they can keep every thought you've ever had on file and use them against you. For ever. You have no idea what I'm talking about, do you?

Evan   No.

Suhayla   Yeah, well, people like you don't have to.

Chris   Hang on, wait, what? The government can see all our browsing history?

Suhayla   Yep.

Chris   Including, like . . .

Suhayla   Yes, Chris.

Chris (*stage whisper*)   The porn?

Suhayla   *Everything*.

Everybody   Oh, shit.

All the boys except for **Samuel**, *plus* **Melina**, *snatch up their phones and start deleting frantically.* **Suhayla** *laughs at them.*

Jordan   Do you not . . . you know? Or is that against your, like, belief system?

Chris   Wanking is in line with everyone's belief system.

Melina   True dat.

The boys make noise.

What? Because I'm a girl? Get over yourself.

Suhayla   I use the dark web, mate.

Rachel   The what?

Suhayla   The stuff they can't trace. Anyway, it's too late. They've already got it. Whatever you've done.

The frenzy subsides into disappointment. Everybody puts their phones down. **Rachel** *storms back into the room and flounces into a chair.*

Rachel   There's graffiti about me in the girls' bogs already. You *twat*, Jordan. You could at least have picked someone better than Andy bloody Thompson. Urgh. And the police are still outside.

Melina   Where?

Rachel   Down the corridor. Talking to the head. Sounds like they're looking for others.

Beat.

Darren   'The dark web'.

Evan   I think I'm starting to hallucinate.

Darren   'The stuff they can't trace'. That's interesting.

Suhayla   You still barking, little doggie?

Evan   Lack of blood sugar.

Darren (*taps his temple*)   Store that away for later.

Suhayla   Woof woof woof.

Evan   I can see Galaxy cake bars floating in the air. As plain as I see you.

Kirsty   Evan. Not now.

Evan   I can though.

Darren   Why would he delete his account?

Suhayla   You tell me, *CSI: (name of local town)*.

Darren   Unless he had something to hide.

He turns and stares at **Jordan**. *A couple of others follow his lead.*

Jordan   How many times?! I don't really know him!

Rachel   But you do, Jordan. You sit next to him.

Melina   You eat lunch with him.

Darren   You've been to his house.

Jordan   Who told you I've been to his house?

Suhayla   His dad's a copper, Jords. Can't you tell?

Darren   You have, haven't you?

Beat. **Jordan** *nods reluctantly.*

Darren   Well? He is one, isn't he?

Suhayla   Here we go. Getting to the point now.

Darren   I know he keeps it under wraps, doesn't make a big show of it, unlike certain people.

A couple of kids look at **Suhayla**.

Darren   But he is one, yeah?

Jordan   Yes, Darren, he is a Muslim.

Darren   There we go.

Chris   What does that prove?

Melina   It is a thing, though, isn't? Like, a reason. Why they took him away. I mean, there has to be a reason why they took him away.

Jordan   All I know is he's a nice lad. I mean, how much do you really know someone? He only came here last month. Been moved from school to school a lot cos of his dad's work. I saw him wandering down the side of the playing field at lunchtime his first day, pulling leaves off the hedge and scrumpling them up into little balls for something to do. No one to talk to.

Samuel   *SoHvaD rap ta' 'e' poHlIj naDev SopwI'.* [I remember you doing that when you got here.]

Olive   Samuel remembers you doing that when you got here.

Jordan   Did I?

A couple of kids nod.

I don't remember. I just thought he could use a friend. So I went over to him.

Suhayla   And is that when he clued you in on his evil plan to blow up the entire town during Physics?

Most of the kids laugh.

Darren   Oh yeah, laugh about it.

Chris   Hey, if it gets us out of Physics, I'm in.

Suhayla (*comedy 'serious' voice*)   'Paris. Brussels. (*Name of local town.*) Where will these evil terrorists strike next?'

Darren   Yeah, go on, make a joke out of it. Because that's the whole point. That's what my dad's been saying for ages. Terrorists are moving to lower-profile targets. The lower the profile, the more likely an attack. This is the perfect place. Shopping centres. Swimming pools. Cinemas. Maybe even a school. This school. And nobody's prepared. Everyone's as clueless as you lot.

Beat as they digest this thought.

Darren   So what's he like then? Quiet?

Jordan   Yeah, I s'pose.

Darren   Bit of a loner?

Jordan   He just moved here.

Darren   A lost soul?

Jordan   What?

Darren   Did none of you read the Prevent stuff Miss Tomlinson gave us?

Melina   I did, yeah.

Kirsty   And me.

Rachel   I started, but it was really boring.

Samuel   *tera'Daq veQ flaws 'e' vItu' Homvetlh.* [I found significant flaws in it.]

Olive   Samuel found significant flaws in it.

Darren   What did the Prevent bods ask us to look out for? Loners. Outsiders. People who struggle to fit in. Here, hang on, I wrote it down.

He fishes out a notepad and reads from it.

'Someone who doesn't know who they are. Someone in search of a purpose. Someone who wants to be noticed. Someone who wants to do something special to stand out, and who might therefore be vulnerable to being radicalised.'

That's him. That is him to a T.

He sits back, impressed with himself. The rest look at each other. Beat.

Melina He's got a point, though.

Kirsty Does he?

Melina I mean, that is what he was like.

Suhayla You're not falling for this, are you?

Melina Wednesday lunchtime, right, he was whispering into his phone in the corridor, really, like, suspiciously, and when I came up behind him, he hung up really quick and gave me the proper evils.

Chris Maybe he was talking to his girlfriend?

Kirsty Does he even have a girlfriend?

Melina In, like, Arabic or whatever?

Chris Maybe his girlfriend speaks Arabic?

Suhayla Are you lot really this thick? Seriously?

Kirsty He doesn't dress like he has a girlfriend.

Rachel Definitely doesn't smell like it.

Melina I mean, not being funny, but would you?

The girls wrinkle their noses in disgust at the thought of shagging Jamal.

Samuel *latlh nuq neH defined SoH DaSov'a', Darren? teenager.* [You know what else you just defined, Darren? A teenager.]

Olive You know what else you just defined, Darren? A teenager.

Suhayla Thank you! The sadly incomprehensible voice of frigging reason.

Samuel *nuv ghaH flaws tera'Daq veQ.* [Those would be the significant flaws.]

Olive Those would be the significant flaws. That's what Samuel says, anyway. But I don't agree . . .

She says something to **Samuel** *in Klingon He shakes his head vigorously. The two have a somewhat animated conversation.*

Jordan   Nah, mate. I'm not having it. I mean, for a start, his mum's lovely. Like, really smiley and that. Amazing cook. All British food, like.

Melina   Are you saying terrorists can't have smiley mums?

Jordan   Well, yeah, as it goes, I am.

Melina   What are you basing that on, Jordan?

Jordan   Because when you watch ISIS videos, Melina, all them lads in the desert in black balaclavas ranting about 'Death to the infidel', very rarely do you see a smiley old lady in the background waving round a Bakewell tart.

Evan   Oh, why did you have to mention Bakewell tart? They are my absolute favourites.

Melina   I don't think that is correct, actually.

Jordan   I will give you a tenner if you can find an ISIS video with a Bakewell tart in it.

Evan   And again!

Melina   Not about the Bakewell tart.

Evan   And *again*!

Rachel   One more, Evan. One more cake reference, and I swear . . .

Evan   I'm trying! It's them!

Melina   About the mum. Because that's the thing, isn't it? A lot of them come from really nice, normal backgrounds. Educated. Well-spoken. That's why they're so hard to spot.

Jordan   And you know this because?

Melina   Because it's well known. Because unlike you, Jordan, I have respect for other people and their needs.

Jordan   Would George agree with that? Cos I'm not sure he would.

Rachel   Oi oi. What's all this?

Melina   Nice. Bring my boyfriend into it. Stay classy, Jordan.

Jordan   You were the one who didn't call me, Melina.

Evan   I've lost it now, what are we talking about?

Rachel   Tarts again, apparently.

Darren   You watch a lot of ISIS videos, do you Jordan?

Jordan   Is this what you think your dad sounds like at work, Daz? Cos I bet *he* doesn't sound like an outtake from *Life on Mars*.

Darren   'All them lads in the desert in black balaclavas.'

Jordan   *Everybody* watches ISIS videos.

Darren   I don't.

Melina   I don't.

Rachel   I don't.

Chris   I do.

All eyes turn to him.

What? It's on my Twitter feed.

Darren   ISIS videos are on your Twitter feed?

Chris   All kind of shit is on my Twitter feed. I like to be informed.

Rachel   Except in class.

Melina   You watch people getting their heads chopped off? Jihadi John and all that?

Chris   Sometimes.

Melina   That's sick.

Chris   No, it's keeping informed. Cos that's the really scary thing, a lot scarier than the chances of ISIS blowing up Wetherspoons: how much people don't know. What about all those army lads you see in town on a Friday night, swaggering in and out of All Bar One, stinking of Lynx Africa? Nobody gives them a second glance, but I bet half of them have done shit just as bad as Jihadi John.

Rachel   No, they haven't!

Chris   Do you have any idea what the army does? I bet half of *them* don't even know what they've done. They just press a button and a little grey smudge disappears. Might've been a terrorist. Might've been a little kid.

Darren   They are protecting this country, you leftie. Protecting *you*.

Chris   They get paid, don't they? Bet Jihadi John didn't get paid.

Suhayla   Ooooh, top corner, Chris mate.

Rachel   My brother is one of those lads. And he doesn't get paid anything like enough for what he goes through.

Chris   Then he should get another job.

Rachel   F you, Chris.

Olive   So is mine, actually. And he knows exactly what he's done. He's got PTSD and hasn't been out of his room for two months.

Chris   Yeah, well, there's always –

Olive   He doesn't sleep. Cries and screams. He'll never be right in the head, the doctors say. Never be back to normal. But thanks for making assumptions about him.

Chris   I didn't . . . I didn't know that.

Samuel (*to* **Olive**)   *vay' vay' Data'nISbogh je jamal doesn't ghaj.*
[That doesn't have anything to do with Jamal.]

Olive (*to* **Samuel**)   Yes it does, he was trying to stop the
things Jamal wants to –

Samuel   *nuq luta' jamal ghewmey DaSov. vaj vay' Qu' ghaH.*
[You don't know what Jamal has done. If he's done
anything.]

Olive   Well they aren't going to take him away for nothing,
are they?

Samuel   *SoHvaD Suq emotional,* **Olive**. *Qa' mr spock* – [You're
getting emotional, Olive. As Mr Spock would say –]

Olive (*emotional*)   I am not getting emotional. And bollocks
to Mr Spock!

She moves away from **Samuel**. *He opens his mouth but nothing comes
out without someone to translate it for him.*

Pause.

Kirsty   I just want to feel safe.

Rachel   So do I.

Melina   And me.

Jordan   Everybody wants to feel safe. That doesn't make
you special.

Melina   When did I say I was special? I'm not the one who
bigs himself up, then pops in thirty seconds like a blown-up
crisp packet.

Kirsty   Why is that wrong?

Jordan   I've not had any complaints from Chloe. Not
compared to what she says about George anyway.

Melina   What? *What*?!

Kirsty   Why is it wrong to want to feel safe?

Darren   It's not wrong. It's normal.

Melina   What are you saying, Jordan?

Jordan   You're a smart girl. You work it out.

Darren   What's wrong is being made to feel like freaks for wanting to feel safe. In our country.

Chris   Do you have any opinions you don't get from your dad? Or the *Sun*?

Darren   I don't read the *Sun*, actually.

Chris   Sorry. *Telegraph*? *Mail*? *Times*? *Express*? Or does Donald Trump just come round personally?

Suhayla   What's Jamal *done*? You don't know he's done anything.

Darren   You don't know he hasn't. Or what he's gonna do.

Kirsty   How can anyone possibly know that?

Darren   The police obviously think they know.

Melina   That bitch.

Suhayla   I'm talking about facts. Facts you don't have.

Darren   Fact one: Miss Tomlinson thought something he did was dodgy enough to report it to the police. Fact two: the police thought it was dodgy enough to take him away.

Melina   That evil fucking *bitch*!

She fights back tears, stews with rage.

Darren   Fact three: he's a Muslim. All Muslims aren't terrorists, but all terrorists are Muslims.

Suhayla   Fuck off, Darren.

Darren   Your turn. What've you got?

Suhayla   Seriously. That is just straight racist.

Darren   Right, so no facts, just the race card. It's always the same with you people. You can't make a proper argument so you play the victim.

Suhayla   Racist prick.

Rachel   He's right though.

Chris   No he's not.

Rachel   Who did 7/7? Paris? Brussels? Muslims.

Suhayla   Who bombs Muslims all over the world? White people.

Rachel   Now who's the racist?

Suhayla   So it's racist to say white people kill people, but not racist to say Muslims kill people? OK then.

Chris   In 2016, right, toddlers have shot more people in America than Muslims. Twenty-three to nil so far, as it goes.

Jordan   There are wankers everywhere.

Kirsty   True.

Jordan   But particularly Stevenage.

Chris   Spitting fire today, son!

Evan   Can we talk about something else? This is getting a bit heavy now.

Rachel   Look who's talking.

Evan   Ha ha. Fat-shaming. So original.

Olive   Shut up, Rachel, you cow.

Rachel   Who asked you? Go back to Klingon, Olive. Ugly nerd.

Darren   This is what makes me laugh about your lot. You rant about how much you hate us –

Suhayla   When have ever I said that? I was born in the same hospital as you.

Darren   So? You'll always be different. You *choose* to be different.

Suhayla   I live two doors down from you! We're in the same class!

Darren   That's what that rag on your head means: 'I'm different. I'm not you. I'm *better* than you.'

Suhayla   What more can I possibly do to fit in?!

Darren   Your lot swagger round rubbing our faces in your difference every single day. But somehow *we're* the problem? We're the ones who are supposed to grovel and crawl and make you feel welcome? In our own country?!

Suhayla   You know what? Yeah, you are the problem. People like you, who refuse to think about what Britain does to the world, all the murders and rapes and exploitation, because if you stay ignorant then you can swan around like *you're* the victims, as if the only reason so many people are pissed off with this country is because they're just crazy and evil and so they need to be locked up or bombed, when it's us bombing them for two hundred years that started all this shit in the first place – yes, Darren, people like you, who can't handle not always being the good guys, you are the problem. Guess what – if you hurt somebody, they're gonna want to hurt you back! And all this bullshit, being the good little copper's son, turning people against me? It's not gonna make Daddy come home, you know. Because Daddy is gone. We *saw* him. He drove away as your mum clung to the handle of his car door, sobbing and shrieking. Because he didn't want to be around you any more. And that is not my fault. It is *not my fault*!

Darren *advances on* **Suhayla**, *real hate on his face.* **Melina** *explodes out of her seat.*

Melina   I've had enough of this. I have had enough of this shit.

She storms over to **Suhayla** *and, on the spur of the moment, pulls her hijab off.* **Suhayla** *shrieks and covers her head. The rest gawp.*
Melina *stands with the hijab in her hand, uncertain of her next move.*

Suhayla   Give that back!

Jordan   What are you doing?

Chris   Give it back, Melina.

Melina (*looks at hijab*)   What's so special about this thing anyway?

Suhayla   Give it *back*. Now.

Melina   I think you've talked enough today.

Kirsty   You're gonna get us in *so* much trouble, Melina.

Melina   Why? It's just a piece of cloth.

Kirsty   You're gonna get us all suspended.

Samuel (*to* **Olive**)   *vay' vay' Data'nISbogh bImejnIS. vay' jatlh.*
[You need to do something. Say something.]

Olive   You do something, Samuel. She brought it on herself.

Rachel   Don't give it back.

Evan   Shut up, Rachel. You're making it worse.

Rachel   Eat a cake, fat boy. Don't give it back, Melina. Until she apologises.

Melina *looks around the room, heart pumping in disbelief at what she's done.*

Jordan   Give it back, Melina. Now.

Melina's *not taking anything from* **Jordan**. *She jumps the other way.*

Melina   Until she apologises. Yes, Rach. (*To* **Suhayla**.) Apologise for what you just said, and you can have your shabby little piece of cloth back.

Suhayla   I'm calling the head.

Kirsty   You're gonna get us all expelled.

Melina   Why? Who's gonna tell? Are you gonna tell, Kirsty?

Suhayla   I'm calling the police.

She pulls out her phone. **Melina** *snatches it from her.*

Melina   Are you, Rachel? Evan?

Evan   Just give them back to her. The phone and the wotsit. And we'll all go back to normal.

Melina   Will we? Don't think we will. (*At* **Suhayla**.) Cos she's not gonna let it go, are you, honey?

Suhayla *makes for the door.* **Melina** *gets in her way. The two girls push and scrap over the hijab. The others watch, not quite believing this is happening.*

Melina   Stop her, Darren.

Darren *is frozen, he can't move.*

Melina   Come on! Big mouth! DO SOMETHING!

Stung into action, **Darren** *steps forward, wrestles* **Suhayla** *off* **Melina***, and hugs her in a bear grip.* **Suhayla** *shouts and screams.*

Suhayla   Get off! Get off me!

Darren   Calm down. Just calm / down

Suhayla   Get / off

Jordan   This has to / stop

Melina   Don't let her / scream

Suhayla   GET OFF ME!

Kirsty   Someone'll hear!

Melina   Make her stop!

Suhayla   GET YOUR HANDS OFF –

Darren *clamps his hand over* **Suhayla***'s mouth.* **Suhayla** *bites his hand hard.* **Darren** *shouts in pain and slaps* **Suhayla** *in the face. Everybody gasps in disbelief.* **Suhayla** *bursts into tears and collapses into a nearby chair. Beat.*

Kirsty   Oh shit oh shit oh shit oh shit.

Chris   What the fuck did you do that for?

Darren   She bit me!

Chris   You hit her!

Darren   On the hand!

Chris   In the face! You can't hit a girl in the face, Darren! Especially a Muslim girl!

Rachel   What difference does it make what kind of girl she is?

Kirsty   Oh shit oh shit oh shit oh shit.

Rachel   That is exactly the problem. That is exactly why we're here.

Evan   What are we gonna do?

Kirsty   What are we gonna do?

Pause.

Melina   Lock the door. Key is in her desk. (*Beat.*) Lock the door.

Rachel *moves to the desk, roots around in a drawer.*

Melina   Other side.

Rachel *finds the key. She locks the door. She puts the key in her pocket. Beat.*

Melina   It's her word against ours. Her word against the group. So the question is, who'd rather be with her than the group?

Beat.

All she needs to do is apologise. All she needs to do is get down on her knees, like she already does five times a bloody day, and beg for our forgiveness. For thinking she's better. For thinking her lot are better than our lot. That's all you have to do, honey. And then we'll let you go.

Suhayla   Stick it up your arse.

Melina   Oh, I think it's you who might be getting things stuck in places, Suhayla. If you know what I mean.

Kirsty   Woah woah woah woah woah woah woah woah woah.

Melina   If things get out of hand. Which they might.

Kirsty   This is too mental now.

Melina   You never know, do you?

Kirsty   This is too mad.

Chris   You've lost it, Melina. You need to stop.

Melina   I didn't start it, Chris. So how can I stop it?

Jordan   Look, Melina, I'm sorry about . . . what I said, OK?

Melina   As you should be.

Jordan   I shouldn't have embarrassed you in public. But you can't –

Melina   Is that what you think this is, Jordan? Oh no. No no no. This isn't about me. This is about *us*. The group. The school.

Darren (*to* **Suhayla**)   I . . . I'm sorry. It'll be alright.

Melina   This is about us doing something special. Protecting each other. Standing up for each other. Fighting back.

Jordan   The only thing you're doing for the 'group', Melina, is getting us into deep deep shit.

Darren   Just . . . please stop snivelling, OK?

He puts an incredibly awkward hand on **Suhayla***'s shoulder. A clumsy gesture of apology. She screams at him and runs to the other side of the room.*

Suhayla   GET OFF ME! I'M REPORTING YOU! I'm reporting all of you.

Melina   Keep her there, Daz. Make sure she doesn't leave.

Jordan   I'm getting Miss Tomlinson.

He makes for the door. **Melina** *steps in his way.*

Melina   No.

Jordan   We'll explain. She'll / understand

Melina   *No*, Jordan. Too late for that.

Jordan   Get out of the way.

Melina   Make me.

Jordan   Out the way, Melina.

Melina   No, Jordan.

Jordan   Don't make me have to move you.

Melina   You heard that. Everybody heard that, right? Jordan just threatened to hit me.

Jordan   I did not . . . I did not! (*To* **Chris**.) Chrissy, go get Miss Tomlinson.

Chris   With my record? Why, d'you want us executed?

Samuel   *vay' Daghaj.* [You go.]

Olive   No.

Samuel   *vay' Daghaj. vay' ghajbogh vay'.* [You have to go. Somebody has to go.]

Olive   You go, Samuel. If somebody has to go, you go.

Jordan   Man up, Chris, and go get a fucking teacher.

Chris   Alright. Alright, yeah.

He moves to **Rachel** *and holds his hand out.*

Chris   Key.

Rachel   No.

Chris   Give me the key, Rachel.

Rachel *takes the key out of her pocket and thinks about what to do with it. Then she shoves it deep into her pants, holds her hands up and grins. Beat.*

Rachel   No one is going anywhere.

Beat.

Melina   This is not our fault.

Rachel   Right.

Melina   This is all gonna go to shit and we'll have records and stuff and it's not our fault. We didn't cause any of this. We didn't do what Jamal did. We didn't bring the police in. We didn't do what she (*Pointing at* **Suhayla**.) says. All we did was come to school. All we ever do is the right thing. So why should we be punished? Why should we have to suffer?

Jordan   No one has to suffer. No one is gonna have a record.

Rachel   You heard what she said. She's gonna report us.

Chris   She won't report anyone, will you, Hayls?

Suhayla   You arseholes assaulted me and are keeping me here against my will. Yeah, I think I just might.

Evan   Just give her back the –

Rachel   NO! No! I'm tired of this! I'm so tired of always being made to feel like everything is my fault!

Kirsty   I just want to feel safe.

Jordan   This is madness.

Melina   What if she's in it with Jamal?

Jordan   Oh, for fuck's sake.

Melina   What if she is though? What is they're in it together?

Jordan   What if they're in *what* together? There is no 'it'!

Rachel   How do you know there isn't, Jordan? You don't know that.

Jordan   How do you know there is?

Melina   Because of this! Because all this shit is happening now! How could all this shit be happening if there were no it!

Kirsty   Why is it wrong to want to feel safe?

Rachel   They could be up to anything! Planning to blow up the school! Planning to do God knows what else! *Nobody knows!*

Jordan   This is proper mad now.

Rachel   There's an easy way out of all this. All she has to do is apologise. Get down on her knees and admit what she did.

Rachel *and* **Melina** *approach* **Suhayla**.

Melina   Get down.

Suhayla   Get fucked.

Melina   Don't push me, darling.

Rachel   Get down on your knees and apologise to us.

Suhayla   Fuck. You. You. Fat. Slag.

Melina   Just apologise and say it never happened, and you can have your minging little rag back, and we'll all go back to normal.

The two girls start to wrestle **Suhayla** *to the ground.*

Kirsty   Woah woah woah woah woah woah woah woah woah WOAH.

Melina   Help us then, Darren!

Darren *steps back, afraid.* **Jordan** *starts wrestling with the door.*

Jordan   Chris, help me bust this.

Chris *moves over to the door.* **Suhayla** *breaks free of* **Rachel** *and* **Melina** *and moves to the other side of the room. She shouts.*

Suhayla   HELP!

Melina *puts her hand over* **Suhayla**'s *mouth and the two of them struggle.*

Melina   Help me then! Or we'll all be in shit!

Olive *and* **Kirsty** *go help* **Melina** *subdue* **Suhayla**. **Samuel** *puts a hand on* **Olive**'s *shoulder.*

Samuel   *nuq Data'? mev!* [What are you doing? Stop!]

Olive *angrily shrugs his hand off. The three girls wrestle* **Suhayla** *to the ground. Murmurs in the corridor.* **Jordan** *and* **Chris** *have nearly busted the door open.*

Rachel   Step out that door and I'll report you to Prevent.

Shocked beat. **Rachel** *is shocked herself, she didn't know that was gonna come out.*

Jordan   What?

Rachel   It's not just the brown ones, is it? It can be anybody.

Jordan   *What?*

Rachel   You go to Jamal's house. You hang out with him every day. You eat his food. You defend him.

Chris   Have you lost your mind?

Rachel   Maybe he's part of it too. I'll tell Prevent he's part of it too.

Chris   This is *Jordan*.

Rachel   How well do you know him, Chris? How well do you know anybody?

Chris   You won't grass.

Rachel   Step out that door and see.

Chris   Nice try, Rach.

Rachel   I'll tell them about you too. How you defend her. How you agree with her. About how maybe you fancy her –

Chris   I do not fancy –

Rachel   And you want to impress her and that's how she got inside your little head and got you onside. Got you and Jordan and Jamal on side.

Chris   *To do what?*

Rachel   I don't know, Chris. You tell me.

Suhayla   HELP ME!

The murmurs in the corridor become loud adult voices. Bangs on the outside of the door. 'What is going on in there?' 'Open this door.' 'Can you hear me? Open this door, now!' **Suhayla** *is pinned to the floor by the other four girls.* **Samuel** *has his face in his hands.*

Darren   We need to stop.

Rachel   What?

Darren   I think we've gone a bit too far.

Rachel   Oh Darren. Dazza. Bottling out when it comes to the crunch. What would Daddy say?

Darren   Shut up, Rachel.

Rachel   You can't talk like that to me. I'm not like her, you know. I'm *English*.

Melina   All mouth, no trousers, Daz. All cock, no bollocks.

Evan   Is that even a thing? I don't think that's a thing.

Rachel   Shut up and hold her down, fat boy.

She grabs **Evan** *and pulls him into the scrum. The noises and shouting from the corridor become louder. Someone rattles the door hard. 'Go get a key!'*

Melina   You started all this. Everything that's happened today is down to you.

Darren   No it isn't.

Rachel   You hit her in the face, Darren.

Beat.

Melina   Nobody pays the price any more, do they? I reckon things would be a lot better if somebody paid the price. Starting today. (*To* **Suhayla**.) Say, 'I apologise.'

Suhayla   Stick it.

Melina   Apologise.

Suhayla   No.

Rachel   Apologise.

Suhayla   NO.

Melina   Say, 'I apologise for all the trouble I've caused today. I apologise for all the trouble my type have caused.'

Suhayla   Stick it up your –

Darren   Just apologise, OK?

Kirsty   Make it go away.

Evan   Just say it, Suhayla. It's the easiest thing.

Rachel   Say it!

Melina   SAY IT!

Class   SAY IT SAY IT SAY IT SAY IT SAY IT SAY IT SAY IT SAY IT!

Melina   Then if you won't say it, honey, we might need to take things to the next level.

She starts to pull off **Suhayla***'s skirt.* **Suhayla** *bursts into a terrified scream.* **Samuel** *leaps from his chair and onto his desk.*

Samuel   STOOOOOOOOOOOOOOOOOOPPPPPP!

WHAT ARE YOU DOING? WHAT THE FUCK ARE YOU DOING?

The class turns as one, stunned. Pause.

I am afraid.

I'm afraid every single day.

I'm afraid that I can't do anything right.

That I'm not worth anything.

That nobody loves me and nobody ever will.

That I don't deserve to be loved because I'm not good enough.

And I know people can see I'm afraid.

And they take advantage.

And so they make me more afraid.

Afraid to speak.

Afraid to think.

And I know you're all afraid too. Underneath. And that's why you pick on me.

But I won't.

I won't let you do this to her.

I don't care what you do to me.

I won't.

He climbs down from the desk, walks over to **Melina** *and takes the hijab from her hand. He helps* **Suhayla** *to her feet and gives her back the hijab.*

Samuel   I am so, so sorry.

He turns back to **Melina**.

Samuel   Come on, then. Do your worst.

Beat. A loud hammering at the locked door. Voices shouting 'We have a key. We're coming in.'

The class looks at one another. Beat.

Samuel (*to everybody*)   Think very carefully. About what you're going to say.

The door opens.

Blackout.

Extremism

BY ANDERS LUSTGARTEN

Notes on rehearsal and staging, drawn from a workshop with the writer, held at the National Theatre, October 2016

How Anders came to write the play:

Anders spoke of wanting to explore the way in which institutions make people act. He writes about 'power' – the power in the room, and the power between students and how the 'Prevent' programme changes that. Anders spoke of how he believed the world is becoming more about barriers and that the Left as well as the Right is increasingly concerned with exclusionary forms of identification (safe spaces and no platforms). The consequence of 'Prevent' is entrusting teachers with the responsibility of identifying terrorists. The play looks at the imposition of an exploitative system and how it changes the dynamic of a group of people. He added that it was written originally for a provincial town, like Plymouth.

The play on the whole is about power. He thinks Suhayla is the wittiest and most confident character, particularly at the beginning. Gender is also an important theme as she is a girl who is not afraid to speak up. It was also a deliberate choice that the violence comes from the girls towards the end.

Everyone in this play is looking to regain power or exercise power. They all feel they have lost something and are looking for a target to lash out at in order to get this power back. 'Prevent' allows them to lash out at Suhayla.

Anders spoke of the dynamic of the play being a slow steady pull of a group of normal people into the orbit of something malicious. He occasionally likened the play to Arthur Miller's *The Crucible*, speaking of how *extremism* looks at people with a certain set of relationships and how those relationships are altered by the creeping influence of this malicious system.

Physical warm-up game and familiarity exercises

- Ask the group to walk around in the room, turn it into a light jog and then speed it up. Ask everyone to freeze and then adjust where they are standing in order to balance the space.

- You could play a large game of 'keep-y upp-y' (keeping the ball up off the ground), encouraging people to stay light on their feet. Every time the ball falls on the floor you have to bow with a prayer position and say 'Wooha!' and everyone else responds. This is a good way of avoiding disappointment when the ball is dropped and encourages people to work as a team. Every now and then when the ball hits the floor, you can ask the group to change position in the space.

- You can then introduce two balls in the space and continue to say 'Wooha!' every time someone starts with the ball. Encourage everyone to be aware of the whole space and the other ball in the room.

- You could then count every time the ball is hit. Introduce another rule that the ball can't be hit by the same person twice in a row. Ask people to treat it gently like a bubble and hit it underarm.

- Ask the group to break off into pairs and label themselves A and B. Person A has two minutes to talk to Person B. This is a diatribe not a conversation so Person B should not talk. Ask them to swap over.

- Ask the group to make a circle again and ask everyone to introduce their partner to the group. Ask them to replace all descriptive words with the name of their partner. So they say two or three sentences and swap key words with their name.

- Ask the group to stand in a circle shoulder to shoulder. Stand in the centre and throw the ball to a person who then has to throw it back, trying to keep a rhythm that stays the same. The next rule is that someone at random can shout 'Go!' and then swap with the person standing in the middle. The person who runs into the middle should try and catch the ball that will just have been thrown. The aim is for the person in the middle to change each time. Encourage people to be bold and shout 'Go!' as often as possible in order to change the centre person. This is a good exercise for focus and teamwork.

Tackling the themes of the play

- Participants were split into groups of five and were asked to do a spider diagram on a large piece of paper noting down the *challenges and benefits* to the director and their theatre company/school group specifically when doing this play.

Some of the responses from the workshop are listed below. It could be useful preparation to consider what your specific challenges and benefits are and how you might begin to approach them.

- The use of 'Klingon' and its role within the play.

- How to make Samuel relatable when he is speaking Klingon all the time. How to make the transition from his use of Klingon to his final speech and make sure it is taken seriously?

- Challenges of casting and the central character of Suhayla. Is it important to have a Muslim actor play the part? If you do cast a Muslim girl how do you deal with the taking off of the hijab ensuring that the young person is comfortable with doing so?

- If you don't have a black or Asian actress for the lead, is it possible to cast a white actress?

- Can characters be split if you have more young actors than there are characters in the play?

- Are you able to swap the gender of the characters?

- What do you do if you don't have a door at the theatre or school? Do you need to create a whole set or can you have a stand-alone door?

- Dealing with the swearing and themes within the play.

- Considering the response to the play based on the backgrounds of your company/audience.

- Is there room for an ensemble and/or moments of physical theatre?

- Dealing with the pace and rhythm of the play and the challenge of line learning.

- Making the fight look realistic.

- Coming at the play from the perspective of adults is challenging, as you need to understand how the young people are dealing with these issues and talk 'with' the students rather than 'at' them.

- The play allows young people from all backgrounds to explore these issues.

Two issues that came up repeatedly in the workshop were whether companies should cast a non-white actor as Suhayla and what to do about the removing of the hijab. Anders warned against groups casting their only actor from an ethnic minority as Suhayla. This passes on a different message, because it means she is already on the outside when at the beginning she's a powerful member of the group (which is why some of less powerful turn against her), and is not necessary as she could come from a number of racial backgrounds.

Ned Bennett, lead director, talked about the action of removing the hijab as being 'abstracted'. It could therefore be represented but not literally carried out. This could be an artistic choice but also a way of avoiding certain actors turning down a part they might otherwise be able to play.

Abstracting and heightening the action

Ned introduced the idea of making ideograms in your production. An ideogram is a symbol that represents an idea or concept independent of any particular language and specific words or phrases. It is about getting to the heart or soul of an idea without literal visual representation. Many of the following exercises that look at ideograms and viewpoints derive from the work of director Anne Bogart.

- Write two or three sentences on what the play is about for *you*. Do not be too analytical or descriptive. Do not try to explain what the play means. You are trying to articulate the essence, the soul. It shouldn't read like a review or an exam answer, e.g. 'The play is about . . .' The aim is to write a short paragraph that expresses the feeling of the play. You might use heightened language or be more poetic. You might end up writing something that is through the eyes of the characters. It shouldn't be too academic. Don't analyse it and instead just write what you feel. Ned gave the participants a few minutes to do this.

Looking at chorus and physical sequences

- In the workshop, a few volunteers read their pieces to the rest of the group.

- Ned split participants into groups of four. In their groups, they read their paragraphs to each other and came up with two themes that best represented each person's response to the play, e.g. a word/phrase/concept.

- The groups were then asked to direct themselves in eight ideograms using the two themes that they had come up with for each person. An ideogram is a graphic symbol that represents an idea or concept. It can have sound but no dialogue or props. It does not have to be a still image.

- The groups then chose one director who had to put all the ideograms together in which they could come one after another or overlap. The aim was to avoid seeing the edge of that particular ideogram when put with the others. They were asked to consider the arc of the story or journey when placing them together.

- Each group showed their sequence back to the rest of the group. This is a useful technique if you want to have a chorus or to explore transitions/physical sequences, or wanted to look at moments like the removal of the hijab and abstracting that moment. This could apply to specific moments in the text, for example when the social media gossip spreads on the phones or when Jamal is deleted from Facebook.

Analytical and practical approaches to the text

Participants were asked to write down the following list:

- What I say about myself.
- What I say about others.
- What others say about me.

Ned asked everyone to get into groups of five. They had to choose one character from the play that they were interested in. Assigning one or two scribes and the others as readers, they had to make a list of quotes from the play under these headings.

This is a useful process for a director to go through. It is time consuming but is a way of analysing the script in a non-interpretive way.

'Points of concentration'

Ned introduced an exercise used by director Mike Alfreds called 'Points of concentration' and his own way of using it with this text. The purpose of the exercise is to feed in the given and imagined circumstances without overloading the actors. The desire is that you get to a point where in theory you don't set the blocking/staging and actors remain present and fully understand their characters' story.

Ned broke it down into three lists:

- *The epic list:* e.g. morality, justice, past, future.
- *Immediate and situational:* e.g. the classroom, other characters, lunch money.
- *The oddly specific:* idiosyncrasies of characters, e.g. chewing gum.

It is useful to break down the text into units and to determine the 'events', that are major changes in temperature/situation. Directors should try to identify the spine of the play for each actor. What is the primary situational obstacle that each character faces in each unit?

This can be a quick way of approaching the text. When you have done these lists it provides you with a number of 'points of concentration' (POC) to give to the actors. The process is to run the scene/whole play with one preoccupation at a time. It is the hope that some POC might open the scene up in new ways.

If your POC was 'violence', you don't want them to play it all violently; rather it is about concentrating on the notion of violence. They might be interpreting someone's movement as violent, noticing someone's language as violent or noticing that they themselves are not violent. It is about exploring the preoccupation in a lateral manner.

'POINTS OF CONCENTRATION' EXERCISE

- Ask your actors to find a space and lie down. On the count of five ask them to push one hand and then the other into the floor. Then ask them to push their heads into the floor and then their bottoms. Then to tense their whole bodies and push them into the floor and then relax.

- Ask them to think of habitual routines that their character would do every day. It should be a simple routine, physically active, and should be able to go into a loop. It shouldn't be too passive like reading a paper. Ask them to jump up and mime their actions all at the same time in the space.

- Then ask them to identify for themselves the primary obstacle within this unit of action. For example if they are getting ready for school then their obstacle is that they are late for school. So something that fuels and activates what they are doing. They need to balance two things – their task, and their obstacle.

- Add a POC, and ask actors to balance this with the other things that they are doing. In the workshop, the first POC was the notion of *time* and Ned encouraged the group to think beyond just being late. The next POCs were *money*, *school*, *sex*, *dreams* and *nightmares*.

This is a useful exercise in allowing actors to become less self-conscious by giving them something to be preoccupied with. Going through all the different POCs one after the other allows for a thorough exploration of character and helps to create mood rather than 'playing the mood'.

Be aware that actors might occasionally dry when they do this work as it knocks them off a set thought pattern that they have got themselves into.

Question and answer session

with Anders Lustgarten and Ned Bennett

Has Jamal been radicalised?

ANDERS LUSTGARTEN   'I want to leave what is not onstage to your imagination. He has been taken out for a reason, but this may be a very tenuous reason. It is not important to me that he has been radicalised. It's more about numbers that need to be interviewed as part of "Prevent". I imagine that Jamal's back story could involve him having distributed pro-

Palestine leaflets rather than overt support for radical Islam.
"Prevent" is fundamentally about repressing political dissent.'

How old do you see the characters as being?

ANDERS LUSTGARTEN   'I thought of them being sixteen to
seventeen. I urge you to get the most out of it for your
school/company. I am not precious about the material. I
would rather you don't take out whole story sections or
characters but if you need to make tweaks you can. It is the
essence of the story that is most important and you need to
make it work for you.'

Casting in terms of race?

ANDERS LUSTGARTEN   'Impossible to answer – diversity of
groups makes this difficult. Focus on power. Be cautious
about making the one black girl in the room Suhayla, as this
might focus on the most obvious thing. Don't go for the
obvious would be my advice. Go with the personalities of the
young people and whom you believe suits roles.'

Gender casting? Is there a possibility of swapping genders?

ANDERS LUSTGARTEN   'I wanted to change the normal trope
that the boys are the violent ones. Suhayla is strong and they
are trying to put her back in the box. I would personally stick
with the girls being girls, but you have the choice and
autonomy to change.'

Why do they remove Suhayla's skirt?

ANDERS LUSTGARTEN   'This is when they lose control and
things get out of hand. The moment of the skirt is the fear of
otherness. That is what "Prevent" is to me. The skirt removal
is about humiliating her and sexual violation.'

Do you see the other characters as having no beliefs?

ANDERS LUSTGARTEN   'Darren doesn't have anything to
hang on to, which is why he wants to take something from
Suhayla. "White male privilege and a strong family" has been
lost and taken from him (regardless of whether or not one

thinks he should have them in the first place). The other characters are in flux and working themselves out. Suhayla is someone with strong convictions who has a model of identity (based on religion). They are afraid of her and want to scapegoat her.'

What would be your suggestion for the door?

NED BENNETT   'The door represents something. It could be a chalk line, or a rope on the floor. It doesn't have to be a literal piece of the set.'

When looking at casting, does it matter if Evan is not a 'large' actor?

NED BENNETT   'No, you can interpret it that he is a greedy character, always thinking and talking about food, so it shouldn't matter about his actual size.'

Can music be used as an underscore?

ANDERS LUSTGARTEN   'Yes, I am not opposed to that idea. My plays are fulfilled by the creativity of others and I don't want to control all aspects.'

NED BENNETT   'You should try to make it as visceral as possible and use all the tools you have in order to do that, including the introduction of music.'

What is the content of the unscripted conversation between Olive and Samuel?

ANDERS LUSTGARTEN   'This is completely up to the imagination of the director and company. It could be the first time that Olive has ever disagreed with Samuel. I consider them to have a deep connection and understanding of each other.'

From a workshop led by Ned Bennett
with notes by Katie Lewis

The School Film

by Patrick Marber

'What are great expectations?'

'It means he's going to be rich. And a gentleman.'

The whole school assemble in the hall to watch 'the school film' which turns out to be an old British classic from the 1940s, in black and white no less. As the young viewers absorb the adventures of the characters in the old story they begin to discover what their own expectations might be.

Cast size
Variable size ensemble of any size or age

Patrick Marber's plays for the National Theatre include *Dealer's Choice* (also Vaudeville and MTC in New York), *Closer* (also Lyric, London, and Music Box, New York), *Howard Katz* (also Roundabout, New York); and *The Musicians* for NT Connections. Other plays include *After Miss Julie* (also Roundabout, New York) and *Don Juan in Soho* at the Donmar Warehouse; and *Hoop Lane* for BBC Radio 3. TV includes co-writing *Knowing Me Knowing You with Alan Partridge, Paul & Pauline Calf Video Diaries* and *The Curator*. Film includes *Closer, Notes on a Scandal, Old Street* and *Love You More*. Radio includes co-writing *Knowing Me Knowing You with Alan Partridge* and *Bunk Bed* (with Peter Curran). *The Red Lion* and *Three Days in the Country* both opened at the National Theatre in 2015.

National Theatre Connections does not
hold any of the rights to the film *Great Expectations*
directed by David Lean. Permission from
the relevant rights holder(s) should be obtained
if you wish to use any aspect of the film
when performing this play.

Notes on the text

This play can be performed by as few or as many young actors as the director is able to or wants to cast.

My instinct is that two is too few and two hundred too many. But I might be wrong.

*

The dialogue is not assigned to named characters. The director and the company can allot lines as they see fit – and thus create coherent 'characters'. Or not.

*

The play is set in a school hall or gym.

The characters in the play are watching a film.

They sit on benches or chairs facing the audience.

The screen is the fourth wall and is therefore unseen.

Costume can be school uniform but doesn't have to be.

*

There are four kinds of discourse in this play:

1 When a character speaks his or her inner thoughts. The majority of the play is in this form.

2 When a character speaks aloud – signified in **bold**.

3 When the majority of the ensemble exclaim or react in unison it is signified in CAPITALS. It doesn't necessarily denote that they are shouting. Though they might be.

4 When someone quotes directly – magically – from the film the line is denoted with the character's name in bold and inverted commas for the speech. The actor might stand up and briefly 'become' the fictional character. Possibly using a piece of costume or a prop. These lines of real dialogue can be allotted to the same actors each time. Or not.

*

The film is nearly two hours long. The play dips in and out of it at selected moments. These time jumps are denoted by an asterisk. The director can demonstrate these gaps or not depending on their preference.

On lights up the actors enter and find seats. Or they might be there already when the audience enters. There may be jostling and minor improvised arguing, etc. They are excited to be seeing a film during school hours.

They settle. Some shushing.

Quite a number of them are playing with their phones.

Adult Voice   Put – Them – Away!

The phones are put away.

Adult Voice   There is only one screen. If I see another screen I will send you back to your lessons. All of you.

Settle down. Se – ttle. WILL YOU SETTLE?!

They settle.

Adult Voice   You are about to see a classic of British cinema.

A few groans followed by shushes.

Adult Voice   Don't adjust your eyes, the film is in black and white.

Pandemonium. Wailing, mock wailing, shushing, a walk-out followed quickly by a walk back in, etc, etc. Finally, focus.

Adult Voice   Enjoy it!

The lights click off one by one and the filmgoers are in darkness.

Sound: two loud beats of the 'J. Arthur Rank Presents' gong followed by the opening music of David Lean's Great Expectations *(1946).*

I'm gonna die!

Noooo!

How long is it?

I love old films.

The filmgoers are now illuminated by the light from the screen. Or so it must seem.

The sound of the film music fades. It can return when or if appropriate. Or not at all.

Ooh, Alec Guinness.

Obi-Wan Kenobi!

Anthony Havelock-Allan.

Wilfred Shingleton.

Ronald Neame.

All the big names.

Ahh. David Lean. *Bridge on the River Kwai. Lawrence of Arabia. Brief Encounter.* Born in Croydon, brought up as a strict Quaker.

Black and farking white.

Great shot. Landscape. Epic.

Small boy.

Pip.

Good runner.

What's he holding?

Sweet face.

Looks like our Stevie.

Graveyard.

Don't like death.

What's that noise?

Oh . . . poor boy . . . he's an orphan.

Flowers for the grave.

Creaking . . .

There's a freaky old face in that tree . . .

I'm scared!

Run, Pip!

Run!

AAAAAGGGHHHHH!!

Oh my God!

The nose on him!

Abel Magwitch, I presume.

Don't hurt Pip!

Chains, a convict.

A file?

Wittels?

Oh, food.

Magwitch   'Your 'eart and liver will be torn out and roasted and ate.'

Ohhh. He's lovely, that Pip.

*

Mrs Gargery.

What a bitch.

Stop hitting him!

Witch.

Nice big lump of cheese.

Tartan waistcoat. Mmm hmm.

Convict on the loose. Two of 'em.

Mrs Gargery   'Answer him one question and he'll ask you a dozen.'

It's quite good this.

Now she's hit him with a spoon.

Psychobitch.

Why did Joe marry her?

*

I strongly advise you not to go back to the graveyard.

Pantry. Good word.

Why is there a rabbit in the cupboard?

Why's it upside down?

Thass a *nice* pork pie.

He's got the wittels.

He's got the big file.

Why is the cow talking to him?

Cow   'Hello young thief.'

It's his inner voice, his guilty conscience.

What, the cow's?

No, Pip's!

SHHHH!

Good scarf.

Second convict!

Nasty scar.

Excellent make-up for 1946.

Magwitch doing tai chi.

Pip   'I think you've got the ague, sir.'

Ague?

I will be using that word.

He's loving that pie.

*

Uncle Pumblechook!

OMG he wants the pork pie!

Poor kid's crapping himself.

She's in the pantry . . .

Soldier.

*

Still wish it were colour.

Marshes.

Where are they?

Kent marshes.

I bet they catch the crims and the baldy's gonna blame Pip.

Good old Magwitch.

Decent.

Joe   'Poor miserable fellow creature.'

Joe Gargery – what a gent.

Do the convicts have to row to Australia?

*

Pip (*voice-over*)   'It was a year later.'

Who's saying that?

Must be older Pip.

The variants from the novel are fascinating. It's a masterpiece of compression. Yes. I'll say that in my essay. Hmm . . . Does it make sense? A masterpiece of compression. A compressive masterpiece?

Ohh. Mrs Garge and Uncle Pumblefatty.

Are they having an affair?

She's *still* furious!

Hope she dies.

Or . . . a comprehensive masterclass in compression. Yes. Perfect.

Pip's got check trousers. Sweet.

Miss Havisham.

I've heard of her.

Wish I'd read the book.

Nothing worse than an enforced playdate with a poshie.

She's pulling his hair now.

She's got to go.

Poor Pip.

He's scrubbed up well.

Cool cap.

I love Pip.

I went in a horse-drawn carriage once. Was it in Spain? Felt a bit embarassed but it was a lovely ride.

'Satis House'. Whass that mean?

Estella   'What name'?

Pumblechook   'Pumblechook.'

Estella   'Quite right.'

Love that.

Same girl.

Jean Simmons.

Here she comes.

Swinging a key like uh-huh.

She's a doll.

Check those bloomers. Big tick.

Oh no . . .

He fancies her.

Don't go there, mate, she is trouble.

Estella   'Come along, boy.'

What a hottie.

Estella   'Don't loiter, boy.'

I'm using that.

Is there a single kind woman in this film?

If only she was in colour.

Another stopped clock . . .

Spooky old house . . .

Estella   'This door, boy.'

Pip   'After you, miss.'

Estella   'Don't be silly, I'm not going in.'

Everyone knocks

OMG!

Cobwebs!

Miss Havisham   'Come close . . . Look at me . . . You're not afraid of a woman who has never seen the sun since you were born?'

It's my nan.

Miss Havisham   'You know what I touch, here?'

Pip   'Your heart.'

Miss Havisham   'Broken.'

It's my sister.

Oh, *she's* back.

Estella.

Don't play cards with her, Pip!

Estella   'But he's a common labouring boy.'

Miss Havisham   'Well, you can break his heart.'

Now that's just mean.

Estella is the spit of Lucy Price in Year 10.

But not as pretty.

Estella   'He calls the knaves "jacks", this boy.'

Knaves?

What's a knave?!

It's a jack!

SHHH!

Estella   'You stupid clumsy labouring boy.'

Will someone throw a turd at her?

Thassit, Pip, tell the old bag you're going home.

Category error – don't admit you wanna see Estella again.

Get out of there, Pip.

Ohh, he's ashamed of his coarse hands.

Ohh, he's sad.

Don't show her!

Estella   'You've been crying and you're near crying now.'

BOOO!!

Girl power!

SHHH!!

*

Older Pip voice-over image of Young Pip awake in bed. He is emotionally detaching himself from his working-class roots. The first stirrings of his 'great expectations'. Must remember this.

*

Oh, man. He comes back to Havershit House and gets a slap from Stella. The abuse is endless.

It's a horror film.

Estella   'Why don't you cry again, you little wretch.'

Pip   'I'll never cry for you again.'

I am *so* Team Pip.

Estella   'In there, boy.'

Yuk.

It's cobweb central.

Is that a wedding cake?

Colour, please!

That is a *mouse* on a cake.

It's like the canteen.

Miss Havisham kept her wedding cake!

For twenty years!

No wonder the guy never married her.

*

Laughter. And again.

The young Herbert Pocket.

Soon to be Alec Guinness.

Laughter.

He fights like me. If I fought.

Laughter.

Estella.

Always spying.

Thinks they were fighting over her.

Vain cow.

Am I like her?

Don't kiss her, Pip!

Have some pride!

He kissed her.

It's quite good, this.

Better than Physics.

*

Huh. Mrs Gargery's snuffed it.

Bit sudden.

A compressional masterwork.

Feel a bit guilty I wished her dead.

The arrival of Biddy.

She seems nice.

At last, a human woman!

I bet she's Joe Gargery's secret lover.

Pip   'Biddy. Biddy, I want to be a gentleman. I'm not happy as I am. I'm coarse and common.'

Biddy   'Who said so.'

Bloody Estella.

Pip   'I want to be a gentleman on her account.'

*

Montage. Pip walks Miss Hav in her wheelchair, Estella blows cold and colder. But Pip is obsessed – a moth to an iceberg. I have to write this down!

Good, she's off to France to be educated as a lady.

Sounds suspicious.

Don't ask her for a kiss!

Oh, what a muppet.

*

Six years later.

An apprentice blacksmith.

Great use of shadow there from Lean.

Who's that tubby in the top hat?

Wow! Pip's twenty now!

John Mills.

He's quite fit.

Mr Jaggers   'My name is Jaggers, I'm a lawyer in London.'

You're not, mate, you're a fat feller in a blacksmith's barn in Kent.

Mr Jaggers   'My communication to him is that he has great expectations.'

Applause and a bit of cheering.

SHHH!

A secret benefactor . . .

Must be Miss Havisham.

What are great expectations?

It means he's gonna be rich. And a gentleman.

*

London!

I wonder if we'll see some black people now?

If it was in colour you'd be able to see that all the buildings are made of cardboard and stuff.

Barnyard's Inn.

Lodging with Mr Pocket.

Bit worried Pip is becoming a git. But maybe that's the point?

The young Alec Guinness.

What a gorgeous face.

It's the boy he had a fight with!

Bit of a coincidence.

Ooh, Pocket's slagging off Estella.

The snooty girl's an orphan!

I'm an orphan.

Miss Havisham adopted her.

And brought her up to:

Pocket   'Wreak revenge on all the male sex.'

Ooh, that's what I call dinner. I'm *so* hungry. Thought I had a sausage roll in my pocket but I must've eaten it in break.

Right. Back story delivered by Pocket. Twenty-five years ago Miss Hav was stood up on her wedding day and has now trained Estella to be a man-killing bullet of vengeance. I *need* a pen and paper.

*

Montage of gentlemanly conduct: learning to dance, fence and box.

Something needs to *happen*.

Still no black people.

I have no memory of eating that sausage roll.

Pip and Herbert Pocket racking up debts.

When's Estella coming back?

Might have a snooze.

Why was it more interesting when he was young?

Where did I leave my sausage roll?

Boring!

SHHH!

Ah! Joe Gargery's paying a visit.

Mr Pip won't like that.

Pip   'In trying to become a gentleman I had succeeded in becoming a snob.'

He better not be rude to Joe.

Joe's top hat is two foot tall!

He's talking all posh.

I do that.

Don't put your hat on the mantelpiece, Joe, it won't fit.

He's dropped it in a tea cup.

We've all done it.

Joe's eyebrows have got to be fake. The left one is alive!

Ooh, Miss Havisham wants to see Pip at once.

Joe 'I'm wrong in these clothes, Pip. I'm wrong out of the forge, and out of the kitchen, off the marshes.'

Poor old Joe.

I must've left it in my locker.

I give up. This film is WHITE.

*

Miss Havisham still rocking the cobwebs.

What does she want?

Estella's back.

A grown woman.

Sexily forbidding.

And he's still a puppy.

Pip 'Do you remember the first time I came here? The time you made me cry?'

Estella 'Did I? I don't remember.'

Pip 'Not remember you made me cry?'

Estella 'You meant nothing to me, why should I remember?'

Sharp intake of breath.

Estella 'You must know Pip I have no heart.'

Give her up!

She keeps warning you off and you keep going back for more.

Story of my life.

Miss Havisham   'Love her. If she favours you, love her.
If she tears your heart to pieces . . . love her.'

Oh, he will, don't worry about that, ya psycho.

Do I dare sneak out to my locker?

*

Estella hits London.

What on earth is that?!

A big furry muff.

I want one.

*

She's met a bloke.

At some rave.

Bentley Drummle.

A human sideburn.

What a cad. Made for her.

Pip's gone green – if it was in colour.

It's dancing but doesn't look much fun.

The Spanish polka.

It won't catch on.

Pip disses Drummle.

And in return she gives Drummle the eye.

She's Beyoncé in a bonnet.

At this point – bizarrely – the entire company could dance the Spanish polka. Or not.

*

A dark and stormy night . . .

Love the smoking jacket.

Someone at the door . . .

Oooh . . .

Magwitch!

He's lost an eye.

I bet he wants wittels. I want wittels.

Why can't Pip remember him?

Cos it was ages ago and he was a kid!

Magwitch is enormous.

Pip's remembered.

Don't mess with him.

Thassit, give the man a drink.

Magwitch   'May I make so bold as to ask how you've done well since you and me was out on those lone shivering marshes?'

OH MY GOD

It's Magwitch!

He's the benefactor!

Ooh dear.

Magwitch   'Yes Pip, dear boy, I made a gentleman of you, it was me what dunnit.'

He wants Pip to be his son!

He wants to move in!

Adults are so demanding.

*

Mr Jaggers.

What a breakfast.

Oh. Magwitch is here *illegally*.

A refugee.

And if he's caught he'll be hung.

Good for Pip!

He's gonna smuggle Magwitch out the country.

*

Bentley Drummle on a horse.

What an arse.

He's dining with Estella.

Pip's got no chance.

Back at Cobweb Mansions . . .

Pip   'I'm as unhappy as you could ever have meant me to be.'

He should've stayed with Joe and Biddy and never tried to be a gentleman.

Thassit, Pip, give Miss H the bollocking she deserves.

Meanwhile, dear sweet Estella is knitting.

Oh no!

Don't tell her you love her!

Idiot.

She doesn't care!

She's dining with Bentley Drummle.

Pip   'How can you fling yourself at such a man?'

Estella   'I am going to be married to him.'

Shiiit!

SHHHH!

Miss Havisham – finally – a conscience!

She's sorry.

Bit late, Miss H.

Pip thunders out in his big cloak.

Slam.

Log!

Log!

Oops . . .

The wedding dress!

Wooompff!

She's on fire!

Oh my God!

Wailing!

Screaming for her life!

Pip, save Miss Havisham!

Run away!

Let her burn!

Save her!

AAAGGGHHH!

Those cobwebs really don't help.

Put her out, Pip!

Too late

Too late

Smouldering.

Dead.

Barbecued.

He's killed her.

It's not good for his gentlemanly reputation.

*

I find myself perplexed. The protagonist (Pip) loves a hateful woman. He is also posing as a gentleman and has just committed accidental manslaughter. None of these things make us like him. He does have a mission to help Magwitch from danger but I can't say I care that much about him either. In short, what are we supposed to care about? Then again, it could be argued that wanting to 'care' is a sentimental and bourgeois response to a work of art. Mmm. I'm on to something here. Yes . . . the fact that we have ceased to care for anyone or anything is Lean and Dickens's way of reflecting the 'uncaring' society of mid-Victorian England. English Essay Prize in the bag.

*

London.

Tea with Mr Wemmick.

Wemmick has worst hair I've ever seen.

Sweep-over over sweep-over over sweep-over – but still bald as an egg.

Unfunniest scene in the history of cinema.

Ah. Some plot. Watch out for man with scar.

He's an informer.

Headteacher called me that. I said I was 'reporting' not 'informing'. He said 'the nuance is moot'.

*

Pip, Pocket and Magwitch feasting on chicken. Or duck. That's it, I'm going for the sausage roll . . .

Exits, creeping silently.

Pocket books them seats on a 'packet boat'.

What's that?

Why is Pip rowing on the Thames?

Still in his top hat.

Rowing is surprisingly difficult.

Oh, it's a steamship.

Enormous.

Beautiful.

Maybe a black sailor on it . . . ? Nope.

Scar man!

He's on to them.

Escape.

Now I care!

A dark old night on the river.

Herbert Pocket is like your bestest bezzy. Never complains.

I'd like a mate like him.

BOAT AHOY! AHOY THERE!

What's Magwitch babbling on about?

Oh, he once had a daughter.

So?

Sausage-roll getter creeps back in and back to seat. Brief complaining from others.

What did I miss?

Everything.

Yeah but what?

SHHHH!

*

The day of the escape . . .

Danger . . .

Two men inspecting Pip's rowing boat.

It's OK, they've gone.

The steamer!

Applause.

What's Pip seen?

Nooo!

Another boat . . .

Police!

And Scarface.

Three boats . . .

Police – steamer – Pip, Pocket and Magwitch –

Policeman   'You have an escaped convict there!'

'I call upon him to surrender and you to assist!'

Row faster, Pip!

Escape!

Faster!

They're gonna crash!

The steamer's gonna kill them!

CRASHHHH!

Magwitch and scar man in the water!

Fighting!

The steamer's gonna shred them!

Pip!

He's saved Magwitch!

He's OK, they're OK.

Scar man's drowned.

Body count is four: Mrs Gargery, Miss Havisham, scar man. And that rabbit.

The cops have got Magwitch.

Pip's plan failed.

Oh . . .

Pip   'I'll never forgive myself for this.'

Magwitch   'I'm all right, my boy, I'm content to have seen my boy. And to take my chance.'

(*Moved.*) Oh . . .

Oh . . .

Dad . . .

*

Packed court room.

Judge   'Prisoners at the bar . . . '

He's put the black hankie on . . .

Tracking shot . . .

Pitiful wretches awaiting sentence . . .

A black lad! The first black face! And he's about to be hung.

Poor old Abel Magwitch.

He doesn't deserve to die.

*

Mr Jaggers.

Voice like lard and treacle.

Whass he burbling on about?

I don't get it.

Estella is Magwitch's daughter!

She's not posh at all.

She's the daughter of a convict and a murderess.

There's a twist.

*

Ohh . . .

Prison hospital.

Poor old Magwitch.

Dying . . .

Magwitch   'Dear boy, I thought you wasn't coming . . . '

Pip   'Are you in pain?'

Magwitch   'Aye. I don't complain of none, dear boy.'

Why do I feel like crying?

Pip   'I have to tell you something . . . '

– 'You had a child once who you loved and lost . . . '

– 'She lived. And found powerful friends . . . '

– 'She's living now. She is a lady.'

– 'And very beautiful.'

– 'And . . . I love her.'

Magwitch . . .

Smiles . . .

Kisses Pip's hand . . .

Dies.

Pip   'Oh Lord be merciful to him. A sinner.'

*

Pip*'s fevered, delirious journey through the London streets ending in his passing out/blackout.*

The company rise and act this sequence using the sound from the film. It could be done in dance or expressionist movement or naturalistically.

On blackout the company are all lying on the floor. They are all 'Pip' as it were.

Fade up of lights.

They slowly get to their feet.

From now on they do not need to return to their seats. They have become a chorus.

A few of the lines where appropriate may be said by all.

And gradually, the company might congregate towards the screen or in a line across the stage as if they now own the story and can tell it to the audience.

*

What happened?

I'm in bed.

Is it Joe?

Yes.

I've been ill for months.

A fever I suppose.

Where am I?

Home.

He says he's brought me home

Joe   'Dear old Pip, old chap.'

Pip   'Ohh . . . Joe . . . '

– 'You break my heart. Please don't be so good to me.'

*

Joe and Biddy are to marry.

Biddy   'One day Pip you'll marry too.'

Pip   'I don't think I shall, Biddy. Not now.'

*

Pip goes to the old house.

Through the metal gate he entered as a nervous child.

He hears voices . . . from his past . . .

Estella   'What name?'

Pumblechook   'Pumblechook.'

Estella   'Quite right.'

– 'Come in, Pip.'

– 'Don't loiter, boy.'

He pushes open the front door.

Estella   'Come along, boy, take your hat off.'

And Pip does so.

He climbs the stairs.

The music is haunting.

Estella   'He's a common labouring boy.'

Miss Havisham   'You can break his heart.'

He holds a lit candle.

He approaches Miss Havisham's room.

He's scared.

Estella   'This door, boy.'

He eases it open . . .

He's in the dark room . . .

Estella   'Pip.'

He's amazed.

Pip   'Estella.'

He still loves her.

Pip   'What are you doing here? I thought you were in Paris with your husband?'

Estella   'I have no husband, Pip.'

Bentley Drummle left her as soon as he was told of her low birth.

Estella says it has simplified her life.

She will live here. Alone.

Pip realises she will become Miss Havisham.

Pip   'Estella . . . '

– 'You must leave this house . . . '

– 'It's a dead house . . . '

– 'Nothing can live here . . . '

– 'Leave it, Estella, I beg of you.'

She refuses.

She says she belongs here.

She still belongs to Miss Havisham.

Pip tells her Miss Havisham has gone.

Estella insists she is still here in this very room.

Pip   'Then I defy her!'

– 'I have come back, Miss Havisham!'

– 'I have come back, to let in the sunlight!'

He rips down the curtains.

Tears them from their rails.

He flings open the shutters.

Light floods the room.

Estella seems to wake from a trance.

And the spell is broken.

Pip   'I have never ceased to love you . . . '

– 'Even when there seemed no hope for my love.'

– 'You're part of my existence, part of myself.'

– 'Estella, come with me, out into the sunlight.'

Estella   'Pip, I'm afraid.'

They hold each other.

And run outside to the gate . . .

Hand in hand . . .

They turn . . .

Take one last look back . . .

And they're gone.

Pause.

THE END.

They applaud the screen. The lights click back on.

Adult Voice   Thank you, everyone. Well done. Please hand in your essays by the end of the week.

A few groans and then everyone leaves.

But one student remains.

He or she approaches the screen/audience.

Thank you, Mr Lean. And Mr Dickens.

And Miss Simmons. And Miss Hunt.

And Mr Guinness and Mr Mills.

You are all dead, I suppose.

Ghosts on a silver screen.

But I will remember you.

The student gazes at the screen as the lights fade to black.

The School Film

BY PATRICK MARBER

Notes on rehearsal and staging, drawn from a workshop with the writer, held at the National Theatre, October 2016

How Patrick came to write the play

Patrick shared his memory of being a ten-year-old in a gymnasium where he watched *Great Expectations* with his fellow pupils in an all-boys school. The David Lean classic was his first experience of a 'grown-up' film and the experience of this has never left him. He remembers feeling frightened at the start of the film and how he and his fellow pupils all identified with Pip. He described this as a powerful experience that united a group of disparate boys. Patrick acknowledged that the character at the end of *The School Film* who thanks the actors and film-makers could be seen as biographical.

In drawing upon this experience, Patrick felt that it would be fun to write a play about a seemingly boring classic film within a modern context and that this could lead to good comedy. This contrast is potent.

Patrick also felt that the play encourages actors to speak out and to have a direct relationship with the audience, which is beneficial in supporting young actors to develop their stagecraft.

Approaching the play

Anthony Banks, lead director, set up a game of charades to start the exploration of the play. The person who guessed the film, play or book then had a go in the centre. This developed so that the person who guessed could also nominate. The game developed into a follow-up exercise where Anthony asked participants to close their eyes and try and remember as much detail as possible from the last ten minutes. He then asked the following questions:

- Was there a performer in the exercise that you felt sorry for?

- Was there a character or performer that you disliked?

- Was there a performer that you fancied?

- Think of the other people in the circle. Did most of them feel older or younger than you?

- Thinking about the background to the characters, did you feel that they were from the same place as you or did you feel you were a stranger in this landscape?

- Do you remember anyone with tattoos?

- Was anyone wearing noisy shoes?

- Did anyone come across as overly confident?

- Did you get the impression people already knew each other?

Anthony then asked participants to open their eyes. The exercise served to illustrate approaches to the play. Putting into context the need to identify the signals we give off when we are the audience and when we are the performer. He explained that the audience is the main character in this play. Finding ways of working on this key element of the play will provoke the questions 'What does it mean to be an audience?' and 'What is the experience of an audience watching an audience?'

The game of charades also served to illustrate the use of an inner dialogue, the need to be humorous, the use of cultural references, the anxiety and dynamic of a silent room, the relief when silence is broken, how eye contact makes us feel involved, an active audience not a passive exchange, the familiar but awkward feeling of 'Is it going to be me next – have I got something to offer?'

In *The School Film*, we are watching an ensemble doing a play wherein they are watching a film. There are many layers to the piece and it may appear to be one thing but is actually made of lots of other elements.

Patrick has left many of the choices about how to realise the play up to the directors, to enable them to match their version of the play with the company that they are working with. This applies to how to develop characters. It is possible for actors to 'play themselves' or to create a character that requires them to transform.

Another aspect to consider when approaching the play is the shared and differing experience of the audience. It is envisaged that there will be people watching the play that know the film well and others who may not have heard of it. It is also important to acknowledge that the audience may be made up of siblings, peers, parents, grandparents and members of the local community. Within this the age range is wide.

It is the responsibility of each director to decide what to say and what not to say in relation to context. Watching the film of *Great Expectations* would be useful, but how and when this is shared will depend on each director.

PATRICK MARBER   'The spirit of the play is warm and should be an embracing experience, it is a joyous life-enhancing play that any age, class, ethnicity, gender can enjoy and is fully accessible to all.'

Themes

The film is about two young people who want to be rich and to better themselves in society, only to find out that love is more important.

Other themes might include:

- Aspiration.
- Celebrity.
- Wealth.
- Materialism.
- Social status.

- Heritage.
- Parentage.
- Affluence and influence.

Structure

Throughout the play an asterix (*) denotes a passing of time. This can take many forms such as dance, montage, movement, a change of position, slow motion or fast-forward.

These moments allow you to explore the story expressively. Patrick stated that the structure of the play puts the director in the position of 'conductor' with each section feeling like a piece of music.

Anthony developed this idea further by encouraging the 'conductors' to embrace moments that surprise the audience, such as the polka moment or when everyone becomes Pip. These magical moments conjure up surprise and the rules of the space that have been set up can be broken to discover this.

Language

The text needs to be spoken outwards and is often an expression of an internal thought and therefore doesn't rely on creating rhythms through dialogue. Patrick spoke about the internalised thoughts having a 'hypnotic spell' quality that should feel as though it is in 'communion' with the audience and through this language they will find a poetry and narrative unison. The text can only really work if the actors have a love of doing it and collectively work to ensure that the ball isn't dropped at any moment.

Patrick explained that the difference between the inner thoughts and the dialogue was that the inner thoughts may be more reflective and the dialogue would be to a neighbour. This may stimulate more of a physical rather than a vocal distinction.

Patrick agreed that the repetition of lines where the same thought could be happening to several characters could be used to create an interesting choral effect.

The text offers descriptions of time and place such as 'spooky old house' that really help to set the atmosphere and are also an opportunity to develop character. Who uses this language and who would be interested in this description? Character and language are intrinsically linked and character is revealed through these moments of description.

Characters and characterisation

Accents in the play can vary – as they do in a group of people.

Patrick shared his ideas about who the characters in the story are. He suggested that it is important to allocate lines so that each character has a through line. The characters need to have a consistent attitude. The actors could play both their student character and a Dickensian character. There are a number of characters that can be found in the text. They are:

IN THE FILM

Pip
Estella
Older Estella
Cow
Miss Havisham
Magwitch
Mrs Gargery
Pumblechook
Joe Gargery
Policemen
Mr Jaggers
Judge
Biddy
Pocket

THE STUDENTS

The cineaste
The pseudo-intellectual (essayist)
The sausage-roll eater
The fashionista
The Pip sympathiser (Mrs Gargery hater)
The Pip admirer
The one fascinated by violence
The one in love with Lucy
The moaner about watching an old film
The one with girl power
The one concerned that there aren't any black characters

The style of the acting will need to take into account who the characters are talking to. This is especially important when the characters are talking to themselves.

It is plausible that actors will play the character close to their own personalities. You could liken the characters' use of inner thought to the character of Hamlet and to imagine the feeling of twenty Hamlets all speaking their inner thoughts at the same time. Actors could personalise this by imagining that the audience are their souls.

Patrick advocated that the actors playing the Dickensian characters should be bold and brave in their characterisation. They should be familiar with the delivery of the character in the film and use this as a launch pad for creating the role. It is important to have a go at embodying the characters/actors from the film and to pay attention to detail regarding intonation, mannerisms and behaviour. They must not try to make the audience laugh but commit to the detail of the role.

Casting

The voice of the teacher should remain a voice, giving a sense of disembodiment. It is important that young people do not play adults. Anthony suggested that this voice offers a theatrical opportunity.

Gender can be mixed up in this play – for example, it is possible for Miss Havisham to be played by a male actor.

Each of the Dickensian characters should be played by the same actor every time they speak (so Magwitch is always the same person, Miss Havisham is always the same person, etc.). These roles would suit actors who enjoy transforming into characters.

Patrick suggested that the actor who plays Pip doesn't play any of the other roles.

It will be important to prepare your character types before casting and to match lines to suit the company that you are working with. You could merge two characters to become one, but it is important to identify who they are separately before adapting to suit the strengths of the group.

The play works well with mixed age groups – it may be worth considering how this might affect positions/relationships within the group.

Production, staging and design

Patrick acknowledged that the play could be challenging and difficult and encouraged directors to experiment with form and to have complete authority over the staging of the play. There is no right or wrong way. When asked about the truth behind the gathering of a group of students to watch a film (and whether this is something that others had experienced at school), Patrick suggested that it may work to imagine that the set-up is that a film club has been instigated by a 'trendy English teacher' and that the film is being shown after lunch. Those students who watch it will miss lessons but will have to write a follow-up essay.

This offers the given circumstances of how the story begins and may influence how characters enter the space or whether they are discovered in the space. What will the audience be looking at before anyone has said anything?

It is envisaged that mobile phones do not feature in the play – they may be put away at the start of the film but do not reappear.

Patrick suggested that the staging shouldn't feel static; inner thoughts trigger inner lives that are active and characters are allowed to move seats, etc. In positioning students, it is vital to ensure that there is scope for distance between characters whose lines follow on from one another to help shift focus and keep the play moving. The seating can be staggered or raked to encourage a sense of surprise of not knowing who will speak their thoughts next. Patrick referenced his play *The Musicians* as having a similar set-up to ensure that actors are encouraged to face out and directly address the audience.

Patrick recommended that part of the rehearsal process should focus on trying out different positions to fully explore how the production will work in space. This will empower actors to own the space more. You could take into consideration that we naturally scan from left to right and that it may be useful for actors to feel where the strong positions in the space are.

Patrick proposed that the Dickensian characters can stand and 'declaim' to fellow students. It may also be possible for everyone to stand on the CAPITALISED text when all speak.

Establishing where the actors' eye-line is is a collective and important decision. It is envisioned that the screen for the film is consistently behind the audience (imaginatively) so that the actors don't limit the reach of their focus. Patrick suggested that the screen should be so believable that the audience will want to turn around to check if it is actually there.

Anthony suggested that eye-line also requires clarity when the Dickensian characters are speaking to one another. This should also be directed towards the audience rather than to each other in the space – but they must make us believe that they can really see one another.

The staging of the play should give a sense that this 'rabble of kids' has the proverbial spotlight turned on them. They become individuals with hearts, souls and a relationship to the film (they don't all have to enjoy the film).

Music and sound

The film soundtrack could be used as much or as little feels necessary for your production (subject to licensing). Other sounds should come from the space such as knocking, crisp packets, wind noises. What is the soundscape of the room and the soundscape of the film? How do they converge/contrast?

Lighting

Lighting can be used to focus on different characters, being mindful that the shift between characters is swift. It may also denote a shift between Dickensian character and student. There is a change of atmosphere after Pip collapses, which may be punctuated through lighting.

Lighting can also help to establish that they are watching a film and may be established at the start of the play – it would be difficult to maintain this flicker throughout and imaginative ways of working with this are encouraged.

Style and technique

Patrick explained that at the moments when the students voice the words from the film, they are *becoming* the character. It is important to trust this as it will work poetically. He emphasised that observing the discipline of the script is essential to telling the story.

There is a differentiation between the film characters and the students. This transformation should be exciting to play. The film characters can have props.

Anthony described the majority of the play as being solitary and advocated the importance of tuning each individual into their role as an ensemble so that they are stylistically the same.

Physical moments such as knocking can be done collectively to add to the sense of ensemble.

Characters are encouraged to break the fourth wall. It is possible to use gesture, but imperative that this still feels like an inner thought where appropriate (for example, 'it's my nan').

It is important not to confuse inner thought with dialogue. It is tempting to make this more conversational, but it can lead to confusion.

It is important that the inner thoughts don't 'flat-line' vocally. The hypnotic quality must feel alive.

There is a distinctive shift in the play once Pip passes out and the actors become a chorus for the last section of the play. Patrick likened this to a Greek chorus where they become the tellers of the tale. This will rely on the actors feeling fully immersed in the story. They all become one in this moment. Patrick suggested that this technique requires discipline and skill and will need to be drilled. Only then can rules that have been set up be broken. He described the play as a dramatic poem in play form where every single line has to be played with intention.

Exercises for use in rehearsals

REHEARSAL GAMES TO ESTABLISH ENSEMBLE

- Hold hands and send a pulse around the circle.

- Stand up and sit down together without a cue.

- Count to twenty-one as a collective, with one person saying one number at a time. Anybody can start the count. Then a different person says the next number – but if two or more people happen to speak at the same time, counting must start again from the beginning.

UNDERSTANDING THE LANGUAGE THROUGH ACTION

Anthony divided the group into four and allocated a section of text to each group from pages 395–399. This section of the text has examples of inner thought, dialogue, Dickensian character and choral speech. The groups were asked to split up the lines and focus on the language of the play. The task was to trust instincts and imagination to ignite the text in whatever way the group chose. Each group had twenty-five minutes to prepare this before sharing.

In the sharing of each section, the rest of the group observed ways of establishing the conventions of the play. All four sections were then pieced together as members from each group were scattered amongst each other. This could be a useful exercise in finding ways to shift focus when the text is coming from different directions.

Anthony and Patrick then redirected each section to bring out different layers and ways of telling the story. The following suggestions were made that could be helpful to consider during rehearsals:

- Encourage actors to not let any air into the text and to pick up on the cues and momentum.

- Encourage actors to play the scene for the smallest theatre. When is there a moment to give the text a beat?

- Play with actors being seated and standing up. What are the differences?

- Encourage actors to ping out the most important word in the line. Ask them to make a decision about how to get the word across. Empower actors to find the juicy word without worrying about the whole phrase.

- Invite actors to try the text using just breath (not whispered) at the same time, isolating them so they can't see each other. Then return to the original formation and voice the text again. What is different? What detail is retained?

- Identify the characters by naming their characteristics (certain, intense, empathetic, bubbly, optimistic, sensual, dreamer, etc.). Once these characteristics have been named, you could encourage actors to explore making opposite choices in the delivery of the text.

- You could add a metronome pulse to the text; explore ways that this unifies the ensemble. Where are the pauses? How do the rhythms impact on the poetry of the language? Repeat the text without the guide. Try this at double speed. Allow this exercise to support the actors' discovery of the pace and patterns within the text.

WATCH THE FILM WITH YOUR SCRIPT

Patrick felt that directors will need to prepare for rehearsals by watching the film with the script and to have a visual memory of the moments in the play that the students are watching. This will help with understanding the play and works towards making the audience feel that they have seen the film themselves.

Suggested references, reading and viewing list

David Lean's film *Great Expectations* (1946).

The Musicians by Patrick Marber, in *Connections 2016*.

Great Expectations, the original novel by Charles Dickens.

From a workshop led by Anthony Banks
with notes by Julia Thomas

Zero for the Young Dudes!
by Alistair McDowall

The inmates at a bizarre summer camp are plotting a revolution. Or has it already happened?

Spending a day watching their schedule of exercise, lessons and meals, a long history of unrest and injustice lies hidden; and as the day wears on, a violent future looms large on the horizon.

Cast size
Variable size ensemble

Alistair McDowall's plays include *X* at the Royal Court, 2016; *Pomona* at RWCMD/ Gate Theatre, 2014 and Orange Tree Theatre/ Royal Exchange Theatre, Manchester/ National Theatre, 2014/15; *Talk Show* at the Royal Court, 2013; *Brilliant Adventures* (Bruntwood Prize Judges' Award, 2011) at the Royal Court Young Writers' Festival 2012, and Royal Exchange and Live Theatre, Newcastle, 2013; *Captain Amazing* at Live Theatre and Edinburgh Fringe 2013 and on UK tour 2014.

Notes on the text

To be staged with a cast of any number of performers.

Genders in each scene have been assigned randomly and should be changed to fit the cast.

Most scenes have a specific number of characters speaking but this can be altered by assigning the lines differently.

The entire cast should appear in Scenes One, Two and Sixteen.

The same actor should perform Scenes Six, Eleven and Fifteen.

The setting is a summer camp.

The time is now.

Maybe the performers wear a uniform or matching outfits.

Maybe the performers remain on stage throughout.

Maybe blackouts would be respite and should be avoided unless stated.

Maybe the audience are the enemy.

A question without a question mark denotes a flatness of tone.

A dash (–) indicates an interruption of speech or train of thought.

An ellipsis (. . .) indicates either a trailing off, a breather, a shift or a transition.

An oblique (/) indicates where the next line of dialogue interrupts or overlaps.

One.
RISE.

The **Campers** *eat cereal.*

They occasionally eye the audience.

Whisper / mutter.

Laugh at something secret.

It's somewhat threatening but hard to tell why.

When the bell or buzzer yells they stand and head to leave
a rabble
half
draining bowls of milk
half
hollering laughing pushing.

Two.
PLEDGE.

The **Campers** *line up to pledge in unison:*

> I PLEDGE MY TRUE ALLEGIANCE
> TO THE NATION THAT SHELTERS, CLOTHES,
> AND FEEDS ME.

> LAND OF MY BIRTH,
> HOME OF MY PEOPLE,
> WHOSE VALUES AND BELIEFS I SHARE,
> AND WHOSE LAWS I UPHOLD AND OBEY.

> I AM GRATEFUL TO BE A CITIZEN OF A COUNTRY
> SO PROSPEROUS, FAIR, AND FREE;
> AND SHALL GIVE UNCONDITIONAL OBEDIENCE
> AND RESPECT
> TO THOSE THAT SEEK TO SECURE

A BRIGHT AND RIGHTEOUS FUTURE
FOR ME
AND ALL THAT FOLLOW.

I PLEDGE MY LIFE AND BLOOD TO THIS CAUSE,
SO HELP ME GOD.

Three.
RUN.

A clearing in the woods that look over the camp.
Two **Campers** *are here in shorts and t-shirts.*
One holds a hand grenade proudly, showing the other.

— When though?
— This morning.
— Just this morning?
— I said.
— Under your pillow?
— Under my pillow, I said.

Pause.

— Four others, too –
— Four others have them?
— At least.
— You saw?
— No –
— You actually didn't *see* though.
— No, but I know because there's, there's like a *nod* –
— You're nodding at each other.
— We're not *nodding* at each other, we're just, you see someone, across the dinner hall or whatever, and you see them, and you look at them, and you just . . . (*Nod.*)
— And that means –
— That means you both, you both *know*.
— That you both have them.
— That we both have them.

Pause.

— Are we allowed them?
— No, we're not allowed them, we're not allowed shoelaces, why would we be allowed grenades?
— But how come you have one then?
— Because I found it under my –
— Yeah, but how *come* though?
— Because someone's putting them under pillows in the dorms –
— Yeah, but *why*?

Pause.

— Is there a plan?
— . . .
— Is there a plan no one told us about?
. . .
Like a secret plan. For the whole camp.
. . .
Do you think?
— I dunno.

Pause.

— Does it smell?
— (*Sniffs.*) No. Not much, anyway.
— Is it new?
— Looks it.
— Looks pretty new.
It's from our war, you think? Not some old war.
— Maybe . . .

Beat.

— Can I hold it?
— Get your own.
— I don't have my own though!
— Put a note under your pillow.
— I just wanna hold it for a few seconds.
. . .

Just for like five seconds.

. . .

Please.

. . .

Just for one second.

Pause.

The grenade is handed over.

— Wow.

She walks around, holding it aloft, rapt.
Inspects it.

— That bit pings off.
— Duh.
— You pull the pin and then when you let it go, that bit pings off.
— I know already.
— We never had these before . . .

Pause.

— OK, give it back now.
— (*Miming throwing it.*) Bloody Japs!
— You had it long enough –
— Bloody Japs! Kamikazes!

It's snatched back.

— Knob.
— (*Grins.*)
— Japs?
— It's racist for Japanese.
— I know.
— When d'ya think they'll tell you the plan?
— I don't know there *is* a plan.
— I bet there is. You don't hand out grenades without a plan.

. . .

Maybe we're going to war again.

— . . .

I dunno.

. . .

Someone's coming.

Another **Camper** *runs on.*

— What are you dildos doing – What's that?
— Nothing –
— It's a hand grenade.
— Oh. (*Beat.*) Have you got a fag?
— No.
— Pfft.

She shoves her hands down her shorts and rustles around.

— I hate cross-country.

Produces a cigarette and lighter after much rummaging, lights it.

— You'll get done if they catch you smoking.
— My socks are wet as fuck . . .

Four.
WASH.

The **Campers** *stand with towels, queuing for the showers.*
Two **Campers** *talk as the line occasionally moves forward a few*
steps.

— The jeeps?
— The jeeps they patrol –
— Yeah, I know which jeeps you mean, but how are you
gonna get one of them?
— Because sometimes they just, when they need to run into the
office quickly they leave them running outside sometimes –
— Not often though.
— Sometimes they do.
— Not often though.
— Well say they do, they do one day –

— For like thirty seconds.
— So in those thirty seconds I get in it and I drive –
— You can't drive.
— I can drive.
— You don't have a licence –
— You don't *need* a licence to drive.
— Yes you do.
— Well, legally, yeah, you have to be twenty-one and have a licence, but what I'm saying is that anyone *can* drive, it's not a hard thing to do.
— I dunno . . .
— It's easy!
— There's the clutch, and . . .
— Trust me, I can drive. I drive the jeep. I wait till they leave it outside the office and I get in and drive it –
— And you just happen to be there when that happens.
— I take my moment – I take my moment and I drive, I drive away wicked fast –
— They're shooting at you –
— And I'm weaving the car –
— You're dodging bullets.
— I'm not *dodging* bullets, I'm just weaving the car, I'm *weaving* it.
— You're getting shot all over –
— I'm not –
— You're like (*Rattling with the impact of a hundred rifles.*) uhuhuhuhuhuhuh –
— I might get *some* minor injuries.
— Your guts all fall out –
— My guts don't fall out –

Another **Camper** *has come on, looking lost.*

— Is this where we go to get our orders?
— Join the queue.
— How come we have to get them in the showers?
— / It's –

— We're having a conversation here.
— But I don't have my towel, I can't –

Others in the line start piping up:

— Hey, no pushing in –
— Who's pushing in?
— Get to the back of the line.
— Move it, dude.

He heads to the back of the line.

— So you're driving –
— Did everyone else get a grenade?
— / Shhh –
— Shut the fuck up, what's wrong with you?
— Moron.

Beat.

— Where do you drive.
— I drive up the hill, up to the woods, where we do cross-country.
— Your guts are hanging out . . .
— My guts are not hanging out.
— You've lost an eye –
— I've got both eyes.
— You're mowing down kids doing cross-country –
— I'm *driving* up there, where the most isolated section of fence is.
— And what?
— And I smash straight through it with the jeep.

Beat.

— What.
— I smash into it –
— It's not one fence, it's three.
— I smash through *them* –
— And razor-wire, and those things with the spikes –
— I'll be going a hundred miles an hour.

— And it's electric.
— . . .
Then —
— That kid ran into it last week and burst all over the place.
— Well, then, I'll —
. . .
Okay,
So,
I'll take the big —
You know the big tarp sheet things we cover the track with
when it rains?
— Yeah.
— I'll have one of those in the jeep —
— So you have to roll up this huge sheet thing.
— I do that before.
— And carry it, have it with you —
— Yeah —
— At the exact moment the jeep is free for thirty seconds —
— I —
— And in those thirty seconds you have to get this thing, I
mean, they're *huge*, those sheets, they cover the whole track —
— I throw it in the jeep, I drive up to the woods, I stop at the
fence, I throw the tarp over the fence so I don't *touch* it, then
I climb up and over and out!

Pause.

— Then what.
— Then,
eventually,
I go round and free all the other camps —
— All of them.
— One at a time.
— Just on your own?
— I've got fantastic muscles and fabulous reflexes.
— There's a few holes in this plan.
— I free the Titches first, because they have the least security.
I get them out and then I have a small army to help me free

the others, free our Generals and everything, and then once
everyone else is free, I come back here, I *lead* everyone back
here (cos by this point they've all voted and made me a
General), and we come and we storm *this* camp, and the
counsellors and the guards are all like 'Hey, isn't that the kid
who escaped just –' BLEGH – head shot!
— This is not even a plan.
— It's a brilliant plan.

Another **Camper** *has come on:*

— Is this where / we –
— (*Both.*) *Yes.*
— It's a terrible plan.
— It's better than whatever it is they've got planned tonight.
— You don't even know what we're doing yet.
— It won't be as good as mine.
— The point is to make a big gesture, not just have one of us
escape. There's no point doing anything if they don't even
notice.
— They'd notice –
— London wouldn't. Kids escape all the time – or they're
shot *trying* to escape.
They don't report it in the capital.
— How do you know?
— Because why would they?
— I reckon I could cause enough of a stir –
— No way.

Another **Camper** *has come on:*

— Is this where we get our orders?
— Why is everyone asking me?
— You're tall.
— How come we have to get them in the showers?
— Do we have to get naked?
— I have a verruca –

— Can everyone shut up? They're just over there, you wanna give everything away?
— The showers are the only place they don't watch us.
— They're scared of people thinking they're paedos so they don't go in the showers, okay?
— Someone did a big shit on the floor in there last week and no one cleaned it up and all the water made it spread round everywhere.
— Yeah, well,
that's the downside.

Five.
DIRT.

There is a huge pile of earth.
Two **Campers** *are steadily moving it from one side of the stage to the other.*
They shovel up a pile, walk it across the stage, and dump it on the growing new pile.

— Sometimes I even forget how long I've been here!
Sometimes I try and, like I'll think, hey, how long *has* it been? And I can't even remember!
I remember how many times I've moved this pile from here to there, but I didn't have to do it every day, and they only started making me do it about a year ago so I can't work it out from that.
How long have you been here?
— Three months, seventeen days.
— You see, you're smart cos I bet you started counting when you got here, but I didn't even think to *do* that. It was so long ago, and I never actually moved camp, I've always been in this one, this is the only camp I was ever even *in*. My unit got cornered in this supermarket and they rounded us up and brought us here and most of them got moved to other places but I'm still here, I've been here the whole time so it's just a

big blur with how much time it actually is, and obviously they don't let you have calendars here, or watches, and there's only the clocks in the dorms and the dinner hall so you can't even really keep track that easy. Some of the kids in my dorm keep scratch-marks on their beds so they know, you know? But I never did that.

They move dirt in silence for a while.

— Sometimes I even forget where I came from in the first place! Haha!

They move dirt in silence for a while.

— Sometimes when I try and remember what it was like before I have a total brainfart. All I can remember is the guns, because I used to work with the armoury? So I'll be trying to remember what toys I used to have when I was really small, but my head'll just be all like M4 Carbine, M4A1, AK47, SA80, L7A2 GPMG, L115A3, M80, And I don't think I had any of those when I was little, unless maybe I had very liberal parents! Haha!

She laughs for a while.

— Oh . . . boy.

They move dirt in silence for a while.

— My parents died in the bombings.

They move dirt in silence for a while.

— Sometimes it even gets in my head when I'm not *trying* to remember.

Like they'll be asking me a question in class, or I'll be in the queue for lunch or doing the pledge or something, and my head'll just be like M4 Carbine, M4 Carbine, M4Carbine M4CarbineM4Carbine, over and over and over making me go mental, or I'll just be totally obsessively thinking of this guy's head I saw blown up once, or this finger I found on the floor of a bank we stormed and my brain'll just be like fingerfingerfingerfingerfingerfingerfingerfinger, you know?

And then whoever asked the question or whatever, they'll be
trying to get my attention, but I'll just be totally spaced out,
and not saying anything, and I'll mess up, and I think that's
why I get dirt duty a lot.

. . .

I never actually obsess on the things that happen *in* the camp,
just the things in the war, isn't that weird?

. . .

. . .

Do you like Harry Potter?
— (*Shrugs.*) It's alright.
— Dumbledore's the coolest!
I once had a dream where I was a wizard, 'cept it wasn't like
Harry Potter, I wasn't at Hogwarts or anything, I was just
here in the camp 'cept I had magic powers, and I was using
them to zap all the guards and the counsellors and then I
used my wand to bust the fences, some of the fences I could
melt with a special spell I had, oh and also I was flying? And
then we all got freed and all of us were running out of the
camp all cheering and everyone was shouting my name
because I was the hero, but then when we got outside
everyone's head just suddenly started melting! Everyone
stopped running and there was this kind of *fizzing* sound and
then everyone's head was all just bubbling and popping like
Rice Crispies and their eyes were drooping down their heads
and their mouths went from big smiles to big frowns and
everyone was like, grabbing at their heads saying No! No!
Don't melt my head! And they all thought it was *me*, because *I*
was the one with the magic! They were all looking up at me
with their runny eyes saying Don't! Stop! Stop melting our
heads! Why would you free us just to melt our heads?! And
I'm like I didn't, I didn't! I'm trying to tell them it's not me,
it's not my fault, but their ears have all melted so they can't
even *hear* me! So I try to do a spell that'll make their heads go
back to normal except now it's like all my magic is *gone*, I can't
do magic any more for some reason, but it's too late anyway
because now everyone's head is just a big pink puddle on their

necks and they're all falling down dead. And then the last one who still has half a head comes up to me and he was trying to keep the shape of it like he was trying to hold melting ice cream into some kind of structure and he looks at me with his eyes that are like dripping yolks and his mouth was all waxy like a candle and he just looks straight at me and just says – Why?
. . .
And then he falls down dead like the rest.
. . .
. . .
. . .
What do you think that means?
— . . .
(*Shrugs.*)

I dunno.

They move dirt in silence for a while.

— How long did they give you?
— Four hours.
— Me too! What for?
— I did a shit in the shower.
— Wow! That takes confidence!
Well I bet this four hours is gonna pass by like nobody's business. They think it's some big punishment to make us do this until our legs don't work any more but I actually take a lot of pleasure from it. Once I get all the dirt from this side to that side I always take a moment and look at it, even if they yell at me, because I like to take a second and notice the impact I can have on the world and the elements around me. Don't you think?
It's much better than solitary too, in solitary it's just so *boring*. No one to talk to. Just *quiet*. *Quiet* all the time. Quietquietquiet. I mean, sure, that's great if you just want some peace, and actually I do sometimes want peace and quiet, but not when I'm on dirt duty, no way, I like to really

cut loose out here. And we have so much in common we can just talk the time away.

We can talk about all kinds of interesting subjects!

Like we can talk about *food*, and what *friends* we have, and what types of clothes we used to wear, and we can tell our war stories, and we can talk about *cats*, and we can talk about keeping fit, and we can talk about the other camps you were at and do like *comparisons* and we can talk about ghosts and scary stories, and we can talk about politics and we can talk about *fruit* and we can talk about where we used to live and we can talk about people we know that *died* and we can talk about *space*, and we can talk about *hair products* –

— Why'd you get dirt duty.

— Talking too much. Hey, what's your favourite type of smell?

Six.

▉▉▉▉▉

Dear Mum,

I am having a really ▉▉▉▉▉ time at camp. The counsellors are all ▉▉▉▉ and one of them told me ▉▉▉▉▉▉▉▉▉▉. I'm sure learning a lot about ▉▉▉▉▉▉ and ▉▉▉▉ There is a lot of time to ▉▉▉▉▉▉▉▉ in here.

I have ▉▉▉▉▉▉▉▉▉▉▉▉▉, and in ▉▉▉▉▉▉ we get to ▉▉▉▉ in the lake and ▉▉▉▉▉▉▉ and sometimes we ▉▉▉▉▉▉▉▉▉▉.

Don't ▉▉▉▉▉▉▉▉.

If they decide ▉▉▉▉▉▉▉▉▉▉▉▉▉▉, then know that I ▉▉▉▉▉▉▉▉▉▉▉▉▉▉. And that everything ▉▉▉▉▉▉▉▉▉▉ has ▉▉▉ into ▉▉▉▉▉▉▉ ▉▉▉ and I am ready ▉▉▉▉▉▉▉▉▉▉▉▉.

All my ▉▉▉▉,

▉▉▉▉▉

Seven.
SOLITARY.

In solitary confinement, a **Camper** *bounces a ball off the walls.*

We watch this for a while.

— Hey.

Pause.

— Hey.
— (*Unseen, outside.*) What.
— How long am I in here for again?

Pause.

— How long am I –
— Two days.
— Two *days*?
. . .
Actual full days?

Pause.

— How long have I done so far?

Pause.

— I said how long –
— Twenty minutes.
— Twenty *minutes*?
. . .
That can't – Twenty minutes, really?

He tries to count the remainder but struggles.

Pause.

He goes back to bouncing the ball.

— How long till lunch?

Pause.

— I said how lo / ng –
— A long time.
— Yeah, but *how* long?

Pause.

— How long though?
. . .
How long though?
. . .
How long till lunch though?
. . .
How long till –
— I'm not allowed to talk to you.
— How come?

Pause.

— How come you're not?
— Because you're in solitary.
— Yeah, but . . .
. . .

Pause.

He bounces the ball for a while.

— How long has it been now?
— I'm not telling you every – What's that noise in there?
— What?
— What are you making noise with?
— This?

He bounces the ball.

— What is that.
— It's a ball.

Beat.

— A ball?
— Yeah.
— You have a ball in there?

— Yeah.
— You're not supposed to have a ball in there.
— Why not?
— Because you're not.
— Why though?
— Because it's solitary.
— Yeah, but, I gotta have *some*thing to do.
— You're not allowed to have a ball in there –
— How old are you?

Beat.

— How old / are –
— I'm not allowed to talk to you.
— Why?
. . .
Are you a grown-up?
— Yes.
— You don't sound like it.
— I am –
— How old are you then?

Pause.

— Like thirty . . . ?
— I'm twenty-one.
— Pfft. That's not that old.
— Stop talking.
— That's not that old at all.

Pause.

— Were you on their side or our side?
. . .
Whose side were you on?
Before.
. . .
Nineteen, twenty, twenty-one . . . You must have been on our
side, right? If you're only twenty-one now.

. . .

You were with us, yeah?

Pause.

— Did you have to go through this camp?
. . .

Did you do one of the camps before you worked here?
— What's it to you.
— I'm interested.

Pause.

— Yes.
— You did?
— Yes.

Pause.

— Did it work?
Like it's s'posed to?
. . .

Did it, like, change you to being on their side?
— There's no sides.
— Yeah, right.
. . .

Were you captured or did you turn yourself in?

Pause.

— You still there . . . ?
— I'm not talking to you any more.

Pause.

He bounces the ball again.

— I bet you did really well to get to be a guard.
. . .

You must've only just got out, too. They only let you out
when you're twenty-one. And only then if you did well.
. . .

Were you one of those ones that did their whole dorm in?

King Rat?

. . .

Do you wanna be a counsellor one day?

. . .

Do you wanna be like the ones / who –
— What are you in here for.
— What?
— Why are you in solitary.

Beat.

— . . .

I wouldn't pull this kid's fingernails out.
— Why not.
— . . .

(*Shrugs.*) I dunno.

. . .

Didn't want to.

. . .

Maybe that's how come I won't get to be a guard like you.
I bet you did anything they –
— Shut up.
— Hey, are you worried what'll happen to you if there's a
breakout?

. . .

Some kids hate the ones who turned even more than the
actual grown-ups.

. . .

Are you worried we'll do all the things to you that your lot are
making us do to each other?

. . .

I bet it'll –
— Be *quiet*.

Pause.

He bounces the ball some more.

Looks around.

He shoves his hands down his pants and pulls his grenade out.
Inspects it.
Picks his nose.

— What time is it now?

Eight.
FEED.

In the dinner hall.
*Two **Campers** serve the lunch line. The one in charge wears an eye-*
patch.
*The lunchline passes in front of them, a few **Campers** at a time.*

— He's a traitor.
— For *that*?
— If he doesn't do it then *they* do it.
— Yeah, but –
— You've not got one? She hasn't got one –

*The **Second Camper** hands a grenade to a **Camper** in line.*

— Vi / va la revolucion.
— Viva la revolucion.
— We all agreed.
— Yeah –
— We *all* agreed. No more violence at their hands.
— I get all that –
— If I'm having my fingernails dragged out, I want it done by
one of my brothers or sisters, looking into their eyes and
knowing it's an unwilling act, done with compassion and
solidarity. I don't want my body mutilated by my oppressors.
My enemy.
— He was a Titch –
— So?
— So you can do that to a six-year-old?
— I can do it knowing the alternative is worse.
He *still* got his nails pulled out, except now by one of *them*.

And they *enjoy* it.

. . .

It's all the same anyway.

. . .

They put some of us in one type of school, the others another.
Some of us get healthcare, some of us don't.
They always wanted us at war with ourselves, consuming
ourselves, all they've done here is made the process more
honest. And I'll take a brutal honesty over a lie.
— You're unbelievable.
— You're an idealist.
— *I'm* an idealist? You thought we could set up the new state
without an economy –
— Because we would have.
— An economy is a, a, it happens *naturally*,
— Him, him –

The **Second Camper** *hands out a grenade.*

— Viva la / revolucion.
— Viva la revolucion.
— Money works based on agreement. And we all agree we
don't want it.
— Whatever you have – trading *fruit*, whatever, whatever it
is, that will eventually become the same system you
destroyed.
— Not on my watch.
— But if we're all taking this pill at twenty-one, then you're
dead.
You've only got a few years to –
— Age corrupts.
— So what's the –
— Absolute revolution has to be absolute.
— You're such –
It doesn't matter anymore, I don't know why we're even –
— Look at the state of you. Look at that – *Look* at it!
— What?!
— Do you have some kind of syndrome? Stop *throwing* the

food at them –
— I'm fine –
— Watch. Watch me. Look at that arm action. If I'm serving you your lunch, I'm *serving* you your lunch. There's commitment. Intention. You serve it looks like you have something wrong with your brain or your arm or both.
— Why's it matter?
— Oh, why's it matter? Sorry for expecting a little pride in your work. Is it too difficult feeding your comrades with essential nutrients and – She needs one, give her one.

The **Second Camper** *hands out a grenade.*

— Viva / la revolucion.
— Viva la revolucion.
— Get your act together dude, fuck. I'm embarrassed to be stood next to you.
— I'm only –

The **First Camper** *picks something out of the food, flicks it away.*

Pause.

— What was that?
— What?
— What you picked out?
— What do you think?

They serve some more.

— Well don't –
— What do you want me to do? Starve them?
— It's –
— This is lunch. Shut up and serve.
. . .
Everything changes tonight anyway.
. . .
Give him his.

The **Second Camper** *hands out a grenade.*

— Viva la rev / olucion –
— Viva la revolucion.
— You don't say it right. Say it better than that.

Nine.
TARGET.

Shooting range.
Two **Campers** *lie on their fronts. The rifles are bolted to the floor.*
They fire.
Start reloading, etc.

— Bollocks.
— It's not –
— That's not true.
— It is.
— It's obviously bollocks.
— It's not, it's true, before they, like, before *this*, before all
this, they used to teach us about it in *schools*.
— You're lying.
— Some of the other kids, the older ones, the ones with
parents still, they said . . .

They're aiming.

Pause.

They fire.

Start reloading, etc.

— They said the grown-ups used to teach us about sex.
— Why?
— What?
— Why would they do that?
— Because – You gotta learn about it somehow.
— What would the point be? For them, what would the point
be for them.
What do they gain?

— What do they gain making us do this?
— They're not *training* us to shoot are they. They're training us to shoot for *them*.
— It's just something you need to learn, it's an important thing, isn't it?
— . . .
I think they're lying to you.
— One of the older ones said that, before, they used to argue about it.
The grown-ups. It wasn't just some thing they all agreed about – Some wanted us to learn, like, really *young. Really* young. And then others didn't want us to learn about it at all.
— Like the army.
— I dunno.

They aim . . .

— I bet the army didn't want us to learn.

Pause.

Fire.

— Aim higher, they go down cleaner.
— If it's so important how come they don't teach us now.
— Because things are different now, they don't want us learning *now*. This was before the war and everything. Imagine if we all started doing it and having babies now.
— We still know about it though.
— Yeah, but they don't *tell* us. And they're rounding us all up and putting us in places like this, and that's *part* of it, it's not just about the war, cos I heard they've started telling the Titches all kinds of stuff about why you're not supposed to do it, and how, like, *God* and all that, and it's like the *opposite* of what it used to be. Cos if we started all doing it *now*, and having babies, and keeping the babies for ourselves, then suddenly there's this whole other group –
— An army –
— A whole other army of kids, in *waiting*, you know?
That we can say whatever we want to, and we can tell them,

you know, we can teach them whatever. And make them do whatever we *want* them to do. They want to control when we have them, and, you know, how *many* and all that.

— I dunno, that still sounds –

Another **Camper** *has sidled up, unnoticed.*

— Hey.
— Oh –
— Don't look at me, they're looking, don't look at me.
— Soz –

They pretend to aim.

The **Third Camper** *looks around for safety.*

— There's a full dorm inspection at ten fifteen.
— Ten fifteen?
— Ten fifteen, you deaf? Be ready at ten fifteen.
— Al*right*.
— Don't be a dick.

They go back to actually aiming.

Pause.

— You're the dick.

He leaves.

Fire.

— I forgot what I was even –
— Sex.
— Oh yeah, well, apparently they did anyway.
— How do you even teach it?
— I dunno . . .
— Maybe they got to watch porn.
— What's porn?
— It's videos of people doing it.
— Oh right, yeah. Well. I guess so.
How else do you learn 'cept by watching?

They take aim . . .

— Apparently everyone used to watch porn. Even grown-ups.

Pause.

Fire.

— *Shit* –
— Fucking hell, you *scalped* him.
. . .
His head looks like a yoghurt lid.
— (*From off.*) Nice job, dickhead.
— He's wriggling all over the place.
— I'm gonna finish him –
— No, you can't, don't. They don't let you do that. Just wait.
You just have to wait.

They watch impassively as the target writhes and kicks.

— Look at him go.

He takes a while to bleed out.

Pause.

— . . .
— Yeah, that was a mess.

Ten.
REVISE.

In class, **Campers** *are silently copying something from one piece of
paper to another.*

Time passes.

— Psst.

Pause.

— Pss –
— What?
— I'm new.

Pause.

— I'm new –
— So?
— So I don't –
— Sh / hh –
— Shut the fuck up –

She leans in.

— I don't get this.

Pause.

— I don't get –
— Get what?
— I don't get what /we're –
— Shut up –
— You just copy it out.
— Yeah, but –
— You just copy it out again.

Pause.

— It's not true though.

Pause.

— It's not –
— *What?*
— Do you have the same as me, cos mine says –
'After a fourteen-day stand-off a battalion under the order of
General Hallmayne stormed the power station outside of
Birmingham and freed the hos / tages –'
— Shut / up –
— Be quiet –
— . . .

(*Quieter.*) 'And freed the hostages who had suffered unthinkable torture at the hands of the Youth Rebels. After a vicious firefight with major casualties on both sides, the stranglehold placed over the city's power by the Rebels was removed, and the station was reclaimed and reactivated, continuing to fuel our homes and businesses today.'

Beat.

— So?
— But –
I was there. We didn't have any hostages. And we held the plant for like a *month*.
— So what?
— So why do we have to write it out if it's not true.
— Are you really that thick?
— I –
— Shut your fucking mouth.

Beat.

— But it's not what happened –
— Why do I –
— Just copy it out, you're supposed to have twenty copies by three –
— . . .
— Copy it *out*.

Pause.

She goes to stand up –

The **Second Camper** *yanks her back into her seat.*

— If you question it, they'll put you out on the firing range –
— It's a *lie*.
— It's *all* lies. They beat us, they get to write whatever they want.
— They'll make the Titches read it –
— Not after tonight.

. . .

Alright?

Pause.

They go back to writing.

Time passes.

Someone farts.

A low chuckle.

Eleven.
[EDIT.]

Dear Mum,

I am having a really [GOOD] time at camp. The counsellors
are all [FAIR] and one of them told me [I AM MAKING
PROGRESS]. I'm sure learning a lot about [SOCIETY] and
[ORDER]. There is a lot of time to [DEVELOP MYSELF] in here.

I have [LOTS OF NEW RESPONSIBILITIES], and in [LESSONS] we
get to [SWIM] in the lake and [LONG DIVISION] and sometimes
we [LEARN PRACTICAL SKILLS].

Don't [WORRY ABOUT ME].

If they decide [I HAVE ACHIEVED MY PERSONAL DEVELOPMENT
GOALS], then know that [I AM THANKFUL TO THE CAMP AND ITS
COUNSELLORS]. And that everything [I WRONGLY BELIEVED
BEFORE] has [PASSED] into [INSIGNIFICANCE] and I am ready
[TO BECOME A PRODUCTIVE MEMBER OF SOCIETY].

All my [RESPECT],

[YOUR SON].

Twelve.

SWALLOW.

A group of **Campers** *sit eating dinner from trays.*
Occasionally another will sit down and join the conversation.

— What about Leicester?
— Yep.

Pause.

— What about Leeds?
— Mm-hm.

Pause.

— What about Birmingham?
— Yep.

Pause.

— What / about –
— What about Sheffield?
— (*Nods.*)
— What about Reading?
— Yeah.
— What about Nottingham though?
— Yes.

Pause.

— Derby?
— (*Nods.*)
— Liverpool.
— Yeah.
— Ipswich?
— Yes.
— Bristol?
— Yes.

Pause.

— Wolverhampton?
— Yes.
— Brighton?
— Yes.
— Harrogate.
— Yes.
— Halifax.
— Yes.
— Oxford.
— Yes.
— Cambridge.
— Yes.
— Durham.
— Yes.
— What about Scotland though?
— Scotland too.
— Glasgow?
— (*Nods.*)
— Edinburgh –
— Yes.
— Inverness.
— Yes –
— Middlesbrough.
— / Y –
— Middlesbrough's not in Scotland.
— No, but –
— Yes, Middlesbrough too.
— The Isle of Man?
— Yes, everything, yes. They're *all* –
— The Titches –
— The Titches too, they're just the same –
— Ireland –
— Ireland.
— Wales –
— *Yes*. Cardiff, Swansea, they're all –
— At ten fifteen.
— At ten fifteen. Everyone is ready for ten fifteen, so just . . .

Don't worry about it.
Alright?

Pause.

— What about London?
— There's no kids in London, bell-end.
— They'll *hear* it in London. They'll know it's all happening.
— How come it's all the same time?
— That's the whole point.
— But what if they don't have a dorm inspection then?
— / Everyone has an inspection at the same time, their
orders are all centralised.
— They all do.
— It's so they can move us from camp to camp easier.
— She never went to another.
— You just went here?
— I'm new.
— Yeah, but, not new to –
— This isn't your first camp though.
— If it was you'd have been here ages.
— I don't, I mean . . .

Beat.

— What?
— . . . my –
my parents kept me hid.
— / For fuck's sake –
— / (*Shakes head.*)
— / Why do we always get sat with these ones –
— Calm down, she still fought. You fought, didn't you?
— I, yeah, I mean –
— Where.
— I did –
— Tell us where.
— . . .
— She's lying.
— I'm not lying, I did.

— So where then.
— . . . Marston Moor.
— / See?
— Me too.
— She's lying.
— Course she's lying.
— Why would she lie?
— She says Marston Moor cos it was so big no one can check.
— I was there –
— Everyone was there. Except her.
— My parents live in York –
— So you just stepped outside to join in then ran home afterwards?
— / No . . .
— Leave her alone.
— Why?
— She's / here now, isn't she?
— Some people had different situations –
— Her situation is that she's a pussy. Let me feel your hands.
— Why?
— I want to feel them –
— Don't listen to him.
— I want to see if they feel like our hands, or if they feel like soft coward's hands.
— / Bit harsh.
— Don't be a dick –
— She didn't fight for tomorrow!

. . .

We're all here –
We're all *meant* to be here, in their eyes.
We gave them *reasons* to lock us up.

. . .

. . .

— *I* fought at Marston Moor.
I did.
And so did thousands of us.

So did kids six-seven years old.
. . .
I took down three power stations, and closed *six* schools.
I held my friends as they bled out in the streets.
They all fought and died because they believed in taking what
was ours by birthright, before *they* used all of it up.
Before there was nothing left to inherit.
. . .
We rose up and fought for our home.
This country. This planet.
Clean air. Housing for everyone. Free healthcare. Equality.
No money. No ownership.
A tomorrow for all of us.
We did all that for *you*. While you sat in your house with your
parents, content with whatever scraps they threw you.
. . .
I should tell them – I should tell all of them they're wasting
time on you, they don't need to force you into anything – you
were never on our side in the first place.
I bet you still *write* to them, don't you.
Don't you?
— . . . we're allowed . . .
— I don't care about what they *allow* us to do.
. . .
When the war started I burned my parents' house to the ground.
. . .
We gathered in the streets.
We tore down the town hall.
The museum.
Schools.
Everything.
Smashed it to pieces.
Nothing left standing.
Everything they thought was firmly in their grasp we
destroyed, because
If you butcher my future, I will massacre your past.

Pause.

— I didn't mean to –
— You didn't fight at Marston Moor.
— I –
— Did you.
— ...
 ...
no.
 ...

Pause.

His point proven, he goes back to his food.

— You make it up to us tonight.

Thirteen.
HOLD.

Night has fallen.
Outside, round the back of one of the dorms, under a dim light,
a **Camper** *stands waiting.*

Time passes.

Eventually another **Camper** *hurries on.*
Very out of breath.

— Hey.
— I nearly left.
— I couldn't –
I couldn't get away –
they were marching us –
one of the guys in my unit did something, so they were
marching us –
and I couldn't get away.
 ...
 ...
I didn't think I was ever gonna get away, I thought they were

just gonna march me to my dorm and then I wouldn't – But
they stopped eventually.
— And you're here.
— I'm here.
— Made it.
— Yeah.
Just.
. . . sweating . . .

She catches her breath.

— I can't stay long.
— No.
— Cos of, well. You know. What we all –
— Ten fifteen.
— Yeah.
— Not long.
— Yeah.
. . .
Nervous!
. . .

Pause.

— I thought cos of – You know. I wanted to try this.
. . .
I thought, I thought I'd try it.
And I nearly missed you!
— Nearly.
— Yeah. Phew. Haha.
— (*Smiles.*)

Pause.

— Do you want to start?
— Oh, yeah. Yes. I mean – I can't stay long, so we, like we
said, so. Yeah.
Have you done this before? I mean, duh, course, course you
have.
Stupid.

. . .
I don't know how to, um, start, so –
— Relax.
— Relax, yeah, yes.
— Just relax, and –

Voices or vehicle noise nearby. They freeze until it passes.

— Close.
— Just relax.
. . .
Breathe in through your nose like this . . .
— . . .
— . . . and then out through your mouth like this . . .
— . . .
— Just keep going like that till you feel relaxed.

They breathe for a while while looking at each other.

— And now I'll start by just getting closer to you.
— . . .
— Really close, okay?
— Oh –

She flinches a little.

— S'alright, just relax.
— . . .
— There, see.
. . .
Just keep breathing.
. . .

She stands very close. They breathe together.

— . . .
— And I'm going to put my head on your shoulder and you
put yours on mine.
— . . .

They gradually come to rest their heads on each other's shoulders.

— . . .

— And then the last bit is just . . .

She brings her arms up to embrace her, closing the hug.

Pause.

The **Second Camper** *raises her arms awkwardly and hugs back.*

Pause.

— This is it?
— This is it.
— . . .

Pause.

— What do we do now?
— We just stay like this for a while.

Pause.

They separate.

— There.
— That's it?
— That's it.
— . . .
— We can do it for longer if you want.
— . . . Nah. That's alright.
— Okay.
— It was pretty good I guess.
— It's nice.
— Yeah. Nice. I guess.

. . .

I dunno . . .

. . .

. . .

. . .

Are you scared about tonight?
— No.
— No.

. . .
Me either.
— We have to take our own tomorrow or they'll force us into
theirs.
— Yeah . . .

Pause.

— I better go.
— Alright.
— I'll see you anyway.
— Okay.
La tierra es vuestra.
— La tierra es vuestra.

Beat.

She leaves.

Fourteen.
CLEAN.

In pyjamas and dressing gowns, the **Campers** *play a spirited and
chaotic game of Blind Man's Buff, a giggling* **Camper** *stumbling
around the washroom with his dressing gown/pyjama top pulled over his
head.*

*Others watch while brushing teeth, yelling, mouths foaming with
toothpaste.*

The game should be played for real, at length.
Lots of laughter, shouts and calls, lots of improvising.

Sometimes the game tumbles into playfighting or wrestling, **Campers**
squirming on the floor in laughter, dogpiling each other, splashing water.

At a peak of excitement, chaos and laughter, a **Camper** *walks in
briskly, heading straight for a sink.*

His arms and torso are coated in blood, his clothes soaked in it.

The energy of the room gradually calms as the **Campers** *all notice their bloodied room-mate frantically washing himself.*

They watch him for a while in silence.

Eventually, one of the **Campers** *goes over and helps him wash.*

One
By
One

They all walk over and
help wash the blood away.

Fifteen.
HOME.

Dear Mum,

I am having a really good time at camp. The counsellors are all fair with me and one of them told me I am a good worker. I'm sure learning a lot about the war and my part in it. There is a lot of time to think about things in here.

I have made lots of new friends too, and in our free time we get to swim in the lake and play sports and sometimes we hear stories about how things were before.

Don't worry about me.

If they decide it's better for everyone if I never see you again, then know that I was okay in here. And that everything I ever did to you through anger has drifted out of me into dust and nothingness and I am ready for a tomorrow that can be better for all of us.

All my love,

Shelby.

Sixteen.
OUT.

The **Campers** *are hurrying to their beds –*

— Hurry up, hurry up –
— Quick, come on –
— Hurry *up* –

They all stand on their beds and look to the door.

The clock above is almost at 10:15.

They watch it tick.

Someone giggles.

— /Shhh –
— Shut up, you'll ruin it –

They watch the clock.

Seconds pass.

— Ready –

In unison, the **Campers** *all pull their grenades from under their mattresses.*

They hold them as if ready to throw.

Seconds pass.

– Pull –

In unison, the **Campers** *all pull their pins.*

The second hand begins to creep towards twelve.
The yells begin –

— La propriété, c'est le vol!
— (*All.*) Property is theft!
— La propriété, c'est le vol!
— (*All.*) Property is theft!
— Tear down fences!

— (*All.*) Burn down walls!
— Tear down fences!
— (*All.*) Burn down walls!

Perhaps we can hear the approach of **Guards**.

— One future!
— (*All.*) Our future!
— One future!
— (*All.*) Our future!
— Seize tomorrow!
— (*All.*) Destroy the past!
— Seize tomorrow!
— (*All.*) Destroy the past!
— A new nation!
— (*All.*) Conceived in liberty!

Footsteps near –
The clock hits 10:15.

— This land is yours –
— (*All.*) This land is ours!

In unison the levers of their grenades are loosed –

Each **Camper** *stuffs his or her grenade into their mouth –*

The doors begin to open –

Black.

Zero for the Young Dudes!

BY ALISTAIR MCDOWALL

Notes on rehearsal and staging, drawn from a workshop with the writer, held at the National Theatre, October 2016

How the writer came to write the play

ALISTAIR MCDOWALL   'I wanted to write a play for a gang or a unit or young people. It seemed the most fun way to fulfil the Connections brief. At first, I was writing about a bunch of kids who meet for a campout and one of them has a grenade. That was a piece with specific characters, but I eventually decided that the best way to fulfil the brief was to write something that could be performed by five kids or fifty kids. So I returned to the original idea of a prison camp. I'd been interested in the kinds of discipline camps popular in America – featured in various documentaries on TV – so I ended up fusing the grenade with the camp, and pursued that metaphor in more literal terms. What's the logical and surreal endpoint of that image of a child holding a grenade?

'The play ended up as a revolution, and that seemed like a fun idea. Kids are often treated slightly like live grenades themselves – possible explosions waiting to happen. The title of the play is half inspired by 'All the Young Dudes', the Bowie/Mott the Hoople song, and a short film called *Zero for Conduct*, by Jean Vigo (this is the film that *If . . .* was heavily influenced by, about schoolboys who start a revolution). A constant influence for me that is more present here than usual is the *Peanuts* comic strip. I'd always wanted to write a play that's like a *Peanuts* strip in presentation. I love the form and tone, and I think it's probably one of the truest representations of the fear, anxiety and depression that comes with growing up.

'I also loved that the adults were never seen in *Peanuts*, and that worked with the form of the play – the adults are all seated in the audience, observing.

'I start thinking about audience very early on in the writing, and for this project the audience was very specific: almost entirely made up of the parents of the actors performing the play. I thought it would be fun and in keeping with the spirit of Connections to make a play that indicted the audience. The kids are telling a story in which the audience are the enemy – I wanted there to be a slight sense that the cast could burst into the audience and start causing havoc – an energy and tone that fosters a bit of unease.

'I'm aware that the play sounds fiddly when you're reading it out for the first time, and at a glance it can be slightly tricky to work out who's speaking. But with a bit of work I hope the format will reveal huge freedoms to you without sacrificing story clarity. You can work out the breakdown on your own beforehand or do mini read-throughs with your groups and explore the best solutions for every scene. It should work with any number of people. There aren't many scenes that can't be split in a variety of ways – a few obvious exceptions being scenes like the solitary confinement one, or the dirt-shovelling scene, or the hug scene towards the end.

'I remember when I was a kid at school, and plays for kids often were very immediately "issue"-based. I presume that nowadays it's the same but with different "issues". I was never as interested in those plays as a teenager (though of course there are some great ones!), and so I've written a play for myself at sixteen, with the hope that others might share my interests. I hope it feels honest. I hope it has the chaotic and mischievous energy of being young.

'Oddly, the play was written in early 2015 and seems to keep getting more relevant. In the context of the whole nation and Europe splitting, the themes underneath the play feel more immediate. It's purely accidental. I was writing a play about these kids at this camp and everything else bubbled up underneath from my unconscious.

'It does feel bleak, though there are some positive elements in there – the kids are able to unify despite their differences and rise up. They lose and end up in these camps, but despite the horrors they're subjected to they remain spirited and human. In the end, though, the ending doesn't feel triumphant, but hollow, empty and tragic. Violence only breeds violence and there should always be another way. With a cast of characters so articulate, a lot of it seems a plea to stop acting and start listening.'

Approaching the play

Vicky Featherstone, lead director, took the group through an exercise to answer some important questions that you and your group should engage with when approaching this play. The key questions were: why are the young people inside this camp and what is the world like outside the camp? Vicky asked the group to investigate what messages there are in the play towards answering these questions.

DISCOVERING FACTS

The best way to investigate messages is to make a list of facts when reading the play. A fact is something that is true before the play begins.

The group came up with a large list of facts, listed here. This is by no means a complete list, but an example of some helpful facts, big and small:

There has been a war.
There are no kids in London.
The kids are plotting a revolution.
There are several camps.
Some parents hid their children.
There are woods surrounding the camp.
There are grenades.
Someone is giving out grenades.

There is no surveillance in the shower.

Kids are being killed.

It has been three years since the war.

Harry Potter still exists in this world.

Power stations, museums and schools were attacked.

The camp is surrounded by three rows of fences, one of which is electrified.

The camp censors letters.

The kids are not allowed to leave the camp, but they are moved about from camp to camp.

Solitary confinement exists.

The Titches are the younger children and they are kept separately.

There is no sex education.

There is centralised control of the camps.

Twenty-one is the official age of adulthood.

There are guards.

There are counsellors.

There are campers.

There is a pledge that they all know.

Children are still forced to do cross-country.

Kids are being forced to punish and harm other kids.

The camps are rewriting history to give to the Titches.

There was a large battle at Marston Moor (*Marston Moor was a bloody battle in the English Civil War*).

Kids are being made to kill each other.

The kids started a war and they have lost the war.

THE CIRCUMSTANCES LEADING TO THE PLAY

Alistair and Vicky talked about how companies should approach this as if it was happening 'now', as if the war that led to the events in the play could start today. Alistair has purposely not suggested a specific regime – we could be

anywhere in the British Isles, and, as a result, companies
don't have to create a fictional foreign regime. These
characters are young people of now, just three or four years
in the future after a revolution and civil war. All the
circumstances that led to the revolution are present in society
right now. As healthcare, economy, environment and
education are threatened and mishandled, the young people
realise that this is the future that they will inherit and they
start a revolution.

Alistair stated that he imagined that this revolution could have
started in one or two schools, and then everyone realises that
it's possible to violently overthrow the adults. Vicky suggested
that this could be fun to work out with your company in
rehearsals: 'How did the war start? Did it start quickly or was
it a cascade effect?' Your history of the play's world should be
precise and logical, and should help to tell the story.

RESEARCH

You could investigate the things present in the world today
that show intolerance or a lack of future for young people.
You could ask your company to research and think about
what things would break them and push them to war or
revolution – they shouldn't make these up, they should be
logical extensions of things that exist today.

It's important for your company to own this play in their own
way. Vicky suggested that you should allow them to discover
this information for themselves, rather than giving it to them.

Themes

Vicky pointed out that although the play has fantastic resonance
with contemporary politics with its themes of war and
revolution, a production should not be weighed down by
these themes. One great thing about this play is the balance
between these themes and the fun of the camp and naivety of
the young people housed there. The playfulness should be

there alongside the weight of the politics and revolution and violence.

Alistair agreed and compared this to the film *M*A*S*H* – in which the themes of army and war sit lightly amongst the well-observed behaviour of characters. Because the kids have been in the camp for so long, they're more concerned about its day-to-day realities – similar to kids in a playground who don't talk about the lessons at school.

Alistair suggested that there is no technology available within the camp. It would all have been confiscated. The spread of information and of revolution in the camp is, instead, 'analogue viral'. You can't pinpoint the one person who started the passing of grenades, it is a viral spread. The slogans that the kids use are examples of this – in every school, stupid slogans and catchphrases spread around and everybody knows them very quickly. The same thing happens in this camp, only they've claimed slogans from Spanish revolutionaries or Woody Guthrie songs.

Structure

DRAWING THE PLAY

Vicky suggested that you could get your company to draw the play to help them get to know the structure of it. You can roll out a massive roll of paper and leave the company alone to draw it together. Ask them questions like: 'What shape is the play? What does it look like visually?' Questions to feed their imaginations.

HEADINGS/TITLES OF SCENES

Vicky noted that it is uncommon for scenes to start with a title, but each one of these begins with a title. You should ask yourself, as a director, what the titles mean in your production and how far do you want to communicate them to the audience.

Vicky led an exercise that could be a preparation for the play. She noted that, when you get into rehearsal, you can easily lose track of the structure of the whole play because you are working on the detail of each scene. This exercise will help you become familiar with the story structure and to see how the story develops through all of the scenes.

In each scene, she asked the group to identify:

- What is the PHYSICAL ACTION of each scene (with a few exceptions, every scene has a defining physical action – for example, the shower queue is moving along)?

- WHAT HAPPENS in each scene?

- What STORY BEATS or MOMENTS carry from one scene to another in a satisfying way?

We also discussed questions posed by the each scene, which are also noted below.

1 RISE (page 437)

- Eating breakfast.

- The camp has finished their breakfast, get up and leave the dining room.

- Eyeing the audience.

Do you need to take responsibility for showing that it's the dining room? Or is the action of eating breakfast enough to achieve this?

2 PLEDGE (page 437)

- Line up and pledge.

- They line up and pledge.

- Unison/conformity.

3 RUN (page 438)

- Showing the grenade.

- During cross-country, campers argue about the meaning of the appearance of the grenades.
- Someone is handing out grenades – this is also the first time that the audience realise that there is a plan.

4 WASH (page 441)

- The young people are queuing for the shower.
- The kids argue about the best plan – it's a moment where there's a plan but the kids riff off it in the way that kids do
- Sense of rebellion/sense of being watched/it's the first time it's clear that they can't get out and they're locked in/the shit in the shower/the first time we know that the rebellion will occur tonight/they can only speak in the shower/lots of different camps all around the country.

5 DIRT (page 446)

- Moving dirt from side to side.
- Someone talks too much.
- The first time we hear specifics about the war/punishments at the camp/shit in the shower.

6 (NO HEADING) (page 450)

- This is up for grabs – no physical action is written – the action is more the censoring of the letter rather than the writing – 'a letter is being written/read/communicated/redacted'.
- They still have parents – they're writing to parents / oppression/punishment.

7 SOLITARY (page 451)

- Bouncing the ball.
- The camper is trying to make the guard talk.
- Whose side are you on/you can go through the camp and become a guard (conditioning process)/they are being told to harm each other (fingernails – King Rat)/twenty-

one being the magic number/grenade/hands down pants/time.

8 FEED (page 456)

- Serving lunch – with a line of people (matches up with 'wash').

- Campers are giving out the grenades to people who haven't already got one.

- Something in the food/the kids are trying to set up a new state, a revolution/punishments ('he's a traitor' refers to the guy in solitary) – everybody is getting a grenade rather than just a few people/first time we hear the slogan.

9 TARGET (page 459)

- Practising shooting.

- Training to shoot for their oppressors – discovering that it's 10.15 p.m. tonight for revolution – arguing about sex education.

- The question of compassion – surveillance – killing someone and moving dirt are given the same amount of weight by the kids, how normal killing someone is.

Vicky noted that it's really exciting when the conversations are dissonant with the action. She pointed out that Alistair has gifted you physical action that will support you to make dynamic action on stage.

10 REVISE (page 462)

- Copying something from one piece of paper to another.

- One camper is fighting for the truth – they're rewriting for the Titches, the victors get to write the history.

- 'If you question it they'll put you on the firing range'.

Vicky pointed out that, in the dramaturgy in this scene and its connection to the previous scene, the audience's sympathies are being managed in interesting ways. In the previous scene, we have been very cold to the people being shot – we have no idea who they are. However, in this scene, we discover that this camper, whom we like, is exactly the type of person who is being shot.

11 [EDIT] (page 465)

• A letter is being written/read/communicated/redacted.

• Replacement words put into the letter – the letter is being edited.

• The language of oppression.

Vicky noted that this is a crucial scene in which you get a fully rounded person in the play, and it's important to allow them to exist in these moments. It is when the audience discovers that not all these kids have been desensitised and regimented.

12 SWALLOW (page 466)

• Eating dinner.

• A girl lies about her involvement in Marston Moor.

• The scale of the revolution through all of the place names and the scale of the event that has taken place – 10.15 p.m. – we hear about the ideals that they are fighting for – past/present/future, who's tomorrow is it, debating about tomorrow.

13 HOLD (page 471)

• Hug and breathe

• One camper calms the other camper down – they learn how to hug and hold each other – one is teaching another how to hug.

Vicky noted that the play gets to breathe a little bit here before it goes into the big ending. The simplicity of this rhythm is crucial.

14   CLEAN (page 475)

- Playing Blind Man's Buff.

- Someone comes on covered in blood and the others clean their friend.

- The first time we've seen blood (the implication is that it's someone else's blood, not that he is injured) – the washing is quite ritualistic, everyone joins in.

Alistair pointed out that it's open-ended as to what has happened to this kid, but it's definitely the first time we see the result of all the things they're talking about. It takes something everyday and childish – the game – and punctures the innocence. This is the most grisly point of the play.

15   HOME (page 476)

- A letter is being written/read/communicated/redacted/issued.

- We're seeing the letter, the original letter, before the redaction process happens, but the letter isn't necessarily being written in this moment.

16   OUT (page 477)

- Blowing yourself up/pulling the pin on the grenades.

- The kids are initiating the end/psyching themselves up.

- The time 10.15 has arrived/first time a physical clock is present and mentioned.

Language

RHYTHM AND FORMATTING

Alistair stated that he builds meaning through rhythm, and so there will be some clues for the actors and director in the rhythm of the text. He discussed the formatting of the text and the clues for the actors that are in the formatting. He said that if a line runs on to the end of the page and a new line, then he's just run out of space on the page. But sometimes a new line will denote a new thought or that a character has interrupted themselves to introduce a new idea. If you look closely at it and say it out loud, there's probably a rhythmic reason for a line break but it's definitely not prescriptive.

Vicky pointed out that a production doesn't need to adhere to every bit of text formatting but a director should ask why it is there and what Alistair has intended.

LIST OF PLACES

It was asked how Alistair would feel about directors substituting other place names that would be more relevant to a particular group. Alistair said that it is broadly OK but he asked that you look at the rhythm of how that list is laid out and try to find place names with the same number of syllables. He did say that you should treat it like a big and careful change, and that if you don't *have* to do it then don't do it.

Characters and characterisation

The play has deliberately not assigned any character names – the play's form has the same gesture as the regimentation of the kids in the camp.

Shelby and the letter

Shelby, the child who writes the letter, is the only time we get a character name – the only individual identity with their own individual needs and wants. Shelby can be a male or female character, and any gender pronouns or references to 'your son' or 'your daughter' can be changed accordingly, as in the rest of the play.

There was a lot of discussion about the letter scenes throughout the whole workshop. Alistair outlined that it is up to each director and each production to decide who has written the letter, whether the letter has been edited to the point that you can no longer tell that it's been edited, or whether it is a child genuinely expressing themselves (and, if so, why they would want to write to their parents considering the revolution). Alistair suggested that, for him, the letter was always innocent, just a child writing to a parent, and that it is made more criminal through the process of redaction.

Anger

Vicky ran an exercise that you could run in rehearsals to give a general attitude to the whole company and their approach to performing the play. She suggested that an attitude of anger, on the part of the young people towards the audience, is a very good starting point.

She asked six people to stand in a line and turn away from the audience. After a count of three, they turned around and just looked at the audience.

Then the same six people turned around again and were asked to think about the thing that made them most angry in England. They were encouraged to be very specific about this thing.

Participants were then asked to stand facing a wall, put their hands against the wall, start breathing into the wall, and put this thing that makes them angry into the wall.

Participants were then encouraged to shout at the wall – to shout at this thing that is making them so angry.

After shouting, participants were asked to turn to face the audience at the same time and to eyeball the audience with this feeling that had been generated.

Participants were finally asked to walk all the way down the room, being aware of us as an audience, and walk out of the door.

This exercise generates a very live relationship between performer and audience. The audience become aware of themselves in the space and they are made complicit within the fictional world.

Vicky suggested that the actors, with this attitude of anger, should be encouraged to play the scenes as kids would; remember that although they have lived through great trauma, they are still children.

Production, staging and design

In general, Alistair stated that you can do whatever you want in the staging of the scenes. The only rules are that you can't change the lines or change the order of the scenes. You should interrogate all of the suggested physical action and suggested objects as written and, if necessary, discover replacements that tell the same story and which have a similar effect for the audience.

Movement of people through each scene

Alistair ran an exercise to demonstrate how each scene could be staged with different numbers of people. He outlined that you should be able to twist and make the play in a way that is tailored to your company's specific strengths without breaking the core of a scene.

The group staged a section of Scene Three ('Run') with two campers, then four campers, and then six campers. You should split the lines between the onstage actors, and be aware of the different stories that you tell by giving particular lines to particular people. In each scene you will discover that there will be one character who is harder to split than the others, and you should be aware of and respect this in the scenes. Alistair also demonstrated how you can use non-verbal actors on stage to build the world of the camp – for example, a runner going through the scene. This runner could then appear in a later scene, and so we have got the idea of the same children being within the camp and a flow between scenes.

To take this exercise to an extreme, Alistair staged the shower queue scene with twenty-four people, all moving rhythmically, and divided the lines between several people in the queue. The main challenge here is to make sure that the dramatic action is clear by assigning the right lines to the right people to tell the story that you have identified in the scene.

Vicky pointed out that each person would have an individual attitude towards the dramatic action (see exercise below about locating attitudes within an actor's body). She also outlined that the whole company should be aware of where the audience's gaze should be focused at any individual moment and they should be supporting the audience concentrating on the right thing in each scene.

Alistair and Vicky agreed that some of the scenes (e.g. the dirt duty, the hug scene) will work better with just two people, and that it would be effective to contrast the large communal scenes with smaller, intimate ones.

Blind Man's Buff

This is the moment when the play explodes off the stage and reminds the audience that these are kids. As long as the story is still told, Alistair is open to interpretation here – it can be long, short, etc. The kids should be allowed to improvise physically and verbally in this scene. The playing is a genuine catharsis for the play – this will be about creating a set of things that they can do on stage so that it appears that it's not especially safe. A blocked, choreographed version of this won't achieve that: it should be a genuine game with milestones blocked within it. It's the opposite to the regimented nature of everything else and you should let your group bring their individuality to this moment.

Costume

A participant asked Alistair if he imagined the campers to be in uniform. Alistair stated that it would make sense, but that it would depend on your production. He suggested avoiding a futuristic uniform or any that would ask the audience to identify with a particular historical period. The task is to make it seem like the camp is in your home town sometime in the very near future. Alistair also suggested that you think about how each person would customise their own uniform, perhaps in the way that they wear them. He suggested that PE kits, and the varying degrees of fitting and suitability, are a good model for thinking about these.

Style and technique

Acting style

Vicky outlined that, in her experience, Alistair writes, thinks and speaks quickly and that this could influence productions of this play. However your production ends up, Vicky suggests that you do not sit in it too much and that, if you flow through the play, you'll start to understand the rhythm and the way he writes.

You should encourage your actors to exist in this world and to perform the given actions without worrying too much about performing a character or emotion. There should be a real simplicity about the performance of this play – just focus on the physical action and in saying the lines in the right order!

Music

Alistair suggested that it is up to you whether you use music in your production. He advised that known pop songs can be troublesome because everyone will have different associations with particular songs and that it could take the audience out of the world of the play. There would be no music in the camp. Vicky suggested that music or soundscape might help to create fear or tension in particular scenes.

Exercises for rehearsals

PERFORMING ATTITUDES

- Ask the participants to draw an outline of themselves on a piece of paper.

- Outside of the body, write the elements of yourself that you're happy to show other people in everyday life.

- Inside of the body, write elements of yourself that you don't usually show other people in everyday life.

- Ask the participants, from these lists, to choose which things they want to bring to their persona in the play. They should imagine that these things are placed somewhere specific in their own bodies.

- Ask the participants to walk around the room and to imagine that their heartbeat is in the specific place that they have located their 'secret thing'.

- While they walk around the room, ask them to locate the 'outside thing' somewhere specific on your body. Participants should be instructed to change their focus between the secret thing and the outside thing.

- Participants should be asked to make eye contact with each other – their feelings when they make eye contact will determine whether they are focusing on the internal or external thing.

This exercise allows performers to locate feelings of vulnerability in their bodies. It means that they don't have to act or perform vulnerability or sadness; it just sits there in their body. It releases them from having to play a character.

LISTENING

Vicky discussed how important it would be to do exercises around listening. They should be aware that they can't say the next thing they're going to say unless they've heard everything that has just been said to them – it's not just about listening for their cues. If they switch off onstage, then the audience could also switch off – especially during the longer speeches.

One potential exercise is to ask people on stage to repeat, out loud, what is being said to them as they say it. This will test their ability to actively listen to what is being said to them on stage.

ACTIONING

- Choose a particular scene, and get the actors in this scene to stand at either end of the room.

- Play the scene – the actors should say the line and physically demonstrate the action of it. For example, they may be trying to pull or push their partner and they should physically do this. They don't need to play what the scene looks like, but rather it is an exercise to discover the energies that underlie the text.

Actioning is important for this play because all the actors should be encouraged to think on the line. Almost no characters have to think about what they're saying, they just say it and the play becomes about action, rhythm and focus.

This exercise can also work for big groups on stage: everyone should be physically active because they are allowed to discover what their action is even when they aren't speaking and there are loads of other people on stage.

Be clear with the participants that this exercise won't work straight away, and that they should trust and be bold with it. Encourage them to get stuck in and involved in the exercise and to not worry about whether it is working or not.

Suggested references

If . . . (dir. Lindsay Anderson, 1968)

Zero for Conduct (dir. Jean Vigo, 1933)

The 400 Blows (dir. François Truffaut, 1959)

'All the Young Dudes', by Mott the Hoople

Peanuts, by Schulz

South Park by Trey Parker/Matt Stone

'This Land Is Your Land', by Woody Guthrie

*From a workshop led by Vicky Featherstone
with notes by Tom Hughes*

The Snow Dragons
by Lizzie Nunnery

Raggi and her friends spend their free time in the woods and mountains around their sleepy fjord town playing games of Vikings, dragons and war. When soldiers occupy the town, they watch from their hut in the mountains while their friends and families are beaten, silenced, abducted . . . Let down by the adult world, they form the Snow Dragons, 'the last line of resistance', carrying out sabotage missions. But this is no game, and true courage requires great sacrifice.

Cast size
8 named parts + chorus

Lizzie Nunnery's first play, *Intemperance* (Liverpool Everyman, 2007), was shortlisted for the Meyer-Whitworth Award. She co-wrote *Unprotected*, awarded the Amnesty International Award for Freedom of Expression (Everyman/Traverse Edinburgh, 2006). *The Swallowing Dark* (Liverpool Playhouse Studio/Theatre503, 2011) was shortlisted for the Susan Smith Blackburn Award. Her new play with songs, *Narvik* (Box of Tricks/Playhouse Studio, 2015), toured nationally January–March 2017. Other work includes *The People Are Singing* (Manchester Royal Exchange Studio, April 2017), a play with songs, *The Sum* (Everyman, May–June, 2017) and *Horny Handed Tons of Soil* (Unity Theatre, Liverpool, July 2017). She has written extensively for BBC Radio and is also a singer and songwriter, performing regularly with producer/composer Vidar Norheim.

Notes on the text

The dialogue suggests Raggi, Sig, Marta and Snorri are girls, the rest of the group boys, but parts can be played by either gender with small changes to the script. The group are all aged twelve to fifteen. Raggi and Sig are the oldest, Odd the youngest. The Trees are ageless. If possible the Trees play instruments but alternatively recorded music could be used.

Setting

A wooden hut surrounded by birch and fir trees, deep in the woods. The woods overlook a little town and a fjord; above are mountains. This world is not always our own, but visually the magical can be contrasted with the very real.

Songs

Scene Two	'Wolf Dance'
Scene Three	'The Bough Breaks'
Scene Five	'Sabotage'
Scene Seven	'Invisible Army'
Scene Eight	'What Will the World Be?'

Characters

Raggi, *the leader*
Sig, *the spy*
Marta, *the worrier*
Snorri, *the storyteller*
Gunnar, *the actor*
Harri, *the fist-fighter*
Odd, *the little brother*
Christi, *the tree climber*
The King, *a very old man*
The Chorus of Trees
   Could be performed by three actors or by as many as twelve.
The Soldiers
   Ideally ten or more actors. Uniforms should be non-specific.
   If necessary, projection and sound could be used for these parts.

Scene One
THE VOICES OF THE TREES

Winter evening in the woods. Snow on the ground. An enormous birch tree centre stage. Something ripples and moves. The voices start as whispers like leaves, getting louder.

— Ask me.

— Ask *me*.

— No one asks *me*.

— This story . . .

— I'll tell it.

— It happened here.

— There were monsters. With long shadows.

— Wild cries and branches snapping.

— My poor broken limbs. My snapped fingers . . .

— There was whispering in the night. It's that kind of story.

— It's the story of a tiny Viking and a tall shining man!

— Leave all that. Don't confuse them.

— It's the story of a monkey child that leapt between my boughs.

— My poor aching arms, my poor shuddering boughs . . .

— Hush.

— Hush.

— Hush about your aching.

— Hush and I'll tell it properly. I've seen it all.

— Here we go . . .

— I've seen warriors hacked to bits with axes. Heads rolling.

— A load of old rot.

— I've had men run through and bleeding against my trunk.

— Nothing but sap . . .

— I've sheltered lost children and runaways . . . Young lovers scaling my sides to see the stars.

— I've seen the northern lights turn in the sky.

— I've seen that a thousand times.

— A hundred thousand times.

— It's boring now.

— Tears have been smeared on my rough skin.

— I've seen a time before time.

— He'll start on about the ice age next.

— I was a seed rolling in the freezing tide!

— Told you.

— I saw the great god Odin ride through this forest – ripping branch from bark.

— (*Moaned.*) My poor branches!

— I saw Thor pull up trees by the roots.

— My trampled roots!

— I saw the very first man sculpted from the ice of the fjord below. If I remember that I must remember something.

— But *this story* . . .

— This story . . .

— Yes, this story.

— This story's about dragons.

— No: children. Children bold as dragons.

— Wild, lost children. Brave, stupid children.

— Nice children, though: I liked them.

— You like everyone.

— How did it start?

— With cries of women and of wolves.

— With blinding flashes in the sky. Living thunder cutting the ground.

— With trees split open. With all the lights of the town turned to darkness.

— No, before that, before that. A boy with horns.

— With a little boy weeping.

— Who can say really?

— Too many things have happened.

— The world's too old.

— I remember.

— It's all lost.

— I remember it all.

Pause as the day darkens. The other **Trees** *murmur dubiously.*

Scene Two
THE RISING OF NIDHOGG

Snorri *runs on banging a marching drum.* **Marta** *circles, flapping and squawking like a hawk, her coat as wings.* **Raggi** *dances on backwards fencing with* **Harri** *and* **Gunnar***, who brandish large sticks. As the drumming get louder* **Christi** *snakes up from behind the enormous birch centre stage, hissing and showing his teeth, his face painted, home-made wings stuck to his back. They all circle* **Christi***.* **Odd** *stumbles on wearing a Viking helmet with horns, holding a* *wooden sword, giggling between asthmatic gasps.* **Sig** *sits high up in another tree and peers through binoculars at the town below.* **Christi** *climbs higher as* **Raggi**, **Harri** *and* **Gunnar** *close in, brandishing their sticks.* **Christi** *hangs upside down, ducking, pulling a branch as a weapon.* **Odd** *runs in circles.* **Snorri** *drums more quietly.*

Raggi (*to* **Harri** *and* **Gunnar**)   Fall back, frail mortals! This dragon dies by my sword.

Harri   I'm not a mortal, I'm a giant. Look at me: I'm being *tall* here.

Raggi (*to* **Snorri**)   Are they giants?

Snorri   Harri, you're a giant. Gunnar, you're an ignoble man.

Gunnar   Why do I have to be the ignoble man?

Snorri   You both get to fight with Odin.

Raggi   Fight me if you dare!

Odd (*to* **Harri**)   Can I be a giant? I can be a giant.

Harri (*to* **Gunnar**)   I'll swap with you if you want, I'm not bothered.

Gunnar   No, I can do it . . . Ignoble man . . . Just give me a moment.

Christi   Come on! All the blood's going to my head.

Gunnar   I can't just turn it on.

Christi   I'll bloody pass out in a minute!

Gunnar (*to himself*)   I'm a wild and sinful warrior – my flesh is weak.

Sig (*to* **Marta**)   I arm-wrestled him earlier. He was quite weak and fleshy then.

Sig *and* **Marta** *laugh.*

Christi   Look, I'm a dragon here – will someone do battle with me?!

Raggi (*to* **Christi**, *in character*)   At last I look into your yellow eye, Nidhogg! Now see me pierce it with my sword!

Odd   In the *eye*. She's going to get him in the *eye*.

Harri   Shut up, Odd, she just said that.

Raggi *advances, fencing with* **Christi** *as he hangs upside down.* **Marta** *circles between them flapping her coat in* **Raggi***'s face. The others dance round the tree howling and stamping.*

Snorri   And so it was at the dawning of Ragnarok, the serpent dragon Nidhogg broke free from his prison beneath the world tree, wreaking his foul vengeance –

Harri   Reeking of what?

Marta   No *wreak*. *Wreak*.

Snorri   And thus he rose up with his trusty hawk –

Marta   That's me!

Snorri   / flapping his stormy wings and pouring his venom on gods and on man.

Odd   And on giants.

Snorri   And on giants!

They cower and shout as **Christi** *flaps his wings.* **Harri** *fences with* **Raggi**, **Odd** *waves his sword.* **Marta** *circles.* **Sig** *watches.* **Gunnar** *tries to climb the tree but* **Christi** *'breathes fire' at him, and* **Gunnar** *falls to the ground as though in great pain.*

Gunnar   I am but a noble man. And he has roasted my blood.

Odd *squeaks with joy at this.*

Gunnar   I will never be vanquished!

Snorri   You're an *ignoble* man. And you *will* be vanquished.

Gunnar *pulls out a red cloth, writhing beneath it as the others fight on around him.*

Gunnar   Sweet life. Sweet death. All one to me . . .

He rolls around, prolonging his death as the others battle on, laughing and shouting, **Snorri** *banging the drum,* **Marta** *screeching like a hawk.* **Odd** *gets tangled up in legs and arms, becoming upset.*

Snorri   As the oath-breakers lie bleeding and Nidhogg spreads his sinewy wings, so the great battle rages . . . and man's evil reaches its bloody heights, bringing with it endless winter . . .

Christi, *swinging his stick around, knocks* **Odd**'s *Viking hat off his head.*

Snorri   The world will end with the freezing of all men's hearts and bones –

Odd *squeals suddenly, grabbing his bare head. They all stop and look at him.*

Odd (*hyperventilating*)   My hat, Harri . . .

Harri   What's up with you now?

Odd   My hat, my hat.

Harri (*approaching*)   Alright, breathe, *breathe.* (*Close.*) Think about nice things. What does Mum say? Chocolate and Christmas – think about that.

Odd (*pointing at* **Christi**)   He hit my hat . . . He . . . Harri.

Harri (*to* **Christi**)   What d'you hit his hat for?

Christi   I'm a *dragon.* Dragons don't care about anyone's hats.

Snorri *puts down her drum and searches around for the hat.*

Gunnar   It's not Christi's fault – he'll always find something to whimper for.

Odd *squeaks, gasping for breath.*

Gunnar   I wouldn't mind – I was dying beautifully there!

Harri   You should have died ten minutes ago – how long does it take?

Gunnar   Why do you even bring him?

Harri   He follows me, doesn't he?

Gunnar   He shouldn't even be playing a giant in a Viking hat. What's that all about?

Harri   He likes the hat, alright? Can't he like a hat?

Snorri *finds the hat and goes to* **Odd**, *placing it on his head. He starts to calm down.*

Gunnar   He *likes* collecting soil. He *likes* licking tree fungus –

Harri (*advancing*)   Because your family's so great?

Gunnar   *My* brother's not a fruit loop. My brother's a policeman.

Harri   Your brother's a traffic attendant.

Gunnar   My brother's keeping this town safe!

Harri   He's a traffic attendant in a town with two roads. If he could do anything else they'd give his job to a signpost!

Gunnar *marches over to* **Harri**, *prodding him hard in the chest.* **Harri** *squares up to him.* **Gunnar** *prods him again.* **Harri** *leaps on him. They wrestle clumsily, energetically.*

Snorri   What are you doing? We've got the great floods to do.

Gunnar *and* **Harri** *roll and scramble offstage, still wrestling.*

Christi (*shouting after them*)   So are we not playing now?!

Raggi (*throwing her stick away*)   Does it bloody look like it?

Snorri   Christi was just about to take flight across the moonless night sky, heralding the end of all things.

Christi   Yeah, I was. (*Beat.*) *Was I*?!

Marta   Can't we ever do a real story?

Snorri   It is a real story.

Marta   Like something that could really happen.

Christi (*jumping down*)   We should do a story with an aeroplane! No, a boat! No, a tank!

Raggi   If you don't want to be here, Marta, no one's asking you to be.

Marta   You said we were gonna search for bear tracks today. We were gonna trap mice.

Raggi   I changed the plan. If it was your group, you could change the plan – *sorry*.

Christi   I could do a story where I'm a fighter. And I can see the fellas, no the monsters, no the soldiers – all coming in the boats and I run at them and throw rocks, no fire, no grenades, but it sets everything on fire – and everything explodes and they have to go back in the sea.

Odd   I don't want to do that story.

Snorri   No one wants a story like that.

Sig (*looking out*)   Your dad's boat's coming in, Raggi. He'll be wanting his dinner.

Raggi   Let him want. He didn't come home yesterday, why should I come home today?

Harri *and* **Gunnar** *roll back on stage, turning and wrestling, roll off again.*

Snorri   My mum said the soldiers are only in the south and they wouldn't come here anyway because there's hardly any of us and we haven't got any money or anything they'd want, so we won't need any rocks or fire or grenades.

Christi   How do we know what they want? No one tells us anything.

Raggi   My uncle's down south. He wrote my dad saying there's thousands of soldiers and they've taken over all the houses. Even the palace.

Marta   You're making that up.

Sig   She isn't. My brother said the same. It was on the radio.

Raggi   They've got everyone trapped and they're not allowed their own radios or newspapers or singing their own songs.

Christi   What songs are they singing then?

Raggi   Enemy songs. That's all there is now.

Odd   Not the palace though. The King wouldn't let them.

Sig   I heard they chased him out. The Prince too.

Raggi   I heard they shot them dead.

Snorri   *Raggi*!

Raggi   It said in the paper.

Odd *covers his ears, hugging his sword.* **Raggi** *shrugs at* **Snorri**.

Snorri (*indicating* **Odd**)   Can we talk about something else?

Raggi (*to* **Sig**)   What's my dad doing? Is he going home?

Sig (*looking around through the binoculars*)   Can't see him. I can see Old Mad Finn breaking bottles against the wall. I can see Gunnar's brother on duty at the crossroads.

Marta   All the police do is stand round these days.

Sig   He's scratching his arse.

Christi *laughs.*

Marta   All just standing in the street watching. Like something's gonna happen.

Odd   They'll know what do to anyway, won't they? The grown-ups.

Christi   They'll have a plan. They don't tell us but . . .

Raggi   You reckon, do you?

Christi   There's probably a plane hidden in these woods – just·in case enemies ever come. Or under the ground – underground tunnels out to the harbour – connecting all the houses.

Raggi   My dad can't even find his way to bed of a night – there's no way he's got an underground tunnel.

Christi   Maybe not him but someone will. Someone'll have it sorted.

Marta   Or boats all ready. And loaded with supplies. So we can all escape.

Sig   What about defending the town?

Marta   They've probably got guns hidden somewhere. If they want to do that.

Snorri   Can we not talk about guns?

Christi   Guns and bombs and grenades and fire. Loads of matches to set things on fire.

Raggi   What is it with you and fire, Christi?

Sig (*looking through binoculars*)   The lights are going out in the shops. We should go back down.

Raggi   What if we didn't?

Marta   They'd come up and get us.

Raggi   What if they couldn't find us?

Sig My brothers'd be up here before dark and dragging me back.

Raggi We'll hide out in the hut. We'll light a fire. It'll be like we're Vikings.

Odd Vikings?!

Raggi Eat all the food we saved. Stay up all night.

Odd Could we eat Viking food?

Raggi Yeah, why not? We'll roast stuff on sticks.

Marta I don't want to sleep in a stinking, freezing hut.

Raggi Who are you saying stinks?

Marta I'm not gonna do it just 'cause you tell me to do it, Raggi.

Harri *enters, elated from the fight;* **Gunnar** *limping behind, panting.*

Odd We're staying out here. With stuff on *sticks*.

Gunnar *lurches at* **Harri** *who shoves him over with one arm.*

Harri What, like here in the woods?

Gunnar Out as in *out*? As in all night?

Raggi Yeah, but Marta's too scared.

Marta I'm not.

Raggi She thinks the dark's got monsters in it.

Marta Did I say I was scared?

Raggi She thinks the trees'll come alive and the ground'll swallow us up.

Marta I'll stay out if it's such a big deal to stay out.

Raggi It is a big deal. It'll be the best thing we've ever done.

Christi   What about wolves?

Raggi   Are you afraid of wolves?

Christi   No.

Raggi   So say it: 'I'm not afraid of wolves.'

Christi   I'm not afraid of wolves.

Raggi   'Cause they want us afraid – the grown-ups. They want us scared so they can tell us what to do, make us feel small. But we're not small. Are we? *Are we*?

Odd   I'm not afraid. (*To his brother.*) I'm not, Harri.

Raggi   All of you.

Harri   I'm not afraid of wolves!

Gunnar   I'm not afraid of the dark!

Raggi   Say, 'I'm not afraid of the dark!'

All (*except* **Marta**)   I'm not afraid of the dark.

Raggi   Marta?

Marta   I'm not afraid of the dark.

Snorri *starts to bang her drum, chanting.*

Snorri   We're not afraid of the dark! We're not afraid of the dark!

The group all form a line behind **Snorri***, stamping and clapping.* **Sig** *slides down from her tree and joins in. They snake through the trees.*

Raggi (*sung*)
A wolf did creep
With blood on his teeth
Howling a wicked tune
But I joined in his song
And we danced the night long
He thought I was a wolf child too

Singing, who's afraid of the dark?

All   I'm not afraid of the dark

Raggi   Who's afraid of the dark?

All   I'm not afraid of the dark

Raggi
If a storm does rage
And the wind does wail
We'll open up the doors and so set sail
To the side of the moon
Where the weird things play
Dance to the rhythm of the ancient ways

Singing, who's afraid of the dark

All   I'm not afraid of the dark

Raggi   Who's afraid of the dark?

All   I'm not afraid of the dark

Raggi
No surrender till the game is over
No rest till the tale's been spun
No ending till we're done pretending
No sleep 'til the morning comes

All repeat the last verse as they dance into the hut, stamping, clapping.
Raggi *lights the fire so it shoots up to the ceiling and they all howl.*
They throw bags of sweets and crisps to each other, tearing them open
with their teeth. They make a dance of preparing their beds, hanging up
hammocks, throwing rugs and blankets. **Christi** *and* **Sig** *swing from*
the rafters. They all chant, getting gradually quieter, down to a whisper
as the night darkens around them, leaving only the fire. This dims as
the children crouch, whispering: 'Who's afraid of the dark?' repeating it
down to nothing. No sound but the worried whisper of the trees.

Scene Three
THE FALL OF THE TOWN

Night. The hut. **Sig** *sits watching the town through binoculars, sweet wrappers beside her. The others are asleep, splayed under rugs or hanging in hammocks.* **Odd** *sleeps fitfully, twitching and squeaking.* **Sig** *whistles a tune. The* **Trees** *murmur outside.* **Sig** *puts down the binoculars to open another sweet, still whistling. A faint rumbling: engines, tramping footfalls far below. She looks out through the binoculars again. The rumbling gets louder. Her whistling stops suddenly. She lowers the binoculars, staring out in shock.*

Sig (*quietly*)   Raggi . . . *Raggi!*

Raggi *doesn't wake.* **Sig** *picks up binoculars again, looking out.*

The **Trees** *speak.*

— Was it *that* night?

— It was a black night.

— Is it that night I remember?

— They came in the dark but so much sound . . .

— Like an earthquake far away.

— Like weather moving in.

— Like voices from under the ground.

— So fast. So sudden.

— They tore through the town.

— The banging on the windows. All the lights turned on.

— One light, two light, three light, four –

— The yells and cries and hammering at doors.

— Echoing. Even up here.

— Singing off the rock.

— They lined them up outside – the ones who fought.

— Dragged them, beat them. Maimed and mauled –

— A boy lying in the road.

— Blood running down his jaw.

— His legs kicking, his brothers calling.

— They pulled them away. Started the engine and slammed all the doors.

— Who told you?

— The birds told me. The ground told me more.

— Everything shaking and trembling.

— And the young girl watching from the woods.

— Watching the town flicker and fall.

— Not so young.

— Young enough.

— Young enough to tremble.

— Old enough to see. And wish to see no more.

Inside the hut.

Sig (*hissed*)   *Raggi!* . . . *Raggi!*

Raggi *wakes, hearing the sounds from below.* **Sig** *beckons, passes her the binoculars.* **Raggi** *looks out, lowers the binoculars. They speak in whispers.*

Raggi   It's a dream.

Sig   It's not.

Raggi   They wouldn't come here.

Sig   They *are* coming. They *are* here.

Raggi   What do we do?

Beat.

Raggi   What do we do, Sig?

Sig   How am I supposed to know? You're the boss?

Raggi (*looking out again*)   All the houses . . .

Sig   All the houses. All the people. They're taking the whole town.

Raggi   You can't *take* a town.

Sig   You can. They are.

Raggi (*looking out*)   There's Mad Finn. He's running round the crossroads with a fish hook. He's coming at them!

Gunshots echo from down below. **Odd** *bolts awake, staring.*

Odd   What's that?!

Raggi   Nothing. It's not anything.

Odd   There was thunder.

Sig   Yeah, it's thunder and lightning. Go to sleep.

Christi (*waking*)   What . . . ? Mum . . .

Raggi   Your mum's not here.

Christi   In my dream – there was . . .

Rumbling engine noises and shouts below get louder.

What *is* it?

Sig   Trucks. Big trucks . . . Soldiers.

Christi *jumps up, grabbing the binoculars.*

Christi   Why are all the lights on?

Beat.

Sig   They're taking the town.

Christi   Why is no one stopping them . . . ? What's everyone *doing*, what are they *doing*?

Raggi They're not doing anything.

Pause. They all look at each other.

Odd What's happening, Raggi?

Beat.

Raggi We can't go home. We . . .

Odd *stares at her. He begins to squeak quietly in fear.*

Sig We'll have to stay up here – just for a while. We have to really be like Vikings now.

Christi Wake the others up – we've gotta tell them –

Raggi *Don't. (Beat.)* Leave them. Can't we let them sleep for now?

They stare out. **Sig** *puts her arm round* **Odd** *and gives him a rough hug.* **Christi** *and* **Raggi** *move in, the four huddling together looking towards the town. The trees sway and sing.*

Trees *(sung)*
Sleep little one while the sky is breaking
Sleep little one while the bough is shaking
Soft and long while the day lies waiting
There'll be time for all things dawning

Sleep little one while the light is creeping
Sleep on and on, while the night lies bleeding
Sleep deep sweet one while the birds are fleeing
Don't dream of day's bright morning

The bough breaks
And dreams are fleeting
The bough breaks
And the earth is weeping
The bough breaks
Every time my sweet thing
The bough breaks

The **Trees** *hum and rock. Shouts echo from below. A loud round of shots suddenly silences the* **Trees**. *The others wake, sitting up sharply. The group stare at each other. Lights down.*

Scene Four
THE RESISTANCE

Early hours, outside the hut. **Raggi** *stands in front of a chalk board on an easel.* **Sig** *watches the town through binoculars.* **Christi** *is up a tree looking down through a toy telescope. The others are assembled looking exhausted, dishevelled, draped in blankets against the cold.*

Snorri   I don't think it's real. Not like how it looks. They're only checking there's nothing here they want, and when they see there isn't they'll just go.

Raggi   It's the town they want. It's the whole country. It's the soil and the woods and the water and the people –

Marta   Maybe Snorri's right. Can't we just wait and see what they do?

Raggi   Any minute them soldiers could be spreading out and heading right at us and you lot wanna sit round pretending it's not happening?

Gunnar   What are we gonna do for food?

Raggi   What are we *what*?

Gunnar   We've nearly run out as it is. There's only one rhubarb and custard left and I'm reasonably sure there's no actual rhubarb or custard in it.

Harri   We've got to go back to town. Haven't we?

Raggi   We're not going back to town.

Marta   Because you've decided?

Harri So we're just gonna live in the woods like bears? Because you realise we're not bears. And bears are much bigger than we are.

Odd With sharper teeth.

Gunnar (*holding his tummy*) I'm hungry already. I think I'm actually really hungry already.

Raggi (*advancing*) Seriously, Gunnar, if I killed you now no one'd come looking for you.

Gunnar What did you just say?! (*To the others.*) Did you hear what she just said?!

Marta She's gone barmy.

Christi He's got a point, Raggi. You can't run an army on empty stomachs.

Marta So we're an army all of a sudden? When did we say we wanna be an army?

Raggi Then what *do* you wanna be? A coward? A *kid*?

Marta We *are* kids.

Raggi We're the last thing this town's got *left*. (*Beat.*) We're the last resistance . . .

Odd What's a resistance?

Marta I bet she doesn't even know.

Raggi Let's say we do go back to the town . . . But let's say we're invisible. Let's say we slip in without a sound, leave without a mark.

Marta This isn't like before. You don't just make something up and then it's true.

Raggi We know every inch of every building, every back street and bush and tree. We know the holes in all the walls and all the sheds and all the attics. We'll make doors come unlocked, tyres burst, windows break . . .

Gunnar   Food disappear!

Raggi   Those soldiers think they've got some sleepy little corner? They'll think the place is haunted by the time we're finished.

Snorri   It's a good idea. But it's an idea, isn't it? It's not . . .

Raggi   Not what?

Snorri   If every grown-up we know didn't know what to do, why do we know any better?

Raggi   Why do you all think grown-ups know so much? What do you all think is so grown up about grown-ups?

Marta   You might want to live up here like a dirty tramp Raggi, but some of us have got things to go back to.

Raggi   What does that mean?

Marta   Just 'cause your dad's an actual loon doesn't mean we should all be trapped up here –

Raggi *runs at her, grappling with her.* **Sig** *jumps down and gets between, holds them apart.*

Sig   They took my brothers. Alright? All three of them. I watched. They tied their hands and dragged them on the ground and drove them away. And Christi's granddad – he was tryna stop the trucks. They kicked him and hit him . . .

Christi *stares at her in shock. She nods at him.*

Sig   We can't just do nothing.

Beat.

Marta   We don't know anything about resistances. We don't know what's going on down there –

Sig   I know where they've made their headquarters. I know where they're keeping their weapons and where the men are sleeping and who their leader is. I know quite a lot actually.

Gunnar We'll need a name. And uniforms. If we're gonna do it properly.

Sig Oh God, here we go . . .

Gunnar If I'm going to *commit* to this –

Odd We should be the dragons.

Gunnar Shut up, Odd.

Snorri What's wrong with the Dragons?

Gunnar It sounds like a football team.

Snorri We'll be the Snow Dragons.

Gunnar Too girly.

Snorri What's girly about snow?

Gunnar What's snowy about dragons?

Snorri We'll rise up from the frozen earth, wreaking our revenge . . .

Gunnar Reeking of what?

Harri (*loudly*) We could get messages through though couldn't we? To the town. To let them know we're okay. Notes or . . .

Raggi We can't risk it.

Marta Or smoke signals. Morse code.

Harri Just so they don't think we're dead or something.

Raggi We'd get caught.

Harri 'Cause my mum'll be losing it. 'Cause she's got bad nerves is the thing –

Raggi No sound, no trace –

Harri She'll think we've run away.

Odd She has got bad nerves, Raggi –

Raggi   They weren't ready. They let us down. Are we gonna give ourselves up like idiots just 'cause they did?

Christi   She's right. Most of them didn't even fight back. Just stuck their hands in the air . . .

Snorri   Maybe they couldn't fight back.

Raggi   We'll fight back. We will if they won't.

Beat.

Odd   So we're Snow Dragons?

Raggi *looks round at them all. One by one they nod. She chalks it up on the board decisively:* THE SNOW DRAGONS.

Scene Five
SABOTAGE

Darkness in the woods. **Raggi** *blows a whistle loudly. Out of the shadows come the group crawling on their bellies. They sing 'Invisible Army' as they snake forwards.*

All
　　If you don't know the woods
　　Then you don't know us
　　If you don't want a fight
　　Then you better back up

　　When the dark night comes
　　And the ghosts rise up
　　If you don't know the woods
　　Then you don't know much

The **Trees** *take out instruments and play dark, rhythmic music – cello, violin, double bass. They rock from side to side as the group rise up, smearing each other's clothes and faces with mud, covering themselves with leaves.*

The group scatters: **Marta** *and* **Snorri** *cover the hut with branches, splash green paint over it.* **Christi** *and* **Sig** *knock spy holes through the roof, appearing with binoculars and telescope.* **Harri** *and* **Gunnar** *place logs which* **Christi** *and* **Sig** *slide down.*

Raggi *blows her whistle and they all fall in line. She leads them in a training exercise played out as a dance: running, skidding, rolling, climbing trees and sliding down again in unison.* **Odd** *lags behind getting the steps wrong.*

The **Trees** *speak.*

— I saw them.

— I heard them.

— The cracking of glass.

— A sixteen-legged creature, slinking like a cat!

— They snaked through the evening, they scattered like rats.

— And nobody knew they were there.

— Did you see?

— Or believe it?

— They were softer than night.

— They slashed all the tyres and snuffed out the lights.

— They flitted round corners, they twisted like kites.

— And only we knew they were there.

— What glory, what stories!

— Each night for a week.

— The soldiers were baffled and kept from their sleep.

— Their boots disappeared and their rations grew feet.

— But never a sound. No never a peep.

— Not a solitary flicker in all of the streets.

— Twisting the sign posts and stealing the meat

— Salt in the water and pins in the sheets

— But nobody knew they were there.

Dawn light fades up. The group pile tins of food, paper, soldiers' boots, loaves of bread. They sit around the hoard, laughing and eating except **Christi** *who sits staring.* **Raggi** *looks through the documents.* **Sig** *chalks up the night's achievements on the board.*

Gunnar   Who got the corned beef?

Marta   Found them stacked up by the water.

Gunnar   Couldn't you've got some mustard?

Marta   I wasn't at the greengrocer's, Harri. I had to slide past three of them on my way back – thought my heart was gonna explode.

Raggi   Where'd the maps come from?

Snorri (*through food*)   Police station. A door was open – I just grabbed everything I could.

Raggi (*of the maps*)   It's the whole county . . . the woods and the mountains.

Harri   Maps and corned beef? I knocked out every headlight on every one of them trucks.

Gunnar   Was I not there as well?

Raggi   There's little black dots all over here . . . Black dots and red lines.

Sig *moves to look.*

Harri   Twenty-five trucks, that's, er . . .

Snorri   Fifty headlights.

Harri   Fifty! Only took us five minutes.

Marta   It's not a competition.

Harri   But if it was me and Gunnar would've won. We probably did win.

Odd   I could do that. I could do something proper next time.

Harri   You guard the hut. That is proper.

Raggi (*to* **Sig**, *of the map*)   What's it mean?

Sig   Whatever it means they won't get far with it now.

Raggi *tears the map up suddenly, furiously, throwing the pieces into the air. The others laugh and catch them – all except* **Christi** *and* **Marta**. **Gunnar** *tries to howl like a wolf but chokes on his sandwich.* **Odd** *smacks him on the back.* **Raggi** *blows her whistle.*

Raggi   Attention! Endurance training – go, go, go!

Gunnar   I'm still eating!

Raggi   Put that sandwich down, Gunnar, it's nearly killed you once already.

Gunnar *throws it down as they all jump in line.*

Raggi (*to* **Marta**)   Not you. You're on surveillance.

Marta   I was stuck up on that roof all yesterday.

Raggi   You'll be stuck up there all week if you give me lip.

Marta   Give you lip? Are you my mum now?

Raggi   I'm worse than your mum: I'm your commander, so button it for once in your life! (*Shouted to others.*) First one to the world tree and back gets pick of dinner!

They all dash offstage. **Odd** *runs the wrong way, then runs after them squeaking.* **Marta** *sticks her fingers up at* **Raggi** *as she retreats. She turns and kicks a tin of corned beef, yelping in pain. She hobbles up on to the roof and picks up the binoculars as* **Christi** *walks slowly back.*

Marta (*muttering*)   'Giving me lip'. No one says anything. Sheep faces, the lot of them . . .

She makes a baaing noise in the direction they ran in, noticing
Christi. *He baahs back.*

Marta   You not one of Raggi's flock, then?

Christi (*climbing up*)   Load of stupid running about shouting,
I thought we were meant to be fighters now, not playing tag
in the woods.

Marta   Better than freezing your bum off up here.

Christi (*sitting beside her*)   You reckon?

Marta   I'm good at running. I'm better at running that she
is and she knows it as well.

Christi   What's the difference though? You reckon any of
this makes any difference?

Marta   Raggi thinks so.

Christi   What do you think?

*She looks at him for a beat then turns away, looking out through the
binoculars.*

I saw my grandad when I was down there. Coming back
out of town, I couldn't help it – took the old turn down the
old street . . . and there he was sat up in our front room
like always. Except he was sitting in the dark. Sat up and
staring . . . And he was so thin and white. And maybe I made
a sound on the gravel or something 'cause he turned and
looked my way and I nearly shouted. I nearly shouted out to
him because he's got no one else. He's got no one but me and
he's in there in the dark on his own. But then I realised . . . he
wasn't looking at me. Just reflections on the glass . . . Like I
wasn't there at all.

Pause.

Marta   It *is* something, all this. It *has* to be.

Christi   I'm afraid all the time. I look alright but inside I'm
just . . . water.

Marta   That's all of us, Christi. That's everyone.

Christi   I liked it before. I liked it when it was a game.

Marta *puts her hand on top of his.*

Christi (*pulling it away*)   What you doing?

She shrugs, looking out again. Beat. He puts his hand on top of hers. Lights down.

Scene Six
BOMBINGS

Night. Roar of planes. Bombs fall nearby: crashing, booming. Lights flash white as the children's terrified faces are caught in tableaux inside the hut. They scramble out of sleep, staring wildly. The **Trees** *rock violently, bend, break, whisper frantically.*

Odd   What was that?

Harri   It was a plane. Was that a plane?

Sig *climbs up and looks out the peephole with her binoculars.*

Odd   It sounded like a dragon.

Harri   Shut up, Odd – just *shut up*.

Raggi   Sig, what's happening?

Sig   The town's on fire.

A bomber flies very close overhead. All but **Sig** *duck down, hitting the ground.*

Sig   Bombers . . . 'bout five of them . . .

It passes close again.

Raggi   Get inside!

Sig *ducks inside the hut.*

Gunnar (*to* **Sig**)   They didn't see you, did they? You didn't let them see you?

Christi   What are they doing? Why take a town then bomb it to bits?

Snorri (*covering* **Odd**'s *ears*)   Don't say 'bomb to bits'. Nothing's being bombed to bits.

Marta   They're looking for someone.

Harri   Funny way to look.

Marta   Trying to scare someone.

Harri   Flatten someone, more like.

Christi   Are they looking for us, Raggi?

Raggi   Don't be stupid. No one knows we're here.

Marta   Don't they? You're sure of that?

Gunnar   We've got to hide. Surely we've just got to run and hide.

Marta   We go down there causing havoc for a week – you don't think someone might come looking for us?

Sig   Everyone get a grip, alright? No one's sending bombers over for a bunch of kids.

Gunnar   We've gotta run. Out. Up into the mountains. We've gotta get away.

Raggi   No one's going running in to the mountains. Are you stupid?

A high-pitched sound suddenly, getting louder.

Marta   What's that – a siren?

The sound becomes clearer: a voice with more voices answering.

Snorri   It's a wolf. It's all the wolves howling.

Bombs fall louder, closer. The trees whip wildly outside. **Sig** *scrambles to the peephole in the roof.*

Sig   They're taking out the harbour.

Gunnar   Don't look. Don't look.

Odd *starts to cry, high-pitched.* **Harri** *shoves him.* **Odd** *continues to cry, hyperventilating, squeaking.* **Harri** *shoves him harder, knocking him over. He rolls on the ground, gasping.*

Harri   Stop it, stop it, stop it. Just stop it for *once*!

Odd *grows more hysterical.* **Harri** *kicks and punches him.* **Snorri** *and* **Gunnar** *rush to separate them.* **Odd** *makes a sudden scramble for the door.* **Harri** *catches hold of his arm.*

Harri   Where would you go? Where'd you think you're going?

Odd   Nowhere. Anywhere. Home.

Harri   And who gets blamed when you fall down a hole and break your legs or get yourself bombed to pulp or crushed under a tree? Whose fault is it when you're ripped to bits by wolves or crack your head open on a rock? Bloody *mine*. 'Cause I'm your big brother, and every way I turn I've got you tied on with a bleeding string.

Odd (*clinging to him*)   I'm scared, Harri.

They grapple for a moment, **Odd** *clinging on.*

Harri   You shouldn't even be here! That's what Mum says. That's what Mum always says.

Snorri   Harri, leave him – you're making him worse.

Odd   What does she say?

Harri   When she gets upset – when you make her cry 'cause you're acting like a mental case.

Odd   I don't. I'm not.

Harri   Like when you kept nicking things. Or kept following round that girl from up the road.

Odd   I don't make Mum cry.

Harri   Just a stupid mistake from start to finish.

A bomb blast even closer. The hut shakes terribly, all the lights are going out. They all hit the floor apart from **Sig** *who ducks down. Pause, as they lie listening.*

Raggi   Snorri, tell us a story.

Snorri   What?

Raggi   Tell us a story.

Snorri   I don't want to.

Raggi   *Please.*

She looks around at them all. They gaze at her in the dark.

Snorri   Right there was . . . There was a . . . There was a little town on a fjord. And one day shadows came swooping over.

Raggi   Not that one.

Snorri   And the shadows weren't monsters, they were machines. And inside the machines there were men.

Gunnar   Tell a good story, Snorri. Tell a proper one.

Beat.

Snorri   But from the mountain tops . . . Odin saw all of this . . . And he went leaping over the woods, thrusting the shadows away with a great sweep of his sword, so the dark machines were scattered like . . . dust . . . crashing against the mountainside.

The bomb blasts are getting further apart, the attack abating.

Snorri   And Odin held out his cloak and scooped up all the townspeople, riding away with them, up past the woods and the mountains and the sky, up to a better place that could never be bombed or broken but looked a lot like home. Like home was before. With the little wooden houses dark red and yellow and green. And the white washing flapping whenever the sun was out.

Christi   And the market stalls with all the same things in the same order and the people having all the same conversations.

Marta   And the fishing boats calling out to each other in the early mornings.

Gunnar   And salt pork ribs on Fridays.

Odd   And trout flapping and squirming on the harbour.

Gunnar   And my mum's at the back door shouting for me to come in. It's the end of the day and there's no more playing out.

Christi   And my grandad's in a grouch 'cause his team lost and I've walked snow in the house again. But I make him a cup of tea and he forgets all about it.

Sig   And there's a crack above my bed where the water gets through in the winter. And I watch it while my brothers snore at night.

Raggi   And there's birds nesting up in the attic with all their soft scratchy sounds.

Marta   And Mad Finn'll be out wandering, singing made-up songs before it's light.

Snorri   And if it snows even the footsteps and the voices'll be put to bed. Buried in the drift.

Harri   And nothing ever changes. Not one thing.

Pause. A bomb falls at a distance. Plane sounds fade. Hush in the woods. They freeze, listening. **Sig** *looks through binoculars, scanning the woods.*

Raggi (*getting up*)   I'll sneak a look at the damage.

Sig   *Wait* . . . There's someone there. Two of them.

Raggi   Where?

Sig   On foot. Can't be half a mile away.

Gunnar *(scrambling in panic)*   They're coming. They're coming . . .

Sig   No it's . . . *Bloody* hell.

She fumbles with the binoculars, dropping them. **Gunnar** *picks them up.*

Raggi   What?

Sig   It's them. Out the paper.

Gunnar *climbs up and looks out.*

Raggi   Who? For God's sake –

Gunnar   Your Majesties.

Raggi *(climbing up)*   Let me see.

She grabs the binoculars. **Gunnar** *drops down and kneels inexplicably, crossing himself.*

Raggi   It looks like them.

Gunnar   Their royal majestic majesties.

Harri   Get off the floor, Gunnar.

Raggi *gives the binoculars back to* **Sig**, *deep in thought.*

Odd   You all said they were dead. I knew they weren't dead.

Christi   What are they doing?

Sig   Walking round in circles it looks like.

Christi   What are they doing *here*?

Snorri   It's the coast. The sea . . .

Odd   They've come to save us.

Harri (*to* **Odd**)   How exactly are they gonna do that?

Snorri   It's the sea they want. The beach.

Sig   Then they're heading the wrong way.

Gunnar   They're probably starving.

Christi   Probably knackered.

Marta   And confused.

Odd   Probably scared on their own in the woods. 'Cause it is a bit scary.

Snorri   Without a map. With all the trees talking.

Harri   They probably think they're surrounded.

Sig   They probably are.

Raggi   What?

Sig   Soldiers on foot from the town. Loads of 'em . . .

Gunnar   Oh God . . .

Sig   Dozens . . .

Harri   What's the plan, Raggi?

Sig   Hundreds . . .

Gunnar   Oh God, oh God . . .

Raggi   Everyone stop for a second. Let me think.

Marta   She hasn't got a plan.

Gunnar   Oh God I'm so hungry.

Raggi (*pulling out a banana, shoving it at* **Gunnar**)   Eat that and shut up.

Gunnar *devours the banana, shoving it in his mouth.*

Snorri   We have to help them, don't we?

Sig   They're gonna walk right into the enemy.

Odd   But the King'll know what to do. The King's the King.

Snorri   We have to get out there and help them.

Gunnar (*through banana*)   There must be a boat. The beach is no good without a boat.

Raggi   Didn't I tell you to shut up?

Gunnar   I'm just saying, if they're getting on a boat, shouldn't we think about getting on it too? Because we're no good to anyone dead –

Snorri   Don't say 'dead'.

Gunnar   And if the soldiers are coming –

Raggi   It's the King and the Prince they're after. It's *them* they want.

Marta   Dead or alive.

Snorri   Can we all stop saying 'dead'?

Gunnar   We get them to the beach. We get out with them.

Marta   No one's getting out.

Raggi (*turning on her*)   Alright 'voice of doom' – screw a lid on it.

Gunnar   We'll probably get medals and all kind of things.

Marta   No one's getting out, Gunnar.

Raggi   Is that how a resistance fighter talks?

Marta   It's how someone facing the actual honest facts talks.

Raggi   It's how cowards talk. Girls like you are always cowards.

Marta   What's a girl like me?

Raggi Nice girls with nice ironed socks and nice tidy handwriting.

Sig (*looking out*) The royals are running. They're going in different directions.

Christi They can hear the soldiers.

Snorri They don't know what to do.

Marta They don't even know the woods. They don't even know the way.

Raggi Then it's a good job there's an invisible army who knows every leaf and branch.

Harri You have got a plan, haven't you, Raggi?

Raggi I'm getting one.

Marta You're having a good time with all this.

Raggi This is what we've trained for.

Marta (*to the others*) Look at her face: she's actually never been happier.

Raggi There's something we can *do* here. Only us. Something that's real and something that matters. Do you not think that's a little bit special?

Marta Our town is on fire. Our woods are overrun –

Raggi Then why are we still talking?

Scene Seven
INVISIBLE ARMY

Deep in the woods soon after. Sounds of approaching **Soldiers***: feet tramping, low but getting louder over the following. The* **Trees** *play 'Invisible Army'. The group put on camouflage.* **Christi** *guzzles lemonade.* **Sig** *is up a tree surveying the woods through binoculars.* **Snorri** *walks through the snow with bits of wood tied to her feet* *leaving 'monster prints'.* **Raggi** *opens a sack, throwing objects to the others: sling-shot, air-rifle, penknife, spade, rope-net, reel of wire, fishing rod. She throws them each a torch.* **Odd** *approaches with hands out but she points him back to the hut. Stamping feet and clicking guns draw closer as great shadows are projected, growing like giants:* **Soldiers** *approaching in lines. The group howl like wolves, then scatter apart from* **Odd** *who trudges off alone.*

Raggi/Sig/Marta/Snorri/Harri/Gunnar/Christi *(sung)*
> You can fool any fool, anybody that you please
> But you won't fool the dark, you won't fool the trees
> You can lay any trap, can catch any prey
> But you won't catch us till a very cold day

The group dance with the **Trees**, *propelled from their branches, swinging and ducking in an acrobatic ballet.* **Christi** *and* **Sig** *drop from branches like bats to check for* **Soldiers**. **Snorri** *lays tripwires.* **Gunnar** *and* **Harri** *dig holes, covering them with nets and leaves.* **Marta** *paints arrows in many directions on the trees.* **Raggi** *plants fireworks.*

Upstage in the dark, **Soldiers** *march in lines, their uniforms flashing between the trees. From high up in a tree* **Sig** *casts her fishing line and reels in a gun, does it again and reels in a* **Soldier**'s *hat. Cries and shouts of* **Soldiers** *below. The group all sing as* **Soldiers** *follow conflicting arrows; point in fear at monster prints on the ground, moving in confusion.*

Raggi/Sig/Marta/Snorri/Harri/Gunnar/Christi *(sung)*
> You can scale any height, you can sail any seas
> You won't fool the dark, you won't fool the trees
> Till the oceans freeze and the beasts rise up
> We're the kings of this kingdom and your game is up

Christi *drinks yet more lemonade and throws the bottle away, belching. Lights of torches flash below; shouts of* **Soldiers**. *He creeps along a branch, turns away and undoes his flies, pisses, showering the men.* **Soldiers** *cry out, fleeing in every direction, falling over tripwires.*

They exit as **Gunnar**, **Harri** *and* **Snorri** *enter upstage.* **Harri** *points in one direction,* **Snorri** *in another. They shove each other before heading off in* **Harri**'s *direction, exiting.*

Music fades as **Raggi** *enters, positioning fireworks on the ground.* **Marta** *follows her softly.*

Raggi (*turning round, hushed*)   What are you doing? You're supposed to be on diversions with Sig and Christi.

Marta   I want a proper job for once.

Raggi   Well, you're not needed, so back off.

Marta   You lay the rockets, I'll watch your back. What's wrong with that?

Raggi (*coming close to her*)   Get it through your ugly skull: I don't want your help, I never asked you to be here, so if you can't take my orders you can go bury yourself in the snow.

She stalks away.

Marta   What's wrong with me, Raggi?

Raggi (*stopping, looking back*)   Seriously?

Marta   What exactly did I ever do to you?

Raggi (*turning away*)   Piss off.

Marta   See, you haven't got an answer.

Raggi (*turning*)   First day of high school. We all had to stand up in assembly and say our names. You stood up and all your mates cheered and clapped. I stood up and you started laughing . . . pointing. Then everyone was laughing and pointing. 'Cause there was a massive hole in my skirt wasn't there? Right round the arse. And I looked at your face . . . and you were so pleased with yourself. So bleeding *sure*. I'm just the skenky girl from down the road aren't I, Marta? Well, not any more. Not out here.

She stalks away. **Marta** *watches her go, then ducks back into the trees, hearing footsteps. She exits.* **Trees** *whisper and watch as* **Harri** *and* **Gunnar** *re-enter upstage, closely followed by* **Snorri***, shining torches.*

Harri (*pointing*)   I'm telling you I know it's faster.

Snorri   It's shorter. It's not faster.

Harri   That doesn't even make sense.

Gunnar   I really think we should just keep moving.

Snorri   The ground's too wet down there. It's nothing but ditches.

Harri   Bleeding girls trying to be in charge . . .

Snorri   Bleeding what?

Harri   What you worried about a few ditches for? Where's your guts?

Gunnar (*low*)   Harri, don't start winding her up, you know what she's like.

Snorri   What am I like, Gunnar?

Gunnar   Well . . . sensitive.

Snorri   Okay . . . why don't you try your ditch-sodden path, and I'll try my rocky path, and we'll see who finds the King first?

Gunnar   Hang on, I don't think we should be splitting up –

Snorri   Why? You worried you don't know the woods? Watch out, Gunnar, you're starting to sound a bit *sensitive.*

She strides off upstage. Sound of stamping boots. **Harri** *and* **Gunnar** *look towards it and exit the other way.* **Soldiers** *run out, guns raised, fall into a pit covered by a net, clamber over each other yelling as they scramble their way out and off. Pause.* **Odd** *enters, moving slowly.*

Odd   Goodbye, ground. Goodbye, sky. Goodbye, snow. (*Picking up a stone.*) Goodbye, stone. I wish I'd known you better.

He drops the stone and trudges on, stops suddenly and listens. Someone breathes heavily. The **King** *stands behind a tree, hidden from* **Odd**. **Odd** *approaches cautiously, listening.*

King   Stay right there. I've got a blade and I'll use it.

Odd *backs away, squeaking in panic, holding up his wooden sword.*

King   What's that sound? Are you man or mouse?

Odd (*hiding behind a tree*)   I'm not a man. I'm twelve and I don't want to be murdered by a tree.

King   By a *tree*? What are you . . ?

He moves slowly out, looking around, sees **Odd***'s hat sticking out.*

King   What are you doing here, child?

Odd   Nothing. I'm disappearing. I'm going up in the mountains to live with wolves. Or be eaten by wolves. Either way I won't be in everyone's way and a mistake all the time.

King   Who says you're a mistake?

Odd   My brother. He's right. I'm always wrong.

King   I used to think like that. I was a weed once. A weed with weak lungs who got dizzy with heights, and couldn't stay in the sun without getting hives. But when I was fourteen my uncle died and something changed. Because when I walked into a room people bowed and called me 'King'. And when they called me that I began to feel taller, to hold my head up.

Odd *peers out from behind the tree.*

King   I began to speak deeper and people began to listen. I was the weed king but a king nonetheless. And I was a good king.

Odd (*crawling out*)   You're not a tree. You're Your Majesty.

King   I've been a good king if I've been nothing else.

Odd   Don't say it like that, Majesty. Like it's over.

King   It *is*, boy. God knows where my son is – the night came between us and the trees closed in. I'll wither with my country . . . because I couldn't begin to save it.

Odd   There's a way. From here I mean. There's a secret way.

King   Don't give me hope – not in vain.

Odd   If you walk a bit that way with your nose towards the mountains . . . past the birch that looks like a skeleton's hand and the three rotten stumps, there's a big rock shaped like a dog's head and under the rock there's a tunnel we dug last summer holidays. It goes out to the edge of the woods and then if you stick to the mountainside but keep the tallest pine in sight . . .

King   A birch, a rock, a tunnel, a pine.

Odd   The tallest pine. If you follow that path you'll come to the beach. And if you come to the beach you come to the water. But you can probably work that bit out yourself.

King   You wouldn't try to trick me?

Odd   No I . . . You're the Majesty. I'm your friend, Majesty.

King   You're more than that. You're my saviour.

He moves to exit but stops, turning back.

Come with me.

Odd   To the beach?

King   To the boat. Away.

Beat. **Odd** *shakes his head.*

Odd   Not without my brother. He wouldn't do well on his own.

The **King** *raises his sword in salute.*

King   Stand tall, little mouse. The world will see a warrior then.

Odd *raises his wooden sword to the* **King** *as he exits.* **Odd** *moves off in another direction.*

Sig *enters clutching her arm, looking behind in alarm, her rod on her back. Her sleeve is torn showing blood and she has blood on her face. She stops, gasping for breath. She leans her face against a tree, crying suddenly and shaking. The sound of someone fast approaching.* **Sig** *looks back in panic, scuttles off into the trees.*

Raggi *enters laying fireworks, her back to the audience. She bends down, moving quickly, lighting fuses. A* **Soldier** *appears downstage with a gun. He stalks towards her softly. As he draws close* **Raggi** *turns, terrified. Just then* **Marta** *swings from on high on a rope, scooping* **Raggi** *up as all the fireworks go off in dazzling flashes. The* **Soldier** *runs around in panic, temporarily blinded.* **Raggi** *and* **Marta** *swing above the woods, laughing and whooping. They jump down from the rope and run offstage, the* **Soldier** *following. As the fireworks fade* **Harri** *and* **Gunnar** *enter, walking backwards and looking up at the sky, down at a compass.*

Harri (*pointing*)   If that's the north star and that's Orion . . . And we came from the south-east and the sea's to the west . . .

Gunnar   Yeah . . ? So where's the path?

Harri   Well, if the town lies south-west in line with the big dipper . . . And the moon's full . . .

Gunnar   You don't know, do you?

Harri   Shut up, I'm working it out.

Gunnar   You *said* you were sure.

Harri   If you hadn't set Snorri off I wouldn't need to be reading the blinking stars.

Gunnar   *I* set her off?

Harri   Well, it wasn't me who called her sensitive.

Gunnar (*turning on him*)   You're never in the wrong are you, Harri? Not ever, not once.

Harri   If you didn't stop for a biscuit every ten minutes we'd 've found the path ages ago!

Gunnar (*prodding him in the chest*)   I need to keep my blood sugar up.

Harri *flails at him and they wrestle clumsily, stumbling backwards in to a ditch, yelling.*

Harri   My ankle!

Gunnar   My head!

Harri   You're head's like a *bloody bowling ball*. You've broke my ankle.

Gunnar   That's not broken, let me see.

Harri *yells in pain.*

Gunnar   Yeah, that might be broken.

A low growl sounds through the trees, getting louder. They gasp and hold their breath.

Gunnar (*whispered*)   That's it . . . of course. I'm going to die here with *you*.

Harri   Don't speak . . . Don't breathe . . .

The shadow of a bear looms above them as the growling continues. They whimper in fear. Suddenly another towering shadow appears: a horned monster. Roaring shakes the trees. The bear shadow turns and flees. **Odd** *walks behind the ditch, holding a torch, still roaring. He listens joyfully as the sound echoes and disappears.* **Gunnar** *and* **Harri** *whimper and sob.*

Harri   Oh heaven, oh my saints above . . .

Odd (*looking down on them*)   Hello, lads.

Harri *and* **Gunnar** *shriek.*

Odd   Do you need a hand out of that hole?

Lights down.

Scene Eight
RAGNAROK

Snorri *enters: a dark shape groping along the ground. She scrambles for the enormous birch centre stage, attempting to climb inside its hollow. Cries are heard as* **Raggi** *and* **Marta** *tumble out of the hollow, yelling and struggling.*

Raggi   Get back. Get back.

Snorri   It's *me*. Raggi, it's *me*.

Raggi's *torch lights* **Snorri**'s *face. She's scratched and muddy, twigs stick out of her hair.*

Raggi   What the hell happened to you?

Snorri   One of them was behind me. I had to run through the bushes forever.

Marta   They're not following?

Snorri *shakes her head, gasping.*

Raggi (*looking round*)   There were ten of them here a minute ago. (*Pointing.*) Came right up to the tree then went off that way – stupid mothbags.

Christi *comes bounding towards them at incredible speed, wearing only one shoe. He hurtles into* **Marta** *and she catches hold of him.*

Marta   You alright? You hurt?

Christi   *My leg* – he had my *leg* – pulled me out the tree! My shoe – look! He's got my bastard shoe.

Raggi   What about Sig?

Christi (*darting around*)   I don't know. I don't know.

Raggi   Weren't you with Sig?

Christi   It all went mad. One of them was throwing rocks and . . . I think she fell, I . . . I heard her shout.

Raggi   Bleeding hell . . .

Snorri   I heard someone crying. When I was coming through the bushes.

Sig *comes climbing down the trunk of the birch, binoculars round her neck.*

Raggi   No. No, if anyone can look after herself it's Sig.

Sig   Too right I bloody can. *Come on*: when have you ever heard me cry?

Marta (*shining her torch on* **Sig**)   What's up with your arm?

Sig   Everyone: torches *off*. There's loads of them down there – every which way.

They all flick off their torches, lit palely by the moon. **Sig** *scales back up the birch, looking out.*

Christi   We should get back to the hut.

Raggi   We tried. They've surrounded it.

Snorri   Odd.

They all look at her.

Odd's at the hut.

Odd, **Harri** *and* **Gunnar** *come scrambling through the trees,* **Odd** *leading the way, holding up his limping brother. They fall down breathless, gasping, pointing the way they came.*

Christi   What? What's going on?

Odd   Back there . . .

Gunnar (*pointing*)   They're . . . They're . . . *There* . . .

Raggi   *Hiding places*. Remember your training: we're not done till we're done for.

They scramble up into the birch's branches. **Christi** *and* **Marta** *huddle together.* **Odd** *climbs a little way and then puts his hand out to* **Harri** *who grimaces in pain as he's hauled up.*

Harri (*pulling close to his brother*)   We shouldn't call you Odd any more. You should get a new name. You should be Bjorn for bear.

Odd   Odd's just fine.

Sig (*looking through binoculars*)   I've got sights on the King . . . moving onto the beach . . . Heading out from the trees.

Odd   And the Prince?

Sig (*scanning*)   There's a light far out . . . A boat . . . He's running, waving.

Odd   And the Prince too?

Raggi   How many are after him?

Sig   No one. There's no one.

Marta   He found the way.

Harri   Odd found the King. Odd put him right.

Snorri   He'll do it. He'll cut loose. He'll sail away.

Odd   And the Prince too?

Sig (*scanning the woods, the beach*)   No. No Prince.

Odd   But the Prince is catching up to his dad. He's running, he's just behind –

Sig   He's not anywhere, Odd. He's gone.

Odd   But . . .

Raggi   What's the position on the boat?

Sig   Close. Getting closer. The beach is clear.

Raggi   There isn't a single soldier?

Gunnar   The soldiers are all here with us.

Pause. Slowly **Sig** *lowers her binoculars.*

Christi   He's not leaving really, though. He's getting out to raise an army, or an air force or both or . . .

Harri   Course he is.

Christi   'Cause there'll be a plan.

Snorri   For all of us. For everyone.

Christi   'Cause he has to come back.

Raggi   When I was little . . . and my Dad'd lock me in my room . . . I'd always believe he was coming back . . . I'd listen to the quiet and think any minute he was gonna open the door and let me out and hug me. Even though he never did. It was always hours and hours and I'd be scared and he'd never be sorry – but I always thought . . . this time he'll realise. This time he'll come and get me and say he's not angry really. And say it's all just pretend.

Marta   I'm sorry for saying your dad's a loon.

Raggi   Sorry for saying you're one of those nice girls. You're not. You're not nice at all.

Marta   Thanks.

They grin at each other. Faint sounds of **Soldiers** *approaching, getting louder during the following. Shouts and whistles: men signalling to each other.*

Christi   What'll they do to us?

Gunnar   Don't ask that.

Christi   Would they kill us?

Sig   They wouldn't kill children.

Harri   Not even them?

Sig   Not even them.

Christi   Not even children who've pissed on their heads?
Not even then?

Raggi   Not even then, Christi.

Snorri (*looking down to the town*)   There's a light on down
there. Can you see?

They all strain to look.

Someone looking out. To see what the damage is . . . To see
what tomorrow is.

Sig   What if I'm an only child now?

Gunnar   Stop it. Don't.

Snorri   Let her say it. We've got to say it.

Sig   What if I never see my brothers again and I'm no one's
little sister.

Raggi   What if my dad's finally gone over the edge with all
this? What if he's locked up in a madhouse or lying at the
bottom of the harbour?

Snorri   What if I get home and my mum and dad aren't
there? The rooms are all the same but there's no one in them.
Or what if they're there . . . but their faces look different. And
they always have secrets from me. And there are things we'll
never say.

Christi   What if my grandad hates me for not coming
back? For not being with him? What if he can't forgive me?

Gunnar   What if my brother calls me a coward for hiding
up here? What if he doesn't say it but he thinks it always?

Odd   What if the school and the streets and the water and
all the other buildings are broken or blown away, or in the

wrong place? What if everything's there but all the pieces are in the wrong order?

Harri   What if Mum's there waiting? Just waiting with a smile on her face. What if all our mums and dads are waiting with tears in their eyes and nothing else matters when they see us again. Not the war, not the soldiers, not the bombs – nothing. What about that?

Gunnar   Tell us a story, Snorri.

Snorri   No. Not now. We are the story now.

Raggi   Too right we are. We're the Snow Dragons. We're the last line of resistance.

Around them the **Trees** *sway and sing.*

Trees (*sung*)
  Don't ask, don't look, don't see
  Some things we cannot speak
  Don't ask, don't try, don't plead
  Some truths we cannot breathe

The Group (*sung*)
  If they take our hands, if they take us home, what will
    home be then?
  If the fight ends hard, or as soft as snow, what will the
    world be then?
  If the road is rocky, if the path is barbed, what will the
    stars read then?
  If the world is spinning, if the world is ours, what will the
    world be then?

A plane flies over. They all look up as the shadow passes over them. Boots tramp closer, louder, heard from all directions. Torchlights flash over the children's faces. The **Trees** *shudder and turn their branches, not wanting to look. The children hold on to each other as the sound reaches a deafening peak.*

End.

The Snow Dragons

MUSIC

Wolf Dance
(Calypso feel)

Lizzie Nunnery

A wolf did creep with blood on his teeth Howl- ing a wick- ed tune I joined in his song We danced the night long He thought I was a wolf child too Sing- ing who's a- fraid of the dark? I'm not a- fraid of the dark Who's a- fraid of the dark? I'm not a- fraid of the dark If the storm does rage and the wind does wail We'll op- en up the doors and so set sail To the side of the moon where the weird things play Dance to the rhy- thm of the an- cient ways Sing- ing who's a- fraid of the dark? I'm not a- fraid of the dark Who's a- fraid of the dark? I'm not a- fraid of the dark Oo oo ooo ooo No surr- en- der 'til the game is ov- er No rest 'til the

tale's been spun No end- ing 'til we're done pre- ten- ding

No sleep til the morn- ing comes Sing- ing who'd a- fraid of the dark?

I'm not a- fraid of the dark Who's a- fraid of the dark?

I'm not a- fraid of the dark Oo oo ooo ooo

The Bough Breaks

Sabotage

Words and music: Lizzie Nunnery
Arrangement: Vidar Norheim

Invisible Army

What Will the World Be?

(Ballad)

Lizzie Nunnery

The Snow Dragons

BY LIZZIE NUNNERY

*Notes on rehearsal and staging, drawn from a workshop with the writer,
held at the National Theatre, October 2016*

How Lizzie came to write the play

LIZZIE NUNNERY   '*The Snow Dragons* is an imagined story
based on actual events. The play is informed by the true story
of a town on the coast of Norway which was bombed by the
Germans in 1942, during which both the King and Prince
travelled through the woods above the town leading to their
escape by boat.

'I heard about this years ago, and came up with an idea
around the question of *what if* there were a group of children
in the forest, and *what if* they could be instrumental in the
plight of the King's escape?

'During the development of the play I changed one of the key
events: in the final version the Prince doesn't survive, aiding a
narrative that doesn't allow a neatly resolved ending and
explores the power of not giving the children everything they
want.

'I have been inspired by the improvisational quality of
children – informed by stories like *Stig of the Dump* and *Robin
Hood*, and excited by the setting of the woods: how woods can
be frightening and also transformative to a group of children
living in this makeshift world.

'Lost innocence and that threshold into adulthood were of
particular interest to me. Most children assume that adults
know the answers and know how to fix problems, and the
play captures the moment when that faith is lost. Within the
narrative the children see how fallible adults are, as it is the
adults who have caused the war.

'The play explores the combination of a universal theme
and an extreme situation – that shift from childhood when

everything is a game, to stepping over the threshold into responsibility and consequence in adulthood.

'It is, at its heart, an adventure story, with elements of fairy tale and myth (all these genres explore loss of innocence). While the content of the story confronts dark truths, the form of the play is not gritty naturalistic drama.

'To the children, the games they play are very real: they get absorbed in them and become taken in by these fantasies, but through the journey of the play they are forced to abandon their games and take on life-or-death struggles, these ideas captured in the line "We are the story now" – a moment when the relationship between content and form crystallises. I hope that for the companies making the work and the audiences seeing it, the play will feel lively, energised and joyous. It's storytelling, dressing up and playing with escapist elements. I encourage companies to move away from the bleak and lean into the natural comedy and spirit of a group of kids seizing a moment and discovering who they can be.'

Approaching the play

James Dacre, lead director, encouraged companies to embrace the magical and the theatrical when bringing the play to life. What is exciting about this text is that it is open to a range of interpretations. The theatrical possibilities need not be bound by resources or budget; what is exciting and inspiring is the ambition and vision that companies will bring to the text.

Read-through

The workshop participants read the play as a whole group; the read-through is the first opportunity to hear the words, and to embrace the lyrical, poetic nature of the text, which takes flight when visual imagery and poetry are read out loud.

EXERCISE: SHORT SYNOPSIS

Immediately after the read-through, you could ask your company to individually write a couple of sentences − a short synopsis of the play. This should include major plot points and encapsulate the key outline of the story. Ask everyone to share their sentences with the group and discuss the similarities/ differences/recurring themes. This is a useful exercise to discover together some of the key narrative choices.

Themes

Resistance

Against . . . Evil? Adulthood? Adults? Something with different values to the protagonists of the tale? Those who threaten their way of life?

The journey of the enemy and that process is important, − from monsters to machines to an enemy with real purpose. Not them and 'us', just 'us'. This is something that characters in the play experience.

Woods

- A constant theme.

- A setting.

Trees

- Mystical.

- Omnipresent.

- Timeless.

- Static.

- Rites of passage.

- Sprawling forest.

- Good and evil and resistance.

They are a stock ingredient of several different mythologies and ancient narratives.

They have an allegorical nature

LIZZIE NUNNERY   'The trees are a kingdom that the children at first have control of – the same with the town, and even more so the woods. They've mapped that world but it can still shift and generate fear in them. This allows us to explore uncertainty and the disruption of constants – that idea of looking at a set of trees and knowing them, but then the light shifts and *everything changes*.'

JAMES DACRE   'The forest is used in a range of plays as it represents being outside civilisation: e.g. *Oresteia*, Molière, *A Midsummer Night's Dream*. It's timeless – somewhere wild and untamed. It's magical and dangerous. Forests can inspire fear in adults because they don't know how to conquer them.'

LIZZIE NUNNERY   'Trees talk directly to an audience. Elsewhere the King is mistaken in thinking a tree is speaking, and a production might use naturalistic tree sounds to show "the voices" of the trees – in this way there is a mix of the literal and the imagined. It's important for the clarity of the story that the children don't "see" the trees, but the trees see them.'

EXERCISE: THREE TERMS

Participants were invited to write three terms that they would use to describe the kind of show they would like to make. Three instinctive aims. The terms should describe the kind of experience they want people to have.

EXERCISE: WHAT THE PLAY IS

James ssplit participants into groups of six and asked them to discuss what they thought the play was, wasn't and what it could be. They were asked to put these thoughts into the following sentences that were shared with the rest of the group:

- What it is . . .
- What it isn't . . .
- What it could be . . .

So, e.g. the play *is* ensemble drama/The play *is not* star-driven.

Doing this early on in your process with your company enables you to put the tent pegs in the ground and all get on the same page.

Here are some of the thoughts from the workshop:

IT IS . . .	IT ISN'T . . .	IT COULD BE . . .
It is stylised	It isn't naturalistic	It could be purely physical
It is ensemble/choral	It isn't realistic	It could be fairy tale
It is combat	It isn't twee	It could be physical theatre
It is conflict	It isn't romantic	It could be spoken word/music
It is adventure	It isn't comedy	It could be a message for today
It is imaginative	It isn't set in multiple locations	It could be about growing up today
It is dark	It isn't past history	It could be social media
It is fun	It isn't a musical	It could be multimedia
It is set in one location	It isn't urban	It could be minimalist
It is ensemble	It isn't naturalistic	It could be Brechtian
It is playful	It isn't indoors	
It is ominous	It isn't little kids	
It is current	It isn't adult	
It is simplistic	It isn't realistic	
It is funny	It isn't musical	
It is a play with music	It isn't comedy	

It is outdoors

It is playful

It is dark

It is full of opposites

It is teenagers

It is playful

It is children

Whose perspective is the play told from?

LIZZIE NUNNERY   'There's potentially a danger if the play is treated as a recollection that the events of the story will all feel past tense. The interaction of the children should be played in the moment. The trees can then be reflective, and offer us as shift of perspective – but even then there is a present tense to what the trees are doing: they are searching, guessing, undermining each other . . . The experience we should feel as an audience is akin to being a child. We want our audience to experience the play with a child's openness. The dynamic that motors the piece is the childlike energy. This is important – it's through their experience that we view the play.'

What is the provocation of the play?

Participants were asked to consider what question might encapsulate the idea, the gesture of the play? What are the key questions screaming out to the audience?

Here are some of their responses to this exercise:

- Can children grasp why their lost innocence is taken?
- Is it possible for adults to view the world as children do?
- How long can children remain children?
- Can children retain innocence when exposed to the adult world?
- How can we protect children from the real world, and should we?

- Where is the line between reality and make-believe?
- Do the children have to accept their reality?
- Can we control our fate?
- Is it possible for young people to influence the future?
- Can children emerge unscathed?
- Can children rule the world?
- Why do we have to be grown up?
- Would war take place if children ruled the world?
- Is it possible for humans to fully escape the evil of war?
- How can we resist becoming machines?

By taking time to think of these questions, you will inevitably bring something of your own value system to your choice of provocation.

Socio-political references

It is a piece that can and should resonate. James encouraged companies to draw direct lines between this play and the homes and the conflict of children – both in terms of places of prosperity and places in conflict. What other associations jump off the page in terms of socio-political references?

LIZZIE NUNNERY   'Hearing it read, I thought why *don't* they use that tunnel that they dug last summer? What's keeping them there? I think it's a heroic idea – that they can't just save themselves – they sacrifice themselves for the future. The King represents the future of the country. Getting out and sailing away is more frightening than staying. The play does have to be current and relevant– it would lack a certain energy if it was just history. You could interpret it to be "nowhere", but wherever you set it, it is definitely set "now" in this sense.'

Lizzie was inspired by stories of children in Bosnia – watching soldiers coming in over the bridge, witnessing the removal of adults. She was interested in the idea of adults taking a group of children's worlds and lives away and also in the adult pressures and challenges that are put on children. Adults are responsible for *breaking* childhood. If we left them alone what would happen?

LIZZIE NUNNERY   'In writing the play I had the performers in mind – looking at the play and wondering what the world would be, the world they haven't inherited yet. There is an important question of what will happen if this war and this world comes to my door? Will I have to deal with this too? What would be the appropriate response? What actions would it galvanise? If the moment arrives, could I be heroic? Raggi enjoys the high stakes of the situation because of the purpose and status it gives her. She knows who she is from the first page – she long ago lost faith in adults. By contrast Marta has been thrown into conflict and is bewildered, scared, angry that Raggi likes it.'

Stage directions

There are helpful indicators in the stage directions that illustrate specific references to place and time. Regarding stage directions describing action/physicality, directors don't have to be reverent to those. It was helpful for Lizzie to write in that way and by being specific you can hopefully understand the intention and energy that drives the action.

Certain stage directions include important story beats that should not be cut. For example:

Marta and Christi – The moment when they hold hands is a significant event in their journeys and therefore essential.

Marta and Raggi swinging on the rope – The important story point is that she saves Raggi from the soldiers. The detail of this action can of course be reinterpreted.

Period

With regards to design and costume, it is not a world crafted with the contemporary in mind– these characters are not in fluorescents and trainers – but neither is it specifically 1940s and you are not required to research the costumes and clothing specifically. It's a piece that will benefit from feeling stripped back.

Food

Lizzie was aiming to create a relatively neutral setting – the fact the food is tinned is important – corned beef and boiled sweets. The food is slightly 1940s, but could still be now.

Geography

Ideally, the setting remains as written, but the most crucial factor if you choose a different setting is that it has to be somewhere near water. The location can't be landlocked as the characters have to be able to quickly access the coast.

Language

If you relocate the play, please do not relocate the language. Lizzie has crafted a slightly heightened script that sits outside specific localities and specific references, lending the style of production to a more imaginary world.

The Viking references should stay – and they could belong anywhere. The Vikings represent the heroic, the big strong people who always fight back and win. Lizzie has avoided specific 'German' references. Another landscape could be used; for example, 'fjord' could be replaced by 'bay' or 'lake'.

Pronunciation

O – din   'I' is 'y'   Raggy   Christy

Music

James suggested to begin approaching the songs within your own restrictions – then look into the function of the songs, how the songs develop the plot, reveal character and explore all the themes at large.

Instrumentation is open – but Lizzie encourages you to lean towards instruments that reflect the style and atmosphere of the world. This is about finding a balance of tone that feels in keeping with the world of the play and the production.

Don't worry about placing music in a *naturalistic* context. The script suggests that the Trees play instruments – this is partly a great opportunity for musicians in the company. Companies don't have to use the melody and sing: they could choose to treat lyrics as spoken text. You may prefer to communicate the words with a foundation of clapping, or rhythm and percussion rather than melody and instrumentation.

For those who may feel an anxiety around *why* people are singing unnecessarily – Lizzie's belief is that it only jars if a production has set up a naturalistic world. As you explore your physical and visual aesthetic, you can use the same choices for your approach to music/songs/singing.

You have total freedom to rewrite the melody and rhythm of the songs; use the words and make what works for you and your company. If you've got talented songwriters/singers/ musicians in your companies, then utilise their talent – that's the exciting thing about making a play with songs.

The songs have a number of different functions. They can be there to provide atmosphere, or to reinforce a theme – 'Bough Breaks' deliberately has a 'hush little baby' quality to it; this idea implies that at some point the bough *will* break for all of us.

A song can instantly pull together an idea that's floating in the play and pulls it into focus. It can accelerate story – in 'Invisible Army' or 'Wolf Dance' you can use the song to make things happen, rather than conveying those events through another dialogue scene, and the action can happen much faster as a result.

If you've got a line in a song that relates to/reflects on a character, the lyric can reveal character in another way.

Don't assume that the dramatic tone of the staging should be informed by the tone of the music.

Sometimes the staging of the song can be in contrast and tell the story better; *then* when you choose to *match* it, it really brings things forward and together.

You could also choose to use bits and pieces of the melodies elsewhere in the play.

The way you use sound design can help you musically too – it can be a key way to express the threat, it can provide an underlying tone (forest and the wind) and provide helpful 'eerie stops' – the use of it, and the *lack* of it, could be played with.

Casting/distribution of roles

Each character should be played by one actor – splitting characters would make the story unclear and the play would lose the precision of the full and crafted journeys that have been written for each character.

Please also keep the lines allocated to the scripted characters. (i.e. don't redistribute lines to different characters). The core of the piece is the specific relationships – e.g. it is important that the brothers are the only brothers.

In addition to the speaking roles of the children there are the Trees. They are open to interpretation and to solo and choric work. You can help your company understand the importance of the Trees in the way you describe them; they are characters and are integral to the plot and structure.

The Trees offer lots of opportunities for performance – they could be three voices or many, or you could approach them

by giving them characteristics – e.g. the Boasting Tree.
Clearly advertise the merits of the trees and soldiers – they
are the musical, physical roles. These parts get to do things
that the speaking parts don't get to do. The Trees are
storytellers, witnesses – they are active.

The 'Staging the Trees' exercise below offers a way to
experiment and relish the opportunity of bringing them to life.

Ages of the characters

Lizzie has written the children as being twelve to sixteen, and
Blue Remembered Hills by Dennis Potter was offered as a good
reference point for those who might be working with sixth-
form/college students.

James reinforced the need to trust the language – don't spend
too much time working hard on making older actors look
young – a lot of it will come from audience's imagination.

Accessing 'play'

There are hundreds of ways to encourage your actors to
openly embrace the playful quality of the text, but broadly
here are a few possible ways in:

'Let's see if your character *would* do that, rather than my
character *wouldn't* do that.' James suggested you could ask the
actors to improvise the 'playful' element of the scene, and
then transpose the dialogue of the scene on to this structure.
It would be possible to treat the building of the den in a
similar way – begin by making a den, then layer the text over
the top.

If you work to create an open, naive, happy-go-lucky spirit in
the room, the young people will access it.

It is also important to address the reasons *why* the children in
the play feel the need to work through these stories in this way.

For some, the key into playfulness could be in the (rural) environment? Perhaps in rehearsing/workshopping the play outside, a different kind of freedom may arrive in the approach to the text.

There are also many computer games that explore these kinds of worlds, for example Dungeons and Dragons on PS4 and Minecraft, and it could be worth opening up a conversation around these reference points.

With the games, you might wish to start by playing games that are much closer to home and then developing the challenge, or exploring the quality of the games that fit the script and the action.

What's key to the exploration of play is finding and animating activities whilst actors are onstage and knowing what they are *doing* there. It's an *active* environment, so the focus should be on keeping the characters (and actors) powering forwards – and not letting the children be still at any time.

James shared a tip for ways to explore the text in the early stages of rehearsals. You could ask your actors to perhaps do a radio play version first – not sound effects, but focusing on the voice and the words. This approach empowers the people in the room to be more imaginative on their feet.

Another way could be to turn the volume off and play it as a silent movie. If the story doesn't hold, then you could ask your actors to go back through their decisions and interrogate their choices. The Litmus test on everyone in the rehearsal room is: if aliens land, not speaking the language, will the story still hold?

Production, staging and design

Design: What are the areas of the visual world that you need to attend to?

James suggested to keep returning to the source for indications regarding the visual world, beginning with the given circumstances. There is snow – therefore there is a wintry feel to the forest. One thing to consider with your companies is whether you set the play in winter. Do you need to be playing temperature? The text often tells you what time of day it is, so this should inform some of the design and lighting decisions.

Playing spaces and configurations

Participants considered the merits of the four most practicable playing configurations. Here are some of the key points that were made:

THE MERITS OF 'IN THE ROUND'

- Good for creating the clearing in the forest.
- The adults will already be in the audience, which makes for an interesting dynamic to play with.
- Trees – they could be standing in aisles, then move away.
- Intimate, claustrophobic setting.
- Removes the requirement for staging as it opens up a more minimalist approach.
- Audience are integrated into the world.
- Good for the fluidity of the play – playfulness and freedom for entrances and exits.
- Democratises things – audience feel immersed in the dynamic of the round.

THE MERITS OF 'END-ON' (PROSCENIUM ARCH)

- Helpfully creates the distance suggested by the narrative.
- Keeps a separation between adults and children.
- 'Behind' the audience in the auditorium is the safety area for the children.

- Digital projection is easier end-on.
- All cast on stage all the time – sight lines are clearer.
- Soldiers could come from the back of the auditorium and 'through' the audience.

THE MERITS OF SITE-SPECIFIC

- Set in a forest – you can have the set and the audience could be in/on the set.
- Natural environment is key for the play.
- Cheaper – and more interesting way of problem solving.
- You could find an area of wasteland or areas of the forest that you could draw the audience's attention to.

THE MERITS OF TRAVERSE

- Maximum amount of space for athletic play.
- Can make the most of the end extremes – town at one end, coast at the other end.
- Can put breaks into the audience configuration and allow actors to get in amongst the audience

Lighting

Light is written into the fabric of the text – it has practical, mystical, technical and narrative roles to play within the script and story.

The participants explored what lighting can offer you:

- Focus – lighting allows you to focus the audience's attention on certain moments or areas.
- You could explore taking light away, gradually moving from daylight to something darker.
- Lighting can help with transitions.
- The use of shadows could help to create scary images

- Using uplight can make things look very tall and downlight to make things look very small.

- Light can completely transform the trees.

- Light can be used to enhance other visual ideas.

- Light can come from the actors themselves; for example, they could all use torches.

Be careful not to suffocate the spoken word for the sake of the visuals – you want the audience to keep listening and the story must speak for itself and the power of the spoken word.

The Soldiers

Sound design could help to put the visuals in the audience's imagination.

The Soldiers don't necessarily have to be played by actors; e.g. they might be represented through shadow/projection with a lot of sound – for example, footsteps marching. The sound of bombs and trees cracking could all be told through sound design.

The enemy could be invisible to the audience and represented through sound, or it could all happen onstage. J.M. Barrie originally wrote *Peter Pan* as a play – the enemy is told through the ticking clock. This is a play about storytelling – a soldier as a shadow means you are saying to your audience 'We are playing'.

The King

The workshop participants explored the questions who/what/ where/why in relation to the King and how he might be represented. Lizzie explained that the key quality the King has is the majestic quality of light – he is magical. Odd is the youngest and Odd sees the King; it could be just a voice and a light, so what the audience sees is Odd seeing the light. The defining characteristic of the King should be that he isn't disappointing. He should fulfil Odd's expectation of the powerful monarch who has all the answers. He should reflect humility alongside nobility – he is a mythical King. You should avoid the audience being confused that the King is in Odd's imagination. The audience *have* to know that the children have helped the King. This is vital to the storytelling. For the children it has to be easier to stay than to fathom leaving.

If you do explore Odd's first sighting of the King only through light, there might also be a moment when the audience sees him as just a man, lonely and lost. It needs to land for the audience that he *really is the King* – this moment anchors down the story.

Fireworks

Participants discussed how to represent the fireworks and some of the thoughts from the discussion are captured below:

- Glitter.
- Lighting.
- Sound design.
- UV paint.
- Projection.

You could ask your company to determine what are the essential qualities of fireworks:

- Sound.
- Shock.
- Human response.
- Surprise.
- Change in colour.
- You don't see the firework, but do see the sky.
- Looking up – vista of the imagination.

The Trees

The Trees should be an integral part of the production. They have a transformative quality and they shouldn't just be treated as a framing device. They are voices, whispering, murmuring a subtle commentary, so you could play around with the way the text can be delivered vocally.

In the workshop, the group was split into four and each group was given one of the following instructions to explore the many possibilities of the Trees.

Staging the Trees

Referencing pages 505–507 of the text:

- *Group 1*. Find a way to tell the story but only with tree-like physicality. Only use bodies and text.

- *Group 2*. Find a way to tell the story as human characters with specific identities and without tree qualities.

- *Group 3*. Find a way to tell the story as a chorus of Trees – you could try simultaneous commentary, unison action, symmetry, a Greek-style chorus.

- *Group 4*. Find a way to tell the story creating the physical visual quality of the Trees – it might be puppetry, or ensemble – an image for the audience of the Trees in space. Explore things rather than people.

This could be a useful exercise to do with your company to generate ideas about what your version of the Trees might be.

Staging the rescue

The group was split into four and, referencing the stage directions from page 545 of the text, given the following rules:

- Choose your staging configuration.
- Be clear on the exact time and place.
- Ensure you convey the given circumstances.

- Make clear decisions on how you're representing the children and the Trees.
- Have an introduction that describes how you will include lighting, sound, set design and any other atmospheric qualities.

This exercise offers a way of exploring the scene on its feet and to have fun playing with different elements. It can allow you to focus your company on some key elements while still keeping staging options open.

References and extra reading

JAMES DACRE   'As the writer, you've read a lot of Norse mythology – how important is it for directors to get immersed in that?'

LIZZIE NUNNERY   'As little, or as much as you'd like. I was looking for *bold* mythology that the children can interpret as black and white. The children *need* that simple view at the start of the play. They're searching for symbols of Good and Evil and over the course of the play arrive at a view that is more complex.'

JAMES DACRE   'Any reason why Norse in particular?'

LIZZIE NUNNERY   'The role of Nature – the belief that man is crafted from ice. The children absolutely connect to landscape, the place and the stories they've grown up with.'

James suggested it was useful to think of yourself as a cultural magpie and in the process of making the work you should encourage your company to explore and share cultural references that speak to them and that reflect the play. No references are bad ones – especially if they unlock things in the play.

Here's a selection that the workshop participants offered:

Nordic myths, *Robin Hood*, *Home Alone*, fairy tales (children with no parents), *Toy Story* at the end, Lost Boys, Peter Pan,

Tiger Lily, *The Goonies*, Grimm's *Fairy Tales*, *The Elves and the Shoemaker* (the elves secretly doing things), *Stranger Things* (children working together).

From a workshop led by James Dacre
with notes by Louie Ingham

The Monstrum
by Kellie Smith

In a cold village on the edge of nowhere, a disease has broken out, infecting the young and transforming them into monstrous creatures. The villagers fearfully watch their children for symptoms of the disease, whilst the Mayor has adopted tough measures for dealing with those who are infected. When Bolek, the local scholar, makes a breakthrough in finding a cure, few are prepared for the gruesome nature of the treatment. But with his own daughter showing signs of infection, there is no choice but to stop this terrible disease dead in its tracks.

A gothic melodrama about the terrifying onset of adolescence.

Cast size
11 named characters + chorus

Kellie Smith was recently awarded a place on the 2016 Channel Four's Pearson Playwright Scheme, and was the Royal Exchange's playwright in residence. Her play *Jonestown* was shortlisted for the 2015 Bruntwood Prize for Playwriting and she recently won a Creative England's iWrite regional partnership with her short film *The Big Day*, which is due to be produced later this year. Previously produced work includes *Black Gold* at Royal Exchange, Studio; *The Sum of Parts* at Liverpool Every-Man; *Blackout* at The Dukes. Her work for young people includes *I* at Liverpool Everyman and *Dog Eat Dog* on tour for Collective Encounters, and her play for children, *The Lost Things*, won Theatre Centre's Skylines showcase. Kellie has also written two afternoon plays for Radio 4, *Can't Live Without You* and *Homeowners*.

Notes on the text

The lines indented in italic can be openly interpreted as song
or spoken word.

The Villagers' lines can be freely divvied out.

As this play has been written for NT Connections there will
be young people playing adult characters. It is important to
play the emotional truth of characters yet there is opportunity
for larger-than-life interpretations that make this play
hyperreal.

Characters

Milena
Bolek

Mayor Wenzel
Lazlo
Preben
Tomis

Radmila
Stanko

Libusa
Mrs Sortov
Mr Koshka

The Villagers
The Infected
Young Man

Snow.

A gust of wind carries in the **Villagers**.

Villagers   Imagine a place
In the highest mountains
Frosted little houses
Shards of glass hanging from a wishing well.

It's so cold here that people's glasses freeze to their faces
Their ink turns to ice before it hits the page
Nothing will grow here
Even a turnip turns to glass
So our people eat horsemeat, and wolf meat
And sometimes even reindeer.

You see
You have to be made of grit to live here
You have to be made of mountain rock
A little old lady will bludgeon a thief with a pickaxe here
People, here they can endure anything
Survive anything . . .

(*To the sky.*) Is that the best you've got?!

Well, almost anything.
Something has
Something has happened here.

We don't like to speak of it.

As you look at this scene
What do you see missing?
Men, women, children
But the youths . . .

My son . . .
My daughter . . .
Control yourself!

They're gone.

It is a terrible thing
Terrible, terrible
It's a disease!

People here
In these parts
They call it . . .

The Monstrum.

They all react to the word.

Which means

Portent,
Omen,
Monster!

There is hysteria.

Villagers
   Our people have lived here for hundreds of years
   And we can cope with almost anything
   Like frozen snot
   And our fingers falling off
   And even permanent brain-freeze.

   But there's one thing that shakes us
   Far worse than an avalanche
   Sends shivers through
   Much worse than a cold snap

   And that something is a sickness called
   The Monstrum.

   It's a terrible thing when you're afraid of your children
   It's a terrible thing when you fear what they have become
   It's a terrible thing when you're locking your bedroom door

And you feel unsure
That these are your children at all.

We look for signs, we look for markings
Warnings of the disease's approach
Hair on the knuckles
Or oozing pustules
And their head may have become ever so slightly larger.

Once it's in the system, it's in the system
This is where the infection truly takes hold
They swell with muscle and fat
Their bones become brittle
And their eyes turn redder than red.

It's a terrible thing when you're afraid of your children
It's a terrible thing when you fear what they have become
It's a terrible thing when you're locking your bedroom door
And you feel unsure
That these are your children at all.

One morning there's a snap and a snarl
And before we know it, they're towering over us
Their hair is now dark
Their hair is now coarse
Some of them are completely covered.

And they're sweating
And they're fevered
And they're rabid.

It's like somebody took my child!

It's a terrible thing when you're afraid of your children
It's a terrible thing when you fear what they have become
It's a terrible thing when you're locking your bedroom door
And you feel unsure
That these are your children at all.

Village square.

Lazlo, *a deadpan-looking boy, rings a bell.* **Mayor Wenzel**, *a fat, worrisome man, is on a podium in front of the crowd.*

Wenzel   We face near-extinction. I do not say this lightly. This is our coldest winter yet. We have barely enough to feed ourselves never mind our animals. The coal shed is mounting up with bodies and it takes days to bury them because the ground will not thaw.

With the spread of this infection we are losing our young day by day. Our commitment to stamping out the Monstrum must be stronger than ever.

I have told you to remain vigilant. To look for signs of the disease's approach. Physical but also a strangeness – a change in appetite. A desire beyond what is normal. A liking for the bloody.

A large, covered cage is rolled out. A weary-looking man, **Preben**, *follows behind.*

Wenzel   Is this your son, Preben?

Preben   Yes.

Wenzel   How long has he been infected?

Preben   He's been showing signs for about a week. (*Quickly.*) But I didn't know – just a little agitation, and his eating –

Wenzel   We tell ourselves it isn't happening.

Preben   I would have handed him over sooner –

Wenzel   But you waited.

He indicates for one of the **Villagers** *to whip off the covering. Revealed is a feral-looking boy gnawing on a bone. The crowd gasps.*

Wenzel   And here he is now.

He picks up a stick.

Preben   Please –

Wenzel   You see why we go to such lengths to protect ourselves from this abomination?

Preben   He is – he was a good boy –

Wenzel   Can you imagine what would happen if we allowed this disease to manifest itself in our little town?

He pokes the stick at the boy –

Just one youth, two youth, three – then suddenly –

Tomis *snaps back.*

Wenzel   What signs did this boy show, Preben?

Preben   He started going out at night.

Wenzel   Typical.

Preben   It was like something had possessed him. He didn't want to work. His teeth. And when he spoke –

Wenzel *prods the cage some more.*

Another snarl.

Preben   I couldn't understand him.

Wenzel   Do I ask too much, when I ask you to report such developments?

Preben   No, Mayor Wenzel.

Wenzel   Where's my son? Where is Lazlo?

Lazlo *is right behind him.*

Wenzel   Oh yes. Of course. Not but a year ago, he was less rabid than this, and what did I do? I cast him out. Out into the wild beyond our houses. Each day afterwards. I prayed. I prayed he would survive. I prayed he would last the winter. More than anything I prayed the Monstrum would leave his system, and he would return to me. And, look. Look at him.

Preben   You are very lucky.

Wenzel   And where is Libusa?

Libusa *raises her hand, shyly.*

Wenzel   Libusa handed her son over, the moment he turned. She dragged him from her home, with her bare hands. Didn't you?

Libusa   I did what was necessary.

Wenzel   Exactly.

Libusa   I think about him every day. I wonder if he's OK out there – if he's ever coming back –

Wenzel   If your sons survive out there, then they return to you as men. Strong. Ready to work.

Libusa   Yes, Mayor Wenzel.

Wenzel   Why would you want to keep such a creature, Preben?

Preben   I – I thought I could help him.

Wenzel   You put us all in danger.

Preben   I'm sorry.

Wenzel   What is our system for dealing with first signs of infection?

Preben   We contain them.

Wenzel   And then?

Preben   We report them?

Wenzel   And then?

Preben   They are assessed.

Wenzel   I doubt there is need for assessment here, is there?

Preben *is quiet.*

Wenzel   I dream of a day that the Monstrum will die out completely. That we will no longer have to live our lives in fear of its approach. Of it rearing its look in our children's eyes –

Preben   Please. Mayor. He is my only son –

Wenzel   Of them one day *turning on us.*

He circles the cage.

I am not going to cast this creature out.

Surprise amongst the crowd.

Wenzel   Today is a very fortunate day for our friend Preben. Many of you have sons and daughters that have presented like his son, Tomis, here, and they have been let loose to survive the wild. Some have returned to you, others – have not. As you know, I have personally tasked Bolek the Scholar with finding a cure, to end this misery. I am pleased to say that just a few days ago he made a breakthrough.

Villagers   What is it? Tell us? Oh thank the Lord. What?

Wenzel   Now, now. Hush. There is still some way to go, but we potentially have something that will stop the Monstrum dead in its tracks. That will stop your children from ever developing these symptoms.

Preben   What is it, Mayor Wenzel, please?

Wenzel   I cannot get into the technical details with you. Most of us cannot understand the intricate workings of the brain.

Preben   The brain?

Wenzel   This infection starts in the brain, we are sure of that much. Bolek has been experimenting on rats, but that research has taken him as far as it can go. Now what he needs is a human subject.

Preben *realises.*

Wenzel   Your son, Preben.

Preben   I – I –

Wenzel   Perhaps it would be a small remuneration for your carelessness –

Preben   Bu – bu – but Mayor –

Wenzel   This is an opportunity for you to have your boy 'reset', Preben. Do you not think half our citizens here would die for the chance I am offering you?

Preben   What if something happens –

Wenzel *hits the cage.*

Wenzel   *It already has happened. Open your eyes.* Here in this place. We live for each other. We do what is best for the whole. That is the only reason that our people have survived out here. That is the only thing that keeps us surviving.

Preben *looks at the cage. Nods slowly.*

Wenzel   Excellent.

He snaps his fingers. The cage is wheeled out.

You will hear soon.

He disappears. The crowd disperses, talking excitedly.

Preben *is left alone.*

Bolek*'s home: a basement lab.*

Bolek *stands sharpening two large ice picks.* **Mayor Wenzel** *watches him, nervously.*

Bolek   In the early days – when I used to be a catcher, if there were a hundred rats and I killed fifty of them the next week there would be two hundred. They wouldn't eat poison.

Or get caught in a trap if I'd used it once. I'd have to lie under the floorboards, very still. Very quiet. You know, I swear that rats laugh. You think I'm crazy but it's true. I could hear them. They are very like us. We're both warm-blooded. Rats eat everything we do. They live where we live. Most important – they suffer the same diseases. They respond to injury and infection the same way we do. They have the same organs. They have very similar brains.

Rats are perfect.

I tried pinpricks. Isolation. Drowning. Some of them became very agitated indeed. Aggressive. Snappy. I peered into their little brains. A little incision, like an Indian scalping, if you will. And I noticed a change. The front part of the brain, it had swelled just slightly. It was darker. Very curious, very curious indeed. I compared this with a rat that had not undergone my programme of stress, and the difference was significant. This led me to deduce that this is where the infection takes hold. This part of the brain holds the madness.

There are wires in the brain. They all have their own function. The ones at the front, I believe they make us feel. They control how we behave. Under my microscope, very intrinsically, I snipped some of these wires in the rat's brains. Snip. Snip.

And the rat was contented. All signs of madness, gone.

Wenzel   You're just going to cut a wire in his brain?

Bolek   Through the eye socket to sever the wire.

Wenzel *has to sit.*

Wenzel   Dear Lord.

Bolek   I have been practising on sheep, and a couple of dead bodies. Ice picks are the best tool.

Wenzel   Will he – the creature – will it feel pain?

Bolek   Ah. There lies the exciting bit.

He retrieves a cut branch of a plant.

The black cherry plant –

Wenzel *quickly moves away.*

Wenzel   The Devil's herb. Don't bring that near me.

Bolek   I'm wearing gloves you see. But it usually isn't too harmful to touch.

Wenzel   That is the Devil plant.

Bolek   Just a useful name to stop children from eating its berries.

Wenzel   Anyone that looks at it –

Bolek   I'm aware of the superstition.

Wenzel   It brings death.

Bolek   It is poisonous, certainly. This is the property I was interested in. Mayor Wenzel, please. I'm not going to touch you with it.

Wenzel *keeps his distance.*

Bolek   The true genius of these experiments is manipulating and blending different properties. The root – highly toxic, but if I moisten it in wine vinegar, you know what it does?

Wenzel   What?

Bolek   It naturally induces sleep. Anyone who smells the right quantities, seeped into a cloth and placed over their mouth, is lulled into a happy, deep sleep.

Wenzel   They don't feel any pain?

Bolek   Not at all.

Wenzel   I'm not sure.

Bolek   You've said yourself if we delay any more, we'll lose that many of our young that this village will grind to a standstill. We will all perish.

Wenzel   Perhaps it isn't as bad as you say. We are identifying cases quicker.

Bolek   How many do you think are hiding infected?

Wenzel   I haven't seen Koshka's son for some time. Come to think of it, Radmila's girl has been absent from church for the past two weeks.

Bolek   We have to act now.

Wenzel   I just want to be sure that you're sticking two ice picks in that Preben boy's head for good reason. People are already wary of you, Bolek. They find you a bit cold, shall we say? And you don't help yourself creeping around the coal shed. Examining dead bodies at night. People still remember all that business with your wife –

Bolek   I pay no attention to idle gossip.

Wenzel   I just need to know that you believe this will be a success?

Bolek   All I know for sure is that nothing gets nothing.

Wenzel   You know, I don't sleep any more. All day long I have people knocking at my door. They want answers. They expect me to have the answers. How can you answer a curse?

Milena *is at the door. She looks unwell.*

Bolek   Milena. I asked you to wait upstairs.

Wenzel   Ah. Little Milena. How did such a beauty come from you, Bolek?

Milena   They're chaining the creature up outside.

Wenzel   This is not the place for young ladies to be, Milena.

Milena   I will be assisting my father tomorrow.

Wenzel   Surely not?

Bolek   Milena is quite accomplished. She has a keen interest in philosophy, the laws of nature and alchemy.

Wenzel   Is that so?

Bolek   One day she will leave here, and she will become a physician. We have worked tirelessly together in finding a cure.

Wenzel   She is a most dutiful daughter. Her and my Lazlo, they give people hope.

Bolek   They do, I am very lucky to have her.

Milena *is scratching*.

Bolek   Mayor Wenzel if there is nothing more, we must prepare for tomorrow.

Wenzel   Yes, yes. I feel I have a much clearer picture of – your – your proposed treatment plan. I will pray that God guides you. We are all counting on you, Bolek – or should I say both of you?

He leaves.

Bolek   Why are you scratching?

Milena   They chained him up outside. I could hear his cries. He'll freeze to death out there.

Bolek   They don't feel the cold like we do.

Milena   Still, maybe I should go out and see that he's OK.

Bolek   You are to go nowhere near that creature, do you hear? Nothing can jeopardise tomorrow The Mayor's on the edge enough. Did you hear what he said? The 'Devil's herb'? These people think the Devil walks around tending to flowers, like some sort of depraved gardener. This is what we must contend with, Milena. The people of this place believe so many things that have no evidence, and they question the things that do. We have much work to do. This has to go completely to plan. It is our chance to get people to finally understand our work. To trust in it. To value it the same as they do any hunter or priest. If it doesn't go to plan, they'll soon turn. Mark my words. They'll have us scuttling under floorboards again. Catching rats to make our living. You don't want that, do you?

Milena   No.

Bolek   Then we must focus our minds. Let's rehearse. Gloves. Masks.

They both put on gloves and masks. **Milena** *wheels out a skeleton strapped to a chair.*

Milena   I place the cloth over the creature's mouth, until he is unconscious.

She prods the skeleton several times with a stick.

The creature is sedated.

She tests the straps.

The straps are secure.

She places a cloth over half of the skull.

I will place cloth over the right side of the creature's skull.

Bolek *picks up his ice pick and a hammer.*

Bolek   The creature appears stable and prepared. I will line up the ice pick with the left eye socket. I will insert the ice pick through the eye socket using a hammer.

He does this.

I will very carefully move the ice pick from side to side to severe the wire that connects the infected front part of the brain to the rest of the brain.

He does this. then removes the ice pick.

Milena   I will place the cloth over the left side of the creature's skull.

Bolek   I will perform the same procedure on the right.

He does.

Milena   I will wipe away any excess blood, and place a bag containing ice over the creature's eyes.

Bolek   We will dispose of masks and gloves and scrub our skin with water.

Milena   If the creature has not come round then I will waft smelling salts under its nose.

Bolek   A checklist. Does the creature – does the boy still appear physically unwell? Is he disturbed? Restless? Does he fidget uncontrollably? Is he fevered? Is he hot? Sweating? Is the boy combative? Resistant? Aggressive? Is he socially hostile or reclusive? Does he suffer dark thoughts? Mental agitation? Can we understand him? Is he able to communicate?

Milena   Will he – will the creature suffer?

Bolek   Milena, when I take you to the city, when we attend a live lecture, they will dissect real cadavers before your very eyes. You need to get over this squeamishness.

Milena   I didn't like what we did to the rats.

Bolek   I don't know what's with you lately, but your capacity for reason seems to be slipping.

Milena   I just want to be sure –

Bolek   Then be sure of me. I am your father – since when have you questioned what I have told you?

He stares at her.

Milena   I'll put the plants in a bucket for tomorrow

Bolek   Come here, Milena.

She does.

What's that on your face?

Milena   What?

Bolek   Is it – is that a spot?

Milena   I caught myself. It's a scratch.

Bolek   Let me see your nails.

She shows them to him.

Milena   I need to cut them.

Bolek *gets out an old medical tin.*

Bolek   We should really start doing these checks each morning.

Milena   I don't need –

Bolek *has a wooden stick in her mouth checking her teeth.*

Bolek   Any tingling in the gums?

Milena   No.

Bolek   Spit.

Milena *spits in a bucket.* **Bolek** *looks at it.*

Bolek   Clear.

He has a tape measure out, measuring her head size.

Seems normal.

He smells her. Then:

Excessive hair?

She shakes her head.

Any strange thoughts?

She shakes her head.

Dark thoughts?

Milena *hesitates. Shakes her head.*

Bolek   Any changes?

Milena   No.

Bolek   *However small.*

He puts his hand on her head.

You're hot.

Milena   We've been so busy.

Bolek   You must get some rest before tomorrow.

Milena *goes to leave, stops.*

Milena   I heard Mayor Wenzel mention Mother. People still whisper about her.

Bolek   They whisper about me.

Milena   They thought she was a witch.

Bolek   There is no such thing.

Pause.

Your mother – something wasn't right in her. She needed help.

There is a howl from outside.

Our work here is more important than ever. You know that, don't you?

Milena   Yes.

Bolek   You're tired. It's an early start tomorrow.

Milena *kisses him, and goes. He looks after.*

Radmila *and* **Stanko**'s *house.*

Radmila *is boiling a pot over a stove, whilst her husband,* **Stanko**, *reads a book.*

Stanko   It says you're supposed to put a whole meal inside one eggshell. That's impossible.

Radmila   There's another page, it says you can use beer.

Stanko   Beer?

Radmilla   You put it in an eggshell next to the fire and wait for it to boil.

She says this picking up a bottle of beer.

Stanko   You're not using my beer.

He snatches it away.

Radmila   I'm not cooking a whole meal either. She's eating us out of house and home as it is.

Stanko   This is ridiculous. A changeling is usually a baby. It's a fairy's baby that has replaced your own.

Radmila   I know that.

Stanko   Dagmar is not a baby any more. Far from it

Radmila   Will you keep your voice down.

Stanko   I'm sick of tiptoeing around this place.

Radmila   You and your drink. Can't you see what this is doing to me?

Stanko   If Mayor Wenzel finds out I haven't reported her –

Radmila   It isn't a disease. She is a changeling I tell you. That up there is not my daughter.

There's a noise upstairs. They both look frightened. They talk in hushed voices.

Stanko   What is she doing up there?

Radmila   I don't know.

*She puts her hand out, and **Stanko** reluctantly hands over the beer.*

Stanko   Is she supposed to drink it?

Radmila   Read on.

Stanko *reads from the book.*

Stanko   'When a mother finds a scrawny ill-tempered, foul-mouthed, yellow-faced babe in the cradle, she knows instantly that the fairies have swapped her baby for this thing.' You see it says there, a baby.

Radmila   Go on further.

Stanko   'If a family whose son or daughter is abducted may receive as a substitute a sickly fairy child, which soon appears to sicken and die, they bury and mourn it, never realising that their own child plucks flowers in Arcadia.' What's Arcadia?

Radmila   Fairyland.

Stanko   'To find out if you have a changeling, place bagpipes at the end of the cradle . . . '

Radmila   We don't have bagpipes.

Stanko   'Boiling eggshells with beer inside is another way of detecting. If a mother boils eggshells in front of a changeling child, it will cackle with laughter.'

He flicks through the book.

Stanko   'Disposing of a changeling.'

Radmila   Don't read that.

She tries to get the book.

Stanko   'Heat a red-hot shovel, shovel the fairy up and cast him onto a chimney fire. Or force a foxglove tea down his throat and wait until it burns out its intestines.' Do you want to kill her?

Radmila *grabs the book. Reads:*

Radmila   'No matter how brutal the punishment of the *fairy*, the original child will return unscathed.'

Stanko   Bolek may have a cure yet.

Radmila   It's the only way.

Stanko   We just have to hold on a little longer.

Radmila   Bolek is a godless man. He believes in nothing but himself.

Stanko   I don't know, Radmila.

Radmila   Each day it gets worse and worse. I creep around this house. I have to leave her dinner outside her door. I can hear her cackling to herself. She speaks in a language I don't understand. Scratching around in that little room.

Stanko   They say maybe it can be treated.

Radmila   So far their solution has been to throw them out into the wilderness.

Stanko   But Bolek says there is something in the brain – they can cure the brain –

Radmila   If we report her we'll never see our real daughter again. She's too weak. She won't survive out there. Is that what you want?

Stanko *hesitates.*

Radmila   The eggshells will confirm it.

After a moment, he nods.

She pours the beer into an eggshell.

Now. How are we going to get her down?

They both look upstairs.

Bolek's *lab. The next day.*

Bolek *is standing over* **Tomis**, *who is unconscious, strapped to the chair. He has his mask on, as does* **Milena**, *who stands nearby. We cannot see the boy's face, just the raised arm of* **Bolek**, *holding his ice pick.*

Mayor Wenzel *stands further away,* **Lazlo** *beside him. Two* **Villagers** *stand by in case* **Tomis** *wakes up.* **Preben** *has been allowed into the room, and anxiously watches from a far.*

Bolek *pushes the ice pick carefully into the boy's eye socket. He hammers it in.*

Wenzel *retches, as do the* **Villagers**. **Preben** *watches in horror.*

Bolek *is wriggling the ice pick about. Eventually he pulls it out.*

Milena *take a bloody cloth off* **Tomis**'s *face and puts it over the other eye.* **Bolek** *performs the same procedure on the other eye, as rehearsed.*

Bolek *passes* **Milena** *the ice pick, which she wipes with the cloth.*

They both remove their masks and gloves and wash their hands. It is a perfectly synchronised routine.

Tomis *remains still.*

Preben   Is he – is he . . ?

Bolek *holds his hand up. Silence.*

They check **Tomis**'s *straps again.* **Bolek** *signals for* **Wenzel**'s *men to be on standby.* **Milena** *looks at* **Bolek**, *who takes a breath before nodding at her.* **Milena** *stands over* **Tomis** *and wafts some smelling salts in front of his face.*

Slowly **Tomis** *begins to come round.*

Preben   Tomis? Tomis?

Wenzel   Quiet.

Bolek   Tomis? Can you hear me? Undo his straps.

Wenzel   Are you sure?

Bolek   Undo them. Please.

The **Villagers** *do. Gradually* **Tomis** *sits up. There is some blood on his face. He looks disorientated. He looks around very slowly.*

Preben   Tomis? My boy?

Bolek   Let him come forward.

Preben *does.*

Preben   It's me –

Bolek   Who is this, Tomis?

Tomis *stares at* **Preben**, *blankly at first. Then he seems to smile in recognition.* **Preben** *smiles too.* **Tomis** *laughs.* **Preben** *laughs.*

Preben   My boy. My beautiful boy.

Preben *hugs him. Everyone gasps.*

Wenzel   My God. You did it, Bolek.

Bolek   I still have to examine him thoroughly.

Wenzel   But look.

He shakes **Bolek**'s *hand vigorously.*

The village square.

The podium. The **Villagers** *crowded round.* **Wenzel** *on his podium,* **Bolek** *beside him.* **Milena** *close by. Every now and then she scratches, increasingly agitated.*

Wenzel   God gave me the wisdom to instruct Bolek to find a cure and through his hands he released us from this terrible disease. We have been tested but we are stronger.

Villagers   Thank God for Bolek! Praise be to God!

Mr Koshka   When can others have the treatment?

Wenzel   I am happy to forward any new cases of the disease to Bolek for treatment. We will no longer live in fear of the disease's approach –

Mr Koshka   My son smells, and he sweats and he sleeps. All morning, I have this great big bear snoring through the ceiling. His hands are twice the size of mine. Thud. Thud. Thud. I hear when he wakes up. And work, he will not. His poor mother running to get his food. And his eyes – he looks at me as though I am nothing at all. As though our work, our business – the business I should hand to him – is no longer fit. I'd clout him if he didn't tower over me. If he didn't frighten me so much.

Mrs Sortov   My daughter is always disappearing into the night. She paints her face and dresses in such an unsavoury way that I think the sweet child I knew is dead. She no longer speaks to me but regards me with such disdain that it sends shivers through me. I lock her door, but she is devious. This creature takes pleasure in tormenting me.

Wenzel   How many of you have been hiding the infected?

Slowly a number of raised hands.

By God, Bolek. Our mission is greater than we thought.

Bolek   But Mayor Wenzel. I haven't had enough time to monitor Tomis –

Villagers   Please – You are our only hope –

Suddenly **Stanko** *and* **Radmila** *rush on.*

Stanko   Help us.

Radmila   Forgive us. God forgive us.

Stanko   We thought she was a changeling.

Radmila   I just wanted my daughter back.

Stanko   I wrapped her up. I wrapped her up like she was a little baby – Please save my daughter, please save her.

Radmila *is crying.*

Wenzel *looks at* **Bolek**.

Wenzel   The Lord stands with you, Bolek, and gives you strength.

The **Villagers** *wait anxiously outside* **Bolek**'s *house.*

Inside: the chair – one new patient after another. A perfect sequence of infected young people being ice-picked one after the other.

Bolek *and* **Milena** *work tirelessly.*

Villagers
    These are our children
    Yes, these are our children
    And who knows what's best for them
    What's right for them?
    Than a parent who loves them
    Yes a parent who knows them
    A parent that looks at them
    And sees their own face reflected.

    Because these are our children
    Yes these are our children
    And who knows what's best for them
    What's right for them?
    Than a parent who loves them
    Yes a parent who knows them.

    A parent that knows them well
    And dare I say, even
    Better than they know themselves

Because these are our children
Yes, these are our children
Yes these are our –

They stop. **Bolek** *has appeared. His apron is blood-splattered. The* **Villagers** *gather round him anxiously.*

Bolek   A success.

The **Villagers** *rejoice.* **Bolek** *is celebrated.*

Bolek's *home: the lab.*

Bolek *is dressed in a nice suit. He is dictating his notes to* **Milena**. **Milena** *is sweating. She's struggling to sit still as she writes.*

Bolek   I knew with the rats, their temperaments became more agreeable after the procedure but I didn't know that the human brain could be so contained. It's as though the subjects have swallowed a happy pill. Life is easy. They take pleasure in small things. They help their parents. They're happy to spend time with them again. They do not long for things they cannot have. They are not controlled by wild emotions. Read that last bit back to me.

Milena   'They help their parents. They're happy to spend time with them again. They do not long for things they cannot have. They are not controlled by wild emotions. Read that last bit back to me.'

Bolek   New page. Mr Koshka reported that his son spent all yesterday chopping wood – one after the other. He said he'd never seen him work so hard without complaint. Mrs Sortov said her daughter now sits with her all day, darning socks. Contented. Village life has returned to a time we'd all forgotten,

Milena   But they're vacant.

Bolek   Vacant?

Milena   After treatment, they're – docile.

Bolek   There is a certain mental dullness, yes.

Milena   Don't you think it's important that we record that?

Bolek   What mental agility do they need to herd reindeer and catch fish? The main thing is that their madness has all but gone.

Milena   But they're not them.

Bolek   Why are you fidgeting, Milena?

Milena   Can I go to my room now?

Bolek   I feel like I never see you.

Milena   We work with each other day in, day out. And then at the end of the day, we work on your book.

Bolek   I thought you liked my book.

Milena   What if there was another way?

Bolek   What are you talking about?

Milena   I found this.

She brings out a journal.

Bolek   Where did you get that?

Milena   It has her notes inside.

Bolek   Give me that.

Milena   Surely we should explore other ideas?

Bolek   Those are the ramblings of a madwoman.

Milena   She writes about healing properties in plants – natural oils that might protect against diseases –

Bolek   Milena, give that to me.

Milena   Why won't you listen to me sometimes?

Bolek   Is this what you want to be? Some madwoman, travelling the countryside with her potions?

Milena   Why won't you let me make up my own mind?

Bolek   She was lucky they didn't string her up in the village square.

Milena   Lucky. I wouldn't call her lucky.

Bolek   You don't speak to me this way.

Milena   Am I like her?

Bolek   I don't –

Milena   Is that what you're afraid of?

She begins coughing.

Bolek   Are you OK?

She is violently hocking something up.

Bolek   Milena?

Milena *pulls a black cherry plant out of her mouth.* **Bolek** *watches horrified.*

Bolek   Wh – what is that?

The both look at it.

Did you eat it?

Milena   I don't know.

Bolek   We need to test you.

He goes and gets his medical tin.

Milena   No.

Bolek   Please, Milena –

Milena   I don't want to.

Bolek *chases her around.*

Bolek   Stay still, for goodness sake.

Milena   Leave me alone.

She jumps onto a table.

Bolek   Get down. I need to examine you –

Milena   Get away from me.

She swipes at him, scratching his arm.

Bolek   You hurt me.

He looks at it. **Bolek** *grabs one of the sedative-soaked cloths, and corners* **Milena**.

Wenzel (*off*)   Bolek? Are you down there?

Bolek *quickly grabs hold of* **Milena** *and sedates her as* **Wenzel** *is making his way down into the basement.* **Lazlo** *follows behind him.* **Bolek** *puts* **Milena** *in a cupboard.*

Wenzel   Ah. There you are.

Bolek *locks the door and spins round.*

Bolek   Mayor Wenzel. To what do I owe this – ?

Wenzel   Don't stand on ceremony. We're friends now, aren't we? How do you like your new workroom?

Bolek   Yes. I've bought new supplies. I'm working on my book –

Wenzel   That's good news. Good news indeed. Look, I need to talk to you about your treatment. Now, I am no man of science, as you well know. And you know how much we all appreciate what you've achieved. You are an upmost valued member of this village, Bolek.

Bolek   Mayor Wenzel – if you don't mind –

Wenzel   I understand you are busy, Bolek. Forgive me. I'll be as to the point as I can possibly be.

Bolek   Yes?

Wenzel   Well – It's just – I've had some people visit me. Parents of those you've treated. And whilst they are eternally grateful to you for curing their children in such a – succinct fashion – they have some concerns.

Bolek   What concerns?

Wenzel   Their children seem to be a little – a little – there's something missing.

Bolek   Missing?

Wenzel   They're not quite – there.

Bolek   Mayor Wenzel, I'm afraid I don't have time for puzzles.

Wenzel   Mr Koshka's boy went out to the storehouse, with no boots on. His feet turned black. He might lose his toes.

Bolek   I fail to see –

Wenzel   And Tomis? Preben took him hunting. He said it was like the boy had never held a bow and arrow before. He practically poisoned himself with the dart.

Bolek   That boy always was an idiot.

Wenzel   Mrs Sortov asked her daughter to give the floor a good scrubbing. She practically wore a hole through the wood scrubbing the same spot. Every day people knocking on my door –

Bolek   All I hear is good things.

Wenzel   They come to me with their fears

Bolek   As I remember they were scared to death of their children eating them before. Would they prefer to go back to that?

Wenzel I'm sure they wouldn't, but perhaps you could speak to the villagers. Assure them that the treatment is sound. Perhaps in time, their children will return to normality?

There's a thump from inside the cupboard.

Bolek Yes. Yes, I can do that.

Wenzel Can you?

Bolek Of course.

He tries to lead **Wenzel** *out. The Mayor stops.*

Wenzel Bolek. There's something I feel I should share with you. It is to remain secret. That is very important.

Bolek *waits.*

Wenzel Lazlo.

They both look at **Lazlo** *standing in the corner. He doesn't react.*

Wenzel Not so long ago. He presented with the symptoms. They worsened –

Bolek Yes. I know. You cast him out.

Wenzel Well –

Pause.

No.

Bolek No?

Wenzel I kept him. In my barn. Tied up of course, until the disease left his system.

Bolek You told everyone in the strictest terms that they must cast their children out.

Wenzel I am not proud of this. I live with it every day. But – haven't you noticed? The Infected that were cast out – the few that returned once the Monstrum has left them – they are strong, capable, young men and women now.

Bolek   What are you saying?

Wenzel   Lazlo – look at him. I can't leave him alone. I'm afraid he might hurt himself.

They look again at **Lazlo**. *He doesn't react.*

Wenzel   I have strange dreams sometimes. That I'm out in the woods. I'm licking sap off a tree, like I'm running. Flashes of something. I'm caught under a wolf. I'm sticking my finger in its eye –

Bolek   You've been under a lot of stress.

Wenzel   Don't you ever dream things like that?

More thumps from inside the cupboard.

What is that?

We hear a sudden squeak.

Bolek   It's a rat. I've trapped inside the cupboard.

Wenzel   You should get rid of those rats, Bolek.

Bolek   I will.

Wenzel   Maybe I've said too much. It will remain between us?

Bolek   Of course.

Wenzel   I'll put a notice up. You can address everyone tomorrow. Times of crisis need people like you, Bolek. You always keep your head.

He pats **Bolek** *on the shoulder and exits.*

Once he has gone, **Bolek** *slowly goes to the cupboard. He opens it. Inside,* **Milena** *is eating a rat. She stands up. Fevered. Red-eyed.*

Bolek *is running.*

He's in the woods.

He stops, he scratches around in the dirt looking for insects to eat. He's feral-like. Gradually, eyes appear in the bushes around him.

The **Infected** *creep out, unnoticed by* **Bolek***. They surround him. They look like they're about to attack him. They make a sound – it's horrifying.*

Bolek *is dragged into a wild dance. It builds – the noise, the frenzy –*

Suddenly **Bolek** *is awake.*

He is in his lab, surrounded by books. He checks himself. He lights a lamp.

He hears scratching.

He goes to a large cage where **Milena** *is sleeping. He watches her.*

The village square.

Villagers   Look at this place.
It has begun to soften
The ice is melting
Revealing something new
Spring creeping through.

We have our children back
A blessing upon our heads
Sleep soundly in our beds
Oh yes
Oh yes.

No longer a snap
No longer a snarl
To disturb our dreams.

Isn't it wonderful?
Aren't we proud?
I'm so proud of my son

My daughter
Oh yes, oh yes, oh yes.

The vllage square.

Bolek *joins the Mayor on the podium. The* **Villagers** *gather round anxiously.* **Bolek** *too appears unsettled. He doesn't look well, though he tries to mask it.*

Wenzel   Your children are no longer the fevered creatures that once tormented you. The Monstrum that locked their eyes and turned them into something you no longer recognised has left them. What you see now are your children in a free and happy state. They are no longer troubled. Out of control. We must thank God that this curse upon our heads has been lifted.

Mr Koshka   Bolek. Sir. Please – my son. Look at him. I ask him what he wants to do each morning and he says, 'I do not know.'

Mrs Sortov   My daughter stares out the window. I ask her what she's thinking, she says, 'I can't remember. It's gone.' I could put a spade in her hand and she would shovel snow all day.

Wenzel   Well, aren't you grateful that you have such an obedient child?

Mrs Sortov   The spark in her eyes. It's disappeared. It's gone. Gone –

Wenzel   I understand that you are all eager for your children to return to complete normality, but let's not let our emotions take over sense. The procedure they have endured is highly – highly –

He is looking to **Bolek***.*

Bolek   Invasive.

Wenzel   Yes, and as such we must give them time to fully recoup. Isn't that right, Bolek?

Villager   But they will return?

Preben *has pushed through the crowd.*

Preben   Please, Bolek. My son is all I have. I must know that he will return to me. I must know –

Wenzel   Calm yourself. Anyone would think we were made of glass. Are your children alive? Are they fit and well? Are they no longer possessed? Then give thanks. We should be kissing the boots of this man, not pestering him with such idiocy. When the farmer plants his seeds, do they pop up the next day? Be patient with your children. Care for them, and in time, they will come back to you. Right, Bolek?

Bolek *realises he's being spoken to.*

Bolek   Yes. All normal behaviours should return.

Wenzel   There. There we have it. There is nothing to be concerned for. Now – let us return to our work, and we shall speak no longer of it.

The crowd disperses unhappily. **Bolek** *rushes off, watched by the Mayor.*

Bolek's *lab.*

Milena's *cage is covered.* **Bolek** *is frantically looking through the journal.*

Bolek   This is how desperate I am. Looking through this hocus-pocus. Fairy tales and sorcery. She grew quite obsessed with it. I think perhaps she had some success, but then she went from the botanical stuff to the bloodletting – see, you don't know, Milena. Suddenly she wasn't banishing demons any more, people thought she was one. And she refused to bow to them. Not even a little. No matter how much I begged. You know, you never had her defiance – till now. I was always thankful for that.

He falls on a page.

This is it. There was a spell that she did. When a child was feverish, she held her hands over the body and chanted. How can I do this? I can't do this.

He takes the cloth off the cage. **Milena** *is immediately at the bars.*

Milena   Let me out.

Bolek   I'm trying to help you.

Milena   Let me out. Let me out.

Bolek   When it's dark – I'll take you out – you can feed –

Milena   Now. *Now.*

Bolek (*reading*)   'I do command and conjure thee, thou who art a true demon – '

We hear whispers off – 'Milena'.

Radmila *enters, unnoticed.*

Milena   Can you hear that?

Bolek   'I summon thee here from this child. I do summon thee by the power filled principally by the Dark Abyss.'

Milena   They're calling me. Can you hear?

Bolek   'By the power and wisdom of the ancient ways – '

Milena   You need to let me out. *Let me out.*

Radmila   I never thought I'd see it. Bolek, 'The Scholar'.

Bolek *shuts the book. The whispering stops. He quickly tries to conceal the cage.*

Radmila   And Milena. Little perfect Milena. Well. Well. Well.

Bolek   It's not what you think.

Radmila   Let's have a look at her.

She almost falls over.

Do excuse me, I've had some of my husband's ale. Somehow it helps.

Bolek   You stay away.

Radmila   My daughter didn't foam at the mouth quite like yours, but she had the same redness in her eyes.

Bolek   It's just a precaution. She isn't nearly as advanced –

Radmila   We tell ourselves it isn't happening –

Bolek   I am treating her.

Radmila   Yes, I saw that. I never thought I'd see the day I'd hear you using your wife's incantations.

Bolek   I wasn't –

Radmila   No need to be embarrassed. When it's your children, you'll try anything. Look at me, offering my beloved daughter up to be butchered by you.

Bolek   I did my best –

Radmila   Then why don't you offer Milena the same medicine?

Bolek   Milena is a bright girl.

Radmila   Too good for it, is she?

Bolek   She is going to be a physician.

Radmila   My daughter is gone.

Bolek   I'll – I'll look at her. I'll see if I can help her. There may be something I can do to – to encourage her mind to make previous connections. I can work with her – her recovery –

Radmila   It's too late now.

Bolek   What do you mean?

Radmila   I took my girl, I walked her to the edge of the woods, and I let her go.

Bolek   You did what?

Radmila   I should have done it in the beginning.

Bolek   She'll never survive out there.

Radmila   That isn't our decision.

Bolek   Are you mad?

Radmila   You need to let Milena go. You must release her.

Bolek   You get away, you old hag.

Radmila   Witch? Isn't that what you called us?

Bolek   You corrupted my wife, you'll not get my daughter.

Radmila   Your 'wife' didn't belong to you. She didn't belong to any man. Any place.

Bolek   There you go with your wicked mouth again.

Radmila   She had a gift. You never believed she could heal people –

Bolek   You sent her mad.

Radmila   It was you that wanted to keep her locked up.

Bolek   All your mumbo jumbo, spirits and magic.

Radmila   You didn't see the things that she did. The things she was capable of.

Bolek   I should have kept her away from you.

Radmila   She had a calling –

Bolek   She had a husband and a child. She had a home, here with us.

Radmila   She was a wanderess –

Bolek   She was a fragile woman that you manipulated for your own amusement.

Radmila   You have no idea, do you?

Bolek   What?

Radmila   Your wife was not some weak young thing. She didn't need your protection. She knew what she was. She knew what she wanted.

Bolek   What do you mean?

Radmila   She wanted to leave you.

Bolek   She didn't leave – she'd lost her mind. She went out in a blizzard –

Radmila   She saved her money. She packed her bag. She left you, Bolek.

Bolek   She disappeared.

Radmila   She didn't want to spend her life weighed down by your cynicism. Your coldness. If she stayed here you would have strangled her spirit.

Bolek   But she – she's still alive?

Radmila   Somewhere out there, she more alive than you'll ever be.

Pause.

Bolek   You kept this from me?

Radmila   I promised not to say a word. She doesn't want to be found.

Bolek   All this time, I thought there was something I could have done. That could have fixed her.

Radmila   Life is to be lived, Bolek. Not controlled. Now –
come. Let us make right with Milena. Let us set her free. It's
what she needs – Look at her.

Bolek   All this time.

Radmila   Unlock the cage, Bolek.

Bolek   And you helped her? You helped her leave here?

Radmila   It was her will. Unlock the cage. It's time to let go.

Bolek *unlocks the cage.*

Radmila   That's it.

Bolek *suddenly pushes her inside.*

Radmila   What are you doing? Let me out, Bolek. Let me
out of here.

Bolek   I haven't fed her today.

Radmila *looks at* **Milena***.*

Radmila   No –

Bolek *puts the cloth over the cage. We hear a scream.*

Wenzel*'s office.*

Wenzel *is loading his gun.*

Stanko   You don't understand, it's been three days.

Wenzel   I don't have time for this.

Stanko   My wife and my daughter – we need to send out a
search party –

Wenzel   Haven't you seen the notices? Last night we lost a
dozen reindeer. A pack of wolves must have been migrating –

hungry. Ripped out their throats. As if we haven't troubles enough –

Stanko   I demand that you help me. It's your duty. It's the reason you were elected –

Wenzel *grabs hold of* **Stanko**.

Wenzel   Sometimes I dream of a nice little town. Cobbled streets instead of mountains. Three hot meals, instead of skinned animals hung over a fire. I dream of lanterns that light up bustling pavements, instead of straggly pine forests and icy bogs. I dream of theatres and dances, instead of five million square miles of nothingness.

But then I remember what my father told me: this place is in our blood. This place is in our blood.

He lets go of **Stanko** *and exits.* **Stanko** *is left alone.*

Night. A snowy field.

Wenzel *and some* **Villagers** *creep forwards with guns. A few hold lanterns but the rest are in darkness. They can hear something – a growl perhaps*

Bolek *suddenly appears, carrying a lantern.*

Wenzel   Bolek. Christ. What are you doing out here?

Bolek   I was just collecting some of the sheep skulls. I use them to practise on. Large eye-sockets.

Wenzel   Don't you know how dangerous it is out here? We could have shot you. And if not, there are wolves on the prowl too.

Bolek   I was just on my way home –

Villager   Sir – there's something in the bushes.

Wenzel   Keep an eye –

Bolek   There's nothing here.

Wenzel   Someone throw him a gun. He's going to get himself killed.

One of the **Villagers** *throws* **Bolek** *a gun.*

Wenzel   It's behind there.

He signals for them all to creep forward, guns ready. **Bolek** *stands back, panicking. There's a sound in the bushes. They all raise their guns,* **Bolek** *suddenly shoots.* **Wenzel** *falls to the ground, as everyone reacts.* **Bolek** *quickly drops the gun, arms in the air.*

Bolek   I – I thought I saw something.

In the commotion he disappears from view.

Bolek*'s home.*

Bolek *is locking* **Milena** *back in the cage.* **Milena** *paces wildly. Blood on her face.*

Bolek   I – I can't take you out any more here. It's too dangerous. I think perhaps it's time we left. I need to pack a bag. We need to go –

Milena   I need out – I need out –

Bolek   I can't understand you.

Milena   Need out. Need out. Need out.

Bolek   Speak normally, won't you?

Milena   Out. Out. Out.

Bolek   I'll read to you. Look, your favourite book. The times you used to read this, huddled in the corner –

Milena   I can hear them calling me. They want me –

Bolek (*reading*)   'For we say that all portents are contrary to nature; but they are not so. For how is that contrary to nature, which happens by the will of God, since the will of so mighty a Creator is certainly the nature of each created thing?'

Milena   I can see lights.

Bolek   'A portent, therefore, happens not contrary to nature, but contrary to what we know as nature.'

Milena   Lights. Lights.

Bolek *shuts the book. Looks out the window.*

Bolek   Dear Lord.

And we hear:

The village square.

Villagers *carry torches.*

The Villagers
  It's a terrible thing when you're afraid of your children
  It's a terrible thing when you fear what they have become
  It's a terrible thing when you're locking your bedroom door
  And you feel unsure
  That these are your children at all
  But these are our children
  Yes these are our children
  Yes these are –

Bolek *is dragged from the house.* **Milena** *too.*

Stanko   Watch its teeth. Tie it up.

Milena *is tied to the chair.*

Bolek   Milena.

Preben   Not Milena. This thing is a creature, isn't it?

Mr Koshka   You told us our children could be fixed.

Mrs Sortov   He kept his own, all this time.

Stanko   Make sure it's nice and tight.

Bolek   Please, you don't understand.

Stanko   I think we do. We do quite clearly.

Bolek   You know my daughter. You know what a sweet girl she is.

Stanko   Same as my own. Same as all our lost sons and daughters. You think she's special?

Preben   She's been the one at our cattle.

Wenzel *appears, helped by his men. He's bandaged round the middle.*

Bolek   Mayor Wenzel.

Wenzel   Let's get a look at her.

Bolek   This is good, Milena. You wanted her and your Lazlo –

Wenzel   My Lazlo is a fine young man. This is a thing.

Bolek   You kept your own son. You didn't release him –

Wenzel   Can someone shut him up?

Bolek *is gagged.*

Wenzel   Now we have a choice, my good people. This creature here is particularly vicious. By far the most advanced stage that we've seen. Perhaps it is too late to do anything for it, and it would be better to put it down.

Bolek *squirms.*

Wenzel   Or perhaps we allow Bolek one last opportunity to atone for his sins, by administering the treatment he so vehemently advocated – on his own.

Two large ice picks are whipped out by one of the **Villagers**.
Milena *struggles.*

Wenzel   I don't think we have time to soak your black cherry plants and sedate her. But you're practised now. I'm sure you can make it swift, Bolek.

Bolek *is released and handed the ice picks. He stands over* **Milena***. Everyone waits.*

Bolek   I – I had a dream too. That I was out there. Out in the wilderness beyond our houses. That I was part of it. That place. Trapping animals. Eating birds. Supping water from a dirty lake. Then, in my dream, the water clears. I see my reflection, and I realise. And I realise – maybe, maybe they are us and we are they. That though I may have forgotten it, though perhaps it has left my system altogether, and only now have I a vague sensation of it in dreams and memories – but undeniably there is something out there that is a part of me. And – perhaps it is necessary, Mayor Wenzel. This disease, as much as we deplore it – fear it. Perhaps it is part of a natural process – perhaps we need it –

Wenzel   Have you lost your mind too, Bolek?

Stanko   Let's get on with it.

Wenzel   There's no use stalling. You cannot halt divine justice.

Calls from the **Villagers***: 'Come on', 'Do it', 'Lets see it'.*

Bolek (*looks at* **Milena**)   I'm sorry.

He raises the ice pick high. He brings is down, severing the ropes.

Wenzel   Get hold of her.

Milena *runs, chased by the villagers.*

The edge of the forest.

The **Villagers** *close in on* **Milena***. Suddenly eyes appear in the bushes. The* **Infected** *creep out from the bushes. The* **Villagers** *recoil in horror.*

Wenzel   Get back. Don't approach them.

He swings his torch at them.

Back. Back.

Milena *joins the* **Infected**.

Bolek   Milena?

The **Infected** *coil round her protectively. Staring at* **Bolek**. *He steps back.*

When you're ready.

He picks up a stone.

A trail to our house.

There is a moment between them, then suddenly the **Infected** *are gone, back into the trees.*

The suddenness of her departure takes **Bolek**'s *breath away.*

Everyone is frozen. It takes a moment before they realise a young man has been left behind. He looks dazed.

Libusa *pushes forward.*

Libusa   Is that my son? Is that my boy?

Young Man   Mother?

Libusa   You're not a boy any more.

Young Man   Where am I?

Libusa   You don't remember?

He looks back towards the woods.

Young Man   No.

She embraces him.

The village square.

A day in the future.

Villagers   Imagine a place
In the highest mountains
Frosted little houses
Shards of glass hanging from a wishing well.

Every now and then you'll hear a howl
A shriek in the night
And you'll know
The Monstrum has arrived
In the eyes of a once dear child.

But no longer do the people fear it
Freeze in terror at the first sign of it.

Instead it is like the slow passing of seasons
The melting ice
The crisp leaf falling
Summer will return again
They will return to us
They will
They will.

We see **Bolek** *leaving his house, putting his coat on. He stands on something – left on his doorstep. He picks it up. It's a black cherry plant. He looks at it. He looks out there.*

Howls in the distance.

The Monstrum

BY KELLIE SMITH

Notes on rehearsal and staging, drawn from a workshop with the writer,
held at the National Theatre, October 2016

How Kellie came to write the play

Kellie writes for theatre, radio and film. She is currently writer
in residence at the Royal Exchange Theatre in Manchester.
She has written a lot for younger audiences, including a play
for small children. Kellie originally workshopped the play
with Chickenshed Theatre Company in London, working on
an early draft with just a few scenes. The idea for the
metaphor came to her very early on in the process. Kellie
loves to work collaboratively. She is interested in form and
how to tell stories in a theatrical and live way.

KELLIE SMITH   'Around the time I was thinking about what
I would write, I was watching my stepson talking to my
husband and thought, 'What is it like to be a child on the
verge of adolescence with your parents watching you and
wondering what kind of teenager you will be? How will you
morph?' I noticed a sense of fear connected with the waiting
of adolescence. The central question of this play is why do we
fear adolescence. I had forgotten what it is like to be that age;
there are lots of things I don't connect with any more. I was
also doing research around the teenage brain and how it
changes during adolescence. I tried initially to write the play
in a naturalistic way but it didn't work, so I needed to give it
its own rules.'

Approaching the play

EXERCISE: DRAWING MOMENTS

Participants were asked to draw what they felt were the three
most memorable moments in the play. Caroline Steinbeis, co-
lead director, stressed that the exercise wasn't about drawing

a masterpiece, but instead, capturing the moments that make the biggest impression on you in some way. She suggested that you should choose the moments you'd most like your audience to go home talking about after the show. Here are some of the moments that the participants chose to draw:

- The lobotomies, clinical and dark.
- The village children queuing up to be ice-picked.
- The dream sequence in the forest.
- Revealing Tomas in the cage, and the villagers standing round, like a Victorian freak show.
- Processing of the children, like a sausage machine.
- Bolek realising that his daughter is infected.
- Villagers fearing an unknown quantity.
- Letting go of loved ones.
- A path of stones left for the children to make their way back.
- Eyes peering out from the forest.
- The chorus of villagers (and how they might look like the trees).
- The visceral description of the operations.
- The Mayor trying to convince the villagers.
- Creatures in the forest.
- Bolek and Milena treating Tomas.
- Opening the cupboard to find Milena eating the rat.
- The cherry tree coming out of Milena's mouth.
- Keys locking doors.
- The moment the parents realise their children have lost their personalities.
- The lobotomy on the skeleton.
- The skeleton, the boy and the work line (three juxtaposing operation scenes).

Participants were then asked to build a timeline of the play by placing their drawings on the floor in the order in which they happen, from the start of the play to the end. The participants reflected on the timeline and found that there were lots of very vivid drawings for certain parts of the play, but then large gaps in other parts. Caroline suggested that you might try this with your company before starting work on the play. Where are the gaps in the storytelling? What does each moment look like? If you can't see a moment then you will struggle to stage it. Ask your cast what the most important moments in the play are for them and for their characters. These images can also start to suggest things about the style or tone of the play.

World of the play

The play begins with the line 'Imagine a place', and that, as directors and theatre makers, is our job. Participants discussed the world of the play and they talked about dystopian worlds, like *The Hunger Games* books and films, where humans are at mercy of those in charge. They talked about stylistic references: the films of Tim Burton, Gothic literature, Munch's *The Scream*. They talked about the play feeling Northern European, Slavic or Baltic. They discussed political power, right-wing dictatorships and corruption. They talked about communities who separate themselves from the outside world: the Amish community, sects and cults in America, etc. They talked about Arthur Miller's play *The Crucible*, and how communities can get away with very extreme laws when they're not under criticism from the outside world.

What implications does this world have on the characters in the play? What is the difference between living in a free world and a society that dictates laws for its members? How does that affect physicality? How does that effect the choices those characters make?

The openness of the text invites you and your company to come up with your own interpretation. It is important to create a common language for the production that you are making. What are the main themes? What are the main events for you? There is so much going on in the play, what are your anchoring points?

Themes

Participants discussed what they thought the themes of the play might be. Below is a list of ideas that came up:

- Fear.
- Conformity.
- The Other.
- The darkness within.
- Truth and lies.
- Dark and light.
- Oppositions.
- Nature/nurture.
- Enlightenment.
- God vs science.
- Science vs pagan world.
- Memory.
- Control.
- Lobotomy.
- Parents and children.
- Authority.
- Change and transformation.
- Isolation.
- Ritual.
- Love.

You could ask your company to look into these themes and ideas. You could ask each company member to do some

research into a theme or an area that takes their interest.
Then at the start of each rehearsal you could have ten
minutes where somebody from the cast presents what they've
discovered to the rest of the group.

It is useful to consider the message of the play. What is the
overarching theme that touches each and every character?
Caroline pointed the group towards a quote on page 622 of
the play. Just before Bolek pushes Radmila into the cage she
says, 'Life is to be lived . . . Not controlled.' The villagers
remember by the end of the play that in order to grow as a
person, you must go out into the forest, you must get away.
If you love something, set it free, if it loves you it will return.

Production, staging and design

Looking at the timeline of pictures on the floor from the
previous exercise, Caroline asked the group to think about
what their set design might look like. What images jump out
of the text? Will your design be full of real objects and set
pieces or will it be something more abstract or physical?
What is useful to have on stage? Will a large solid piece of set
get in the way of the fluid, wild nature of the piece? Could
bits of set be on wheels? There are many different locations.
How do you want to stage those places? Is there one particular
aesthetic that could bring it all together?

What does the cold environment mean for your costume
design? Do the characters need to be layering up? How are you
going to show snow? Where will you locate your production
in the world? How can you tell that story to the audience?
Caroline suggested that something as simple as a fur-lined hat
could immediately transport an audience to Eastern Europe.
What will the different characters wear and what will that tell
us about those characters? What is it normal to wear in this
world? Is there a dress code? Who breaks it . . . ?

It is important to establish a viewpoint for your production.
Will the audience see the story from the eyes of the children,

being forced into horrific operations? Or will they see it from the eyes of the parents, having to cope with the infected Monstrum? Or is it both? Does the forest have a different identity considering who is looking at it? For the parents is it a scary place? For the children is it a place of hope?

Sam Pritchard, co-lead director, suggested that you could create a 'mood board' with your company, finding images and reference points for the kind of aesthetic you want to achieve in your production.

Force yourself to make decisions so you can question them later, go down an alley and see where it takes you; if it is a dead end you can always come back, but you need to explore by making choices.

EXERCISE: RULES OF SOCIETY

Caroline and Sam asked participants to come up with ideas for what the rules of this society might be (both public rules and unspoken rules). Here is a list of what the group came up with:

- *Rule 1.* Everyone has to come to the town square when the bell rings.

- *Rule 2.* Your elders are always right; there is a structure of hierarchy attached to age.

- *Rule 3.* Nobody is allowed to leave the village (Mayor: 'We face near extinction').

- *Rule 4.* Don't deviate from the norm (and yet everyone is constantly pushing the boundaries of the norm).

- *Rule 5.* Report all children who have contracted the disease (yet everyone breaks that rule).

- *Rule 6.* Everything is for the greater good.

- *Rule 7.* Emotions are not to be trusted; they should be contained and controlled. (This tells you something about the physicality of these characters' – they won't be running around hugging each other!)

- *Rule 8*. People forget (Why do they forget? Do they force themselves to forget? There seems to be a collective sense of amnesia in the play; the parents don't remember that at some point they were in the forest themselves).

- *Rule 9*. What goes in the forest stays in the forest! (no one knows what happens in there, people are afraid of what they don't know).

- *Rule 10*. You have to get married and stay with your family (Bolek's wife disappearing is not normal, marriage is sacred).

- *Rule 11*. The Mayor is in charge. (How do you get to be Mayor? Does the Mayor change?)

- *Rule 12*. Fear the Monstrum.

- *Rule 13*. Report anything suspicious.

- *Rule 14*. CONTAIN. REPORT. ASSESS.

- *Rule 15*. Everybody breaks the rules.

- *Rule 16*. God exists and the Devil exists. Witchcraft is real

- *Rule 17*. Superstition is part of life.

- *Rule 18*. Life is hard. Life is cold. Life is violent. (Humans are here to survive.)

Participants then considered what they know to be true about the world. Below are some of the answers that came up:

- It is a world of traditional male and female roles.

- This village is far away from the modern/civilised world.

- There is a sense of timelessness; there is no specific mention of when the play is set.

- There is an organised structure of scientific enquiry.

- Operation and physical intervention as a cure exist within this society.

- It is cold – the play begins in winter.

- The seasons change within the play.

- There is a form of democracy; it is not a totalitarian state.

- There is a binary reality, a sense of black and white and right and wrong.

- There is no external factor that influences the play. The exception might be the weather that could be directly or indirectly affecting the action.

- The outside world does represent the possibility of escape.

- There are mountains.

- There are different types of animals.

This is a great exercise to do with your cast. You could ask them to choose ten commandments for the village. Don't worry if they are different from the ones above. It is a brilliant way to start to understand the world the characters live in. What is it like living in a town that faces near extinction? A town that reports anything suspicious? A town run by an all-powerful dictator? Which characters break the rules? Which are allowed to function outside the rules? This is a society that is permanently on the brink of terror or fear; people feel it all of the time.

You can find the answers to these questions in the play and it is important that you continually refer to the play when you're writing the rules. If there is no clear answer in the play you should make the nearest possible conclusion.

EXERCISE: LOCATION/EVENT/PLOT

Scene numbers are not marked on the script but it was suggested that a new scene begins every time the play changes location.

You could split your company into smaller groups and give them each a few scenes to look at. Ask them to answer three questions for each scene:

- *Location:* What is the location of the scene?

- *Event:* What is the most important event in the scene? An event is a moment in the play that changes something for every character on stage.

- *Plot:* A brief description of what happens in the scene.

Below are the suggestions the group came up with. You might find different ideas with your company.

SCENE ONE (page 585)

- *Location:* Snow, cold, highest mountains (the Overture).
- *Event:* The villagers finally say the word 'the Monstrum'.
- *Plot:* The villagers talk about the malevolent force that is taking their children away.

Kellie has put the text in italics to suggest a change in performance style (song or spoken word). This is the first big ensemble moment to really get your teeth into.

SCENE TWO (page 588)

- *Location:* Village square (denoted by the sound of a bell).
- *Event:* The Mayor says he won't cast the creature (Tomis) out.
- *Plot:* The Mayor discusses the Monstrum with the villagers: 'we face near extinction'.

The challenge here is that the Mayor has a lot of text; it's a big undertaking for a young actor. You could possibly think of ways to divide up the text between a few actors.

SCENE THREE (page 592)

- *Location:* Bolek's laboratory.
- *Event:* Milena is scratching (she is becoming unwell).
- The Mayor and Bolek discuss the nature of the experiment: 'I just need to know that you believe this will be a success'.

SCENE FOUR (page 601)

- *Location:* Radmila and Stanko's house.
- *Event:* 'If we report her we will never see our daughter again'.
- *Plot:* Radmila and Stanko hide their child from the Mayor and the village.

SCENE FIVE (page 604)

- *Location:* Bolek's lab.
- *Event:* Tomis' smile of recognition (the seeming success of the operation).
- *Plot:* The operation on Tomis seems to have been a success

SCENE SIX (page 605)

- *Location:* Village square.
- *Event:* Bolek says 'I haven't had enough time to monitor Tomis'.
- *Plot:* The Mayor tells the villagers that the operation has been a success.

SCENE SEVEN (page 607)

- *Location:* Outside Bolek's house.
- *Event:* Bolek says: 'A success'.
- *Plot:* The villagers await the outcome of the operations

This is an incredible sequence (the lobotomies on the skeleton, then the boy, then the long work line of children queuing for the operation). It is also potentially the second song in the piece.

SCENE EIGHT (page 608)

- *Location:* Bolek's new improved laboratory.
- *Event:* Milena pulls a black cherry plant out of her mouth.
- *Plot:* A scene of revelations, Bolek realises his daughter is infected, the Mayor admits that he has broken the rules, Milena is found eating a rat.

SCENE NINE (page 614)

- *Location:* Bolek's dream (takes place in the woods).
- *Event:* Bolek wakes up (we realise it has been a dream).
- *Plot:* Bolek remembers being in the woods in the form of a dream.

SCENE TEN (page 615)

- *Location:* Village square.
- *Event:* It could be the conflict between the positive message the villagers are putting across and the reality of the situation (lobotomised children!)
- *Plot:* The parents talk themselves into believing that everything is OK.

SCENE ELEVEN (page 616)

- *Location:* Village square.
- *Event:* Bolek rushes off, watched by the Mayor.
- *Plot:* A quick downturn in mood as the villagers complain about the procedure and the effects on their children, the Mayor's confidence is challenged – who is in charge?

SCENE TWELVE (page 617)

- *Location:* Bolek's laboratory.
- *Event:* Bolek pushes Radmila into the cage.
- *Plot:* Radmila's reveal. Bolek tries to use his wife's old spells to cure his daughter. We learn that his wife didn't die, she left him.

SCENE THIRTEEN (page 622)

- *Location:* The Mayor's office.
- *Event:* 'This place is in our blood'.
- *Plot:* Stanko demands help. The Mayor loads his gun.

SCENE FOURTEEN (page 623)

- *Location:* A snowy field at night.
- *Event:* Bolek distracts the villagers by shooting the gun.
- *Plot:* While hunting wolves, the Mayor and some villagers discover Bolek and give him a gun. (Is Bolek hunting for meat for his daughter, or is he trying to find her in the bushes?) Bolek shoots the Mayor.

SCENE FIFTEEN (page 624)

- *Location:* Bolek's laboratory.
- *Event:* They hear the villagers approaching.
- *Plot:* Milena is becoming hysterical. Bolek reads to her from a philosophical text.

SCENE SIXTEEN (page 625)

- *Location:* Village Square.
- *Event:* Bolek cuts the ropes and saves his child.
- *Plot:* The villagers look for payback from Bolek.

SCENE SEVENTEEN (page 627)

- *Location:* Edge of the forest.
- *Event:* Milena joins the infected.
- *Plot:* Milena's departure from the village. A young man comes back from the forest.

SCENE EIGHTEEN (page 628)

- *Location:* Village square.
- *Event:* 'No longer do the people fear it'.
- *Plot:* A day in the future, the villagers reflect

SCENE NINETEEN (page 629)

- *Location:* At the door of Bolek's house.
- *Event:* A howl in the distance (is this a communication with his daughter?)
- *Plot:* Bolek finds a black cherry plant on the doorstep of his house.

You could then challenge your group to identity the main event of the play. The 'penny drop' moment that reveals something to all of the characters.

In the workshop it was suggested it could be the moment where the young man returns from the forest (in Scene

Seventeen). It is the moment everyone realises they don't need to be afraid any more. It is the moment you ratchet up to. In terms of sound design, lighting design, work with actors, it all builds to this moment.

The above exercise is a great way of getting your company inside the play. You could even draw a literal graph of the different peaks and troughs in the play, noting where the action hits its highest peak. This will help you find the dynamics in the piece and keep your audience engaged.

EXERCISE: DRAWING THE MONSTRUM

Deciding what the Monstrum looks like is an important aesthetic choice for your production. Ask your company to draw what they think the Monstrum looks like.

Is the Monstrum a full-on monster? Or a version of the child who has been infected? Is the monster only a monster in the eyes of the parents perhaps? Is it the adult's perception of monsters/young people? Are they feral zombie-like creatures? Or are they actually quite normal when they appear? Kellie suggested that this decision is totally up to you. She also hasn't made a decision as to what happens in the woods, so that's for you to discover too.

The question at the heart of the play is how we think about adolescence, how we fear it. Your choice in staging the Monstrum monster somewhat depends on how strongly you want to give the audience the answer. Kellie stressed that every moment in the play is a metaphor.

KELLIE SMITH   'Don't get too worried about the literal rules; remember the bigger idea to the play. Challenge your students to think about what the parallels might be in the real world. The play is open for your imaginative interpretation. You can make choices that other scripts might not allow you to make. Embrace it.'

EXERCISE: PHYSICALISING THE MONSTRUM

Another way of exploring the Monstrum could be to create a five-seat line up, with one of the following representations in each chair. Ask those in each chair to consider the physical attributes of the disease.

1   A pre-Monstrum childhood.
2   A full Monstrum adolescent.
3   A post-ice-pick Monstrum.
4   A post-woods youth.
5   An adult.

EXERCISE: STAGING THE STAGE DIRECTIONS

You could set your company the challenge of how they might stage the opening stage direction: '*Snow. A gust of wind carries in the villagers.*' You could allow them to use anything they can find in the room; instruments, paper, chairs, tables, cushions, brooms, electric fans, their bodies, etc.

When you set a devising task like this, you are not looking for finished performances, just seeds of ideas. If you're working collaboratively, you'll need to bring all of those seeds of ideas into one big idea. Don't worry about getting it right or wrong, just look for the moments that work.

The participants each showed their attempt at staging the opening stage direction. The group reflected on some of the most effective things they saw:

• Paper crunching underfoot sounds like snow.
• Sweeping in the villagers as a group of snow, leaving one person on stage each time.
• Using musical rhythms and percussion.
• Torn-up paper, thrown into the air as each person enters.
• Using a fan to blow paper into the air.
• Using physical lifts for villagers to fly in on the breeze.

- Creating the sound before you see anything visual.
- Doors bursting open.

It is then the director's job to ask: What is most clear? What is most vivid? How can those different elements be brought together to create one image? As director you are the editor of ideas; you layer them up to create complex and beautiful images.

ENSEMBLE EXERCISE: STAGING A 'GUST OF WIND'

The participants were split into groups of five. Each group was given a very specific set of parameters or a provocation.

- *Group A* – to create a gust of wind only using vocals.
- *Group B* – to create a gust of wind only using instruments.
- *Group C* – chorus work, look at the first four lines of the text (speaking a line each).
- *Group D* – chorus work, look at the first page of text (speaking a paragraph each).
- *Group E* – chorus work, nominate just one person to deliver the text.

This is a useful exercise in allowing your company to generate their own material, which you can then edit, drawing together different elements to create a layered idea.

There is huge potential for ensemble work in this piece. The villagers are a really interesting collection of characters. Who could they be? Are they quiet and ethereal? Or are they bestial and dangerous? Or maybe they're comical and broadly drawn? Violent and bloodthirsty? What does the writing suggest? What are the clues in the play that tell us who these people are?

When working with a large cast the challenge is often how you keep everyone engaged in rehearsals. Caroline suggested you should always try and work collaboratively. If you're looking at a small scene with a couple of characters you can still explore it as a group. Find questions and challenges with each scene for the group to explore. Or send them away to work on the big challenges of the play. You might also try leaving casting until later in the process so that everyone stays invested in the work for as long as possible (not just their bits).

It might also be useful to consider the power of one person on stage speaking. While it is often very effective to have a large number of people on stage, sometimes having one, or one voice, can be really powerful as it focuses the audience and really makes them listen.

EXERCISE: STAGING THE LOBOTOMIES

You could run a similar exercise to look at ways of staging the lobotomies. Split the group into four, giving each a provocation or set of restrictions. This is a great way to start the devising process and to encourage your cast to be imaginative and playful in their work:

- *Group A* – find staging solutions for the lobotomy of a skeleton.
- *Group B* – find staging solutions for the first real lobotomy (of Tomis).
- *Group C* – find staging ideas for the sequence where the villagers bring their children for lobotomies.
- *Group D* – find staging ideas for the check-up of Milena.

When you are rehearsing the lobotomy procedure, make sure you get the cast to repeat it many times over so they can learn the precision of the process, so that the detail is well practised. Perhaps the most effective way of showing violence onstage is often to show us the reaction to the violence. Try using your ensemble reactions to give the audience a sense of how nasty the operation is. Each of the three times we see the lobotomy procedure it should feel different. First it's a new process they are working out using a skeleton as a dummy; second they try it for the first time with a live patient; and finally it is a routine that has become well practised. By this third time you can aim for the economy of the idea. We know what it is now, we know how horrible it is, the story we want to tell is of a conveyer belt, don't worry about the individuals in this bit, think more about the choreography of bringing in lots of patients.

EXERCISE: GENERATING HIGH STAKES

Ask for two volunteers to read part of the scene between Radmila and Stanko.

Ask the actors to read the text to each other slowly and clearly to get a sense of what happens. The emphasis should be on clarity, so keep the staging as simple as possible.

Next, ask the actors to play with their internal tempo. You could give one of the characters a time pressure, then ask the other to speed up their internal tempo. It is important to avoid the word 'speed' with your cast. It is more important to think about tempo, or speed of thought, trying to connect the urgency of the scene to what the characters want or don't want to happen. Playing with tempo immediately lends an interesting dynamic to the scene; there is more tension and the actors have something to play against. The tempo of the character might also suggest something about the intellect of the character: if they speak slower, do they also think slower? Another useful way to do this is to play with tempo on a scale of one to ten. Doing this allows the actors to play the tempo more specifically. What would that scene feel like if the character had a tempo of nine instead of three?

You could then ask the actors to play with tension and physicality. For example, ask one of the actors to play with high physical tension and the other with low physical tension. Consider what this dynamic does to the scene.

You could encourage actors to 'take out the air'. Often characters don't have to think about what they're going to say before they say it; try pushing the actors to think on the line instead of before it. Young people often think that a pause can be dramatic, but unless the playwright has written a pause in, or you feel like it is important for the shape of a scene, then avoid it. A simple instruction like 'Take the air out' can immediately make the scene dynamically more interesting. Don't start fast, let people become familiar with the text first and then increase the tempo. Make sure people can walk before they run.

Another way to access the stakes of the scene is to make sure every actor understands every line of dialogue. Ask the students to translate each line into their own words (as you might do with Shakespeare). This encourages the actor to really investigate the thought of the line. What are they really saying? What do they really mean? This will help with clarity of thought and also clarity of vocal delivery. You can also get the actors to ask the questions 'who?'and 'what?' with each line. It will help drive the emphasis of the line to where the key bit of information is.

When looking for the stakes of the scene you might also want to consider where the characters are. How could the size of the space affect the dynamics of the scene? Who might be listening in to their conversation? What is outside the space?

Language and style

Kellie referenced *Metamorphosis* by Franz Kafka as a great example of a piece that works as a metaphor and it feels important that a production of *The Monstrum* embraces the metaphor fully. However, there is the possibility of breaking the metaphor at the end because what the audience has watched up to that point has been a manifestation of the adults' fear, rather than the objective reality. What you offer the audience in those final moments could feel more real.

With regards to pronunciation, Kellie stated that the main thing is consistency within a production. The names have been inspired by Russia. The 'Russian-ness' could be very important or it could be more mythic. Bolek could be pronounced like 'bullock', or with a stress on the second syllable. With Libousa, you could emphasise the 'lie'.

There are two very different styles of text within the play: the text that is non-italicised and the text that is italicised. There should be a qualitative distinction between the two.

The participants discussed what the differences could mean. They suggested that the italics could be the subconscious, or what is not allowed to be said within the community. There could be a public–private distinction. You could speak directly to the audience during the non-italicised text. There could be something more connected in the delivery of the non-italic text. Or even the opposite could be true.

EXERCISE: EXPLORING LANGUAGE AND STYLE

There is much narrative detail and exposition in the non-italicised text; we are introduced to the Monstrum for example. To explore the shifts in language and style you could set the group a challenge.

Divide the group into five and ask them to explore the section of non-italic text on page 586. In the workshop, groups were given ten minutes for this exercise.

Task 1: Find a way to interpret this section of non-italicised text

It is a terrible thing
Terrible, terrible
It's a disease!

People here
In these parts
They call it . . .

The Monstrum

They all react to the word.

Which means

Portent
Omen,
Monster!

There is hysteria.

Task 2: Find a way to interpret the following section of italic text

> *Our people have lived here for hundreds of years*
> *And we can cope with almost anything*
> *Like frozen snot*
> *And our fingers falling off*
> *And even permanent brain freeze*

Each group was given a set of images to use as inspiration and each group had a slightly different focus, as outlined below:

GROUP ONE

Task 1. Focus on the different villager characters as discrete individuals.

Task 2. Raise the emotional temperature of the community.

Feedback: There are interesting choices to be made about how the text is divided and when voices all come together. Seeing individuals brought out the humanity of the group. Laughing was used to mark the shift in the action, which could be useful as a way of moving between one chorus style to another.

GROUP TWO

Task 1. Focus on the pack version of the chorus.

Task 2. Move into a chant.

Feedback: There is an option for the italic text to act in conversation with the non-italic text.

GROUP THREE

Task 1. Focus on creating a sound world of some kind, either vocal or percussive.

Task 2. Charting the creation of –the Monstrum.

Feedback: You could treat the italic text as though it is a different genre; you could be almost teaching your audience the symptoms of the disease in the chorus.

GROUP FOUR

Task 1. Focus on having a very direct conversation with the audience.

Task 2. Focus on moving into unison

Feedback: The structure of the exercise has brought out extremes. Can you create a style that could be consistent throughout the whole production? It might be useful to explore the physical environment as a way of creating the change between different styles.

GROUP FIVE

Task 1. Focus on a street scene that establishes the daily lives of these characters.

Task 2. Focus on a shift into working in physical rhythm.

Feedback: This exercise allowed for the participants to discover that the movement into the italics allows an expression of something that is not heard in the dialogue. This could be compared to a musical, when characters sing when they can't express what they want to in words.

EXERCISE:
SHAPE AND SCALE OF MOVEMENT IN AN ENSEMBLE

Begin by asking the group to take a gentle and neutral journey around the space, acknowledging other people, finding comfort and easiness in this, but not engaging for too long. Then introduce the idea of a speed index, from one to ten. Ask the group to explore a level five, then to take it down to one, then building up the scale all the way to ten, before going back to five.

You can then introduce a scale index, again one to ten, which could explore people vs environment, character, how small or large your world is. Level one is at its smallest, most constrained and level ten is at its largest, most expressive. When exploring scale, the speed can be any level.

You can then try and combine the scale and speed indexes. For example, you could ask the group to explore the speed at level two and the scale at level nine, then the speed at level ten and the scale at level four.

One scale on its own can feel general, particularly when working on exaggerated levels, but there is something useful about the intersection of the two.

Discussion: the mother's notebook

The group discussed how you might stage the important story of the mother's notebook. It is easy to overlook this detail in a play full of challenging staging and characters, but it is really important. The mother is a fluid character: she is the only one who got away from the village, she doesn't adhere to the structures and rules that bind the rest of the village. Is the notebook a piece of her mother? A memento of her mother? Does Milena have the book on her the whole time? If so, could there be a moment earlier in the play where we catch a glimpse of the book? Could Bolek find Milena looking at the book? Could you use a scene change to tell this part of the story? If this is a play of secrets, maybe you could use the scene changes and transitions to show the audience these secrets?

What does the notebook look like? What is in the notebook? Does it have anything else in it – cuttings, pressed flowers or maps? The book signifies the character of the mother, so you should really investigate what it looks like and what it means to Bolek and Milena.

Discussion: Milena eats the rat

There is a challenging moment in the text where Milena, in a crazed frenzy, devours a rat. It is a tricky image to get right but has the potential to be incredibly powerful. What is the prop? Does it have to be a whole rat? Could it just be the tail hanging out of her mouth (often what we don't see is more powerful than what we do)?

What is the sound of eating a live rat? Can you hear the rat squeal? Could she eat the rat like a corn on the cob?! Could you hide some actual food, like melon or apple, inside a prop? Could it be something expressive? Eating something that clearly isn't a rat, like a plate of spaghetti bolognaise?

Do we even need to see the rat being eaten? Could we hear the noise and then when the door opens we see the girl covered in blood with bits of rat body in her hands? Could you backlight it so you don't see the detail of her eating? Could you explore the reality of this moment; is it that we see through the eyes of the parents as opposed to fact?

Discussion: cherry tree

Similarly challenging is the moment where Milena takes a cherry tree out of her mouth. The participants discussed ideas for staging this moment. Could actors make the shape of trees with their bodies? Could you use shadow puppets, or bits of branches to create shadows on a backcloth? Or is there a technical solution that uses projection?

Is it more literal? Could you use a cherry tree branch that you hide with some clever staging and then reveal in her hands? Is it the cherry that's an interesting texture? Could she be throwing up black cherry, staining her mouth?

The properties of the black cherry plant (also known as deadly nightshade) were used as a sedative. It represents the mythology, the fear of the unknown and the woods. The narrative of the plant is important to track throughout the play.

Characters and characterisation

How close can you get to a real-world contemporary version of an adolescent? The tone of the play acknowledges the humorous side of the grotesque. The humour in the play lies behind some of the adult behaviours, Bolek's sense of grandeur for example. There are two layers to this world: the facts of what has actually happened and then the adult response to that. You might want to explore or give a physical language to what they think the Monstrum might be like, compared to what it actually is. Is adult behaviour normal? Is it useful to have a heightened adult characterisation to help us understand that they are misguided and unaware of their own behaviours?

Casting

The play offers ample opportunity to create roles for villagers and the infected.

Patriarchy seems to be one of the main driving forces in this play. You can change this with your casting if you choose to. You could, for example, cast all the leaders of the town as women.

It is important to pay attention to existing relationships within the play, so that you don't pull focus with any additional roles you create. For example, if you give the Mayor a wife, this might pull focus from the fact that Lazlo follows the Mayor around.

Certain roles are more technically demanding than others. Bolek for example, needs to be played by someone who can own the language. The Mayor could be a role that is embraced by a comic actor. Stanko and Radmila have comic potential and with Radmila there is opportunity to land a surprise on the audience.

With all casting choices, it helps to understand the context that you are working in, consider the story and how your young people will best tell that story.

Question and answer with Kellie and Caroline

What are your feelings about the moments of music in the play?

KELLIE SMITH   'I heard the moments as song but I want to leave it open for people to approach it in different ways. I've never written a musical before, but I got a sense of the heightened, *Sweeny Todd*-like musical style in those moments. I enjoyed the bigness of musicals in previous NT Connections festivals, especially on the stage of the Olivier. You should embrace the size of it. The italics suggest that those sections are tonally different. They could be sung. They were partly inspired by the overture section in Tim Burton's film *The Corpse Bride*, where they're getting ready for the wedding. The characters in that are grotesque and Gothic.'

CAROLINE STEINBEIS   'No music is provided, so you can create your own version of the songs. Keep it as simple as possible. You might want to start with a simple round as a way of creating music. Always ask yourself when is music useful? What are the limitations and possibilities of using music in your piece?'

Is the play set anywhere specific?

KELLIE SMITH   'No. But when I was writing it I read about a small Russian village called Oymyakon. It's the coldest permanently inhabited place in the world. They struggle to bury bodies in the ground because it's too hard. This piece was inspired by the conditions of that place.'

How should we approach the horror and gore of the play?

CAROLINE STEINBEIS   'Quite often the things you don't see on stage are the things that make your imagination work harder. It's useful not to show everything. Nothing is more powerful than the imagination. For example, the covering of the cage before Radmila is eaten (all we hear is the scream as the cage is covered over). Showing less is always more.'

Can we change words or cut the text?

CAROLINE STEINBEIS   'I would say only change words where absolutely necessary. It should only ever be a last resort. You've made a choice in doing this play. If you are switching gender you might want to swap some words to make sense of it. Alternatively, you could leave it as it is. One thing you can consider, if you're running heavily over time, is taking scenes out of the play. If you need to take stuff out, you might want to look at cuts to Scene Eight. You might also look at cutting the scene with the Mayor in the office (Scene Thirteen), and possibly also the following scene (Scene Fourteen). That should help you. But only do this if you're really running over time. If you don't edit carefully you might lose something from the text.'

What are the rules for using copyright material (music) in the production?

CAROLINE STEINBEIS   'My instinct is always to avoid it where you can. It's much more interesting to get the cast singing or playing music. If you do want to consider using copyright material, then the usual copyright rules will apply.'

Suggested references, reading or viewing list

Tim Burton films, particularly *The Corpse Bride*

Gothic literature

Dystopian worlds, like *The Hunger Games* (books and films)

It could be helpful to research the science and history of lobotomy: it is interesting because the pre-frontal cortex is the part of the brain most affected by growth in adolescence. There are some very interesting Ted Talks about the pre-frontal cortex and the brains of teenagers.

Kellie referenced a man called Walter Freeman who invented the ice-pick lobotomy through the eye socket. It was apparently cheaper and quicker, severing the nerve connections. In pictures they would have bruised eyes but they didn't often go blind.

Edvard Munch's *The Scream*

Amish communities, sects and cults in America

The Crucible by Arthur Miller

Metamorphosis by Franz Kafka

From workshops led by Caroline Steinbeis and Sam Pritchard
with notes by Ed Stambollouian and Miranda Cromwell

Participating Companies

20Twenty Academy
Aberconwy
Aberystwyth Arts Centre Youth Theatre
Acorn Young People's Theatre
ACT 2 Academy
Alnwick Playhouse Youth Theatre
Ardclough Youth Theatre
Arts1
artsdepot Youth Theatre
ArtsEd Extra Youth Company
Astor Youth Theatre Company
Barbara Priestman Academy
BDC Company
Bedford College
Bilborough BTEC
Bishops High School
Blatchington Mill School
Blue Bee Productions
Bodens Performing Arts
Borders Youth Theatre
Bournside Drama
Brackley Youth Theatre
Bridge Academy
Bridgend College
Bristol Grammar School
Broadland High School
Burnage Academy for Boys
CAM Theatre Company
CAPA College
Carmel College
CAST Ensemble LTD
Castleford Academy
Chadsworth Stage School
Chagford Youth Theatre
Chapter 4 (Mansfield Palace Youth Theatre)
Chesterton Youth Theatre
Chichester Festval Youth Theatre
Chichester High School Sixth Form
CHS

Churchill Theatre Connections Company
City of Westminster College
Clapton Girls Academy
Class Act Drama Academy
CoLA
Colchester Institute
Collision
Coppice Performing Arts School
Cornwall College
CoTeens
CRE8@KLA
Creative Learning Stoke-on-Trent
Curve Young Company
CYA at HOME
CYGNETS (Cheshire Youth Group for New and Emerging Talent on Stage)
Delante Detras Theatre Company
Drama Lab Jersey
Droylsden Academy's No Limits
DSLV
Dudley College Performing Arts
Dukies Youth Theatre Group
Eden Court Young Company
Epping Forest College
Fallibroome Academy
Felixstowe Academy
Felpham Community College
First Floor
Flame Theatre Company
Flying High Young Company
Fred Longworth High School
Fusion Project
George Dixon Academy
Get Stuck In
Gildredge House
Grand Young Company
Great Glen Youth Theatre
Green Shoes

Greig City Academy/GCA KS5 Drama Company
Griese Youth Theatre
Gulbenkian
GYP
Halesowen College
Harris C. of E. Academy
Hemsworth Arts and Community Academy
Hinchingbrooke School
Hinde House School
HMS Theatre Company
HMTP
Home Spun Drama School
Horizon International School
Hornsea School & Language College
Huntingdon Youth Theatre
IGS Theatre Co
In Yer Face Productions
Indelible Arts Youth Theatre
InterACT Youth Theatre
Invergordon Academy Youth Theatre
Jackass Youth Theatre
JAM Productions
JASPA Lincs
John Cabot Academy
John Lyon School
John Willmott School
Kildare Youth Theatre
Kindred KYT
King Edward VI Five Ways School
Kingsley Bideford Community Theatre Company
Kirkcaldy High School
Knightswood Secondary School
Lakeside Youth Theatre
Lammas School
Langdon Academy Theatre Company
Langley Theatre Workshop
Langtree School

LAUNCH Theatre
Limitless Academy of Performing Arts
Lincoln Young Company
Lipson Cooperative Academy
Lister Company of Actors
Lochaber Youth Theatre
LOST Youth Theatre Company
LSC Expressive Arts
Lyme Youth Theatre
Lymm High School
Macrobert Young Company
Malta Drama Centre
MAPA (Millbrook Academy Performing Arts)
Mark Rutherford School
Marple Drama
Matravers School Drama Department
Mishmak Youth Theatre
MK College Performing Arts
Montage Theatre Arts
NCN Actors
New College, Swindon
NMPAT County Youth Theatre
North Durham Academy
Northampton College
Northern Lights Theatre Company
Norwich Theatre Royal Youth Theatre Company
Nuffield Youth Theatre
Oakgrove Integrated College
Octagon Connect
Odd Productions/Galashiels Academy
OP and MCS Young Company
Orange Tree Theatre Connections Company
Ormiston Rivers Academy
Oslo International School
Outloud Productions
PACE Youth Theatre
Page2Stage Youth Theatre

Patrician Youth Centre
Peploe-Williams Academy
Perfect Circle Youth Theatre
Perth High School
Petchey Players
Pike and Musket
PlayActing Drama Celbridge
Plough Youth Theatre Seniors
PRC
Prestatyn Hgh School
Procrastinate
Pump House CYT
Pursue Theatre
Queen's Theatre Cut2
Rainham Mark Grammar School
Range High School
Ravens Wood School
reACT
Reading Rep in collaboration with
    Artemis Studios
Richmond Shakespeare Society
    Senior Youth Theatre
Ripley St Thomas CE Academy
    Youth Theatre
Rotherham College
Royal & Derngate Young
    Company: Connect
RUTC PERFORM
Sandbach School Theatre
Scarborough Sixth Form College
See&Eye Theatre
Sgioba Dràma Òigridh Inbhir Nis
Shadow Syndicate
Shazam Theatre Company SCIO
Sheffield People's Theatre
Sherborne Girls
Sherman Youth Theatre
Shotton Hall Theatre School
SMSJ Theatre Company
Soham Village College
Something Wicked This Way
    Comes
South Hunsley School
SRWA Youth Theatre

St Brendan's Sixth Form College
St Clement's High School
St Ives School Youth Theatre
St Joseph's RC High School
St Marylebone School
St Monica's Theatre Company
St Peter's
St Richard's Catholic College
St Saviour's and St Olave's
    School
St Thomas More
Stafford Gatehouse Youth Theatre
Stage-Fright Whitty Theatre
Stanley Park Drama
Stockport Academy
Story Makers
Stratford School Academy
Strode's College
Suffolk New College Performing
    Arts
Sundial Theatre Company
TAG
The Blue Coat School
The Blue Room Theatre
    Company
The BRIT School
The Canterbury Institute of
    Performing Arts Acting
The Customs House Youth
    Theatre
The Drama Studio
The Garage Young Company
The Hastings Academy
The King's School
The Lowry Young Company
The Marlowe Youth Theatre
The MidKent Players
The Minster School
The Pauline Quirke Academy of
    Performing Arts Enfield
The Redhill Academy
The St Leonards Academy
The Stow Company
The William Allitt School

The Winston Churchill School
The Young Actors Company
Theatre Royal Plymouth Young Company
Theatre Royal Stratford East Youth Theatre +
Thurso High School – Eden Court Creative
Tiptoe School of Performing Arts
Tomorrow's Talent
Trowbridge Arts Youth Company TAYC
Twyford Drama Company
Unlimited Theatre
UROCK Company
Wadebridge School
Waid Academy
Walsall College
Walton Acting Company
Warwick Arts Centre Connections Company
Wellington School
West Yorkshire Drama Academy
Westfield Arts College
wgytc
WHAT Theatre
White City Theatre Project
Winstanley College
Wokingham Youth Theatre
Woodbridge High School
Woodrush High School
Worthing College
Yew Tree Youth Theatre
Young and Talented
Young and Unique @ CCCC
Young Lyric
Youth Arts Centre Isle of Man

Partner Theatres

Aberystwyth Arts Centre
The Albany, London
artsdepot, London
Bristol Old Vic
Cast, Doncaster
Chichester Festival Theatre
Derby Theatre
Eden Court, Inverness
HOME, Manchester
The Lowry Centre, Salford
Lyric Hammersmith, London
Lyric Theatre, Belfast
Marlowe Theatre, Canterbury
Northern Stage, Newcastle
The North Wall, Oxford
Norwich Garage
Norwich Playhouse
Octagon Theatre, Bolton
Queen's Theatre, Hornchurch
Royal & Derngate, Northampton
Sheffield Theatres
Sherman Cymru, Cardiff
Soho Theatre, London
the egg, Theatre Royal Bath
Theatre Royal Plymouth
Theatre Royal Stratford East, London
Traverse Theatre, Edinburgh
Warwick Arts Centre

Copyrights

Performing Rights

Applications for permission to perform, etc. should be made,
before rehearsals begin, to the following representatives:

For *Three*
Knight Hall Agency Ltd
Lower Ground Floor
7 Mallow Street
London EC1Y 8RQ

For *#YOLO*
The Agency (London) Ltd
24 Pottery Lane
London W11 4LZ

For *FOMO*
David Higham Associates
7th Floor, Waverley House
7–12 Noel Street
London W1F 8GQ

For *Status Update*
Forced Entertainment
502 The Workstation
15 Paternoster Row
Sheffield S1 2BX

For *Musical Differences*, *Extremism*, *The Snow Dragons*
and *The Monstrum*
Curtis Brown Group Ltd
Haymarket House
28–29 Haymarket
London SW1 4SP

For *The School Film* and *Zero for the Young Dudes!*
Judy Daish Associates Ltd
2 St Charles Place
London W10 6EG

National Theatre Connections Team 2017

The National Theatre

National Theatre
Upper Ground
London SE1 9PX

Registered charity no: 224223

Bloomsbury Methuen Drama Modern Plays
include work by

Bola Agbaje
Edward Albee
Davey Anderson
Jean Anouilh
John Arden
Peter Barnes
Sebastian Barry
Alistair Beaton
Brendan Behan
Edward Bond
William Boyd
Bertolt Brecht
Howard Brenton
Amelia Bullmore
Anthony Burgess
Leo Butler
Jim Cartwright
Lolita Chakrabarti
Caryl Churchill
Lucinda Coxon
Curious Directive
Nick Darke
Shelagh Delaney
Ishy Din
Claire Dowie
David Edgar
David Eldridge
Dario Fo
Michael Frayn
John Godber
Paul Godfrey
James Graham
David Greig
John Guare
Mark Haddon
Peter Handke
David Harrower
Jonathan Harvey
Iain Heggie

Robert Holman
Caroline Horton
Terry Johnson
Sarah Kane
Barrie Keeffe
Doug Lucie
Anders Lustgarten
David Mamet
Patrick Marber
Martin McDonagh
Arthur Miller
D. C. Moore
Tom Murphy
Phyllis Nagy
Anthony Neilson
Peter Nichols
Joe Orton
Joe Penhall
Luigi Pirandello
Stephen Poliakoff
Lucy Prebble
Peter Quilter
Mark Ravenhill
Philip Ridley
Willy Russell
Jean-Paul Sartre
Sam Shepard
Martin Sherman
Wole Soyinka
Simon Stephens
Peter Straughan
Kate Tempest
Theatre Workshop
Judy Upton
Timberlake Wertenbaker
Roy Williams
Snoo Wilson
Frances Ya-Chu Cowhig
Benjamin Zephaniah

For a complete listing of Bloomsbury
Methuen Drama titles, visit:
www.bloomsbury.com/drama

Follow us on Twitter and keep up to date
with our news and publications
@MethuenDrama